# AMERICAN GLOBAL STRATEGY AND THE "WAR ON TERRORISM"

Terror is not always the effect of force, and an armament is not a victory. If you do not succeed, you are without resource; for, conciliation failing, force remains; but force failing, no further hope of reconciliation is left.

—Edmund Burke, *Speech on the Conciliation with the Colonies*, 1775

… (T)he moralizing politician, by glossing over principles of politics which are opposed to the right with the pretext that human nature is not capable of the good as reason prescribes it, only makes reform impossible and perpetuates the violation of law. Instead of possessing the *practical science* they boast of, these politicians have only *practices*; they flatter the power which is then ruling so as not to be remiss in their private advantage, and they sacrifice the nation and, possibly, the whole world.

—Immanuel Kant, *Perpetual Peace*, 1795

# American Global Strategy and the "War on Terrorism"

HALL GARDNER
*American University of Paris, France*

## ASHGATE

Published by
Ashgate Publishing Limited
Gower House
Croft Road
Aldershot
Hampshire GU11 3HR
England

Ashgate Publishing Company
Suite 420
101 Cherry Street
Burlington, VT 05401-4405
USA

Ashgate website: http://www.ashgate.com

**British Library Cataloguing in Publication Data**
Gardner, Hall
   American global strategy and the "war on terrorism"
   1.War on Terrorism, 2001- 2.United States - Foreign
   relations - 21$^{st}$ century
   I.Title
   327.7'3'0090511

**Library of Congress Cataloging-in-Publication Data**
Gardner, Hall.
   American global strategy and the "war on terrorism" by Hall Gardner.
      p. cm.
   Includes bibliographical references and index.
   ISBN 0-7546-4512-6
1.  United States--Foreign relations--2001- 2.  War on Terrorism, 2001-  I. Title.

   JZ1480.G367 2005
   327.73'009'0511--dc22

                                                                    2005013076
   ISBN 0 7546 4512 6

Printed and bound in Great Britain by Antony Rowe Ltd, Chippenham, Wiltshire.

# Contents

# Preface

After being told that "American global strategy" was the subject of this book, the typical response has been, "Does Washington really have one?"... The problem is that a truly "global strategy" worthy of the name has been lacking since the collapse of the Soviet empire. During the Cold War, Washington had largely followed a script called "NSC-68," but since the end of that perilous period, most measures have been taken in an *ad hoc fashion* without a true "global strategy" in mind—even after the horrific attacks of 11 September 2001.

The purpose of this book is consequently to provide a critical approach to the way in which the US has thus far approached the questions of "terrorism" and the rise of the new "threats" from a perspective of what I call *non-traditional*, or *alternative*, realism. The book thus seeks to provide an alternative strategy to that proposed (and implemented) by contemporary "neo-conservativism" (also known as "conservative internationalism") since 11 September 2001. The intent of this book is to develop a truly *irenic* global strategy that seeks to put an end to the "war on terrorism" and deal with the "new threats" through concerted and multilateral engagements—for the most part in the effort to achieve reconciliation between conflicting states and between state and anti-state factions. The book's long-term goal is to point the way toward new systems of local, regional and global governance, with greater degrees of civic participation—in what can be called confederal "world democracy" that seeks to strengthen regional cooperation and to achieve a modicum of sustainable development, order and justice.

I would like to thank Villa Piazza, Allison Sanders, Mikko Lähteenmäki, and Jung Woo Lee for their help in preparing the text. I would also like to thank my editors at Ashgate for allowing me to further elaborate on a number of points raised in my previous edited book, *NATO and the European Union: New World, New Europe, New Threats* (Ashgate, 2004). The chapters in this book are based, in part, on various lectures I have given at the *Georgetown School of Foreign Service* in the seminar of John Ikenberry; at the *Johns Hopkins Paul H. Nitze School of Advanced International Studies*, under the invitation of David Calleo; at the *Institut d'Etudes Politiques de Paris*, where I teach a section of *Enjeux Politiques*; at the *American University of Paris*; at the *École Militaire* in Paris for the *Collège InterArmées de Défense*; at the *Institut Universitaire d'Etudes du Développement* (IU) in Geneva for the conference "Pakistan, North Pakistan at the Crossroads of Central and South Asia" invited by Claire Galez; and at the May 2003 session of the *World Political Forum*, under the invitation of Mikhail Gorbachev.

Once again, I thank my family for persevering through this project.

# About the Author

Hall Gardner is professor and chair of the Department of International Affairs and Politics at the American University of Paris. He completed both his M.A. (1982) and Ph.D. (1987) at the Johns Hopkins Paul H. Nitze School of Advanced International Studies (SAIS). He also taught at the Johns Hopkins-SAIS-Nanjing Center for Chinese and American Studies (1988–89) and at the Johns Hopkins SAIS-Washington (1989–90) before coming to the American University of Paris in the Fall of 1990.

His book publications include: *Surviving the Millennium*: *American Global Strategy, the Collapse of the Soviet Empire, and the Question of Peace* (Praeger, 1994); *Dangerous Crossroads: Europe, Russia and the Future of NATO* (Praeger, 1997). He is editor of, and contributor to, *Central and Southeastern Europe in Transition: Perspectives on Success and Failure* (Praeger, 2000); *The New Transatlantic Agenda: Facing the Challenges of Global Governance* (Ashgate, 2001); and *NATO and the European Union: New World, New Europe, New Threats* (Ashgate, 2004).

Introduction

# Labors of Hercules
# Without End in Sight

During the Cold War, the US and Soviet Union had tacitly collaborated in restraining, or "double containing," the power potential and capabilities of both major and minor powers, including Germany/Europe, Japan, China, the two Koreas, India and Pakistan—as well as many other lesser states throughout the developing world.[1] US-Soviet collaboration in this "double containment" was partly a result of the formation of opposing "spheres of influence and security" and through the partition of Europe. In addition, the US and Soviet Union often kept strategically positioned states in the developing world as "weak" as possible by playing the differing sides against each other in violent wars.

In the aftermath of Soviet collapse, the US has become the world's lonely *hyper-puissance* (in the critical French coinage). The US is the only state capable of "restraining" many of the emerging powers, but not without increasing difficulties. Washington has thus continued efforts to "mono-contain" Japan by tightening its alliance in defense of Taiwan; it has also attempted to channel or restrain, as much as possible, an enlarging European Union (EU) by means of expanding NATO membership into former Soviet space. At the same time, however, the US has had troubles restraining China, among other states. It is not entirely ironic that China, following Soviet collapse, would begin to strengthen its military and nuclear capabilities. It is also not entirely ironic that both India and Pakistan would almost simultaneously explode nuclear weapons in 1998 or that both North Korea and Iran would threaten to obtain nuclear capabilities.[2] It likewise should not have been entirely unexpected that the collapse of Soviet controls over Afghanistan and central Asia, not to overlook the loss of Soviet influence throughout the "Greater Middle East," would have permitted the emergence of pan-Islamic movements. The latter have not entirely surprisingly sought to destabilize as many "corrupt" Arab-Islamic regimes as possible—in addition to attacking Russian, European and Indian interests as well as American.

The US, by itself, did not "cause" the new global disorder. Yet, the roots of the present crisis to a large extent lie in the general failure of US diplomacy to establish new and more concerted norms for international action in the post-Cold War era. Here, most crucially, the US had refused to engage in multilateral diplomacy, involving Russia, Pakistan and other regional powers, in an effort to work toward a resolution of the vicious conflict in Afghanistan—a "sin of omission" that, in many ways, opened the door to pan-Islamic insurgency, once the Taliban came to power, then joined by *al-Qaida*. (See Chapter 5.)

1

Moreover, in placing emphasis upon NATO enlargement to the exclusion of a more concerted US-Russian-European approach to European and global security, Washington missed opportunities to develop a far-reaching, multilateral approach that could have dealt more effectively with actual and potential crises. The Clinton Administration did engage in *informal* "Contact Group" formulas to handle the complexities of the Bosnian crisis. (See Chapter 7.) Yet the Yeltsin administration proposal in 1992 to meet *more formally* with NATO in a "19 plus 1" framework to deal with overall strategic questions affecting all of Europe and the world was only accepted a decade later by the Bush administration in May 2002—after the 11 September attacks.[3] Concurrently, while the US did pressure the UN to streamline its operations and cut costs in the 1990s, proposals to reform the UN Security Council (UNSC), and to "strengthen" the organization in the face of multiplying peacekeeping operations throughout the world, stalled miserably.

Once the Bush administration arrived in power, it appeared that American policy was beginning to retrogress to a Cold War stance as US relations with both Russia and China plummeted. The attacks on the World Trade Center and Pentagon ironically gave the Bush administration a new lease on life, but it is still not clear that a real "global strategy" capable of dealing with the full extent of the global crisis has yet to evolve. The US military intervention against *al-Qaida* and the Taliban in Afghanistan obtained UN, NATO, EU and Russian support—in what appeared to represent a new US-led "multilateralism." Yet positive worldwide support and sympathy for the US after the 11 September attacks rapidly began to fade as a result of its essentially unilateral intervention in Iraq—an action taken against the counsel of the UN Security Council and key NATO allies, France, Germany, as well as Turkey.

President George Bush, the father, was often criticized for his apparent lack of foresight ("the vision thing"), and particularly for not "going to Baghdad" at the end of the 1990–91 Persian Gulf War. President George W. Bush's efforts to make up for his father's ostensible inadequacies, however, have taken the US and the Middle East/ Persian Gulf to the brink of disaster. The belief that the Americans would be treated as "liberators" revealed the self-inflated nature of the George Bush, Jr.'s "vision thing" which, by contrast with the father, has now come to haunt the son. Whereas the father's "vision thing" may have erred on the side of the prudence of the traditional realism, the son's "vision" has been blurred by the arrogance of neo-conservativism. (See Chapters 1 and 2.)

In May 2003, National Security Advisor Condoleezza Rice was purported to have counseled President Bush to "punish France, ignore Germany and forgive Russia." This strategy appeared to represent an attempt to drive a wedge between France and Germany, as the two major US Allies that had opposed "pre-emptive" war with Iraq, while mollifying Russia, whose opposition to the Iraq war was less noisy—in an attempt to gain European concessions in respect to Iraq's post-war reconstruction and peacekeeping. In general, the US could play the UK and Germany against France (always the "reluctant ally") during the Cold War. Yet, in the post-Cold War period, it is clear that not only do France and Germany need to work together, but the US also needs to work with the Europeans—if the EU is not to disintegrate into disaccord and rivalry.

Recognizing the fact that its first term "strategy" tended to alienate the key allies of the Cold War, Germany and Turkey, as well as France, the second term Bush administration has promised to engage in a new multilateral approach, with strong US support for the European project. This appears true despite the fact that the principal "multilateralist" of the first term Bush administration, Colin Powell, decided to step down. Here, the US needs strong multilateral supports in dealing with Iraq, the war on terrorism, plus the Iranian and North Korean threats to develop nuclear weaponry. That more than 1,500 US servicemen have thus far lost their lives in Iraq for a very uncertain cause, and at rapidly mounting financial and political costs, has awakened official Washington to the need to work in as concerted a fashion with its Allies and the UN, as much as is possible.

On the one hand, Washington has expressed a questionably sincere *mea culpa* for not having previously engaged more consistently in a "multilateral" fashion with its friends and Allies. On the other hand, the second term Bush administration has continued to assert the necessity to engage in the essentially neo-conservative (and neo-liberal) goal of "democratic globalization." Expanding the geographic scope of the former "axis of evil," Washington intends to confront the "outposts of tyranny" in which "America stands with oppressed people on every continent ... in Cuba, and Burma, and North Korea, and Iran, and Belarus, and Zimbabwe"—in the words of now US Secretary of State, Condoleezza Rice.

The question now is whether Washington will truly build upon its promises for a new multilateralism. The key dilemma is this: Multilateralism can work in those few areas where the US does not have substantial interests at stake. But in areas where the US has substantial interests, or where the problematic states involved (Iran and North Korea, for example) regard present US policy as the source of the problem, it is appears dubious that multilateralism will succeed—unless either the US or its partners change their policies. The question thus remains whether the Bush administration will ultimately need to "bite the bullet" and negotiate directly with the very regimes that it has denounced as "outposts of tyranny"—despite the reluctance of its neo-conservative ideologues to do so.

While the US will need to engage in special force operations against groups such as *al-Qaida*, for example, it will also need to engage in a more clever global strategy—if it is to ever wind down the "war on terrorism." As a key step toward a diplomatic end to the "war on terrorism," the US should work with the Quartet grouping of the UN, EU and Russia in order to bring a fair resolution to the Israeli-Palestinian conflict, while concurrently looking to achieve "good governance" in the "Greater Middle East"—where really possible. Likewise, the US must work behind the scenes to ameliorate geopolitical and nuclear tensions between India and Pakistan—in the diplomatic effort to wind down the "war on terrorism." Washington will need to engage with a highly instable Russia, as the latter seeks to expand its interests while confronting its own version of the "war on terrorism." The US must strive more effectively to check closer Russia (and EU) military ties with China, plus prevent conflict over Taiwan.

Much like the ancient half-man half-god, Hercules, the US has been confronted by a number of new "threats" and challenges to itself and world stability. Much like the ancient images of Hercules, but in a flashier, high tech, cinematographic form, the US has begun to engage in a number of dangerous and potentially unending "Labors"—which involve both sub-adventures and misadventures. Having defeated the Lion of Nemea (the Taliban), at least in appearance, the war with the multi-headed Lernean Hydra of global terrorism continues, while the US has thus far failed to capture the Ceryneian Hind (bin Laden). The US did capture the Erymanthean Boar (Saddam Hussein) alive—although the resistance to the American "occupation" has not yet subsided. Washington has not yet been able to manage the Stymphalian Birds that plague the Middle East—although the largely unexpected death of Yassir Arafat may have stimulated some progress along the Road to Peace.

The new American Hercules has additionally not yet figured out a more clever stratagem to flush the nuclear waste from the stables of the North Korean Augeias, nor has it been able to capture and contain the nuclear capabilities of Iran, become the three headed dog, Cerberus—so as to fling its nuclear capabilities back into the pits of Hades. Other crises may soon confront the US in dealing with Europa and a Turkish Minos. What adventures or misadventures may await the US and Russia as they seek to tame the man-eating Horses of Diomedes? Will India and Pakistan be able to capture Geryon's cattle, as the latter seek to destabilize peace negotiations between New Delhi and Islamabad? In what adventures or misadventures will the new American Hercules engage in the conflict zone surrounding the belt of Hippolyte and the Amazons? Will the US and China go to battle over Taiwan and the oil-coated apples of the South China sea, guarded not only by a hundred-headed dragon, but also by the Hesperides, the nymphs, with strings of pearls, who were daughters of Atlas?

In his twelve labors, numerous challenges confronted Hercules, resulting in significant errors of judgment and considerable "collateral damage." The American cinematographic version may attempt to cover up many of those errors as possible through the flashy manipulation of the global media, but he cannot altogether escape those errors of judgment and his culpability. Even that all-powerful mythological figure did not "succeed" in his labors—without seeking the advice of the gods (to obtain legitimacy) and, at least sometimes, without the help of his friends. It appears, however, that the contemporary American version may require a significant re-working of the script: Many of these issues (which originated both before and after Soviet collapse) need to be addressed as rapidly as possible—before a number of grievances result in "blowback" in contemporary slang—or else explode to the surface in Clausewitzian terms.

In this regard, the American Hercules may need even greater assistance than did the ancient one—in the assumption that his present friends and Allies will not, in the very near future, decide to part company altogether. Alternatively, it is also possible that the American version could abandon his tasks, and withdraw back into his more traditional pre-World War II isolationist shell due to an unwillingness to bear the burdens of empire and military intervention—in feelings of political-military impotence and socio-economic self-loathing.

**Chapter Outline**

Chapter 1, *Reflections upon the 11 September Attacks and "Pre-emptive" War in Iraq* critically examines the post-11 September decision to expand the "war on terrorism" beyond the immediate threat of *al-Qaida* to a war against "every terrorist group of global reach." The Bush administration then expanded that conflict to an additional dimension that included a war against "rogue states," which not only involved so-called "pre-emptive" war with Iraq, but also political-military pressures upon the two other "axis of evil" states, North Korea and Iran. The US tendency to "demonize" various regimes as members of the "axis of evil," or as "outposts of tyranny," risks a further widening of the conflict without a clear goal or end in sight. The chapter additionally questions whether Bush administration policy will be able to achieve its goals of liberal "democratic federalism" in Iraq after having attempted to *impose* its will by force—following in the footsteps of Great Britain and previous empires in history.

Chapter 2, *The Roots of American Neo-Conservatism: Neo-Timocrats or Moralizing Politicians?*, traces the historical and ideological roots of the new American interventionism, and the rise of the "neo-conservatives," who have taken the helm in the formulation of policy in respect to both the "war on terrorism" and war on "rogue states." It is argued that although many, but not all, neo-conservatives identify themselves with the Republican Party, the phenomena transcends the considerations of political parties—in that the neo-conservative urge for unilateral American initiatives has its roots in the political and social history of US continental, and then overseas, expansionism (going back to security concerns raised by Alexander Hamilton). Despite the deeper historical nature of the phenomena, the contemporary form of neo-conservative ideology has its roots in the 1970s in that it represented a reaction to particularly American versions of liberal and radical thought. Instead of viewing American "imperialism" in a *negative* light as was common during the Vietnam war era and after, neo-conservatives argued with great conviction, that American imperialism (or what they prefer to call "leadership") has its *positive* "virtues" in bringing "democracy," capitalist development, and "rule of law" to tyrannical regimes. The chapter critically examines neo-conservative policies in respect to Soviet collapse, opposition to "balance of power" politics and to "appeasement," and the relationship between democracy and "regime change"—a term coined under the influence of political philosopher, Leo Strauss. The chapter argues that one can depict neo-conservatives in Platonic terms as "neo-Timocrats"—but that they rightfully fit the category of "moralizing politicians" in Kantian terms.

Chapter 3, *The Question of State versus Anti-State "Terrorism": Who is Terrorizing Whom?*, identifies the political-ethical dilemmas involved in the expanding "war on terrorism" which has been aimed against "every terrorist group of global reach," in President Bush's words. The chapter attempts to clarify the concept (there are over one hundred definitions) by identifying four differing forms of "terrorism": *anti-state terrorism*, *state-supported terrorism*, *totalitarian terrorism* and *street terrorism*. The chapter furthermore reviews the "clash of civilizations" thesis, particularly the view of history as a "progression" from the "wars of princes" to the "wars of religions/civilizations," as developed by Samuel Huntington (and as adopted by bin Laden, among others). The chapter argues that while the number of "terrorist" organizations with religious ideologies do appear to be on the upswing, there are still more secular-type organizations than religious ones, in quantitative terms. Moreover, both religious and secular organizations have more in common than might first meet the eye. In developing concepts from Thomas Hobbes and Edmund Burke, the chapter argues for an approach that seeks to *reconcile* the "dialectical" interaction between conflicting anti-state and state "terrorisms"—a policy option, which, in some cases, may prove more plausible in the long term than one that seeks either "eradication" or "regime change."

Chapter 4, *The Risks of Nuclear Proliferation*, analyzes the successes and failures of American efforts to stem nuclear proliferation. It looks at the present global and regional crises brought about by Israeli, Indian and Pakistani acquisition of nuclear weapons, with a particular focus on the apparent Iranian and North Korean quests to obtain a nuclear weapons capability. It looks at EU, Russian and US policies in respect to proliferation and then outlines a number of related policy positions: The first is that of strengthened international inspections and reform of the Nuclear Non-proliferation Treaty (NPT). The second is economic sanctions and "containment." The third is the Proliferation Security Initiative (PSI). The fourth is to threaten, if not use, force. (The latter option could range from covert actions, to pre-emption and surgical strikes, to direct military intervention.) The fifth option is to try to "manage" the spread of nuclear weaponry. The sixth is a "nuclear free weapons zone." The seventh is the implementation of "Regional Security Communities" which would engage in *real dialogue* and multilateral diplomacy. In a critique of both *neo-realist* and *neo-conservative* approaches, the chapter argues that efforts to dissuade both Iran and North Korea from controlling their own nuclear fuel cycles may ultimately mean *regime recognition* as opposed to *regime change* (but without necessarily ruling out far reaching *regime reform*)—given the appropriate negotiated conditions and conditional security *assurances* leading to *security guarantees*.

Chapter 5, *Manipulating US Global Power: Pakistan, "War on Terrorism" and Strategic Leveraging*, explores Pakistani efforts to manipulate US policy both before and after the 11 September 2001 attacks on the World Trade Center and Pentagon. The purpose is to better explain contemporary Pakistani foreign policy in its geo-historical context—in an area of the world in which nuclear weapons, oil, drugs and "terrorism" make a very explosive concoction. The chapter consequently analyses how the deeper roots of the 11 September 2001 attacks stemmed from the conflict in Afghanistan. In that conflict, the US: 1) coaxed the Soviet Union to intervene; 2) totally ignored the domestic Afghan political struggle once the Soviet Union withdrew, thus permitting the Taliban to come to power, to be joined by *al-Qaida*; 3) turned its back as Pakistan (and India) sought to obtain a nuclear weapons capability. Not only was Pakistan able to acquire a nuclear capability, but the A. Q. Kahn nuclear "network" then assisted the efforts of states such as North Korea and Iran, among others, to develop a nuclear capability as well. The chapter consequently looks at how the relatively poor state of Pakistan has been able to manipulate its geo-strategic position and acquisition of nuclear weapons, to assert its interests in the "war on terrorism" in respect to Kashmir, despite US demands for the "illiberal democracy" to take more decisive steps toward "democratization." Finally, the chapter advocates the need for Indian-Pakistani "reconciliation"—as a diplomatic step to put an end to nuclear "brinksmanship"—as well as the "war on terrorism."

Chapter 6, *The Global Ramifications of American Military Expansionism*, outlines geo-strategic and political "hotspots" throughout the globe. The chapter first examines the expanding US military strategy and the Pentagon's global basing plans. It studies the global ramifications of "pre-emptive" war in Iraq; the effects of NATO and EU enlargement upon Russia, Ukraine and Belarus as the NATO and EU "borderlands"; American and EU ties to China. It looks at conflicts in the Balkans, the Caucasus, Turkey, Iran, and Central Asia, as well as efforts to achieve peace in the Middle East, including the domestic and regional consequences of the Iraq crisis—as affected by pan-Islamic strategy throughout the Arab/Islamic world. The chapter also scrutinizes US relations with the "outposts of tyranny" of Zimbabwe and Cuba; "narco-terrorism" in Columbia, as well as rising tensions between Japan, China and the two Koreas. The chapter concludes with a discussion of the potential emergence of new political-economic "blocs," whose formation largely depends upon the three key "pivotal" states, Ukraine, Turkey and China. It is argued that the break-up or potential shift in alliances of any one of these three key states could spark major power conflict.

Chapter 7, *"Clash of Democracies" or New Global Concert?*, questions whether the US and EU, despite holding "common" values and norms may continue to "clash" over foreign policy—and clash over how to best engage in the war/fight against "terrorism." A clash in perspectives appears to be developing precisely because the US and EU rank their values and interests very differently, and because their governmental structures, processes and goals are very different as well. The chapter argues that contrary to the "end of history" argument, which posited the triumph of the liberal democratic "idea," the US and EU are in the process of developing very different "ideas" of democracy, which will strongly influence the ways in which they interact. The US possesses a federal model with a very strong executive branch; the EU is in the process of adopting an amalgamated and *consensual* model of "social democracy," which goes beyond a loose confederation, with a much weaker executive than the US model. The differing American and European "ideas" of "democracy" are in an intense competition on a global scale with other conceptions that include "national democracy," "illiberal democracy," "participatory democracy," and "world democracy." The chapter consequently explores the differing nature of EU and US foreign policy formulation, clashing EU and US strategic visions, as well as the dilemmas posed by Wilsonian efforts to "export democracy" linked to "national independence" or "self-determination"—and the general US reluctance or failure to support *confederal* and *consensual* models of governance. The chapter then examines the question of UN *legitimacy*: By contrast with neo-conservative views, it is argued that the original conception of the 1948 Vandenberg Resolution—that sought to initiate the North Atlantic Treaty and simultaneously "strengthen" the UN—needs to be more fully adopted in contemporary circumstances. The chapter concludes by proposing a radical restructuration and reinvigoration of the UN Security Council—and considers the formation of a "World Citizen's Assembly"—as a step toward the establishment of a *confederal* "world democracy."

Chapter 8, *Transcending the International Disequilibrium*, analyzes American global strategy and proposes policy options intended to transcend the post-Cold War disequilibrium. The chapter argues for the establishment of a more "equitable" security relationship between the US and EU. It first advocates the creation of Euro-Atlantic Euro-Mediterranean security communities upon the basis of joint NATO-EU-Russian security guarantees under general UN mandates. The chapter argues that multilateral peacekeeping forces could move beyond Europe and into the Caucasus, for example, and possibly into Iraq. The latter option assumes that the US, France and Germany can resolve their differences—the dilemma arising, in part, due to the fact that European critics of the war do not want to give the US a *post-facto legitimacy* for "pre-emptive" intervention. Concerning North Korea and Iran, the US and its partners need to engage in *real dialogue* over the questions of nuclear proliferation, Weapons of Mass Destruction, state repression and human rights abuses, and support for "terrorism"; here, the US may need to engage in *regime recognition*, as opposed to *regime change*, but not excluding far reaching *regime reform*. Efforts to halt nuclear proliferation in the Middle East likewise mean bringing the Israeli nuclear deterrent under international safeguards while simultaneously guaranteeing the security of a new Israeli-Palestinian "confederation." This latter goal can be achieved through overlapping NATO-EU-Russian security guarantees involving the deployment of multinational peacekeepers in specified areas under a general UN mandate—once, and if, the two sides can reach a political settlement.

The chapter critically scrutinizes US and EU relations with Russia and China, and asks whether Russia (and ultimately China) can be brought into a larger US-EU confederation involving power sharing arrangements and regional security accords. The chapter proposes a peaceful settlement of the China-Taiwan dispute through the formation of a loose China-Taiwan "confederation" based upon the principle of "one China with cooperating states and differing systems" (instead of "one China, two systems.") Finally, the chapter argues that the world is entering a *danger zone* that is largely a consequence of the exponential growth of US, Chinese and worldwide energy consumption (particularly oil). This *danger zone* will stretch into the mid–21$^{st}$ century as the US and the other major industrial powers attempt to shift from an oil and fossil fuel based energy infrastructure to an infrastructure based upon hydrogen fuels, microchips, and alternative energy resources. During the period of transition, it is possible that a number of major geo-strategic and political economic crises could spark both major and minor power conflicts—much as has already been forewarned by US intervention in Iraq. To prevent the real potential for major conflicts to erupt in the coming years, it will be necessary for US to work to formulate a truly concerted global strategy—and as swiftly as possible before it potentially withdraws into isolation and self-criticism, exhausted with the heavy burdens of its Herculean tasks.

# Chapter 1

# Reflections Upon
# the 11 September Attacks
# and "Pre-Emptive" War
# in Iraq

It is possible that had the United States heeded the warnings of Mikhail Gorbachev (in respect to American support for the Afghan *mujahedin*, who were once upon a time depicted as "freedom fighters"), the horrors of the 11 September 2001 attacks on the World Trade Center and Pentagon might never have taken place. Certainly, had the US shaken hands with Mikhail Gorbachev in the late 1980s over Afghanistan, it is dubious that the pseudo-Islamic Taliban would have come to power. Instead, the US, having initially taunted Moscow into intervention in 1978–79,[1] turned its back once the Soviet Union was forced out, largely indifferent to the fate of the Afghan people, and what kind of regime might eventually take control. It is also possible that had the US really shaken hands with Gorbachev, the specter of terrorist actions, as well as the threats posed by proliferation of Weapons of Mass Destruction (WMD), would probably not have reached quite the same order and magnitude as today. Not only did the US taunt the Soviet Union into intervening, but also, contrary to its stated policy on non-proliferation, it looked the other way as Pakistan sought to develop a nuclear weapons capacity.[2] (See Chapter 4.)

There is, of course, no way to know for certain what could have happened had a different path been taken. And such speculation should absolutely not be interpreted as nostalgia for that grotesque, ideologically charged era dubbed the "Cold War" with its superpower cravings.[3] More pertinently, however, there *should be* a clear-headed recognition that the collapse of the old bipolar world order has led to the emergence of a new global *disequilibrium*—in which the US has now *seized* the predominant role, yet without adequately formulating the new rules for the global system—and without offering new goals for an emerging *global society*.

It was evidently not the first or the last time that the US would fail to heed friendly advice. In late 2001, the US did obtain UN Security Council support for the war against *al-Qaida*, which had allied with the Taliban in Afghanistan. In the period 2002–03, the US appeared to engage in a multilateral approach through the UN summits of 2002–03, but Washington refused to heed the friendly counsel and warnings of its own allies, France and Germany, as well as that of Russia, in respect to the potentially destabilizing regional and global consequences of military intervention in Iraq. In chastising France in particular for its opposition to so-called "pre-emptive" US-UK military intervention in Iraq, Washington largely ignored the fact that it was the *Quai d'Orsay* that had first led the charge to Kabul in October 2001 in support of UNSC Resolution 1368. The latter had provided international legitimacy for a military operation in Afghanistan led essentially by the United States, with more limited assistance from the UK.

Relations between the US and Europe subsequently became more fractious as US policy tended to play the UK, Spain, Italy, and eastern European states, particularly Poland, against France, Germany and Belgium, taking advantage of already existing political disputes within Europe. These US actions appeared intended to impede European efforts to achieve unity, and likewise risked the alienation of Russia as well. At the same time, much as the two Cassandras of the "old Europe" forewarned, the US and its coalition partners appear bogged down in the Iraqi quagmire, and may well be sinking into quicksand.

As of January 2005, the US Army has been operating on the assumption that the number of American troops in Iraq would remain above 100,000 through the year 2006. For fiscal year 2006, the Bush administration has requested an additional $82 billion for spending on Iraq alone. Part of this request would be used to establish fourteen "enduring bases" in Iraq, in the plausible, but not absolutely certain, assumption that the new Iraqi government would permit a long-term American military presence. By the law of "opportunity cost," this expenditure will cut into of other possible ways to spend those same funds on domestic American security concerns, international development assistance (such as the UN Millennium Development Goals, the Global Peace Operations Initiative, and future funding for democracy, development, and political transitions), among other initiatives.[4] The Congressional Budget Office has estimated that the war in Iraq, and other military operations against terrorism in general, could cost at least $285 billion over the next five years.[5]

## 11 September and Pearl Harbor

The 11 September 2001 attacks by pan-Islamic militants on the World Trade Center and Pentagon, two of the primary US symbols of power and influence, has consequently raised an acrimonious debate within the US as to who was responsible for letting such attacks take place and how best to deter and prevent such acts from taking place in the future. There were those who argued that the 11 September catastrophe was much like Pearl Harbor in that Washington had more evidence of plans to attack than it was willing to reveal. But there has been no smoking gun to prove that the Bush administration had possessed hard evidence of an imminent attack to take place *on the day* of 11 September. Certainly, there were clues that the Federal Aviation Administration could, and should have, been more thoroughly investigated; the FBI and CIA could have done a better job in communicating with one another.[6] In the cases of both 11 September 2001 and 7

December 1941, it does appear that a shortage of translators prevented critical information from getting into the right hands at the right time. At the same time, 11 September conspiracy theories across the political spectrum abound, while the Pearl Harbor analogy raises even more portentous concerns for the future of this conflict—that has now re-awakened the "Sleeping Giant."

The debate over 11 September and US foreign policy then became even more acrimonious following the Bush administration's decision to opt for "preemptive" (really preclusive) war with Iraq in March 2003 in order to eliminate the possibility that Iraq may have acquired, or would acquire, Weapons of Mass Destruction (WMD). After chasing the Taliban from Kabul (but without thoroughly eradicating the *al-Qaida* leadership or the Taliban for that matter), the Bush administration continued to focus almost obsessively on Iraq, in the belief that Saddam Hussein would eventually seek revenge for his defeat in the 1990–91 Persian Gulf War. Bush administration officials argued that multilateral diplomacy and sanctions would not prevent the Iraqi regime from ultimately developing nuclear weaponry—and that even if Saddam Hussein did not possess nuclear weapons or other weapons of mass destruction (WMD) at that time, he would ultimately possess such capabilities.[7]

The Iraqi threat thus began to take precedence over efforts to track down and eliminate *al-Qaida*—in respect to the significant amount of financial and military resources that were used to pressure, and then overthrow, Saddam Hussein. "Regime change" represented an option that the administration of George Bush, Sr. had first considered, but then ruled out in 1991. President Clinton, rather than intervening in Iraq directly, engaged in two *coup d'état* attempts; both, unfortunately, failed.[8] The passage of the 1998 Iraqi Liberation Act—pushed by neo-conservative lobbyists—additionally impelled the Clinton Administration to confront the issue.[9] President Clinton consequently sought to contain Iraq by preventing Hussein's military machine from functioning effectively through a devastating bombing campaign in 1998. General Anthony Zinni, Commander in Chief of the US Central Command from 1997–2000, argued, "The sanctions were working. The containment was working. He had a hollow military, as we saw. If he had weapons of mass destruction, it was leftover stuff—artillery shells and rocket rounds. He didn't have the delivery systems. We controlled the skies and seaports. We bombed him at will. All of this happened under U.N. authority. I mean, we had him by the throat. But the president was being convinced by the (neo-conservatives) that down the road we would regret not taking him out."[10]

Neo-conservative factions within George W. Bush's administration, however, argued that Clinton's strategy had totally failed. Despite the frequent and effective US-UK bombing of Iraqi military facilities since 1998, the "neo-conservatives" believed that direct military intervention represented the only available option. The Bush administration consequently waged a propaganda campaign to convince American and world opinion that Iraq possessed considerable WMD capabilities; yet the truth of the matter was that Saddam's brutal military machine was not so gradually crumbling; his threat to acquire nuclear weaponry was largely bluff.

The Bush administration, and Defense Department in particular, likewise manipulated the 11 September attacks by linking Iraqi support for various terrorist activities with *al-Qaida*—in what has been dubbed a "noble lie" in neo-conservative circles (see Chapter 2). Although Saddam Hussein's intelligence services and *al-Qaida* may have engaged in some tenuous contacts, it appears dubious that Saddam had infiltrated the organization or coordinated planning in any way with bin Laden's group. In effect, the Bush administration was able to take advantage of the 11 September attacks to expand the "war on terrorism" to a war on "rogue states"—but without any clear end to *either* conflict in sight.

Here, the analogy to Pearl Harbor possesses ramifications that are even more ominous. From a historical perspective, major acts of "anti-state terrorism" have often resulted in significant *overreaction* by those states attacked. (See Chapter 3.) The nature of counter-reaction and counter-terrorism is largely dependent upon how state elites in power at the time of the attacks choose to manipulate those attacks for domestic and international political purposes. It is quite possible that, as the wars on "terrorism" and on "rogue states" continue to drag on with no clear "victory" in sight, that one side or another might ultimately opt to utilize some form of weapon of mass destruction—as the US itself did in revenge for Pearl Harbor and for other Japanese actions during World War II.

It is also possible that other states, following in American footsteps, could take up the banner of "pre-emption" or else use brutal tactics in their efforts to eradicate "terrorists" or other political opponents. After the US intervention in Iraq, for example, India initially threatened to engage in preemptive strikes—if Islamabad did not stop its support for *jihadi* "terrorism." (See Chapter 5.) In September 2004, Israel threatened to intervene in Syria or Iran, much as it previously threatened to intervene in Iraq—that is, if the US did not act to stop Iran from developing WMD. After the September 2004 hostage crisis in Beslan, Northern Ossetia, the Russian military chief of staff threatened to "take preventive strikes against terrorist bases in any region" while Russia simultaneously modernized its multiple warhead ICBMs. (See Chapter 6.) US military intervention in Iraq likewise appears to have convinced the other "axis of evil" states, North Korea and Iran, that the possession of nuclear weapons represents a form of prestige that will ostensibly bring greater international respect. These weapons, regardless of their costs, could consequently serve as a deterrent against a potential attack—and permit these countries to pursue their regional interests.

Moreover, the US intervention in Iraq has become a rallying point for *jihadi* groups throughout the Arab/Islamic world. *Al-Qaida*, which ostensibly aligned with the partisan group of the Jordanian Abu Musab al-Zarqawi in October 2004 in attacking US and coalition forces in Iraq, has warned of a repeat of major attacks in the US or Europe. Bin Laden's apparition on *Al-Jazeera* television, just before the November 2004 US presidential election, symbolically indicated that the US had not yet captured the world's most wanted man. This appeared true contrary to ubiquitous pre-election rumors that bin Laden had already been imprisoned and that the Bush administration was waiting to display him to the world media just a few weeks before the American elections (much as had already been done with the captured Saddam Hussein).

## From Indifference to Holy Wrath

At the time of the Korean War, George Kennan, in *American Diplomacy* (1953), compared the US with a "prehistoric monster." Kennan essentially argued that Washington could have "taken a little more interest in what was going on at earlier date" and "prevented some of these situations from arising instead of proceeding from an undiscriminating indifference to a holy wrath equally undiscriminating."[11] The problem thus appears endemic to the making of US foreign policy, but must ultimately be surmounted—if a modicum of global peace and justice is ultimately to be achieved. The inconsistent pattern of US diplomacy has tended to repeat itself under both Democrats and Republicans: Deadlock or war is the result.

Kennan's observation appears particularly pertinent when one regards how the US supported the Afghan *mujahedin*—which President Reagan once called "freedom fighters" and—then, in 1985, even more preposterously—the "moral equivalent of the founding fathers." Moscow had very clearly warned Washington that continued support for the Afghan *mujahedin* could well backfire against US interests. Congress itself was well aware of the possibility: The Congressional debate as to whether to sell Stinger shoulder-held missiles to assist the Afghan "freedom fighters" combat Soviet gunship helicopters had raised the question as to whether these weapons might ultimately be used against American and European interests. The US Congress opted to provide Stinger weaponry, which helped achieve victory for the Afghan resistance, but at the price of putting such weapons in the hands of pan-Islamic extremists. Once the Soviet Union finally withdrew, the United States abruptly withdrew all support for the country itself, leading Afghanistan to fester in limbo. Washington simply washed its hands of the matter, departing from the country in "undiscriminating indifference" in George Kennan's words. By 1993–94, the Taliban had largely taken over, and had overthrown the Soviet-backed regime of Mohammed Najibullah; it was then joined and assisted by *al-Qaida*, once bin Laden was forced from the Sudan to Afghanistan in 1996.[12]

The US initially believed that the Taliban, even with its xenophobic character, would bring "order" and "stability." The US thus tolerated the Taliban (even if it harbored major "terrorist" groups) in the hope that the latter would cooperate in helping develop energy resources and pipelines in central Asia.[13] (See Chapter 6.) It was only after US intervention in Afghanistan in October 2001 (symbolically backed by both the UN and NATO), followed by the rapid "defeat" of the Taliban in December 2001, that the US attempted to work with each of the domestic Afghan factions, and with all the regional powers, including Russia, in the effort to reconstruct the country. Yet only recently have the Americans begun to realize what the British had realized in the late 19th century: Given the highly fractious nature of Afghan politics, bringing peace and development to the entire country will prove to be a long-term venture, primarily because aid and investment will not be forthcoming without strong commitment to political and military security.

Although some progress has been made, successes have been minimal. NATO peacekeepers, which have been under political pressure to move into the countryside, have had major difficulties in controlling Kabul alone. In general, NATO sees its mandate as that of focusing on peacekeeping, and not in engaging in police work or in investigating narcotics and criminal activities. The fact that opium production has skyrocketed after the US-led intervention in 2001, however, has raised questions as to whether the international assistance that does arrive is simply sinking into a black hole, and precisely where opium profits are going.

After each of its post-Cold War interventions, Washington soon found itself confronted with a new form of *short war illusion*. Although the American high tech war machine rapidly achieved "victory" in Kosovo, Afghanistan and Iraq, its post-conflict peacekeeping (and counter-insurgency) has proved to be a long term endeavor—*to a large extent due to the fact that the geopolitical disputes at the roots of each of these conflicts had not been thoroughly addressed or resolved.*

Washington has thus failed to consider the long-term repercussions and, one might add, the much needed financing for the post-war reconstruction, peacekeeping, police enforcement, state and society building—wars that concurrently brought about (or else exacerbated) significant refugee crises and internal population displacement, not to overlook significant "collateral damage" to civilians. Moreover, prior to almost all of its post-Cold War military interventions, now including Iraq, the US has appeared to promise a "Marshall Plan." Yet, US (and international) funding has only trickled in, as the amount pledged did not always materialize. State and society building has then taken a backseat—opening the door to both "gray" and "black" market libertarianism.[14]

In this regard, many of these latter issues and problems stem precisely from the fact that Washington did not thoroughly address the roots of the dispute before or after the conflict, and because Washington did not initially work in true concert with regional states and other significant powers to help find a diplomatic resolution *at the outset* of the crisis. One can thus add to George Kennan's point that once the US does act in "a holy wrath equally undiscriminating," Washington seems incapable of comprehending that it will still be confronted with ongoing political- social- economic and ethical dilemmas—not to overlook long term peacekeeping—even after "victory" has been declared.

## Rhetoric of "Demonization"

The provocative nature of US foreign policy rhetoric and discourse has thrown fuel upon long simmering disputes. Inflammatory and bellicose rhetoric, such as the "axis of evil," which merges simplistic religious "good versus evil" dichotomies with misleading references to the global struggle of World War II, appears designed to obtain domestic popular support for US policies through the manipulation of the mass media. The catch phrase "war on terrorism" represents the perfect formula for perpetual conflict. The term provides no direction and provides no foreseeable resolution, particularly once it was confounded with the war on "rogue states."[15] There will be no end to this conflict as long as established governments and anti-state actors continue to counter-accuse each other of engaging in acts of anti-state "terrorism" or "state terrorism." The choice of the term "war" implies that primarily military means will be pursued; the term "terrorism" is, in effect, meaningless, as it has more than one hundred definitions. It seems the US cannot even define what it is struggling against, let alone determine how to "fight" it. (See Chapter 3.) Even more problematic will be deciding which groups might be fighting for "legitimate" causes as "freedom fighters" against *real* state repression, and which groups might represent "terrorists" without a "just" cause.

On 20 September 2001, President Bush stated, "Our war on terror begins with *al-Qaida*, but it does not end there. It will not end until every terrorist group of global reach has been found, stopped, and defeated." The fact that the Americans see themselves in a "war" and that the Europeans see themselves in a "fight" indicates a significant difference in how to define the "enemy" and reveals divisions in precisely which strategy and tactics to apply to differing groups, and how to reconcile opposing factions, if possible. Here, for example, the US and Europeans have disagreed over whether to label *Hamas* and *Hizb'allah* as "terrorist" groups. The Russians have denounced American and European calls to work toward a political solution for the crisis in Chechnya and the Caucasus. The difference in perspectives illustrates the tremendous difficulty in achieving a truly multilateral and concerted US-EU-Russian approach to these crises.

The rhetoric of "rogue states" thus raises questions of "double standards"—in which nefarious foreign policies, crimes against humanity, or lack of democratic practices of selected governments tend to be singled out, while equivalent actions of US allies, US-supported regimes, or even by the US itself, are largely overlooked, if not totally ignored.[16] It seems to have been quickly forgotten that the Cold War had often been characterized as a "balance of terror" in that both the US and Soviet Union manipulated their own brands of nuclear "terrorism" as the ultimate threat to obtain geopolitical concessions, short of going to war. These "double standards" (that only the US, Russia, and other permanent five ("P-5") UN Security Council members possess the legal right to develop nuclear weaponry) leads other states to copycat the "P-5"—and thus brandish the ultimate weapon. Attacks on "double standards" have consequently led to counter-protest that the US has become the predominant "rogue state," as regarded in its refusal to abide by international laws and treaties that Washington itself had worked to formulate, and in respect to the US decisions to modernize nuclear weaponry.[17]

Most poignantly, the tendency to *demonize* the leaderships of particular countries and the refusal to "divest diplomacy of the crusading spirit"—a position that violates the elementary principles of "classical realism"—boxes the US into a corner that makes war, or else, a further deterioration of diplomatic relations, almost inevitable.[18] The rhetorical depiction of Belarus, North Korea, Iran, Zimbabwe, Burma and Cuba as "outposts of tyranny" by US Secretary of State Condoleezza Rice in January 2005 spreads the geographic scope of the crisis, but does not necessarily represent a significant improvement over the "axis of evil" concept. Designating these states as "outposts of tyranny" may shift away from the religious connotations of the "axis of evil" but it does not answer the question as to how these states can best be reformed. Options include containment and sanctions; the threat and possible use of force; open support for civil society movements against the regime; and multilateral engagement of the major powers; or some form of combination of these options.

The problem raised here is that it is nearly impossible to engage in *real diplomacy* and reach compromises, or gain some concessions, once the leadership of a particular country has been labeled a "tyranny" or some other derogatory term. Such an ideological position tends to foreclose an *open examination of a whole range of viable diplomatic options and opportunities*. The consequences of such an ideological approach may well prove counterproductive on essentially three levels. The first is that the potential failure to press US friends and allies into engaging in similar democratic reforms will magnify accusations of "double standards." A failure to press US allies to reform can cause these "outposts of tyranny" to dig in their heels against positive reforms, while efforts by the US to be "even-handed" in response to international criticism, and thus press US friends and allies to reform, could possibly cause a backlash among those allies as well. The second problem is that Washington may ultimately need to thoroughly negotiate with some of these very same leaderships in order to prevent a further deterioration of the country or the regional situation, particularly as the threat to engage in "regime change" may prove ineffective or else dangerously destabilizing. The third problem is that perceptions of excessive pressure on some of these states may spark a backlash by their major friends or allies. Without a truly concerted and *differentiated* approach to each of these "problematic" states (as well as to others), it is dubious that *unilateral* US measures and pressures will bring about positive results.

Not only is the term "war on terrorism" dangerously misleading, but the American tendency to demonize its opponents oversimplifies issues by focusing on individual leaders rather than examining the more complex sources of conflict. The domestically oriented politics of media demonization tend to foreclose the very possibility of working out possible compromises as negotiated deals tend to legitimize the power of the very state leadership or "terrorist" organization that has repeatedly been denounced as the epitome of "evil." While a leader may publicly claim that it is impossible to deal with "terrorists," secret diplomacy may prove necessary to break the deadlock. The question remains: Which groups or regimes to "appease"? Which ones to "co-opt"? And which ones to "eradicate"? As shall be argued, efforts to dissuade Iran and North Korea, for example, from acquiring WMD may ultimately mean "regime recognition" as opposed to "regime change" (but without necessarily ruling out far reaching "regime reform")—given the appropriate negotiated conditions (see Chapters 4 and 8).

## The Deeper Questions Posed by Iraq

The Bush administration's tendency to demonize Saddam Hussein made a possible diplomatic solution close to impossible. If not fully understood why the regime acts the way it acts, efforts to intervene by force may well backfire and may even make the overall situation even worse. Trying to understand the way the latter regime worked does not, in any way, represent an apology for Saddam Hussein's horrific crimes, use of torture and chemical weaponry, and his policy of *tarhib wa-targhib* ("terror and enticement") that involved a mix of terrorizing elite opponents of his regime and cooptation of the general population, particularly the Shi'a.[19] Yet it does mean that Washington needed to fully comprehend the complex nature of that regime, its history and its strategy and more carefully analyze the reasons why Baghdad opted for war with Iran followed by its invasion of Kuwait—before attempting to modify the regime's behavior through military intervention.

During the Cold War, for obvious reasons, Washington totally ignored the torture of members of the Iraqi Communist Party. More pertinently, the US totally looked the other way concerning the Iraqi use of chemical weaponry and other war crimes during the 1980–88 Iraq-Iran "war of cities"—in the fear of Iranian victory. In this conflict, Saddam Hussein sought to decimate the Kurdistan Democratic Party (KDP), for example, which had allied itself with Iran.[20] At that time, Washington believed Saddam Hussein represented the "lesser evil," as compared to the radical Shi'ite leader of Iran, the Ayatollah Khomeini. (In 1985, Iran, not Iraq, was listed as a supporter of state terrorism.) Washington likewise ignored NATO member Turkey's actions in the brutal repression of the Kurdistan Workers Party (PKK), after the latter began a violent struggle for "independence" in 1984. The issue of Iraqi war crimes and "crimes against humanity" came to the forefront of Washington's rhetoric *only* after the August 1990 Iraqi invasion of Kuwait and after Operation Desert Storm—when the uprisings of the Kurdish *peshmerga* ("those ready to die") and of Shi'ite militants were brutally repressed by Hussein.

Even more profoundly, the *demonization* of the entire Iraqi leadership (and not just those individuals accused of war crimes) through the "de-Ba'athification" of the former regime in 2003, which resulted in the removal of highly trained Ba'ath party members, security officials, military officers and teachers (some 450,000–500,000 individuals) from their previous posts, has worked to further inflame the insurgency.[21] In late October 2003, the US did take belated steps to attempt to re-integrate ex-Ba'athists into a new Iraqi army and police force, but even this fact has not yet helped to end the guerrilla war—or break the newfound "alliance" between the Ba'athists and pan-Islamic extremists. Efforts to justify the de-Ba'athification of Iraq in 2003 by comparing it to the de-Nazification of Germany in 1945 represent an exercise in selective memory. The US moved away from a "corrective" to a "constructive" peace in both cases—but in far more controlled circumstances in the case of a divided Germany, which was under the tight occupation of US, UK, French, and Soviet forces.

## Alternative Options

The option of "vigilant containment"—which would not have ruled out the possibility of another coup attempt—was dismissed.[22] Another coup attempt was also ruled out.[23] The Franco-German-Russian proposal in late 2002–03 for more muscular weapons inspections, which would have put an international force on the ground within Iraq, and begin to affect "regime change," in the view of French Foreign Minister Dominique de Villepin,[24] was likewise ruled out. Purported back-channel pleas by Saddam Hussein to arrange a political settlement that would have included Iraqi cooperation in fighting terrorism, full support for any US plan in the Arab-Israeli peace process, as well as "free elections" after two years, were dismissed as a hoax.[25] Evidently, the US believed that Hussein would continue to play cat and mouse; it thus refused to trust any promises, and ruled out secret negotiations.

Franco-German warnings of even greater chaos in Iraq, possibly including a potential destabilization of the entire region, if the US did intervene unilaterally, went unheeded. Yet once the US decided to intervene, in the (false) argument that no other options were really feasible, then Washington needed to go all the way, to supply sufficient military and police forces—to guarantee stability, to protect lives, government complexes, and archeological treasures, and not just oil facilities.[26] Certainly the actual military intervention was rapidly executed, and caused less "collateral damage" than initially expected. Some of the refugee crises that were expected did not materialize; neither did a number of other feared humanitarian or health crises develop.

Yet it appears that very little thought was given to post-war planning, and that warnings of numerous Washington think tanks (and of the State Department itself) were ignored. Instead the Bush administration only took half measures in order to cut costs, so that post-war "planning" for a number of possible and clearly foreseen contingencies was largely non-existent, and reflected a technocratic and instrumentalist cost-cutting approach that ignored the political role of military deployments for peacekeeping, but also for deterrence against terrorist attacks and reassurance for the general population.[27] Moreover, while the US concerned itself with searching for Weapons of Mass Destruction, which it was unable to find, it totally ignored the safeguarding of Weapons of Conventional Destruction. As much as 350 tons of high explosives were stolen from one site, among other sites containing significant quantities of weapons which the International Atomic Energy Agency (IAEA) had been monitoring *before* the US intervention—thus providing additional ammunition to those resisting the coalition forces.[28]

The Bush administration likewise needed the post-war support of its allies, yet it succeeded in weakening and dividing the two multilateral organizations that could best help the US reconstruction effort: the UN and NATO. The Bush administration succeeded in alienating not just France (which has always been a reluctant ally), but Germany and Turkey as well, the two states that had been the most loyal to the US during the Cold War. In addition to the Bush administration's initially obstinate reluctance to bring in the UN fully, violent attacks against UN headquarters in Baghdad (August 2003), which killed UN envoy Sergio Vieira de Mello, among others, appeared intended to forestall any option that might help provide international *legitimacy* to a new Iraqi government.

The belief that the Americans would be treated as "liberators" appeared to provide the US with a green light to engage in whatever actions it deemed necessary to deal with the insurgency, the size of which was largely unanticipated, despite warnings by numerous critics (see below). Prisoner abuse and torture at *Abu Ghurayb* prison (where the US detained several thousand common criminals, individuals suspected of "crimes against the coalition," as well as leaders of the insurgency) shocked world opinion, once exposed in the global media—in terms of its overt efforts to humiliate those taken prisoner *by using methods that dishonored and degraded the values held in esteem by Islamic culture itself.*

Such outrageous behavior by low rank US military personnel (tolerated, if not instigated, by individuals at the highest echelons of American government) has seriously undermined the credibility of US leadership in general, all the more so in the eyes of those for which the Americans have claimed to be fighting.[29] This appears true even if Hussein (who had detained as many as 50,000 in the same prison confines) had practiced such torture and executions actions on a much greater scale. The situation is complicated by the fact that Iraqi prisons are still being run by many of the same individuals, utilizing similar techniques.[30]

Along with the US inability to sustain a modicum of domestic stability in post-war Iraq, such actions were combined with Bush administration claims that the US was not entirely subject to all sections of the Geneva Convention. This is not to overlook accusations that the US has primarily been concerned with access and control of high quality, potentially low cost, Iraqi petroleum reserves, due to rising US and world demand for oil. Furthermore, the failure to uncover significant quantities of WMD, the prime factor which had provided the initial pretext for the war, have all represented factors that revealed the hypocritical pretence and double standards of taking the "high moral road" that American neo-conservatives had proclaimed as a political-ethical justification for *preclusive* intervention in Iraq. Credible estimates that as many as 100,000 civilians may have been directly or indirectly killed since the March 2003 US-UK intervention (which did not include the numbers killed in the US siege upon the Sunni/Ba'athist stronghold of Fallujah in November 2004) are disquieting to say the least.[31]

In addition to Sunni Ba'athist insurgency, the US and the coalition forces have had to deal simultaneously with *al-Qaida*, *Ansar al-Islam*, and Iranian infiltration into Iraq, plus local mafias. These partisan groups (which may number as many as 40,000 active fighters and around 200,000 militant supporters, according to Iraqi intelligence) not only seek to disrupt the formation of a new government, but also intend to ultimately expel coalition forces from the country.[32] Much as *al-Qaida* and other organizations obtained training in fighting the Soviet Union in Afghanistan, the next generation of pan-Islamic militants appears to be gaining combat experience in Iraq against the United States.[33] More ironically, US intelligence had severely underestimated the depth and extent of the Sunni resistance (combined with foreign forces)—despite the fact that the nature of Ba'athist strategy appears similar to the concept of a "stay behind" group which NATO had been planned in case of Soviet invasion of Europe. (See Chapter 3.)

In this regard, Washington, with roughly 150,000 over-tasked troops in Iraq is stuck in quicksand in which it will prove very difficult to extricate itself, despite its efforts to turn the conflict over to the Iraqis themselves.[34] NATO itself has been divided as to the training of Iraqi peacekeepers, as opponents of the war (Belgium, France, Germany, Greece, Luxembourg, and Spain) prefer to avoid action or work directly with an Iraqi government with perceived *legitimacy*. If Iraq is not to slip into an even more protracted conflict—it is highly probable that the US and its allies (or an increasingly internationalized force) will remain in Iraq for decades. However, much as General Wesley Clark put it, "simply adding more troops won't let you succeed."[35]

## Iraq, Geohistory, and "Democratic" Progress

The French had tried to warn the Americans based on their own experience in Algeria—but to no avail. There the French deployed close to 400,000 men to suppress roughly the same number of insurgents in Iraq and failed to do so in a bloody war that lasted from 1954–1962. Given the fact that the Bush Administration has been determined to erase the Vietnam (followed by the Somali) "syndrome," the US experience with guerrilla warfare in Vietnam, and the severe problems faced in the "Vietnamization" of the conflict (training South Vietnamese forces to fight against the Viet Cong), has largely been ignored as well.

Cheered on by neo-conservatives, much like their 19th century British jingoist counterparts, in the belief that most factions of Iraqi society would welcome the US as "liberators," Washington refused to see itself as one of a long line of powers that have conquered or occupied Baghdad. These invaders have included Great Britain, the Ottoman Empire, the Mongols, the Seljuk Turks, the Iranian Shi'ite Buwayhids. One cannot also overlook the capture of Ctesiphon, ancient capital of the Iranian Parthian and Sassanid Persian Empires, by Rome and then Byzantium, as well the previous invasion and occupation of Babylon then under the rule of Darius III of Persia by Alexander the Great of Macedonia/Greece.

Today's situation in Iraq, however, may prove even more difficult and dangerous for the Americans, than did military intervention for the last major power to occupy Iraq, Great Britain. One wonders if UK Prime Minister Tony Blair had forewarned George W. Bush, Jr. of the British experience in "liberating" Iraq from the Ottomans in 1917–33.[36] In 1920, it took more than one year for the British to repress the Sunni, Shi'ite and Kurdish uprisings, which largely took place in the countryside and not in the major urban centers, as is the case today. It then took more than a decade to grant Iraq a semblance of sovereignty. The British were able to rule *through* an essentially Sunni elite and a constitutional, yet authoritarian, monarch, King Faysal, placed in power by British agents T.E. Lawrence and Gertrude Bell.[37] The British were additionally impelled to use force (including diplomatic and military steps to block Turkey from obtaining Mosul) in the effort to integrate a very artificial state made up of conflicting ethnic and religious factions that was formed in the aftermath of Ottoman collapse. The largely *artificial* nature of the Iraqi state and society has represented the key geo-historical factor that eventually set the stage for the horrific violence that characterized the regime of Saddam Hussein.[38]

The question posed here, however, is whether the American intervention will be able to bring about *qualitatively* different results than those imperial occupations of the past, thereby instituting a well developed and diversified economic infrastructure (going beyond a petroleum based economy). The other interrelated question is whether Iraq will develop a positive superstructure based upon a balanced "democratic-federal" government and rule of law founded upon "majority rule" with "minority rights." These questions are presented in the terms of classical Marxist conceptions of the "regenerative" aspects of imperialism (in which imperialism is regarded as "annihilating Asiatic society" and laying "the material foundations of Western society," e.g. its entire political-economic system).[39] These questions are also not so ironically posed in terms of the rationalizations of neo-conservatives who regard imperialism as a *positive* force for global democratization and for global capitalism (see Chapter 2).

Despite claims to the contrary, British intervention in Iraq can hardly be said to have brought "democracy" and "regenerative" capitalist development. It thus appears dubious that "democracy" can be imposed *from the outside* by force: Moreover, the US decision to remove Ba'athist elites from power, coupled with the fact that continued political-economic instability has tended to frighten off other elites and investors, has raised serious questions. Having invested billions of resources in the military intervention, and in a continued "occupation," will the US be able to sustain a new "democratic federalism" in Iraq? Even if a new "democratic federalism" and "capitalism" can ultimately be instituted, will the new Baghdad necessarily engage in pro-American policies? Or will the consequences be much more negative, with Iraq unable to get back to its feet again, bogged down in domestic and regional turmoil?

## "Democracy" and the Greater Middle East

Arguing that the Israeli-Palestinian peace process appeared to be going nowhere in part due to Iraqi intransigence, and that the policy of "double containment" against both Iraq and Iran had failed, Bush administration neo-conservatives contended that US military intervention, followed by "regime change" in Iraq, would also initiate a process of "democratization" throughout the entire Middle East/Persian Gulf region.[40] The Bush administration's 2003-04 "Greater Middle East Initiative" accordingly claimed that its goal was to set the stage for the "democratic" reform of the entire region.

It was, however, not made very clear what "democratization" meant for Arab monarchies, authoritarian Arab governments, the Islamic Republic of Iran (as well as for the Palestinian Authority). There was no clear guidance as to how these states could somehow go beyond feasible measures of "good governance" involving limited social reforms, permitting freedom of press and assembly, and the guarantee of political and human rights. There is consequently a great difference between the potential for "good governance" that *could be* practiced by monarchical and authoritarian regimes, versus the very different forms of "democracy" that have been practiced by the US and Europeans, among other states—and which generally took centuries to develop. Moreover, it was not clear how "democratic" change in domestic power structures would necessarily change the elitist nature of foreign policy behavior for the better—particularly for states in highly anarchical shatterbelt of the Middle East/Persian Gulf region.

Despite a number of critical, largely unanswered questions, neo-conservatives nevertheless argued that knocking out the Iraqi regime would not only work to convince the Islamic Republic of Iran to halt its nuclear program, but it could also undermine the control of Iran by Islamic ideologues, and eventually cause the Mullahs to fall from power. Neo-conservatives also asserted that Saudi Arabia and other Arab monarchies would begin to reform. (Municipal elections did take place in Saudi Arabia in January 2005, with the *promise* that women could participate at a later date, yet no one expects the Saudis to transform into a constitutional monarchy overnight!) It was additionally argued that US intervention in Iraq would set the stage for the Israelis and Palestinians to reach a peace settlement through the concept of "sequencing"—the elimination of Saddam Hussein in exchange for an Israeli-Palestinian peace settlement.[41] Here, however, it appears that the largely unexpected death of Yassir Arafat at the end of 2004, more so than the elimination of Saddam Hussein, appeared to stimulate Israel to engage in negotiations with the Palestinian Authority—at least initially. (See Chapter 6.)

Bush administration neo-conservatives have consequently advocated a controversial form of "democratic peace theory," which is presently confronted with at least two strenuous tests (in addition to continuing tests posed by conditions in Haiti, Bosnia, Kosovo, Afghanistan, Georgia, and now Ukraine, among other states). Just following the election of the new Palestinian Prime Minister, Mahmoud Abbas, in January 2005, Israel initially cut off all diplomatic relations. A truce was then established: but that truce will only hold if the Palestinian Authority can restrain all militant factions and if "democratic" Israel does not engage in additional military incursions—and if it abandons settlements in Gaza and continues to retract from significant portions of the West Bank, among other actions. The second test of this version of "democratic peace theory" will be the question as to what type of government will emerge after the January 2005 elections in Iraq. Questions remain as to whether a democratically elected Iraqi government will be truly representative of both majority and minority political, ethnic and religious factions. Questions also remain as to whether the new government can work to incorporate minority groups that have been effectively alienated, including the Sunni Moslem and Christian communities, among others, and whether the new government will be effective enough to deal with continuing acts of insurgency and terrorism that are presently undermining full Iraqi recovery.

The problem remains, however, that the contentiously illusory prospect of the "democratization" of the entire Middle East/ Persian Gulf area has additionally been coupled with not-so-veiled threats of US military intervention directed at states, such as Syria and Iran, that have supported "terrorism" or that have intended to develop WMD. In effect, if the US ultimately made good on its threats, or if regimes failed to "democratize" in ways that Washington approves (i.e. by adopting policies more or less acceptable to Washington), the US could opt for future interventions (assuming there is sufficient "democratic" support for such engagements). The dilemma, however, is that intervention in Iraq has opened a new front that diverts attention, resources and manpower from the initial focus on *al-Qaida*, and thus risks US overextension by limiting the possibility of military intervention in other regions, such as North Korea or Iran—if deemed "necessary." (See Chapter 4.) The situation in Iraq likewise exposes the US and coalition forces to weapons of conventional destruction—in a very costly war of attrition that makes the long term prospects for peace, social reconstruction and reconciliation in Iraq even more remote.

Without concerted attention, there is a real possibility that the civil war in Iraq (which, in effect, is already raging between rival ethnic and religious factions, as well as foreign pan-Islamic militants) could enlarge, possibly resulting in interventions by regional states. Washington's promises to establish a new form of "democratic federalism" thus threaten to degenerate into "sectarian chaos" based upon tribal, ethnic, religious and mafia power brokers, as opposed to more secular political criteria. Instead of achieving a stable "democratic federal" model as initially promised (and idealized) by Washington, a different type of either "communal" or "theocratic" government could emerge.

It will accordingly prove to be a superhuman challenge for a "democratically elected" and "moderately" Islamic, more or less pro-American, Iraqi regime to hold its coalition together.[42] This is true due to the need to eradicate "corruption" within the US-backed transitional authority and to check Iranian and radical influence among the Shi'a. It may also prove necessary to limit Kurdish claims to "relative autonomy," which includes demands for political control of oil rich Kirkuk. It is most crucial to win support from Sunnis and other factions alienated by US intervention, while effectively smothering "terrorist" activities, yet averting acts of Shi'ite and Kurdish vengeance—while risks of significant "collateral damage" will continue to haunt all forms of military action against insurgency.

Furthermore, even if a "democratic" Iraq can ultimately emerge from the present chaos to obtain nominal independence, it is highly likely that the new government will take exception to US political and economic policies, despite its being fostered by Washington. No matter what kind of government is ultimately formed, it will seek a further reduction, if not the repudiation, of what it considers "odious" debts. The latter had largely been forced upon the country by the Iraqi dictator in the 1980s during the war with Iran (with the tacit support of the US,

France and Russia). It is certain that the new government will additionally press OPEC for higher oil prices to pay the massive costs of its political, social and economic reconstruction—contrary to the initial, largely unstated, hope that "regime change" would help to lower the price of oil.[43]

## Roots of the New Global Disequilibrium

The new post-Cold War global system can be generally characterized as a highly unstable *polycentrism* in which states and other significant actors, possess highly uneven, if not totally lopsided, geo-strategic, military-technological and political economic *power capabilities*, as well as highly uneven, if not *unpredictable*, levels of socio-cultural, moral, ideological and media *influence* within civil society. In this respect, states, as well as intergovernmental, anti-governmental and non-governmental actors, multinational corporations and other forms of organizations and institutions, possess differing goals, interests and perceived political *intent*—as they seek to expand, sustain, and at times retract, their position of *relative* power and influence within a *dynamic* global and regional "equilibrium." States, and other forms of actors, operate in conditions of disproportionate resource and ecological scarcities, highly uneven vulnerabilities, and in general accord with historically changing international laws and norms. The latter may or may not be effectively "supervised" or "enforced" by international regimes, such as the Concert of Europe, League of Nations, and the UN, in differing historical epochs.

The Cold War system could be depicted more specifically as a "five-dimensional double containment" dominated by an essentially bipolar US-Soviet structure, and characterized by a mix of discord and collaboration. By contrast, the post-Cold War period can be largely described as a multidimensional "mono-containment" in which most of the collaborative aspects of the US-Soviet relationship have largely collapsed, particularly following NATO enlargement into eastern Europe. In this perspective, the US, as the predominant hegemonic power, has been attempting, largely single handedly, to contain, or else *channel* or *co-opt*, the power capabilities and intent of a number of emergent or re-emergent powers— while simultaneously seeking to "contain," "isolate" or "eradicate" a number of emergent "threats." The end of the Cold War has consequently resulted in the collapse of the *collaborative* aspects of the US-Soviet "five-dimensional double containment" coupled the emergence of new powers and actors and subsequent transformations in power relationships and in political intent among former "friends" and "enemies."[44]

The first and foremost level of Cold War "double containment" was that both "superpowers" not so inadvertently preferred to keep Germany and Europe partitioned for as long as possible, so that a unified Germany/Europe could not ultimately exercise its burgeoning political-economic power and influence *against* the interests of either Washington or Moscow. Both "superpowers" likewise preferred to keep Japan militarily weak and China and Taiwan divided. By generally siding with key opposing states in various regional conflicts, Washington and Moscow kept the semi-peripheral Eurasian rimland and Middle East/Persian

Gulf shatterbelt regions in perpetual tension. The two superpowers likewise tended to keep the peripheral "developing" world in perpetual tension (often by supporting armed partisans of differing ideological camps), and thus providing only limited self-serving military and economic assistance that generally supported pro-Western or pro-Soviet elites in power.

Following Cold War phases of détente and confrontation involving the US-Soviet "double containment" of a number of emerging powers, the post–1991 era following Soviet collapse can thus be characterized by US efforts to "mono-contain" a number of rising powers. The first, and most crucial, level of "mono-containment" has been to check the *potential* for Russian *revanche* by a *preclusive* NATO enlargement to as many eastern European states as possible, while simultaneously seeking to *channel* and *co-opt* Russia into taking a pro-American, pro-European stance through a tenuous largely incomplete US-Russian "diplomatic revolution."[45] Yet, at the same time, such a diplomatic revolution also represents a potentially risky process in that it involves a fundamental re-assessment of American (and Russian) relations with former Cold War enemies as well as friends.

The second level has been to contain a militarily and economically rising China, and prevent the unification of China and Taiwan on Beijing's terms. The third has been to check Japanese efforts to move toward greater political-economic and military independence, and to bring Japan closer to the US in the defense of Taiwan. The fourth level has represented an effort to prevent a newly unified Europe from implementing a truly common foreign and defense policy. The fifth has been to keep emerging nuclear *upstart* or *parvenu* powers in the Eurasian rimland (such as India and Pakistan) and Middle East/Persian Gulf shatterbelt region at permanent loggerheads—but without provoking nuclear war—or else eliminate threats by "regime change." The sixth is to sustain developing countries with limited military and economic assistance, and consequently *channel* the rise of emergent peripheral powers. Finally, the US seeks by itself, or with the help of its Allies, to check or eradicate pan-Islamic or other "terrorist" movements by extending the US military outreach throughout much of the world.

US unilateral intervention in Iraq, coupled with the uncertainties posed by shifting US alliance relationships and commitments, sets a dangerous precedent. Such uncertainty threatens to hurl Europe and the world back into inter-state rivalries, in which both *emergent* and *re-emergent* powers may begin to form countervailing alliances, including linkages with pan-Islamic movements or other "terrorist" organizations. The tenuous and uncertain nature of shifting American alliance formations and fumbling efforts to cope with a number of emergent or re-emergent powers and "terrorist" threats raises the risks of regional, if not major power conflict—but only if an engaged concerted diplomacy cannot soon be implemented.

## Multilateral Options

The roots of the new global disequilibrium, of course, do not rest solely in the *preclusive* US-UK intervention in Iraq. They also reside in the inability to establish new modes of global governance and security through a concerted strategy. US reluctance to reach out to an expanding EU and to a retrenching Russia, and to implement new systems of security in Europe, is most fundamentally at the root of the post-Cold War crisis. One simply cannot expect to achieve peace and security in much of the developing world—if one cannot absolutely guarantee peace within Europe itself. History has revealed that horrendous fact far too often.

The American belief that NATO enlargement represents a panacea for European security is disquieting. NATO—even as a quasi-reformed organization— simply cannot guarantee the security for *all* of Europe, that is, without fully and openly engaging in political-military coordination with each of the key states in the region in such a way as to permit both power *and* burden sharing. NATO enlargement risks alienating those states that are still not included as "full" members, most crucially Russia—despite the formation of the NATO-Russia Council (NRC) in 2001–02 in the months following the 11 September attacks. The NRC represents an important step in the right direction, but one that is not sufficient, that is, without more formal arms reduction/elimination accords and greater forms of power sharing. NATO enlargement also tends to ignore the crucial role that EU member states can play in European security, as well as states that do not presently wish to join NATO in its current form.

From the perspective of American interests, NATO enlargement, as presently conceived, risks the overextension of NATO's political will and resources. Most problematically, it raises exaggerated hopes as to the US ability to defend all "full" NATO members in all possible types of disputes/conflicts. The fact that Washington appears to be stretching itself out to confront crisis after crisis in central Asia, the Persian Gulf, the South China sea, as well as Africa, raises fears that the US might not necessarily come to the defense of Europe if needed. It also raises fears that Washington will engage forces only selectively, or that it might drag Europe into unwanted conflicts.

It is accordingly in the interest of the Europeans (and the UK as well) to construct new systems of European and global security—while it is concurrently in the interests of an *enlightened* American global strategy to help foster the development of those systems—in that Washington cannot possibly manage all these disputes single-handedly through "mono-containment." The world must not ignore the fact that the situation throughout Eurasia remains uncertain—despite the apparent *entente* between Russia, NATO and an expanding EU concerning the "war on terrorism." Present disputes over global geo-strategic, political-economic and socio-cultural concerns still need to be thoroughly addressed and resolved through a concerted and truly "multilateral" strategy—before complacency and indifference once again breed tensions and conflict.

# Chapter 2

# The Roots of American Neo-Conservatism: Neo-Timocrats or Moralizing Politicians?

In his classic text on American foreign policy, *The Arrogance of Power*, Senator J. William Fulbright, stated: "The inconstancy of American foreign policy is not an accident but an expression of the two distinct sides of the American character. Both are characterized by a kind of moralism, but one is the morality of decent instincts tempered by the knowledge of human imperfection and the other is the morality of absolute self-assurance fired by the crusading spirit."[1]

In the post-Cold War era, American foreign policy is still divided between two distinct viewpoints. It is the "multilateralists" who are best characterized by the "morality of decent instincts tempered by the knowledge of human imperfection"; it is the "neo-conservatives" who are best characterized by "the morality of absolute self-assurance fired by the crusading spirit."

## Neo-Conservative Ideology

The doctrine of "neo-conservatism" seeks to develop and implement America-first, and essentially *unilateral*, global strategies; it represents a *national universalistic* and *unilateralist* tendency in American geo-strategic thinking that is characterized by "absolute self-assurance fired by the crusading spirit." While the actual term "neo-conservative" was coined as a derogatory term in the 1970s, the general world outlook (*Weltanschauung*) has asserted itself in a number of periods throughout American history.

The primary goal of the neo-conservative agenda during the Cold War was to impel "democratic" change in the Soviet system, and secondarily in China, among other Communist states. The primary post-Cold War goal of neo-conservatives has been to implement "global democratization"—in that the collapse of the Soviet empire, as a countervailing military power, has largely provided Washington with a free hand to engage in the policies that it sees fit in order to achieve its ends. Since 11 September 2001, neo-conservatives have been engaged in three simultaneous struggles: the "war on terrorism"; the effort to eliminate weapons of mass destruction

27

(WMD); and the determination to engage in the "democratization" of both major and regional powers—with the primary focus on *selected* states that oppose American policies.

Another term for neo-conservatives is "conservative internationalists." Neo-conservatives themselves utilize this term to distinguish their position from both communist internationalism and more traditional and "prudent conservatism"—in which some isolationist variants have been dubbed as "paleo-conservative." As it openly advocates radical changes in the global and regional *status quo*, neo-conservative ideology represents an anathema to traditional conservatives and has very little relationship to "traditional" or "classical" realism. The latter generally seek to implement policies designed to sustain the "balance of power" of the *status quo*—rather than attempt to alter that *status quo*. Other labels for neo-conservatives include "democratic internationalists" or "democratic globalists."[2]

In this regard, neo-conservatives seek to merge or synthesize aspects of "neo-realism" and "neo-liberalism" into a new doctrine. Here, neo-realism, generally argues that state concerns with *security* should take precedence over concerns with *power* (as previously argued by "classical" realists, such as Hans Morgenthau). By contrast, neo-liberalism generally supports the global extension of liberal democracy and free trade. Neo-conservative ideology consequently seeks to merge both neo-realism and neo-liberalism. Neo-conservatism argues that the US, as the world's leading power, as it is no longer checked by Soviet counterforce in a bipolar era, needs to take the lead in extending "democracy" and "free trade" throughout the world. This may be accomplished by the overthrow of "tyrannical" states through the imposition of tough sanctions, or through support for revolutionary political or civil society movements, or if necessary, by the use of direct military intervention.

## Background

The term "neo-conservative" was intended to be derogatory; it originated in the 1970s to describe former "liberals," "socialists" or "leftists" who became disillusioned with radical thinking (often after a revelation of seeing themselves as "naively" following the ways of the anti-Soviet left, usually as social-democrats, Maoists or Trotskyites).[3] While most neo-conservatives tended to flock to the rightwing of the Republican Party, the Democrat Party has attracted a significant number as well—often calling themselves "hawkish" democrats.

Neo-conservatives represent a mix of "born again" evangelical Protestants, fervent Catholics, Jewish intellectuals, former intellectuals from "New York City" democratic left, or else democrats who turned "far right" Republican, as was the case for Ronald Reagan himself. Some were influenced by the American civil rights movement, which they see as an ideal for other societies to emulate in the struggle against "tyranny." Still others were already conservative democrats, but who opposed what they saw as the "leftward" tilt of the Democratic Party. Such a diverse variety of individuals do not necessarily agree on overall tactics and on all specific issues, but they do generally agree to the general goal of an "America-first" strategy, and the willingness to use force to achieve their objectives.

What might be the common denominator of this very diverse crowd is not so much a common religion, as Samuel Huntington might argue (Protestant, Catholic and Jewish religions are all represented). But rather, an elitist technocratic and global geo-strategic and political economic perspective that is willing to use force in the belief that there are military-technological "solutions" to generally intractable geopolitical problems. In this regard, neo-conservatives tend to downgrade diplomacy as a means to resolve conflict. Claiming to think in the long term, they tend to be insensitive as to as the socio-cultural and ecological impact of their policies, but concurrently seek to upgrade political "morality" and American "values" and "virtues" as an ideological basis for foreign and domestic policy decision-making. But, here, there is a tendency for neo-conservatives, as *political moralists*, to confound *values* with *interests* and *morality* with *expediency*.

## Mercantilism in the Name of "Global Liberalism"

In part as a reflection of their "radical" roots, neo-conservatives tend to argue, as did both Karl Marx and Leon Trotsky (but generally without concrete reference to either thinker), that imperialism and colonialism play a "positive" role in breaking down traditional societies and that forceful action can open the doors to the development of capitalism and democratic liberalism. Although they disdain the term, neo-conservatives regard "imperialism," coupled with permanent "democratic" (rather than "socialist") revolution, as "progressive" in the sense that it ostensibly impels developing countries to adopt the image of the highly developed "democratic" countries.

The key motor for global political change, however, is not the united proletariat, or civil society as a whole, as Marx and Trotsky would argue, but rather, the elites of the predominant or "leading" state of the international system. "Democracy" in this view can ostensibly be *imposed* by elites *from above*—and need not necessarily arise *from below* from civil society. In this regard, free trade "imperialism" and "liberal democracy" can be fostered by the *predominant* state or states. Neo-conservatives claim to distrust "big government"; yet, at the same time, they contribute heavily to what President Eisenhower dubbed the military-industrial (and university) "complex" in his Farewell Address.

Yet in contrast to classical liberal *laissez faire* policy, as it pertains to the international political-economic system, neo-conservatives generally believe that more audacious, and potentially interventionist, steps must be taken in order to bring about "positive" political and economic change throughout the world. As "global populists," neo-conservatives accordingly "borrow" strongly from supply side economics; they advocate hefty tax cuts for investors and engage in heavy deficit spending. These measures are generally coupled with heavy defense spending and neo-mercantilist incentives to press arms sales abroad, in order to boost business (and ostensibly create jobs)—regardless of the risks posed by heavy government borrowing. Sales of F-16s to Poland (dubbed the "contract of the century") represents one example of neo-mercantilist neo-conservative policies (see Chapter 7) as do US AID contracts to major American multinational corporations to develop Iraq (without competitive bidding on grounds of "national security").[4]

Neo-conservatives argue that huge public deficits only represent a small percentage of the GDP and that the US economy is large enough to ultimately pay back debts owed to foreign lenders. (The US deficit in 2005 should amount to about 3.5 percent of the nation's gross domestic product, a figure that is still below the budget deficits of the Reagan era.) Yet this point ignores the often unmentioned fact that more than 80% of the Federal Government's $2.3 trillion budget cannot be cut to pay back debts—without a significant sacrifice in entitlements, and in military and domestic "security" expenditures. Not afraid of spending borrowed money, neo-conservatives are capable of acting for ostensibly idealistic causes, but only when key US geopolitical interests are at stake. The forgiveness of Mexican and then Iraqi debts (under Ronald Reagan and George W. Bush respectively), and a major aid package to the Indian Ocean region in early 2004 with a focus on Moslem Indonesia (after the Tsunami struck and devastated much of the region), represent specific "idealistic" actions designed to serve long term US interests. (See Chapter 8.)

It is interesting to note that while Reagan economics supported a strong dollar (which generally assisted American overseas investors), the administration of George W. Bush, Jr. has permitted the dollar to fall quite drastically against a generally rising (but also overvalued) Euro. This latter fact theoretically stimulates exports, and may possibly help increase investment within the US, but it has simultaneously frightened creditors, who have begun to accept the Euro as a reserve currency—a fact that may ultimately impel the US to tighten its deficits.[5]

**Reaganite Roots**

Many had expected George Bush Jr. to follow in the footsteps of his father, but this has not at all been the case. The administration of George Bush Sr. was often critiqued as being much too "prudent" and lacking the "vision thing." George W. Bush, the son, has consequently attempted to prove through forceful and decisive action that he does possess the long range "vision" that his father did not. George W. Bush accordingly surrounded himself with many of the neo-conservative strategists and evangelicals who had promoted Ronald Reagan's cause. It was ostensibly in meeting with evangelical Christian leader, Pat Robertson, in the course of his father's campaign for the presidency in 1988, that George W. Bush realized the importance of attracting the evangelical vote, which, in turn, helped him win the governorship of Texas, and which likewise helped him to outflank both his democratic, as well as his more moderate Republican, opponents.

While Arizona governor Barry Goldwater (with strong backing from Ronald Reagan during his failed presidential election campaign) probably represents the forerunner of the Cold War neo-conservative movement, contemporary neo-conservatives give more credit to the populist Ronald Reagan for bringing the movement to power. (By the time Reagan ran for the presidency, Goldwater himself had begun to oppose the Republican Party's turn toward the religious right and away from more moderate and "libertarian" principles; for this reason, Goldwater is regarded as having abandoned the neo-conservative cause.)

Former CIA Director during the Reagan years, William Casey represented an interesting case of a neo-conservative, with a different background as a Catholic Knight of Malta, educated by Jesuits. He fervently believed in augmenting the outreach of the Catholic Church in order to counter Communism in eastern Europe and in Central America. The CIA quietly supported the Solidarity movement in predominantly Catholic Poland, with Pope John Paul II's support, while it concurrently sponsored violent "freedom fighters" in Nicaragua, and state sponsored terror in El Salvador and Guatemala against militant radicals and peaceful reformers, as well as Catholic advocates of "liberation theology." In a criss-crossed "civilizational" alliance, CIA director Casey likewise supported the cause of pan-Islamic forces against the "evil empire" in Afghanistan.[6]

The influence of neo-conservatives began to rise with the initial 1976 challenge of Ronald Reagan to the moderate wing of the Republican Party, led by former President Gerald Ford. In essence, Gerald Ford had been unable to unify Southern voters; Reagan, in the 1980 election campaign, appealed to the "Sun Belt" and won every Republican primary in the South and West, while denouncing President Carter's impotence in handling the hostage crisis in Iran. By claiming to uphold "religious" and "family" values, Reaganites called themselves "social conservatives" opposing both libertarian philosophy and big government "liberalism."

In 1984, Ronald Reagan then went on to defeat the "liberal" pro-union Democratic Candidate Walter Mondale, who only won the Electoral College votes of his home state of Minnesota plus those of Washington, DC! George Bush, Sr. (who is regarded as a New Englander while his son, George Walker Bush, is regarded as a Texan) then lost to a southerner, Bill Clinton (former Governor of Arkansas). Once Clinton stepped down after two terms, his former Vice President Al Gore, from Tennessee, and who tried to appeal to conservative southern voters, barely lost to George W. Bush, Jr. but in the Electoral College, not by the popular vote.

In terms of specific policy-makers, the administration of George W. Bush Jr. (2000-04) can best be compared with the first term of the Reagan administration (1980-84) as opposed to the single term administration of George Bush, Sr. (1988-92). This is true as many key officials of the George W. Bush Jr. worked in the Reagan administration. James Baker, as a more traditional realist, had tried to weed the Reaganites out of the administration when he was Secretary of State for George Bush, Sr. The prime exception was Paul Wolfowitz who served as Under Secretary of Defense for Policy from 1989 to 1993, under then Secretary of Defense Dick Cheney for matters concerning strategy, plans, and policy.[7]

The Reaganite neo-conservatives were able to spring back once George W. Bush was elected in a highly contested election in 2000, in which Al Gore, former Vice President under Bill Clinton, won the popular vote by more than 500,000 votes, but did not win the Electoral College. George Bush Jr. accordingly won the majority of Electoral College votes, including those of the key state of Florida by a very slim majority. Gore's appeal to the Supreme Court for a recount of votes in Florida lost in a close five to four vote. Four of the five US Supreme Court Justices, who had blocked a recount, had been chosen by Ronald Reagan. Of the two Supreme Court justices appointed by then President George Bush Sr., one opposed a recount, while the other did not. At the same time, had the Florida votes of third party candidate, Ralph Nader, gone to Al Gore, the latter would have more clearly defeated George Bush in Florida. It might then have been possible for Al Gore to win both the popular vote and the Electoral College, without a recount. The fact that the Supreme Court had largely decided the nature and process of the American election in the year 2000 has led critics to comment that George W. Bush was appointed, but not elected. Moreover, the fact that the election was determined by a Supreme Court decision has raised questions as to the general understanding of democracy as "majority rule," coupled with still changing definitions of "minority rights". (See Chapter 7.)

While many observers predicted that the drive to get voters to the polls in the 2004 elections would bring in more Democratic voters, the drive to increase voting populations actually brought a Republican victory, thus leading the neo-conservatives to believe that they had a clear mandate. In essence, Bush won the votes of the American southwest and "heartland" while John Kerry, the democratic candidate, won the east and west coasts, and areas along the Mississippi river that are most exposed to international trade and cultures. Yet the fear of terrorism, and the unwillingness to change leaderships in the midst of a real "war," played a large role in securing the re-election of George W. Bush for a second term.

**Neo-Conservatives and the Question of Soviet Collapse**

The experience of contemporary neo-conservatives stems most directly from the Reagan era, yet their historical roots go deeper. During the Cold War, the neo-conservative outlook was generally represented by the first *Committee for the Present Danger* in 1950, for example, which sought to alert the country to the Soviet "threat," as formulated by National Security Doctrine NSC-68, a doctrine that gained support just after the invasion of South Korea by North Korea. NSC-68 consequently engaged the US into a far more extensive campaign against the global Communist threat than previously determined, in the effort to contain, if not roll back, the Soviet Union. (Paul Nitze's doctrine resulted in the militarization of containment in the views George Kennan.)

It is not clear when, or if, Washington had actually planned for a Soviet break-up—and for its consequences. In the 1950s, it had been common to say that the Soviet system possessed the "seeds of its own destruction." But American containment policy went far beyond that outlined by one of its "neo-conservative" founders, Paul Nitze, one of the original members of the *Committee for the Present Danger* (see below). For Nitze, the purposes of the Cold War were not to break-up the Soviet Union, but rather, to "democratize" it, and impel it to withdraw from eastern Europe. In fact, Paul Nitze in NSC-68 had warned very strongly *against* breaking up the Soviet Union: Overall US objectives did "not include unconditional surrender, the subjugation of Russian peoples, or a Russia shorn of its economic potential." The latter, Nitze argued, "would irrevocably unite the Russian people behind the regime that enslaves them."[8] It was thus not contradictory for Nitze to advocate integrating the new Russia into the US and

Europe, after Soviet collapse in 1991, and to warn against isolating Russia through NATO expansion—in advocating a more realistic strategy of *cooptation* that has generally been opposed by contemporary neo-conservatives.[9]

Efforts to impel an implosion of the Soviet empire were strengthened by the "China Card," as played by the Nixon, Carter, and then the Reagan, administrations. Richard Nixon and Henry Kissinger had argued that the opening to China should serve to "counter balance" Russia; Nixon himself had urged recognition of China as early as 1960. Neo-conservatives, however, opposed Nixon's strategy of détente (and were, to a certain extent, skeptical of the "China Card" as well). Paul Wolfowitz (a Republican) and Richard Perle (a Democrat) both served as assistants to Democratic Senator Henry "Scoop" Jackson, who had founded the *Coalition for a Democratic Majority* and who led the opposition to the Nixon-Kissinger strategy of détente with the Soviet Union, and who have subsequently been regarded as taking on Senator Jackson's torch.[10] Moreover, it was also Senator Jackson who refused to grant MFN status to Moscow through the Jackson-Vanik amendment, which was ostensibly aimed at forcing Moscow to open up its emigration policies. (See Chapter 6.) Perle and Wolfowitz were additionally protégés of Albert Wohlstetter, the author of the classic Cold War article "Balance of Terror" which was highly influential in developing the US policy of deterrence and the concept of Mutual Assured Destruction (MAD).[11]

Although not generally considered a neo-conservative, but certainly a "hawkish democrat," it was President Carter's National Security Advisor Zbigniew Brzezinski, who asserted that China should be impressed in the service of American global strategy as an "active" strategic counter-weight *against* Moscow. The Reagan administration continued Brzezinski's efforts to play the China card, which involved high technology assistance, and a lowering of Coordinating Committee on the sales of restricted military and dual use technology for China alone, and which gradually led to a significant augmentation of China's power potential—despite China's continued threats to Taiwan.

From this perspective, the roots of Soviet/Russian instability and the break-up of the USSR can be traced, in part, to the "China Card" which forced Soviet preparations for a possible two front war. Following US intervention in Vietnam in 1964 in the aftermath of the trumped up Gulf of Tonkin incident, American global strategy increasingly linked NATO, Japan, China. American alliance formations then helped to push up Soviet defense spending to the detriment of its agricultural and consumer sectors: Soviet defense procurement grew at a rate higher than its GNP while Moscow became a net importer of grain. The Soviet far eastern military build-up then cost its already strained economy two, perhaps three, times the cost of its build-up in Eastern Europe. Soviet forces committed to China accounted for roughly 25% of Soviet defense spending; Soviet forces deployed in Afghanistan and central Asia in the 1980s added another 10% as did Soviet crack down in Eastern Europe.[12]

It was during the oil crisis of the early 1970s that the option of seizing oil fields in the Persian Gulf began to circulate in neo-conservative circles. By 1976, following the US withdrawal/defeat in Vietnam, the neo-conservative outlook was best represented by the "re-emerged" *Committee for the Present Danger*, which opposed détente with the Soviet Union with the argument that US military strength and nuclear capability was falling behind that of Moscow, through a "window of vulnerability." During the 1980s, the *Committee for the Free World* (founded 1981, now defunct) helped to lead anti-Communist crusades in Afghanistan, Angola and in other countries in Africa, and in Central America, among other regions. Combined with efforts to play the Beijing against Moscow, forcing the Soviet Union to build up its military defenses against NATO, Japan, as well as China, neo-conservatives hoped to roll back, if not implode, the Soviet Empire.

In this regard, the Reagan Administration adopted the doctrine of "horizontal escalation" which was intended to roll back post–1975 Soviet gains throughout the world. The strategy was based upon the concept that rough US-Soviet nuclear parity, with the US venturing toward superiority in delivery capabilities (but not necessarily in explosive "throw-weight") would be able to match Soviet threats across the board—without escalating to nuclear war. Here, the Reagan Administration largely utilized surrogate fighters to beat back Soviet-backed regimes or Soviet-supported movements. US support for anti-Soviet movements would not-so-inadvertently set off a number of seemingly permanent brush fires throughout many regions (as in Angola) that would be difficult to put out, even after the Cold War was "over." (Secretary of State George Schultz of the Reagan Administration was, however, able to draw the ANC away from Soviet influence in South Africa through secret diplomacy rather than through repression—and in working with the leadership of F.W. de Klerk. See Chapter 3.)

A number of deaths in the politburo ultimately led to the rise to power of Mikhail Gorbachev in 1985, but even then, Secretary of State Dick Cheney and Paul Wolfowitz continued to warn that Gorbachev remained a significant "threat" to US interests. By the time George Bush, Sr., had entered the White House, an article called "To the Stalin Mausoleum" by "Z" indicted Gorbachev's reforms and "Gorbiemania"; the article hinted of the inability of USA to stop Soviet collapse and was reputed to be the Bush administration's equivalent to George Kennan's 1947 "X" article.[13] Gorbachev's unilateral retractionist policies had given Washington the excuse to argue that such a "change" in the Soviet system had occurred; but at the same time, subsequent US administrations began to take advantage of Soviet/Russian weaknesses, rather than engage directly with Moscow. Then Secretary of Defense Richard Cheney warned that Soviet instability was a greater danger than its military expansion. Uncertainty and fear of Soviet instability soon replaced the Cold War fear of a Soviet attack on Western Europe.

Even after Soviet collapse, neo-conservative Paul Wolfowitz, and his deputy I. Lewis Libby, prepared the initial February 1992 Pentagon Defense Planning Guidance (DPG) draft which warned of the worst case scenario of a "resurgent/ emergent global threat" (REGT) should a *revanchist* Russia, perhaps linked to a rising China and India, come to the forefront at the turn of the millennium. The February 1992 DPG draft accordingly argued that the US needed to pursue a strategy of global dominance versus the emerging "threats" posed by Russia, China, India—if not Germany and Japan. It was argued that the latter allies would attempt to obtain greater political-military independence from the USA. The February 1992 DPG document thus not only sought to counter Russia and China, but it also sought to prevent the emergence of European-only security arrangements, which would "undermine" NATO. The first draft also considered extending East and Central European nations security commitments similar to those extended to Saudi Arabia, Kuwait and other Gulf states; this position actually stopped short of advocating "full" NATO membership for eastern European states, as would become policy later in the decade under Presidents Clinton and Bush, Jr. The first draft also sought to guarantee access to vital raw materials, primarily Persian Gulf oil, which has been a demand of neo-conservatives ever since the OPEC-induced rise of oil prices in the 1970s.

After the leak of the first draft, the more pragmatic "realists," or traditional conservatives, James Baker, Brent Scowcroft, and Colin Powell pressed then Defense Secretary Dick Cheney to radically modify the document.[14] The later May 1992 DPG draft called for a "democratic partnership with the new Russia," and then toned down the apocalyptic assessment of the February draft, parts of which had been leaked to the New York Times.[15] (Yet regardless of apparent doctrinal shift in 1992, the US has still been attempting to limit the rise of Europe and Japan as potential military powers.[16])

In the post-Cold war era, neo-conservatives initially supported some aspects of Bill Clinton's neo-liberalism—but only when it was regarded as asserting US global interests. Neo-conservatives pressed for the expansion of NATO to as many eastern European states as possible, but were upset when the Clinton administration decided to take in only Poland, the Czech Republic and Hungary. In 1997–98, when a number of neo-conservatives began to move against the Clinton administration's multilateralist policies and support for the UN, they formed the *Project for a New American Century (PNAC)*, which pressed for US military intervention in Iraq, among other unilateralist, America-first, policies.[17] Many, but not all, neo-conservatives tended to support the Clinton administration's war "over" Kosovo in 1998. Traditional conservatives, such as Henry Kissinger, in addition to so-called "paleo-conservatives," such as Patrick Buchanan, had both opposed the latter conflict.

A new *Committee on the Present Danger*, which defines itself as bipartisan, once again "re-emerged" just after 11 September 2001—in order to "fight terror."[18] By 2004, neo-conservatives appeared to have won a major "victory" by expanding full NATO membership to the Baltic states, and to most other former Warsaw Pact countries—despite Russian protests. (See Chapter 6.) Neo-conservatives have additionally attacked President Putin for "undermin(ing) democracy" and for taking steps toward an "authoritarian regime"—but without fully analyzing the complex situation in Russian in comparative or historical perspective.[19]

**The Question of Pre-Emption**

In that they do not accept the sovereign rights of all states as a given, neo-conservatives are generally not supporters of "containment" and prefer "roll back" and "regime change" of unsavory governments and "rogue states."

Neo-conservatives and neo-realists differ upon key questions relating to nuclear proliferation and the questions of "imminent" threat. Neo-realists believe that nuclear proliferation is generally impossible to stop or must be "managed" in such a way that only "responsible" states should obtain a nuclear capability. Neo-realists argue that nuclear weapons are largely developed for defensive purposes, and work to restrain states from attacking, actually minimizing the chances for war. At the end of the Cold War, neo-realist John Mearsheimer, for example, argued that responsible states, such as Germany and Ukraine, should be permitted to obtain or retain nuclear weaponry.[20] In essence, nuclear weapons seek to preserve the status quo, obtain prestige for isolated states; they are intended to *preserve* regimes rather than permit "regime change."

By contrast with neo-realists, neo-conservatives oppose any further spread of nuclear capabilities, but seek to maintain clear US nuclear and military predominance. Here, the question of the nature of what makes a truly "imminent" threat tends to divide neo-realists and neo-conservatives. (See Chapter 4.) Neo-conservative Richard Perle justified the Israeli attack on the Iraqi Osirak nuclear reactor in 1981, and the US military intervention in Iraq in 2003, as "pre-emptive" in the sense that both actions were designed to prevent Iraq from ultimately obtaining a nuclear enrichment capability. This is true even if Baghdad did not possess a nuclear weapons capability at the time of the attack; the problem was when to strike before the threat became "unmanageable."[21] In many ways, neo-conservatives have extended the concept of "pre-emption," that the Clinton administration developed, into a policy of *preclusion*. The Bush administration's National Security Presidential Directive-17/ HSPD "National Strategy to Combat Weapons of Mass Destruction" (12 December 2001) represented, in effect, a step beyond Clinton Administration policy, using the 11 September 2001 attacks as rationalization. It was argued that the US now requires "new methods of deterrence" against those states that were aggressively pursuing WMD and their means of delivery.[22]

## Opposition to "Balance of Power" Politics

Neo-conservatives do not adhere to traditional concepts of "realism" or even "neo-realism"; they generally oppose "balance of power" politics and believe in proactive foreign policies and military strategies designed to throw the other side "off balance." In many ways, neo-conservative opposition to "balance of power" politics and the push toward more unilateral, if not *preclusive* policies, in the Middle East/Persian Gulf, stemmed from the failure of "balance of power" to change the situation in the Middle East.

The US tended to play neo-realist "balance of power" games by supporting both Iraq and Iran, for example, during the "war on cities" in the 1980s. This is true in that the US may have initially encouraged Saddam Hussein to intervene in Iran, which was inciting Kurdish and Shi'ite rebellion in Iraq, according to former Iranian President Bani Sadr. By 1982–83, the US definitely tilted more fully in support of Baghdad (with the engagement of Donald Rumsfeld)—so as to prevent Iranian victory.[23] Washington consequently looked the other way when Saddam Hussein repressed the Kurdish *peshmerga* who had aligned with Iran; when Saddam used chemical weaponry against Iranian human wave offensives, particularly in 1986 to prevent the capture of the Fao peninsula; and when he used chemical weapons in August 1988, against Kurdish fighters and population.

The fact that neo-conservatives loathe the concept of "appeasement" (see discussion below) helps to explain their demand to overthrow the Saddam Hussein regime, following the latter's invasion of Kuwait. President Bush's refusal in 1990 to "go to Baghdad" had angered both Paul Wolfowitz and Richard Perle. At the time, however, the more prudent realists in the Bush Sr. administration—such as Richard Cheney (then) and Brent Scowcroft, as well as George Bush Sr.— supported the President. As George Bush and Brent Scowcroft put it after Desert Storm: "While we hoped that a popular revolt or coup would topple Saddam Hussein, neither the United States nor the countries in the region wished to see the break-up of the Iraqi state... However admirable self-determination for the Kurds or Shi'tes might have been in principle, the practical aspects of this particular situation dictated the policy.... Had we gone the invasion route, the US could conceivably still be an occupying power in a bitterly hostile land."[24]

While Brent Scowcroft continued to oppose US military intervention in Iraq after 11 September, Richard Cheney flip-flopped sometime after 11 September. Initially, he opposing intervention in Iraq in 1991, but then openly supported intervention in August 2002—largely in the presumption that Saddam possessed, or would soon possess, a significant WMD capability. Like Scowcroft, former Secretary of State James Baker, who had served in the administration of George Bush Sr., had publicly urged that the US should not intervene in Iraq without the support of the UN Security Council. (There has been much speculation that George Bush Sr. had strongly disagreed with his son's decision.)

According to former Bush Jr. administration official, Richard Clarke, it was Paul Wolfowitz, who had first urged President Bush to find out if Saddam Hussein had been involved in the 11 September 2001 attacks against the World Trade Center and Pentagon.[25] In the view of Secretary of State Colin Powell, neo-conservatives such as Dick Cheney "had an unhealthy fixation on *al-Qaida* and Iraq that caused him to misread and exaggerate intelligence and the threat." Powell also stated that Cheney, Wolfowitz, vice presidential chief of staff, Scooter Libby and Douglas J. Feith, undersecretary for defense policy who pressed for US intervention in Iraq—were all part of "a separate little government."[26]

## Unilateralism versus Multilateralism

Neo-conservatives do not necessarily oppose multilateral initiatives, but they argue that such initiatives may prove weak-kneed and ineffective, or that such "multilateral" ventures are, in reality, US-led. They thus put the threat to use force up front and argue that the United States must take its role as an "eagle" seriously. The US must extend its talons and demonstrate its resolve to use force in order to make certain that its policies will be respected, *if not feared*—by both "democratic" and "non-democratic" states alike.

According to neo-conservatives, Europeans (including both European conservatives and Euro-socialists) often support concepts of "liberal internationalism" and "multilateralism" to suit their own political purposes (in the quest for greater European unity).[27] Robert Kagan, for example, makes a distinction between "principled multilateralists" and "instrumental multilateralists."[28] He argues that Europeans only pretend to be "principled multilateralists" by advocating that all decisions go through the UN Security Council (UNSC). The European position accordingly argues that a major power cannot promise to abide by the decisions of UN Security Council and then act unilaterally—if the decisions of the UNSC do not please that power, for whatever reason. Yet as Kagan argues, the Europeans themselves will, just like the US, opt for unilateral measures when it suits their national interests to do so. (Unilateral German recognition of Croatia in 1991—against the policy of the US, EU and UN—represents a case in point.)

In contrast with the Europeans, Kagan argues that American realists, such as former Secretary of State James Baker, tend to take a more pragmatic approach to the UNSC, and thus can be defined as "instrumental multilateralists." From Kagan's perspective, "the core of the American multilateralist argument is pragmatic" in contrast with European pretence. This is because most American multilateralism "is a cost-benefit analysis, not a principled commitment to multilateral action as the cornerstone of world order." Kagan thus quotes James Baker as arguing in respect to military intervention in Iraq that, "the costs will be much greater, as will the political risks, both domestic and international, if we end up going it alone."[29]

Baker's assessment, according to Kagan, may be correct, but Baker's argument only points out the fact that the US was willing to go to war "alone" regardless of the opposition of three members of the UNSC, except the United Kingdom. In this view, "instrumental multilateralism" is only a variant on "unilateralism." As specific examples, neo-conservatives argue that a whole series of bilateral and international accords represent a means to restrain unilateral US actions and interests. The 1967 ABM treaty (the cornerstone to the theory of Mutual Assured Destruction and Cold War deterrence), for example, was seen as a hindrance to the development and deployment of national Ballistic Missile Defenses. Yet rather than carefully revise the ABM treaty with Russia, so that both sides could provide input, the Bush administration dumped the treaty unilaterally—placing American (and world) security in the hands of an untested and undeveloped technology, and potentially alienating Russia.

The US similarly opposed the International Criminal Court (ICC) as an infringement upon US national sovereignty; neo-conservatives believe that is up to the US (and no other power) to decide issues of legality, morality and justice. (In "good" company, the US and the People's Republic of China are the only two members of the fifteen permanent members that have not ratified or signed the treaty establishing the ICC—as of 2004.) Neo-conservatives claim to be strong formal believers in civil and political rights; yet their own opposition to war crimes, crimes against humanity and genocide appears *selective* and not universal. Non-democratic states that oppose US policies (such as the so-called "outposts of tyranny") are condemned, while the actions of non-democratic states that generally support US policies (such as Pakistan, Saudi Arabia, Egypt, Uzbekistan,

Kyrgystan, among others) are generally ignored—as are the actions of democratic states *outside* their immediate territories, as is the case for Israel.

Neo-conservatives accordingly tend to pick and choose according to political-moral criteria, and can thus be accused of "double standards."[30] It is consequently difficult to maintain legitimacy for one's actions (outside possibly forgivable "collateral damage" and "errors of judgment" in the stress of wartime)—if one is increasingly accused of doing precisely what the opposition is doing. The problem raised by the neo-conservative insistence upon the use of force, and by the promulgation of unilateral US interests, is that the US risks losing credibility and creating even greater animosities. By not acting as an "honest broker" between two or more conflicting sides, US policy may force reformist groups into joining the violent opposition. The dilemma then is to press allies to engage in reforms where possible, but then prevent "extremist" factions from obtaining the upper hand.

Neo-conservatives retaliate by arguing that "double standards" are inevitable: one standard for "democracies" and one standard for the "rest"—except when the rest are one's Allies. But even here, neo-conservatives, such as Kagan, argue that the US may have to go it alone and bear the moral and legal consequences; the Europeans are simply unable to accept the international reality of "double standards." In Kagan's view, democracies in the US and Europe are quite capable of keeping law among themselves, but they must be willing and capable of using force outside their territories against those states that are ostensibly incapable of sustaining law and order. (See Chapter 7.)

## "Democracy" and "Regime Change"

The question is raised, why press for "democracy" or else engage in "humanitarian intervention" in some states, but not others? Why intervene in Afghanistan, Kosovo, Haiti or Iraq, rather than Russia, China, North Korea, Iran, Rwanda or Sierra Leone? Why should the US favor self-determination for East Timor and Croatia, but not Chechnya or Tibet, or Kosovo? In response, Paul Wolfowitz argues, "foreign policy is not about consistency… it is rather about discrimination, the application of judgment and the balancing of competing but valid claims—and all this in circumstances that inevitably vary in significant ways."[31] Here, Wolfowitz reveals himself as somewhat more of a "realist" than as a typical neo-conservative; but one can also question whether intervention in Iraq, among other Bush administration actions, has showed any real *discrimination*.

Once again, more of a realist, Wolfowitz does recognize that states that are helped by outside powers along the route of "democracy" may actually turn against the interests of the very states that initially supported their path to "democracy." Wolfowitz admits that support for democratic movements does not always create allies, but is better in his view to support such movements; he believes that support for democracy, even if it works to counter US interests in the short term, may work in the long-term national interest of the country, as well as in the American interest. Despite the fact that the US more or less supported steps toward Filipino democracy (against the Marcos *cleptocracy* that the US had originally placed in power), Manilla then turned against American interests by ousting US military bases (the Philippines may be reconsidering that position, however). Likewise, just as NATO-ally Turkey has strengthened its democratic process, it voted in 2003 against the deployment of US troops upon its territory as a launching pad for US intervention against its neighbor, Iraq.

Wolfowitz concedes that Vietnam and Haiti represented cases in which the US military failed as a "democratizing" force; yet the same situation appears to be repeating itself in Iraq—in that the US military appear to be sinking into a quagmire, if not quicksand. It is possible that if Iraq ultimately gains a modicum of sovereignty, it could likewise oppose US policies, in this logic. Even the hand picked Iraqi National Council, for example, vehemently opposed US-initiated proposals in November 2003 to bring 10,000 Turkish troops into Iraq as peacekeepers, in areas outside Iraqi Kurdistan. Such a presence, it was argued, could provoke Iran or Syria to intervene or else raise fears of Turkish occupation. (The very proposal makes one wonder if the Bush administration knows anything about the region and its culture and history, in that the British had previously "liberated" Iraq from Ottoman/Turkish controls in 1917–21!)

Moreover, after Iraqi elections in January 2005, to be followed by a Constitutional convention, Washington may ultimately find the new government hostile to US interests. The new Iraqi government will most likely demand significant cuts in Iraq's massive foreign debts (following the concept of "odious" debt)—if not threaten default and attempt to augment oil prices as much as possible. Should Iran acquire a nuclear capability, Iraq might want to acquire the same—that is, if the US refuses to provide Iraq with security guarantees, or if the US withdraws and the new Baghdad seeks total independence.

One furthermore wonders to what extent the US can tolerate even ostensibly democratic states that do not abide by its interests. To what extent can the US universally support "democratic" movements across the board—in that true democratization could actually destabilize key US allies? To what extent can the US back even democratically elected regimes that might ultimately oppose US interests, for example, through nationalization or expropriation of property? What if "democratic" elections bring to power radical Islamic governments, as almost happened in Algeria in 1992, and could happen in Pakistan? (See Chapters 3 and 5.) On the other hand, to what extent can states, *without* deep-rooted democratic traditions, truly adopt *substantial* "democratic" practices? And lastly, as the foreign and military policies of even "democratic" states are generally the least transparent, and the least effectively supervised by democratic oversight and through "checks and balances," how does that fact affect the neo-conservative faith in "democracy" as an apparent panacea for the world's ills?

## Historical Roots

Although the events of 11 September helped to catalyze the recent militarization of US foreign policy, and helped propel the neo-conservatives to the forefront, American actions can be explained, in part, by domestic factors—in that the proportion of resources going into the Pentagon throughout the Cold War has dwarfed those going into the State Department. US Federalism as a system of "checks and balances" has increasingly been challenged by forces of "national universalism"—a tendency that appears to be accelerated by "the war on terrorism" in which the Pentagon has been gaining in political influence over the State Department. In this battle, the Pentagon had outmaneuvered US Secretary of State Colin Powell in the first Bush administration, as Powell preferred to engage in a multilateral approach to the question of Iraq.[32] President Eisenhower had warned of the increasing centralizing tendencies of the military industrial (and university) complex: The danger is that if the Pentagon continues to hold a monopoly over analysis and policy implementation, without competing interpretations, Washington may tend to opt for military solutions to problems that may be best handled by diplomacy.

One can trace the deeper 19th century roots of neo-conservativism to President William McKinley and the 1898 Spanish-American War. This was America's first major *preclusive* venture into *overseas* imperialism (not overlooking US intervention in Hawaii, the face off between the US and Germany over Samoan isles, and multilateral intervention in China's "Boxer Rebellion," along side the Europeans, and the corresponding support for the "independence" of Panama and the canal zone from Columbia). The Spanish-American war resulted in taking Cuba to "liberate" it from Spanish tyranny, human rights abuses and General Weyler's "re-concentration" camps that were intended to separate civilians so as to prevent guerillas from living off the land. The primary purpose of the Spanish-American war was to end the instability posed by factions resisting Spanish rule—to free the Caribbean of foreign influence (including Germany and Great Britain). The 1903 Platt amendment then maintained Cuba (and Puerto Rico) under US hegemony, including US controls over Cuban foreign policy and rights to coaling or naval stations. (Thomas Jefferson, who believed in "conquest without war," had coveted Cuba as early as 1823 and feared that Spain might hand it over to Britain after Mexican independence. In an early expression of "neo-conservatism," the 1854 Ostend Manifesto stated the American desire to purchase Cuba, rather than agree to a multilateral English, French, American guaranty of Cuba to Spain, in order to put an end to "extreme oppression"—but upon the threat that the US would support Cuban insurgency against Spain, if Madrid did not sell out.)[33]

In the Philippines, the US engaged in its first colonial Vietnam-like conflict, involving scorched earth campaigns and re-concentration camps (similar to those of the Spanish in Cuba).[34] It was America's duty, according to President McKinley "to educate the Filipinos, and uplift and civilize them, and by God's grace do the very best we could by them." (Ironically, Filipinos were predominantly Catholic, except for the Moslem Moro minority, in which factions continue to resist the government today.) Manila, under the governorship of William Howard Taft, was intended to become the American version of Hong Kong. It is said that President William McKinley, perhaps much like President George W. Bush in relation to Iraq, thought that "God" supported the intervention. After McKinley's assassination by the anarchist Leon F. Czolgosz (see Chapter 3), William Howard Taft then became president and advanced the cause of "dollar diplomacy." He employed "Roosevelt's corollary" to intervene in Nicaragua and other Latin American countries to protect American investments, and check foreign influence.

Going deeper into US history, the neo-conservatism has a historical precedent in the Radical Republicans, including their leaders Thaddeus Stevens and Charles Sumner. The Radical Republicans supported the powers of the Federal government over those of the individual southern states; they thus opposed the concept of "states rights"—in addition to laws that permitted racial discrimination. This is not to argue against the freeing of the slaves, but to point out that the abolition of slavery represented a *by-product* of the war, and was not an original *goal* of that war. The primary aim of the war was to sustain the Union, and hence to impose the powers of the Federal Government over the powers of the individual states of the Confederacy.[35] As the war began in 1861, President Abraham Lincoln, in fact, waited until 1863 before emancipating the slaves, in the effort to create a "fifth column" to undermine southern opposition. William Appleton Williams put the issue this way: "Despite its long history, including the considerable achievements of societies which practice it, slavery is evil. But that truth fails to define either the question or the answer. *For so is empire.* The irreducible question is whether or not one uses one evil, empire, to destroy another, slavery."[36] Radical republican efforts to crack down on the South after the Civil War then resulted in the formation of the Ku Klux Klan that became a "state within a state"—that used "terrorist" tactics against newly free Blacks and other minorities, including white Catholics.

The Mexican-American war in the 1846–48, stemming from American skirmishes with the Mexican army, permitted the US to expand its territory farther southwest, and provided greater socio-cultural support for Manifest Destiny, at the same time that it weakened the Mexican dictatorship, after Jackson had, of course, recognized the independence of the state of Texas in 1837. Perhaps roughly comparable to the Bush administration's doctrine of "pre-emptive" strike, President Jackson's United States Force Bill of 1833 authorized the use of whatever force necessary to execute laws. Intended to nullify South Carolina's own nullification of the "tariff of abominations," Jackson's 1833 Force Bill was seen as a precursor to the American Civil War, after Jackson had dispatched troops to South Carolina ports to ensure importation of affected northern products, a tax that was imposed by the North and that would weaken the latter's steps toward commercialization. President George Bush and his advisor, Karl Rove, have admired Jackson's populist, unapologetic, and forceful policies.[37] It appears that the neo-conservatives, who, in Colin Powell's words, formed a "separate government" in the first Bush administration, represent the equivalent to the "kitchen cabinet" of Andrew Jackson.

One can furthermore find elements of neo-conservative foreign policy advocacy in the "war hawks" in the war of 1812, such as Henry Clay and John Calhoun, most of whose members were Democrats from southern or western states, and who strongly criticized Thomas Jefferson's unsuccessful diplomatic efforts and who were enraged by the impressment of American sailors by England. The war hawks (who were opposed by the New England Federalists) urged the invasion of Canada, in the belief that French Quebec would rise against the British, who were at the time engaged against Napoleon. The US did not win that "second struggle for liberty," however. Once Napoleon was defeated (prior to Waterloo), British forces landed upon US territory and burnt the White House in 1814. The Treaty of Ghent in December 1814 returned the situation to the *status quo ante bellum*. The French Canadians did not secede, but the war did open the door to greater American expansion against the Indian tribes, resulting in forced relocation into tribal reservations, led by then general, Andrew Jackson.

And here is the key thesis: *In many ways the historical debate between the power of the federal government and "states rights" within the USA itself, a debate that was at the roots of the US Civil War, in which Southern states used the concept of "states rights" to protect an agrarian economy and the institution of slavery, is now being played out on a global scale with American government challenging the traditional concepts of "state sovereignty" in a new wave of overseas imperialism—in the name of "global democratization."*

In neo-conservative ideology, the so-called "right" of "state sovereignty" can no longer be used as an excuse by lesser powers (at least those not aligned with the US) to engage in human right abuses, war crimes, and genocide. Nor can the so-called "right" of state sovereignty be used as an excuse to acquire Weapons of Mass Destruction (with some exceptions) that could potentially destroy humanity. Hence, American military intervention in Kosovo, and then in Iraq, without clear UN mandates. To a large extent, the neo-conservative *Weltanshauung* stems from the American revolutionary perspective: The belief that through its Constitution, the American people had found the ultimate way to organize society. This has led US leaders to criticize the behavior of other states in accord with the "American way" and to urge intervention against tyranny to help others find the path to "freedom" and "prosperity." American experience with the civil rights movement has also been regarded as an exemplary path for non-democratic states to follow (as if these reforms took overnight!). At the same time, as previously pointed out, as neo-conservative ideology emphasizes national values, as opposed to universal ones, and as it emphasizes American historical experiences, as opposed to the specific historical experience of the societies it seeks to "liberate," it is not clear whether all states are ready to adopt to American standards of government. Moreover, the approach appears selective: the horrific abuses of some states are singled out, while those abuses of other states, or the possession of WMD, are either downplayed or ignored for reasons of "expediency"—or *raison d'etat*.

Furthermore, the clash between the rights of the US Federal Government and rights of state sovereignty has been exacerbated by the apocalyptic fears provoked by the events of September 11, the attacks against the two symbolic centers of US military and economic power, the World Trade Center and the Pentagon. These latter events have consequently evoked the fears of one of the American founding fathers, Alexander Hamilton, whose articles in the Federalist papers are the closest in spirit to the security "obsession" of contemporary neo-conservatives, which derives, historically, from the attempt, and then failure, to conquer Canada in the American Revolutionary War. Britain's control of Canada appeared to represent a permanent threat.[38]

Alexander Hamilton expressed the classical views of the American defense posture and fear of perpetual insecurity in Federalist Paper No. 23:

> The authorities essential to the care of the common defense are these—to raise armies—to build and equip fleets—to prescribe rules for the government of both—to direct their operations—to provide for their support. These powers ought to exist without limitation: *Because it is impossible to foresee or define the extent and variety of national exigencies, or the correspondent extent and variety of the means, which may be necessary to satisfy them.* The circumstances that endanger the safety of nations are infinite; and for this reason no constitutional shackles can wisely be imposed on the power to which the care of it is committed.

While such exigencies that potentially threaten the US, if not all mankind, with total destruction exist in contemporary circumstances, a distinction must be made between those dangers that can be eliminated by patient diplomacy; those that can be more easily foreseen and prevented beforehand; those that need to be contained, and those that may need to be eradicated by force. Nevertheless, even if the use of force is chosen, it is still possible to engage in force that involves concerted multilateral action with the backing of the UNSC. Not to engage in concerted diplomacy and action is to take the risk that other states and political movements might simply withhold assistance that could be desperately needed. Major states may additionally engage in unilateral actions or else form new coalitions and alliances to challenge the interests of the US and its allies.

At present, there appear to be no international institutional structures that can "contain" the United States. The US might be able to work within a reformed UN (see Chapter 7), but this prospect seems out of the neo-conservative agenda. At present, there also appear to be no major powers on the global level that could combine in such a fashion as to provide appropriate (and positive) "checks and balances" upon such a quest for power "without limitation" as suggested by Alexander Hamilton. As powerful states can move into neutrality or even bandwagon in support of the US, the formation of a countervailing alliance is not inevitable. At the same time, however, a hostile coalition of states alienated by the American quest for hegemony, and that aligns itself with pan-Islamic forces, and which, in turn, could use methods of asymmetrical warfare, as well as nuclear blackmail, should not be entirely ruled out. To prevent such a hypothetical coalition from coalescing in response to a forceful and unilateral American foreign policy, an alternative strategy should be formulated. Such a policy would be for the US to begin to "self-limit" its quest for power, in the formation of a truly multilateral policy, in which the US leads some, but not all actions—in the enlightened understanding that such a quest for power "without limitation" is self-defeating in the not-so-long term. (See Chapter 8.)

## Opposition to "Appeasement"

For neo-conservatives, the failure to stop Communism and then Fascism represented the two blunders of the 20th century. Opposition to the 1936 Munich Agreement that "appeased" Hitler in the Sudetenland, permeates the writing of many neo-conservatives. Here, neo-conservatives argue that had France intervened against Hitler in the Rhineland, for example, it might then have been possible to overthrow the Nazi regime. They also condemn the fact that US-UK-French military intervention in Russia after World War I had failed to prevent Lenin from coming to power.

In the neo-conservative perspective, both Nazi German and Soviet crimes against humanity have been protected by false principles of "national sovereignty"—as have those of the People's Republic of China, Serbia, Iraq, among others. The implication that the US may have "appeased" many of these regimes, or else failed to eradicate totalitarian regimes, appalls them—in that appeasement, in their mind, appears to imply a loss of *political honor*, and results in American recognition of heinous tyrannies. The crime of "appeasement" thus represents the crucial foreign policy question for historian Donald Kagan, as well as for his son, the political theorist, Robert Kagan, for example.[39]

By contrast, the very concept of "pre-emption" in order to overthrow tyrannies, and engage in regime change, as often advocated by neo-conservatives, reminds the more historically minded Europeans of the Schlieffen Plan, Hitler's Operation Barbarossa, as well as the Japanese strike at Pearl Harbor, or Mao's decision to cross the Yalu, which were all plans that advocated pre-emption before the situation became worse.[40] The Europeans, with a more tragic sense of history, tend to argue that states need to be cajoled and persuaded to change policies through dialogue, and that the threat and use of force can be counter-productive.

The question raised here is whether the *categorical* anti-appeasement anti-dialogue approach of the neo-conservatives is appropriate in all situations and circumstances, and whether or not such a hard line strategy and tactics may exacerbate crises rather than work to resolve them—precisely because such an approach fails to see any legitimacy in other perspectives, and in "competing, yet valid claims" in Wolfowitz's own words. Not all policies of "appeasement" necessarily end in disaster (Great Britain engaged in a policy of appeasement the US after the Civil War, for example, despite General Sherman's March to the Sea). Furthermore, it may be practically impossible to isolate, reform or eradicate all tyrannical regimes by force—all the more so as the very process of eradicating such regimes can cause considerable bloodshed and "collateral damage."

Another overlooked issue is that policies of "roll back" are often accompanied by policies of appeasement of "lesser evils" due to expediency. As the Europeans (and later the Americans) were unwilling to take on Nazi Germany, Fascist Italy, Imperial Japan *and* Soviet Russia simultaneously, an "appeasement" of the Soviet Union—as the state that appeared the *least threatening* to US, British and French interests—became the logical geo-strategic choice—despite the moral vacuity of playing "evil" versus "evil." In the 1991 Persian Gulf War, US policy "appeased" Syria in Lebanon at the same time that the US under a UN mandate forced Iraq out of Kuwait. (In 2005, the US, France and the UN have begun to pressure Syria out of Lebanon with uncertain repercussions.) In the Bosnian conflict, the US largely appeased Croatia (which had engaged in ethnic cleansing, but to a lesser extent than Serbia) to form a Moslem-Croat alliance against the "greater evil" of Serbia. From the late 1960s, the US has largely "appeased" Communist China in order to build up a strategic counterweight to the "evil" empire, the Soviet Union. But one can question—which of those two really represented the "greater evil"?

## Neo-Timocrats or Moralizing/Despotizing Politicians?

The University of Chicago philosopher Leo Strauss, who argued that one of the key philosophical problems was how to best *defend* the values of democratic societies against their enemies, has ostensibly influenced the thinking of neo-conservative factions in the administrations of Ronald Reagan and George W. Bush. The Bush administration's concept of "regime change"—meaning a total transformation of the model of the society in question rather than a simple change of government in the narrow sense—is said to have stemmed from Strauss' argument—in that "regime" is the term that Strauss used to translate the Greek *politeia* (which is generally translated as Republic).[41]

The concern here is not so much with the philosophy of Strauss *per se*, but more with how it has been vulgarized by his followers—in the formation of an ideology, if not a cult.[42] Based on the Platonic aspects of Strauss' neo-conservative followers can be called neo-Timocrats, i.e. those who rule not by reason but by the spirited, honor-loving, and warlike aspects of their soul. In this regard, neo-conservatives see themselves as defending American "values," but in the process, they assert that their values are superior to those of other states and civilizations (as well of those of domestic rivals)—in a form of "national universalism." Moreover, as they appear willing to trample upon their own self-proclaimed "values" in support of the "virtue" of a greater cause, through the "noble lie," they tend to confound universal *values* with their particular *interests* involved in asserting those presumed values at particular times and places for reasons of expediency.

Neo-conservatives claim that they are not afraid to impose their "values." They argue that "Strauss's devastating critique of the distinction between 'facts' and 'values' has gradually made itself felt within contemporary political discourse: 'Virtues are now spoken of more often, and values less. And arguments that not too many years ago would have been dismissed as illegitimate attempts to 'impose one's values'—a semantic trick used to end debate on important matters before it can begin—are now more frequently acknowledged to raise serious questions of principle.'"[43] Here, however, even if one grants the neo-conservative argument that opposes *extreme* multicultural "relativism," the problem remains that even among liberal-democratic cultures that claim to possess common "values," those values may not necessarily be held in the same rank, order or sequence. Of the values "liberty" and "order," for example, liberty may come first in some political cultures, but order and stability may be held in priority in others.

The next problem is to identify those cultural values that are truly "universal" as opposed to those values that are specific to particular political cultures; yet even those "universal" values, which may be considered absolute and unchanging, in fact, change from era to era, and may be implemented in practice in different, and potentially, incompatible ways. Although both the US and EU may stand for "democratic" values, this does not prevent substantial differences in their approaches.[44] Nor does it prevent these very different democracies from engaging in different forms of decision-making processes, or from possessing very different interests, which, in turn, are affected and influenced by very different *priorities* in values. (See Chapter 7.)

The other neo-conservative presumption is that states have permanent "friends" and "enemies," and that states remain in a permanent struggle to sustain their "values" against *presumed* enemies.[45] In fact, however, values and interests of democratic states change from epoch to epoch in differing circumstances: Particular states may be considered "friends" and "allies" in one epoch, enemies in the next, as has been the case with US relations toward the Soviet Union. As the friend-enemy dichotomy is actually never permanent, but always relative to geo-historical circumstances, a constant *re-evaluation* of international geopolitical interests and relationships represents a fundamental aspect of changing international dynamics, and can help *prevent* conflict with *presumed* enemies.

Given their attachment to Plato and Hobbes, one can accordingly question neo-conservative commitment to truly democratic *practices*—as opposed to decision-making by an elite or a "philosopher-king"—as if there could be such an individual in today's highly complex world that is highly dependent upon expertise of individuals in differing scientific, economic and technical fields. The question raised here is not a question of the rights of an "elite" to make decisions, or even the necessity at times to make decisions in secret, *but whether elites in power are obtaining all pertinent information—and are open to listening to a whole range of policy options.* Are they listening to all available options, or are they both closing themselves off to expertise and variety of policy options, in a form of "kitchen cabinet" *group think*? Here, open discussion (in the form of *multiple advocacy*) becomes absolutely necessary, even if decisions must be made in secret, as was the case during the Cuban Missile crisis when President Kennedy permitted a free and open debate in secrecy within his cabinet—in discussing options ranging from pre-emptive strike to diplomacy and appeasement.

In this regard, neo-conservatives, who can be depicted as a "moralizing politicians" in Kantian terms, tend to praise democratic *formalities* and *ideology*, but not necessarily democratic *practice* and *real dialogue* in supporting a culture of political compromise and the free and open debate of issues with those of opposing viewpoints. Serious questions arise as to the sincerity of their democratic convictions (and their willingness to engage by established international laws and conventions)—particularly when democratic dialogue ends in severe disagreements. The Straussian vision argues that the rule of a "good" tyrant is better than misrule under law. But this latter position depends upon whether that tyrannical leadership is truly capable of "good" governance, whether the elite is capable of listening to all possible options—or whether the ostensible "goodness" of the leadership is mystified and then broadcast through propaganda.

The essential theoretical point made here is that in the increasingly complex contemporary world, a neo-Platonist worldview of a philosopher king, or even an elite decision-making body, represents a complete anachronism. In contemporary conditions, in which there are a variety of competing elites and rival factions within civil society with diverse outlooks, as well as divergent levels of technical expertise, effective decisions can only be made after *open* consideration of all possible options, a position which is closer to that of Aristotle than to Plato. Today's world appears far more complex in political, social and technological terms than that of Plato's ancient Greece, and yet, seemingly incapable of surpassing the linkage between democratic governance, the refusal to relinquish alliance formations (NATO), and drive for imperialism—the essential concerns of Thucydides![46]

Neo-conservatives accordingly can be regarded as a mix of "moralizing politicians" and neo-Timocrats—those who rule not by reason but by the spirited, honor-loving, and warlike aspects of their soul. Timocrats differ from oligarchs, democrats, tinpots and tyrants (and, of course, philosopher kings). Out of four types of dictatorships, *timocrats* rule by means of low repression and high loyalty, as compared to tinpots (low repression, low loyalty), tyrants (high repression, low loyalty) and totalitarians (high levels of repression and loyalty.)[47] This point appears to adequately describe today's post–11 September 2001 circumstances that so far appear to involve *relatively* low levels of domestic repression as compared to previous historical epochs. The repression appears relatively very low, and loyalty relatively high—so far. At the same time, however, the grotesque torture of Iraqi suspects in Abu Ghurayb prison, the imprisonment without trial of those suspected of having contacts with *al-Qaida* or other organizations, as well as censorship by the Defense Department of points of view that do not support, or that are critical of, Bush administration policies concerning the "war on terrorism" and intervention in Iraq, raises real questions. (See Chapters 1 and 6.)

## A Kantian Critique

The neo-conservative mind does not retreat from the ostensible necessity to tell the "noble lie" in order to achieve their political objectives—ostensibly in the service of greater "virtues." The question, however, is where lies the line between the "noble lie"—told to improve or ameliorate a very bad situation full of inconstancies and contradictions in which there are few alternatives—and the "big lie" reminiscent of that of Hitler and Goebbels, which was told to expand the national power and corrupt interests of one particular state and party. At the roots of the problem is the question of correct analysis and correct prognosis. The rationale for military intervention in Iraq was characterized by a number of myths, if not outright deceptions, many propagated by either official Washington or its neo-conservative cohorts (or both)—and that were designed to gain domestic American and international support for the costly military intervention.

These deceptions included: the myth that Iraq possessed an *imminent* threat in WMD in the form of nuclear weapons and missile delivery capabilities; the direct linkage between Saddam Hussein and *al-Qaida*; that the US military presence would not last more than a year as Americans would be welcomed as "liberators"; that the intervention would result in a post-war "democratic peace" for the Iraqi people, despite the widely conflicting interests of secular, religious and ethnic factions within Iraq; that a future Marshall Plan would be available to develop Iraq; that Iraqi oil wealth would be immediately exploitable and profitable; that it was necessary to eliminate Saddam Hussein before seeking a "fair" resolution to the

Israeli-Palestinian conflict; that unilateral military intervention would initiate the process leading to the "democratization" of Arab/Islamic states in general. (The sudden death of Yassir Arafat probably did more to spark Arab-Israeli peace talks and regional "change" than the elimination of Saddam Hussein, see Chapter 6.)

In Kantian terms, neo-conservatives fit the depiction of the "moralizing politician... (who )... by glossing over principles of politics which are opposed to the right with the pretext that human nature is not capable of the good as reason prescribes it, only makes reform impossible and perpetuates the violation of law. Instead of possessing the *practical science* they boast of, these politicians have only *practices*; they flatter the power, which is then ruling, so as not to be remiss in their private advantage, and sacrifice the nation and, possibly, the whole world.... Their task is not to reason too nicely about the legislation but to execute the momentary commands on the statute books; consequently, the legal constitution in force at any time is to them the best, but when it is amended from above, this amendment always seems best, too."[48]

Moreover, it appears Kant would have also opposed the neo-conservative concept of "regime change" by preemptive action, in that he argued quite explicitly that "No State Shall by Force Interfere with the Constitution or Government of Another State"—even if that state is "despotic." In Kant's view, nothing can really justify intervention in the "rights of an independent people struggling with its internal disease." Such intervention "would itself be an offence and render the autonomy of all states insecure." On the other hand, Kant argues that it may be justified to support a faction of a state that has broken in two parts due to "internal dissension" —in that the state no longer possesses a "common constitution" and lies in a "state of anarchy." It is thus the process of determining precisely when a country has entered into a "state of anarchy" that it might be possible to justify concepts of "humanitarian intervention"—or other acts of international interference in state's disintegrating sovereignty.

As their justification of intervention in Iraq revealed, the neo-conservatives are masters of Kant's three sophisms:

- *Fac et excusa* which seizes "every favorable opportunity for usurping the right of the state over its own people or over a neighboring people," for which "the justification will be easier and more elegant *ex post facto*, and the power can be more easily glossed over, especially when the supreme power in the state is also the legislative authority which must be obeyed without argument."
- *Si fecisti, nega.* "What you have committed, deny that it was your fault... if you have conquered a neighboring nation, say that the fault lies in the nature of man, who, if not met by force, can be counted on to make use of it to conquer you."
- *Divide et impera* in that if the concern is "foreign states," then "it is a pretty safe means to sow discord among them so that, by seeming to protect the weaker, you can conquer (or rule over) them one after another."

To further paraphrase Kant, it is not that neo-conservatives are ashamed of revealing these three sophisms "but they are ashamed only when these maxims fail, for they still have political honor which cannot be disputed—and this honor is the aggrandizement of their power by whatever means."[49]

It is clear that the American people and the world were told a number of "noble lies" in order to justify "pre-emptive" (really *preclusive*) intervention and "regime change" in Iraq. Yet, from the neo-conservative perspective, those "noble lies" were "necessary" to achieve the "virtues" of their greater aim. Moreover, if that unilateral intervention proves "successful" in the coming decades, then those "noble lies" will largely be "forgiven." If, however, that intervention does *not* prove "successful" over time, then the neo-conservatives will try, if they can, to re-write history—at least in their public discourse, regardless of the actual and future strategic-political-economic-social and ethical costs.

Much as Machiavelli, and leaders such as Abraham Lincoln (a neo-conservative hero), observed, the *means* chosen are really much less important than the *ends* to be achieved. At the same time, those ends must be *perceived* to be "successful" and used as a further step for the aggrandizement of personal and/or national power.[50] Even if the actions taken were not ultimately perceived as "successful," that is, in respect to the originally stated goal, then the aims and goals need to be re-formulated so that whatever end is finally achieved, it will somehow appear to be "successfully" achieved. Ironically, their stated "values" (however strongly supported by "virtue") will be imperceptibly altered—contrary to their stated belief in support of "universal" values. Otherwise, if the ends are not ultimately regarded as "successful" (however their values may be re-defined), there will be a loss of *political honor*, possibly resulting in a fall from power (which is the worse!). The trick then is to turn failure to one's own advantage—even if that failure was largely self-inflicted.

It is in this sense that the refusal to accept a loss of *political honor* potentially represents the root cause of war, and, in the post-11 September 2001 crisis forewarns of future conflict, *as honor must still be defended...*

# Chapter 3

# The Question of State versus Anti-State "Terrorism": Who is "Terrorizing" Whom?

The Bush administration's declaration of a "war on terrorism" has exploded a field of landmines that will continue to plague both domestic and international politics for years to come. Having declared war on "every terrorist group of global reach," it is not at all clear precisely what is being fought against and where such a war is heading. "War on terrorism" can easily become a "war without end"—in that the concept of "terrorism" represents an undefined entity that various leaderships can readily manipulate for political purposes.

In order to move beyond stereotyped, one-dimensional conceptions, it is thus important to develop as clear understanding as possible, one that deals with the multiple facets of terrorism. By identifying the multiple facets of terrorism, the ultimate hope of this Chapter (even if this sounds utopian) is to work toward the abolishment *all* forms of "terrorism" as a political tool. More pragmatically, however, the immediate purpose is to find ways of reconciliation between groups and states that counter-accuse each other of engaging in acts of "terrorism," wherever possible. It shall accordingly be argued that acts of "terrorism" take on essentially four different, but not necessarily exclusive, forms: (1) anti-state terrorism, (2) state-sponsored terrorism, (3) totalitarian terrorism and (4) street terrorism. Furthermore, it is argued that, in ideological terms, both "religious" terrorism (which manifests itself in the ideology of the "clash of civilizations) and "secular" terrorism (as manifest in "radical" ideologies) possess a number of aspects in common despite the differences in their beliefs and ultimate goals.

## Definitions: "Anti-State" versus "State-sponsored" Terrorism

While it may be risky to add yet another definition (there are more than 100 definitions), "terrorism" can be defined as a largely *psychological* tool of "strategic leveraging" utilized by both anti-state partisan revolutionary groups and by state leaderships. The latter possess a whole range of possible threat options intended to

51

achieve domestic and/or international ends, depending upon their capabilities, intentions, and *will to power.*[1]

"Terrorism," which has perhaps been best defined as "propaganda by deed,"[2] often involves the *staged*, if not theatrical, utilization of either *discriminate* or *indiscriminate* violence by either anti-state groups or state-supported partisans who are fighting for a self-propagated cause.[3] In the effort to manipulate emotions and to cause fear and panic, these groups, individuals or states then seek to demonstrate by concrete actions an iron will to use violence—even if that means martyrdom and/or mass murder. Such groups and individuals generally seek to obtain either official and/or popular *recognition* for their respective causes through the effective use of the mass media, if possible—assuming they do not desire to keep their involvement secret for whatever reason. The fact that mass communication and the internet has increasingly weakened the ability of states to control the free flow of ideas within their borders has apparently given "anti-state" propagandists an advantage; yet this fact does not permit state leaderships from trying to manipulate the media as well.

The key goal of anti-state "partisans"—who have some form of political goal in mind and who are not engaging in terror for "terror's sake"—is not so much the conquest of territory, as has been the case in more traditional wars, but rather to destabilize governments and undermine popular support for specific leaderships. Such groups generally seek to instigate both social and interstate conflict—and, if possible, bring new political factions into power by assassination, revolution or *coup d'etat*. Terrorist actions may seek to purposively exacerbate the existing class and ethnic tensions within a society, as well as among differing states, in an effort to then capitalize on dissent and conflict. Attempting to impel change in the electoral process, if feasible, by means of intimidating voters, or else by threatening public officials, cannot be ruled out as another form of "terrorist" tactic (tactics utilized by both Hitler and Mussolini, who transformed from revolutionary agitators into "totalitarian terrorists").

The nature of the political cause evidently differs from group to group, as do the nature of the tactics, which may involve varying degrees of *discriminate* or *indiscriminate* violence. Such tactics are generally intended to weaken the will of the opponent to fight or resist, or which often seek to force the overextension of the opponents' capabilities and resources through wars of attrition. *Discriminate* violence may be used to pinpoint specific enemies and in the quest to gain more supporters; *indiscriminate* violence may, by contrast, be used to display force capabilities, or else to sustain the allegiance of those individuals who are fighting for whatever cause through the proof that the group is still capable of using force.

By the late 20th to early 21st century, there has now emerged so-called "post-modern" terrorism in which the symbolic message and psychological effect (often obtained by effective use of the international media) of extreme and indiscriminate violence is often more important for the terrorist group than the precise role or function of the specific individuals who are actually attacked. In symbolic terms, attacks on the World Trade Center (in 1993 and 2001) parallel Anarchist bombings on Wall Street in September 1920, for example; yet the horrific effects of 11 September 2001 was evidently more potent and catastrophic than the latter.[4]

The more shocking and theatrical the event, the better to advertise the cause; the object of such attacks is, in part, to wake the "complacent" up to the crimes, sufferings, and inequalities that are ostensibly instigated by the *geopolitical- socio-economic system as a whole.* Unlike 19th century terrorism, which was generally directed against specific leaders, the goal of much of post-World War II terrorism, as well as 21st century anti-state terrorism, has been a more general protest and struggle against what has been regarded as *systemic* political-economic forces combined with the *structural* violence caused by territorial divisions governed by colonial or neo-colonial regimes. In this regard, anti-state secessionist movements often seek "independence" (ironically, in an increasingly interdependent world) based upon actual or imagined communities. Pan-Islamic propaganda, for example, seeks to awaken populations to the breadth of the Islamic world before Spanish *reconquista* and subsequent European imperialism—which was intended, in part, to circumvent and weaken the Ottoman empire.

**The Question of Legitimacy**

Both established state leaderships and anti-state partisans are in a battle to claim and sustain *legitimacy* for their various causes and for their use of violence to achieve those causes. State-supported terrorism, guided by elites in power, or in association with those elites, may seek to undercut potential popular support for either *legitimate* (generally reformist) political parties or else violent "revolutionary" or "terrorist" groups that are considered *illegitimate.* Yet, in distinction to state-sponsored or state-supported partisans, anti-state actors attempt to *build* their legitimacy against their "oppressors." In this regard, *legitimacy* is never a "god-given" right but is *constructed* over time. Communist members of the French *maquis*, for example, used their resistance against the Nazi occupation in order to obtain a certain degree of legitimacy in post-1945 French politics despite their loyalty to the Soviet Union during the Hitler-Stalin pact.

In essence, acts of terrorism challenge the claims of state leaderships to provide security for their citizens; the authority of state leadership is consequently undermined because traditional *realist* options, which involve a mix of rewards and punishment, may not work against individuals willing to face death—the ultimate punishment—for their cause. The fact that terrorism threatens the power, influence and *legitimacy* of the state leadership often causes the latter to over-react. In this regard, there is a great temptation for state authorities to use the "war on terrorism" as an excuse to violate civil liberties, and to repress freedom of speech and non-violent protest. The fear is that journalistic investigation could expose state "secrets" (or illegal actions of the state), for example; the advocacy of specific, even non-violent, causes or reforms could be construed as support for "terrorism."

States, which generally possess the power of law and legitimacy on their side, may consequently use a wide range of means to contain or repress domestic protests or insurgencies. Imprisonment, assassination, differing forms of torture, "death squads," summary execution, indiscriminate bombing, "ethnic cleansing," rape *en masse*, represent a number of possible means. State authorities may additionally seek the backing of more powerful states to gain support for counter-terrorist activities and to repress rebellions. In the latter case, states that are more powerful may support acts of "terrorism" precisely because they do not want to exhibit their influence and activities openly.

The response of states, whose authority and legitimacy may be questioned by acts of protest, whether peaceful or violent, may thus be that of "terrorizing the terrorists." State leaderships additionally use the threat of external terror (threats coming from outside the state) in order to obtain and sustain both allegiance and obedience, and to repress dissent. In *The Politics*, Aristotle argued that "the distant fear must be brought home"—in that elites seek to preserve their power and influence and obtain both domestic and international allegiance to their goals by manipulating real and imagined (or exaggerated) fears that their "constitutions" and basic freedoms might be subverted by enemies abroad, or at home. On 11 September 2001, the "distant fear" was brought directly home—with a vengeance. By contrast, during the Cold War, the "distant fear" appeared to be somewhat more abstract, except *within* states where strong communist movements existed.

The key dilemma is then how to determine whether the causes and goals of specific groups are, in fact, *legitimate* (other than by proving one's superiority through the use of force and violence). Some groups, labeled as "terrorists," may be willing to accept possible compromise or reconciliation and mediation—if such compromise is at all politically feasible. Others may continue to uphold their values and beliefs as *absolute* and remain impervious to compromise in the belief of the "virtue" of their cause and that their cause must necessarily and absolutely *supercede* or *transcend* that of the other (as is the case in the deterministic Leninist conception, or often in belief of divine justification). The nature of revenge and counter-revenge, coupled with the illegality, if not immorality, of violent actions, as well as the "irregular" nature of "terrorist" warfare, furthermore makes possible reconciliation with either partisan groups or states that use "terrorism" as a weapon of warfare much more than difficult than is the case with more traditional warfare fought by *mutually acceptable* standards.

**Totalitarian "Terrorism"**

State leaderships that most fear domestic opposition to their claims to legitimacy may engage in severe forms of repression, in the process of enacting "totalitarian terrorism." The nature of "terrorism" transformed from its late 19th, into its more violent 20th century, manifestations—with the rise of early 20th century total warfare, and with the *systemic* nature of repression in totalitarian societies. It can be accordingly argued that officially supported "state terrorism" during the 20th century has, from a historical perspective, instigated far greater collective crimes against humanity, than did specific acts of anti-state terrorism, sponsored by either individuals or anti-state partisan groups. The burning of the Reichstag, for example, which was really more of an act of "sabotage" than of "terrorism," was manipulated by Adolph Hitler as a pretext to galvanize a far more dangerous

National Socialist political movement, and to engage in other acts of "state terrorism." Hitler's use of "state terror," in taking advantage of socio-economic instability and uncertainty, was intended to impose a new *Weltanschauung* and overthrow the permissive weaknesses of liberal democracy that, in Hitler's view, undermined the authority of the state and thus permitted "terrorism" to thrive.[5]

It is also not surprising that partisan forces themselves not infrequently seek vengeance through terror after seizing power—and in many cases tend to exaggerate or overcompensate their retribution for "crimes" of the *ancienne regime*—as has proved the case in the French, Russian, Nazi German, Chinese and Cambodian/Khmer Rouge revolutions, among others.[6] As was the case for the both the Soviet Union (which, under Stalin, not-so-ironically sought to "nationalize" international Marxism) and for Nazi Germany, totalitarian states actually thrive on indiscriminate terror as their very essence. It also cannot be ignored that these continental states were very influenced by the overseas behavior and the political-ethics of "race and bureaucracy" of the European colonial powers.[7] The quote attributed to Stalin, "The death of one man is a tragedy. The death of millions is a statistic" illustrates the absolutely cynical attitude of those who propagate any form of hyper utopia in the name of *raison d'etat*. In addition, it should be pointed out that the Soviet Gulag and Nazi concentration camps were, in many ways, intended as *preclusive*: In expectation of resistance, both Stalin and Hitler sought to eliminate both *actual* and *potential* political "enemies."

The rise of totalitarian methods of controlling populations since the 19th century (generally during periods of domestic or international conflict) can be seen in the following examples: American Indian reservations; early twentieth century Cuban "re-concentration" camps (of General Weyler) and similar American camps in the Philippines as a result of the Spanish American war; British camps in South Africa (for Boer families); the Soviet Gulag (here one can also include forced migration of numerous ethnic groups within the ex-USSR); Nazi concentration camps (modeled after Soviet camps); Japanese slave labor camps; US internment camps for Japanese-Americans; the Chinese *Laogai* prison camps (which detain both political dissidents and criminals); the Khmer Rouge and North Korean work camps; as well as ex-Yugoslav Serbian, Croatian, Bosnian, as well as Slovenian camps in the Bosnian war (1990-1995) among many other examples. Saddam Hussein's centers of torture, such as the infamous *Abu Ghurayb* prison, which housed as many as 50,000 prisoners, can likewise be mentioned. US detention centers in Iraq (although not at all as extensive as those under Hussein), and in Guantanamo for *al-Qaida* fighters, likewise fit into this general category of response—in which Washington has attempted to justify and rationalize its failure to follow the Geneva Convention in response to the irregular and illicit nature of "terrorist" warfare. Evidently, living conditions (and methods of interrogation and torture) differ substantially from camp to camp.

For Hannah Arendt, the fundamental difference between modern dictatorship and previous tyrannies was that terror is no longer used only as a means to exterminate and frighten opponents, but "as one instrument to rule masses of people who are perfectly obedient."[8] One can add to this theory that 20th century totalitarian societies can use modern technology and propaganda much more *systematically* to control and mobilize their populations than was the case in ancient China, for example. In an early prototype of modern totalitarianism, the Qin dynasty (221-206 BC), once the First Emperor *Qin Shi Huangdi* had finally conquered the Kingdom of Chu, began the process of integrating the country in breaking down all regional independence and standardizing all aspects of society. It likewise engaged in the burning of Confucian classics and regional histories, and in burying alive some 460 scholars—as a deterrent to any one who might oppose the new emperor. What has been called "oriental despotism" appears to differ from modern forms of totalitarian terror only to the extent in which the state can *systemically* control or manipulate the systems of communication, manipulate thinking, in addition to *impelling* obedience by perpetually threatening the physical being and security of the domestic society.

### The Question of 'Street Terrorism'

Despite the fact that "terrorism" is primarily a political-psychological phenomena, one cannot overlook the more *apolitical* form of *street terrorism*, which represents the indiscriminate criminal expressions (muggings, kidnapping, rape, murder) of the rage and jealousy of a permanent underclass. The latter can provide the recruits for gangs, pirates, mafias and drug dealers; but it is also possible for partisan elites to manipulate such individuals for political purposes through contract killing, for example, or other "terrorist" actions, as in Mexico City, for example. In addition to air hijacking among other actions, targets of terrorist groups often include oil pipelines or other energy facilities, as in Columbia, Iraq, Afghanistan, and Saudi Arabia or along shipping routes, such as the Straits of Malacca.

Poverty, by itself, does not necessarily create "terrorism"; however, the precarious and uncertain nature of global market forces may lead to fears for one's survival that is generated by job loss without a social or personal safety net. Even a plunge in personal and social status may lead certain individuals toward "terrorism" to avenge their personal or familial losses and suffering during periods of joblessness or else anxiety; certain individuals may, though sympathy or for purposes of self-identification, seek to avenge the "terror" that is ostensibly suffered by whole groups or classes who are perceived to be oppressed.

It is true that "weak states," which are unable to effectively police their territories, often open themselves up to terrorism and paramilitary activities (as in Baghdad following the US intervention). Yet "stronger," more effectively managed, states may also tolerate paramilitary activities if the authorities are sympathetic, or else reluctant to crack down, as has been the case for the Ku Klux Klan, for example, in the United States in the past. Rich countries that do not provide civil liberties for their citizens, or which do not appear to live up to their stated ideals, may be more likely to give birth to terrorists (the American Weather Underground during the Vietnam war or else in Saudi Arabia today) than poor countries. If the latter do protect the rights of their own citizens, they may be less likely to produce terrorists. At the same time, individuals, whether from poor or rich backgrounds, may decide to engage themselves in particular causes that they believe to be "just" and that might involve acts of "terrorism."

If societies cannot fully integrate the poorest members of the community by working to provide meaningful employment (or somewhat ironically by providing them with the option of police or military service if other employment opportunities are not available), alienated individuals of these sectors of society can provide the *recruits* for partisan activities involving acts of "terrorism."[9] Here, for example, thousands of *Madrasas* schools in Pakistan and Afghanistan provide food, shelter, as well as dogmatic pan-Islamic interpretations of the Koran, for impoverished young men. These alienated individuals, however, cannot be considered "terrorists" unless they use violence to achieve political goals; nor can the laws defining acts of *politically-oriented* terrorism be equated with acts of *apolitical* "street terrorism" and other violent criminal acts.[10]

The precise division between political and criminal acts of violence is not always clear; yet the increasing linkage between terrorism and criminality appears to be an integral aspect of the creation of a separate "black" and "gray" "libertarianism" that subsists in the shadows of the liberal "free trade" global market. Unable to base themselves upon truly popular support, and not able to obtain significant state financing as was often the case during the Cold War, a mix of secular and religiously-oriented anti-state terrorist groups (not to overlook leaderships of "failed" states) have sought to survive through illicit arms and drug trade, and other mafia style activities. This is true for the Peruvian *Sendaro Luminoso* as well as for the Columbian Revolutionary Armed Forces (FARC) and its rival, the National Liberation Army (ELN), as well as for the post-Taliban Afghanistan (see Chapter 6). In this regard, the "war on drugs" is increasingly related to the "war on terrorism," yet it is not clear that either "war" is succeeding.

In sum, terrorism, whether utilized by states, anti-state organizations, totalitarian regimes, or "street terrorists," is generally chosen as a tactic precisely because it represents a less expensive, and more *deceptive*, way to counter-attack armies and police, or for state authorities to eliminate political enemies. Moreover, non-state supported "terrorist" operations do, of course, need sources of funding and may raise funds through kidnapping, drug smuggling, theft and bank robberies, as well as through legitimate business and charities, etc.[11] It has become a cliché to say that terrorist organizations have become "non-governmental organizations" (NGOs), yet some of these groups might create false fronts as non-profit organizations. At the same time, many of these organizations may also obtain secret state, in addition to private, financial assistance. Here, CIA involvement in the Iran/Contra affair in the 1980s represents a prime example of a state-supported organization in the quest for self-financing.

Seeking to cut off funding may be one of the most effective ways to decimate some groups, depending upon exactly *how* those groups are funded.[12] The dilemma, however, is that in the age of globalization, there is at least US$1 trillion laundered across states annually. Groups and states of all kinds can accordingly fund their violent political actions through both legal and illicit activities, using sophisticated methods of moving funds across borders.

## The "Clash of Civilizations" and Terrorism

One of the risks of the "war on terrorism," as generically defined, is that in lashing out against *all* forms of presumed anti-state terrorism is that the conflict could spread to an even wider number of organizations and states. The National Intelligence Council's 2020 report argues that civilizational movements—religious adherents that include Muslim militants, Christian evangelicals, Hindu nationalists, as well as Jewish fundamentalists, among others—will generally rise in numbers in the period 2002–25. This fact, along with increasing rivalry over oil and energy, opens a "danger zone" in that more and more individuals are becoming "activists" who tend to see the world in Manichaean "good vs. evil" terms, and who tend to "connect local conflicts to a larger struggle."[13] In this regard, the "war on terrorism" could begin to involve *both* "civilizational movements" (in Immanuel Wallerstein's terms) *and* blocs of states regarded as "civilizations" (in Samuel Huntington's terms).[14]

A number of pundits have accordingly argued that the wars of ideologically inclined guerrillas, and of the secular "terrorist" cells of the Cold War, have been superseded and replaced by wars of fanaticism in the post-Cold War period. It is consequently argued that these kind of ideologies seek to affirm the presumed values of one civilization, ethnic group, culture or religion against those of another, in a "clash of civilizations" particularly once major states become involved.[15] Appeals to religious texts, or to civilizational values, increasingly appear to provide a deeper *legitimacy* for a number of groups or movements than do the works of Marx, Lenin or Mao. Bin Laden, for example, subscribed to the "clash of civilizations" thesis in a 21 October 2001 interview.[16]

Empirical evidence has generally pointed to the fact that the identifiable number of religiously oriented anti-state groups has tripled between the mid–1960s to the mid–1990s. Thus while the number of "terrorist" groups with ostensibly religious goals has been growing and now represents roughly one quarter of all such groups, roughly three-quarters of anti-state groups still base themselves on some form of secular ideological or nationalist goals.[17] Thus, despite their high visibility, and the general impression of horror created by the millenarian aspects of their "passionate intensity" (to cite W.B. Yeats poem *The Second Coming*), terrorist organizations with religious ideologies still do not represent the majority of anti-state terrorist groups in post-Cold War circumstances.

## Explanatory Factors

Political-economic crises, instability and unpredictability, much as Karl Marx argued in the Communist Manifesto in the mid 19th century, challenge the viability of religious and cultural traditions and values in socio-economically destabilizing circumstances of world capitalist development—which "terrorizes" individuals with the fear of unemployment and the inability to "make a living." In such instable conditions, individuals and groups may turn to "terrorist" acts in an effort to preserve differing religious, cultural, linguistic or civilizational "values," as well as personal and group identity, in the face of the homogenizing tendencies of "globalization." Opposition to women's rights, seen as fostered by "westernization" and "liberalization," for example, represents a factor fueling militant Islamic movements. But these influential socio-economic factors do not explain why these movements adopt *particular* kinds of ideologies in specific eras.

One explanation for the adoption of religious values is that apocalyptic expectations at the end of the second millennium (by the Gregorian calendar) play a role in the apparently burgeoning *appeal* of religiously oriented groups. These groups generally possess more destructive goals (without clearly articulated goals) in the effort to oppose a vaguely defined "hegemony," "globalization," "internationalization," or a "world government." Here, the Japanese international cult, *Aum Shinrikyo* (The Supreme Truth), for example, which was founded in 1987, based itself on millenarian expectations, in predicting world war between the US and Japan. In 1995, members of the group attacked the Tokyo Metro with poison Sarin nerve gas.[18] Still legal (and controversial) in Japan, it ostensibly renounced its violent past in 2000 and changed its name to *Aleph*.

Such apocalyptic groups may also possess the intent to resist the dominance of another ethnic or religious faction, or even eradicate a minority group. The April 1995 bombing of the FBI building in Oklahoma by Timothy McVeigh, who allegedly had ties with White Supremacist groups, and who sought to revenge FBI actions against the mystical Branch Davidian sect (an offshoot of Seventh Day Adventists) in Waco, Texas, represents one extremist apocalyptic movement that opposed perceived US governmental support for "one worldism." (Here, a number of very different "white supremacist movements" appear to be a permanent feature of the American landscape since the end of the Civil War, when Ku Klux Klan in 1866 had essentially established a "state within a state" in the post-bellum South.)

The general aims of such groups may include demands for secession, or to expand control over specific territories in accord with irredentist claims, or else efforts to construct independent and ethnically "pure" states. Sikh movements, such as the *Dal Khalsa* (1978) in India for example, seek an independent Khalistan (Land of the Pure); Jewish movements, such as *Kach Chai* founded in 1971, seek to establish *Eretz* Israel. Irredentist Pathan movements (which backed the Taliban) have supported the formation of Pushtunistan, which would link the Pathan provinces in north Pakistan with those in southern Afghanistan by abolishing the hated Durand Line, the frontier drawn up by the British in 1893.

While purporting to speak for "pure" doctrine and ostensibly immutable values, many (but not all) anti-state, as well as pro-state, partisan elites and partisan groups tend to manipulate religious ideology for *specific*, rather than ostensibly *universal*, geo-strategic and political economic purposes and goals and have often arisen in response to *specific* historical events and circumstances. Here, for example, The *Sh'ite Hizb'allah* (Party of God) was founded 1982 after the invasion of Lebanon by Israel. The Sunni *Hamas (Zeal)* and *Islamic Jihad* organizations were founded in 1987 with outbreak of the first Palestinian *Intifada*. Both represent the more militant offshoots of the Moslem Brotherhood, which was founded in 1924 following the break-up of the Ottoman Empire.

More specific interests have been mixed with religious demands: Bin Laden's propaganda has referred to businessmen whose contracts were not honored by the Saudi government. His followers have struck oil facilities and foreign worker compounds in an effort to drive oil prices up and force foreigners out. The kidnappers and assassins in Pakistan of reporter Daniel Pearl in February 2002 demanded that the US resume F-16 sales or else return the money that had not been received after Pakistan had purchased the planes. (The US had blocked delivery due to Pakistan's testing of nuclear weaponry, and fears that Pakistan could redesign the planes for the deployment of nuclear warheads.)[19]

### Confounding Civil War and the "Clash of Civilizations"

The civil war between "Catholics" and "Protestants" in Northern Ireland has been dubbed a clash of civilizations (even if it essentially represents an intra-Western conflict), and which has involved acts of terrorism, including the attempted assassination of former Prime Minister Margaret Thatcher. Yet the root cause of the conflict is political: The clash between the goal of a united Ireland, supported by Nationalists and Republicans, and the goal of maintaining strong links between northern Ireland and the UK, as backed by Unionists and Loyalists. Religion is thus not the root of the issue—although it is in the background. In this regard, questions of religion, language and culture exacerbate the nature of the conflict through acts of discrimination and segregation.[20]

Nor is the formation of such groups necessarily the result of apparently irreconcilable religious, or civilizational values. On the contrary, the pluralistic aspects of the world's major religions and civilizations, which generally call for cooperation among differing beliefs, *are often downplayed or dismissed in order to suit a particular group's confrontational, violent and extremely divisive, tactics and often utopian aspirations, that are often intentionally designed to create fractures and dissent within the same religion*. In this sense, religious-oriented groups may seek to manipulate religious belief, on the one hand, while such movements themselves may be manipulated by *both* secular *and* theocratic states, as well as by anti-state movements, on the other.

The wars in ex-Yugoslavia (with use of ethnic cleansing, rape *en mass*, and internment camps) have been interpreted as one of the prime examples of the "clash of civilizations" in the post-Cold War era.[21] First, the clichéd depiction of the ex-Yugoslav conflict as an "ethnic" struggle ignores that fact that significant numbers of ethnic Serbs and Croats opposed the war. These, in turn, may have lost positions of power and authority because of their political opposition. Moreover, what distinguished ex-Yugoslavia before its civil war and disaggregation was precisely the *commonality* of its culture, language, as well as the generally nonchalant attitude of Yugoslavs toward religion in general. The break-up of the federal state that had been forged by Marshall Tito was, in reality, driven by rival ex-Cadre "ethnic entrepreneurs" who sought to sustain power by *constructing* a new post-Communist legitimacy based upon so-called civilizational values and a *mythological* past. (Now each region is claiming to have developed a separate language as opposed to what was once called "Serbo-Croatian.")

In historical terms, the *commonality* of Yugoslav culture does not derive from ancient times, but stems more from the region's submersion into the Ottoman Empire. While rarely admitted, the cultural and linguistic similarities of Yugoslavia were in large part a consequence of the socio-cultural effects of the region's former integration into the Ottoman empire, combined with the effects of the Ottoman confessional or *millet* system—but as the latter later interacted with 19th century western conceptions of nationalism.[22]

**Intra-Civilizational Conflicts versus "Criss-Crossing" Alliances**

The clash of civilizations thesis does not explain why groups of the same civilization with ostensibly similar goals may fight with one another, such as the National Liberation Front of Corsica and its rival, Armata Corsa (which sees itself as fighting for national self-determination and against Corsican "Maffyas"). The civilizational thesis does not explain deep political divisions within Kurdish groups, for example, between the Marxist-oriented PKK, the ostensibly democratic PDK, and the nationalist leaning PUK—which have all clashed with one another. Nor does it really explain disputes between southwestern "Bible Belt" Protestantism and more "traditional" east coast Episcopal Protestantism!

The clash of civilizations thesis also does not really explain mutual support for groups that do not belong to one's own religion or ethnic group. Even fundamentalists of different sects can find common cause depending upon political circumstances: Both pan-Islamic and Christian "fundamentalism" opposed Communism during the Cold War. Both evangelical Christians and strict Moslems oppose free wheeling *libertarian* and *radical* ideologies. What has been called "Christian Zionism" strongly supports the state of Israel, despite the historical disputes between the two religions. A "clash" between very different religions or civilizations is thus not at all necessary, particularly if the groups possess common interests against a common foe, or hold common "values" and interests.

Essentially ideological and cultural issues of religion and civilization generally do not help explain the geo-strategic and political economic complexities of a number of conflicts, even within what Huntington calls "torn states." On example is tacit Orthodox Russian and Shi'ite Iranian cooperation against Chechen independence (Chechens are largely Sunni Moslem, but many follow the Sufi branch of Islam.) Even more complex is more overt Russian and Iranian support for Christian Armenia (which is 94% Armenian Apostolic) *against* Azerbaijan (which is 93.4% Muslim, predominantly Shi'a). The conflict over the Nagorno-Karabakh enclave (largely Armenian populated) has remained unresolved since 1994. Azerbaijan, on the other hand, is backed by the US and Turkey. The latter is 99% Sunni Moslem, presently under a "moderate" Islamic leadership of the Justice and Development Party, which compares itself to the German Christian Democratic Union and other Christian Union parties.

In another example of criss-crossing of religious ideologies, the Lord's Resistance Army in Uganda has been fighting for twenty years for a government in

Uganda based on the Ten Commandments; yet it allegedly received support from the Islamic Government in Sudan in the 1990s. In return, Uganda allegedly supported the Sudanese People's Liberation Army, at least until 1999 when Sudan and Uganda agreed to end support for either group. As many as 2.5 million people may died in the period 1999–2001, in which many more were probably killed by Ugandan security forces than by the Lord's Resistance Army.[23]

## Pseudo-Historical Progression

Much as the general concept of a "clash of civilizations" is off the mark, so too is the basic concept of sequential steps and ostensibly necessary "progression" from secular ideological to religious/civilizational movements as Samuel Huntington purports in his largely *pseudo-historical* chronology of wars of princes, nations, ideologies, and religions/civilizations.

As defined by Huntington, the latter so-called "progression" confounds concrete political classes ("wars of princes") and wars of specific state leaderships (depicted as abstract "nationalist" forces engaged in "wars of nations") with pure abstractions ("wars of ideologies" and "wars of civilizations"). In a illusionary slight of hand, Huntington thus moves from the concrete to the abstract—as if the so-called wars of nationalism, ideologies and civilizations did not possess concrete and specific proponents in the form of elites, political parties, social groups, and partisan movements, etc.

Huntington's interpretation thus implies that the "war of civilizations" arrives only in the late 20th and 21st centuries. Wars of other epochs (such as the Crusades and the Thirty Years War) ostensibly did not possess facets of religious/ civilizational propaganda manipulated by powerful and influential elites of their respective times. Huntington's historical schema thus falsely implies that Imperial Germany's *Kulturkampf* and Britain's *pan-Anglicism* (during the "war of nations"), or else Hitler's National Socialism (during the "war of ideologies") did not possess "civilizational" overtones.[24] In order words, religious or "civilizational" propaganda has certainly been an integral factor of many of the major conflicts throughout history, but is not at all unique to the contemporary crisis. At the same time, however, contrary to Huntington's emphasis, it remains an *instrumental* factor that has been manipulated by both elites and counter-elites that oppose the domestic and/or international *status quo* throughout history.

Huntington's conceptualization also implies that the "clash of civilizations" is primarily *between* the peoples that make up the major powers and who have held essentially immutable (and non-reconcilable) values over the long durée. Huntington thus tends to downplay potential "clashes" within the same civilization. Yet in many revolutionary situations, an internal dynamic of revenge and counter-revenge takes places within the same ethnic, religious or "civilizational" grouping, and a spiral of dissension and violence becomes established that is very difficult to break. In Arabic, this is called *fitna* (dissension), and was specifically warned against in *The Koran* in passages dealing with *jihad* or Holy War—in that causing "dissension is worse than killing."[25]

Major conflicts can thus be sparked by "intra-civilizational" schisms, such as that which has afflicted Islam between Shi'ite, Sunni and Sufi Moslems, or else that which plagued the Catholic Church in respect to the split between the Roman Catholic and Greek Orthodox churches, followed later by Lutheran rebellion, not to overlook schisms within Protestantism itself, between Calvin and Luther. Included in the concept of schism, should also be the profound differences in outlook between the two states of Great Britain and America, violently acted out in both the American Revolution and War of 1812, despite the fact that both peoples belonged to the same English-speaking "civilization."

By downplaying "clashes" *within* the same civilization, and even those *within* Western civilization itself, Huntington's analysis reveals itself to be absurdly *ahistorical*. The false nature of "clash of civilization" presumptions likewise may lead such analysis to poorly predict the future in which a number of states that *predominate* within differing "civilizations" may forge alliances that actually cut across states belonging to the same civilization. Unless some form of loose *confederal* arrangements can ultimately be forged, for example, "Confucian" Taiwan, even if not backed by the US, would remain in permanent tensions with "Confucian" China—precisely because the elites and general public of both states do not *rank* the values of that Chinese civilization in the same ways. Despite distant origins in a common culture, the historical and linguistic backgrounds of Taiwan and China are very different—in addition to the fact that the leaderships of both *states* possess very different interests.

In general, contrary to the Huntington thesis, so-called "civilizational" movements tend to rise in prevalence not in some form of historical progression, but in periods of the socio-political disaggregation of states, such as the period during the Thirty Years War, or after the collapse of former empires, including the Soviet Union. As noted above, the decline of the Ottoman "Sick Man in Europe," along with its confessional or *millet* system of governance, lay in the background of pan-Serbian acts of terrorism that helped to spark World War I. At that time, Serbs likewise engaged in acts of ethnic cleansing to obtain a greater Serbia—but then backed by France and Russia against Imperial German interests in the Balkans. With the advent of World War II, Nazi Germany would support Croatian interests.

### Historical "Dialectics" of State and Anti-State Terrorism

Huntington's thesis likewise does not help to explain the essentially dialectical transformation from late 18th century aspects of "state terrorism" to 19th century "romantic" actions to 20th century conceptions of state-supported and anti-state terrorism. The issue raised here is that the contemporary post–1945 use of the term "terrorism" has, in effect, overturned its original meaning.

In this respect, a term that first referred specifically to the use of "terrorism" by state authorities for domestic repression or against foreign opponents has evolved to imply the use of violence against state authorities for political purposes, to simplify the definition. It is consequently this historical reversal of meanings of "terrorism" that is at the very root of the dilemma as to how to best deal with the contemporary phenomenon of so-called "post-modern terrorism" and its emphasis upon political symbolism as "propaganda by deed." The double-faceted and "dialectical" nature of "anti-state terrorism" and "state terrorism" must be thoroughly explored if it is at all possible to truly eradicate all forms of "terrorism" as political options or tools in the affairs of both state and anti-state actors.

The modern usage of the word "terrorist" consequently refers, more often than not, to a conception of *guerrilleros*, or groups who violently oppose the leadership of a particular state or states, and which may or may not possess backing from *legitimate* authority. It is a term that originated from the Spanish bands who had resisted Napoleon's conquest of Spain.[26] The Spanish resistance to Napoleon, in turn, stimulated the Prussians, and other national partisans to resist French domination as well. In arguing, "It is necessary to fight as a partisan wherever there are partisans,"[27] Napoleon opened the door to the key political-ethical dilemma of fighting "terror" with "terror."

The term "terrorism" itself originates from the use of terror by those who seized state power in France, and implies a "system" or "regime of terror," or those who supported "reign of terror" from March 1793 to July 1794.[28] In July 1790, the French Jacobin, Jean Paul Marat, who established the Committee of Surveillance, had justified the reign of terror: "Five or six hundred heads cut off would have assured your repose, freedom and happiness. A false humanity has held your arms and suspended your blows; because of this millions of your brothers will lose their lives." Marat's assassination by Girondist Charlotte Corday provoked a Jacobin backlash against both the Girodins and monarchists.

In contrast to late 18th century state terrorism in France, the terrorism of the mid– to late–19th century had been characterized by a self-prescribed morality and by highly abstract political "ideals" in that it argued for *discriminate* attacks against only those individuals responsible for the accused offence. The failure of the 1848 revolutions to succeed, however, led to considerations of more drastic, but still limited, actions, in the 1890s. The latter became the "Golden Age of Assassination" in the West. Here, 19th century anarchists often justified their violent anti-state actions in criticizing the often-arbitrary nature of *raison d'état, as well as upon the general failure of the state itself to obey its own rules, regulations and legal obligations, and its own self-proclaimed morality and values.*[29]

A more general change in social attitudes toward violence came about with concepts of total war and the advent of World War I.[30] Terrorism then developed into the more cynical *indiscriminate* forms of modern 20th century terrorism based upon futuristic hyper-rational, hyper utopian visions, as discussed in terms of "totalitarian terrorism." The latter likewise involved self-sacrifice for the greater cause, whether secular or religious, whether of the political "left" or "right."

## Historical Efforts to Control Anti-State Terrorism

One of the prime examples of early 20th century terrorism was the September 1901 assassination of President William McKinley (believed by anarchist Leon F. Czolgosz as responsible for the new overseas American imperialism). This action led President Theodore Roosevelt to denounce the new international anarchist "threat" and demand that all anarchists to be returned to their country of origin.[31] US fears of anarchist and communist movements then set the stage for the Palmer raids of 1919 at the end of World War I.

Yet, interestingly enough, in 1904, when Germany and Russia urged states to sign an international protocol in St. Petersburg to share police information, the US refused to convene. Washington was afraid to entangle itself in European affairs; it feared the rise of Imperial German power, and it had no federal police to enforce its crackdown. Italy, likewise, refused to participate in an international protocol for fear that if Anarchists were returned to their countries of origin, Italy's domestic troubles might be worse than its international ones![32] (See also Chapter 2.)

By contrast, in 1972, once it had become the leading hegemonic power, the US wanted the UN General Assembly to pass a convention against "international terrorism," largely in order to stop the hijacking of commercial aircraft and kidnapping of diplomats, among other actions. Yet, the UN General Assembly was unable to endorse US propositions. (Here, in addition to Cuban and Puerto Rican air-hijacking, Israel's defeat of Arab armies in 1967 had led Palestinians to adopt more radical "terrorist" methods.) In opposition to US demands, socialist states and so-called "Third World" states attempted to extend the laws of war to those so-called "terrorists" or anti-state actors who were struggling for self-determination, or against colonial rule, alien occupation, or "racist" governments.[33]

One can see similar concerns in the post-11 September 2001 war on terrorism today, for example, in Pakistan's refusal to fully crackdown on all *jihadi* groups. This is because the Pakistani government had supported many of the *mujahedin* in the 1980s during the war against the Soviet Union in Afghanistan, and had continued to support a number of these groups in their battle to free Kashmir versus India. A number of Islamic states refuse to crack down on the former freedom fighter, bin Laden, for fear of retribution. Moreover, the US, Europeans, Russians and Chinese do not always see eye to eye as to which groups represent "terrorists"—and fear that a full exchange of information may reveal state secrets.

**Secular versus Mystical Aspects of Terrorism**

Both anti-state (as well as pro-state) "terrorist" ideology—that sanctions the use of extreme and indiscriminate violence—need not be "religious" in the sense of appealing to traditional religious doctrine. Both religious and non-religious elites may create their own mystical faith based on secular visions. Or they may re-invent religions or alter religious concepts of the past, as has taken place with the concept of "jihad."[34] This can also be the case with certain "born again" interpretations of Christianity, particularly when Christian "just war" doctrine is interpreted as a factor to legitimize war and when killing is sanctioned *outside* the state. Or, *within* the state, Christian doctrine has been manipulated to justify killing those who engage in abortion, which has been regarded as "slaughtering the innocent" by militant Christians and likewise compared to the Holocaust.

Both secular and religious anti-state terrorist groups often consist of disillusioned "idealists" who believe that society does not live up to its own stated ideals. Animal rights advocates have attacked animal testing laboratories, and have poisoned consumer products to publicize their causes; anti-abortion activists have assassinated doctors who practice abortion. During the Vietnam War, the Weather Underground (a splinter group of the non-violent Students for a Democratic Society) attacked US military research facilities to protest against the fact that the US was not living up to its own principles in Vietnam or else was engaging in discriminatory practices against minority groups at home. National Bolshevik activists in Russia proclaim their actions (throwing eggs and tomatoes at public figures) as "velvet terror." Likewise, pan-Islamic radicals attacked Moslem leaderships for corrupt practices and for not practicing "pure" Islamic Shar'ia law.

The aim of such pro- and anti-state elites is often to find "innovative" systems of belief and alternative visions and values that might appeal to a significant number of adherents or supporters (by finding a belief system that suits the lowest common denominator of people with similar outlooks). Alternatively, such groups may attempt to sustain the passionate loyalty of small number of "elite" revolutionary "cells." The innovative pan-Islamic worldview, for example, sees itself as both *incorporating* and *transcending* revolutionary aspects of Marxist-Leninism—as a tool to counter and undermine the predominant Judeo-Christian and the liberal-democratic *Weltanschauung* (of the so-called "Zionist-Christian crusaders"). Or such groups simply take the *risk* that their struggle will ultimately gain supporters, if not in their lifetime, then in the next. Yet they also take the *risk* that their violent actions will not prove to the long-term detriment of their cause.

Such belief systems, which are intended to help rationalize and justify acts of terrorism, must also be convincing and encompassing enough (although not necessarily rationally coherent) for a member of that group to sacrifice his or her life for the "cause." Killing others within the same society is generally condemned by moral law, as well as by most systems of ethics. The fact that killing can take place without official state sanction or approval (as is the case in respect to warfare, capital punishment, and, from some perspectives, abortion and euthanasia) generally means that individuals must ultimately accept some form of highly abstract, if not dehumanizing, indoctrination in order to engage in such violent actions. Terrorist movements also have to break taboos against killing citizens of the same clan, religious group, or society. The building of a rationalizing myth is thus intended to both justify illegal actions and to help *legitimize* the cause—*for that cause to be successful in the future.*

One can thus argue that all organizations, whether deemed "legal" (and state indoctrinated) or "illegal" (outside the parameters of state law) and that demand individuals to sacrifice themselves for a greater cause, possess religious or quasi-religious legitimacy. Any demand for self-sacrifice requires "a leap of faith," or a "leap into the absurd." This is true whether one dies for "god," "freedom," or "country," or for other abstract "causes." The glory of god and religion does not, however, necessarily possess a higher legitimization than ideologies that are based upon more secular grounds such as "solidarity," "permanent revolution," "historical inevitability," "freedom," "democracy," "nationalism" or "patriotism."

The call to self-sacrifice may accordingly involve a mix of motivations, including religion, political ideology, and patriotism. The more militant and isolated partisan groups become, the more they may become dogmatic, making ultimate compromises even more difficult. Yet the most important motivation for the turn to violence, and for self-sacrifice, is not the ideology *itself*, but the personal experience of actual repression or injustice, or the knowledge of repressive acts presumably experienced by others—in which the causes of that repression or injustice can ostensibly be traced to a particular enemy or opponent. It is the role of ideology to explain what has happened and provide direction as to "what is to be done."

Self-sacrifice in the name of revenge for the deaths of others in the same society or family may thus be one of the key rationalizations for waves of "suicide bombing" or "martyrdom," for example, in Palestine and Iraq. Moreover, even secular justifications for the use of extreme violence possess elements of myth and mysticism that promise personal transcendence and new dignity—in addition to social transformation, as an outgrowth of the violent act. Such quasi-religious arguments (within secularly based philosophies) are represented in the works of Georges Sorel, Frantz Fanon (with supportive introduction by Jean-Paul Sartre), as well as Andre Malraux. Thus, even secular revolutionists, much like established religions and nationalist movements with strong religious overtones, have also produced their own myth of martyrdom and philosophy of "liberation" from the fear of death—although the believers are often burdened with an intense paranoia.

Except for a few die-hards, the appeal of Marxist-Leninism has generally collapsed in eastern Europe and in the ex-Soviet Union, as has been the case for Maoism in China particularly following the brutal repression of the Chinese Democracy movement in June 1989. Yet the myth of Che Guevara, in addition to the "success" of Mao's revolution, continues to stimulate resistance (and "terrorist" actions) against governments in Central and Latin America, and elsewhere, in India, Nepal and Sri Lanka, as well as in Italy, for example.

The Maoist branch of the Communist Party of Nepal, or CPN(M), began a "people's war" (*jana yuddha*) in February 1996 with the aim of abolishing the monarchy. Their demands include political, economic, social, and security sector reform; the establishment of a secular state; and nationalist demands such as staving off Hindi cultural influence in Nepal. The Nepalese government invited the CPN(M) to join peace talks, yet the rebels walked out of negotiations in August 2004, ending a seven-month cease-fire, in a conflict that has cost 10,000 lives so far. In February 2005, King Gyanendra decided to assume full power, saying the step was "crucial to fight Maoist rebels."[35]

Naxalite groups in India, such as the People's War Group (PWG), mainly active in the southern Andhra Pradesh state, and the Maoist Communist Center of West Bengal and Bihar, seek to defend the poor and establish a classless society. Former professor, Abimael Guzman (Comrade Gonzalo), leader of the *Sendero Luminoso* (Shining Path), which is regarded as responsible for the deaths of up to 30,000 people, sought to create a form of syncretism between Maoism and traditional Inca and native Peruvian cultures. Although Peruvian authorities began an effective crackdown in the 1980s, narcotics trafficking (narco-terrorism) may have given the organization a new lease on life in the 1990s despite the capture of its fearless leader in 1992. His 1993 declaration of peace with the Peruvian government had helped split the movement.

These more secular revolutionary anti-state ideologies have tended to develop in Latin America, for example, as the predominant religion, Catholicism, has generally been regarded as closely aligned with Latin American governments and with the region's history of imperialism and colonialism. Conversely, such secular ideologies have also developed in Asian countries where Hinduism (with its social hierarchies) and Buddhism (with its escapist *ethos*), among other religions, may not have appeared to play a positive role in the socio-political development of the region. Leninist North Korea, for example, in repressing its own people and supporting "terrorist" acts, such as the kidnapping of Japanese citizens for ransom, still claims that its philosophy of *juche* (self reliance) has granted it autonomy from the capitalist world system. By contrast, the political and historical nature of Islam as an essentially *oppositional* religion versus previously established Christianity and Judaism permits its various interpretations to remain a rallying force to be manipulated by different political claimants.

From this perspective, depictions of contemporary conflicts in terms of a clash of religions, ethnic groups, or of civilizations tends to mask the effort of cynical elites to attempt to expand their influence by *instrumentalizing* religious ideologies and/or by manipulating potential adherents through considerations of religious, ethnic, or clan membership. Although it still does not represent the basic ideology of the largest number of anti-state groups, religion is no longer necessarily regarded as the "opiate of the people" in the secular theories of Karl Marx—but can be *instrumentalized* as an "amphetamine for the people."[36]

## Weapons of Terror

States and anti-state actors develop novel technologies of death designed to "terrorize" opponents often in the belief that new technologies or innovations will deter the enemy or cause the opponent to stop fighting or surrender. In addition to the development of weapons ranging from the crossbow to the atomic bomb, the development of the submarine, for example, represented a novel technique of warfare that could "terrorize" the adversary.[37] Similarly, it has been dreamed that if weapons could create fears of absolute terror, then war could be abolished.[38] Yet, the invention of the H-bomb, for example, has not brought with it an end to war— even against those states that possess such weaponry. It is still debatable whether the spread of nuclear weapons will prove to be an effective deterrent—particularly as this weaponry becomes miniaturized and more useable.

In the 19th century, Anarchists regarded dynamite as a great "equalizer" between partisans and government forces. At the 1899 Hague conference, the US opposed banning the "dum-dum" bullet, which expanded upon impact, for example, due to its efficacy in maiming guerrillas in the Philippines. (The British first developed the soft-leaded "dum-dum" bullet for use at the Northwest Frontier in India/Pakistan in the late 19th century.) Today's advanced "dual use" technology provides anti-state partisan movements effective explosive capabilities as seen in the 11 March 2004 attacks in Madrid, among other attacks using sophisticated weapons of conventional destruction, such as plastic explosives, like Semtex. An additional issue is the fact that both states and anti-state partisan organizations may gain access to chemical or biological weaponry or other forms of WMD, or seek to poison food and water supplies, or attack vulnerable chemical factories (or nuclear power plants). Historically, states, such as Venice and the Ottoman Empire, have used biological weapons such as plague as weapons of war.

Primitive tactics of terrorism include beheading, scalping (also a form of bounty) and cannibalism, actions that are intended to act as a deterrent by literally annihilating any presumed respect for the individuals cherished by the other side. One out of many horrid acts of state terror throughout history was that of Vlad Tepes who impaled some twenty thousand Turkish prisoners in 1461 in an ultimately failed effort to offset a Turkish invasion, but which initially repulsed Mohammed II back to Constantinople in disgust, before he returned to conquer Transylvania in 1462.

Now known as "asymmetrical warfare," what were once known as "irregular" tactics, are not entirely "novel." Partisan groups often radically altered traditional rules of engagement precisely because they could not match their opponents in terms of true military "parity." The British, for example, dubbed the American Revolutionary hero, Francis Marion, the "Swamp Fox" for his tactics of attacking, and then quickly retreating, to swamps and forests—tactics learned from the Cherokee. The Apache leaders Cochise and Geronimo became mythological figures for their resistance to US settlers and troops. As previously mentioned, Prussia learned from the Spanish guerrillas fighting Napoleon, and developed a concept of total resistance. Mao Ze Dong, Ho Chi Minh, and Che Guevara further improved modern guerrilla tactics, as did T.E. Lawrence, also known as Lawrence of Arabia, who had helped Saudi Arabia secede from the Ottoman Empire.

The "post-modern" tactics of *al-Qaida* may have been to a certain extent derived from the *ghazi* (religious warrior) tradition in Afghanistan, but more important was the up-to-date training by the CIA. Air hijacking, beginning in the late 1950s by Puerto Rican and Cuban groups, the taking of American embassy personnel hostage by Iranian students, plus suicide bombing tactics in Beirut during the Lebanese civil war, may have also been influential.[39]

From a "globalizing" perspective, it cannot be altogether ruled out that the Japanese Red Army Faction (with a Kamikaze tradition) may have had some limited influence on the nature of terrorist tactics, air hijackings and suicide bombings in the Middle East in general—in that argued that the Israeli-Palestinian struggle was the forefront of the battle against international imperialism.[40] Most pertinently, one certainly cannot ignore the extent to which Israeli "terrorism," which accompanied the emergence of the state of Israel, has influenced both Arab and Iranian "terrorism."[41]

Cold War rivalries between the US and the Soviet Union additionally did little to restrain "terrorism"; CIA-KGB cloak and dagger operations exacerbated it. Both the USA and USSR supported surrogates and terrorist activities, as they battled it out behind the scenes beneath the nuclear "balance of terror." Both states and anti-state actors hence rationalize the development of WMD (such as the "poor man's atomic bomb"), as well as their own "terrorist" actions upon the basis the actions of the major powers that ostensibly set the standards. They argue that so-called "responsible" states: 1) possess such weaponry in their arsenal; (2) may violate the spirit of international laws through the use of controversial weaponry that are considered "inhumane" and not necessarily in accord with Geneva conventions (such as Napalm, Agent Orange, cluster bombs, fuel air explosives, depleted uranium ordinance). Accused of "double standards," the major powers have not necessarily restricted their use of the different forms of non-conventional weaponry. (On the question of "double standards," see Chapter 2.)

## Terrorist "Internationals"

The formation of a "terrorist international" made up of different nationalities is not an entirely new phenomenon either. The break-up or forceful division of states and empires often leads to the creation of diasporas that seek to re-connect through *irredentist* claims. The so-called "Arab Afghans" (who may be neither Arab nor Afghan) who have been associated with *al-Qaida* do not represent a unique phenomena, and may be supported by both Sunni and Shi'ite Moslems.[42] As previously discussed, another "terrorist" internationalist grouping included the Anarchist "International" of the late 19th century (although not all Anarchists supported violence or terrorism). The Communist International prior to World War II was active in the Spanish Civil War against Franco, for example.

In the age of "globalization," worldwide immigration and recurrent international refugee crises have permitted the possible formation of international cells, "fifth columns" and "sleeper agents" of differing nationalities and ethnic groups, as have the break up of empires into rival states, leaving enclaves of various national groups who often look back to their former motherland in support of *irredentist* claims. The membership of Menechim Begin's Zionist *Irgun Zvai Leumi* consisted of individuals from the Jewish Diaspora of different nationalities from eastern Europe and the Middle East and Persian Gulf, as well as from the United States, the United Kingdom as well as from *Eretz* Israel itself. The actions of the *Irgun* included the bombing of the King David Hotel, then the hang out of British officers, which was in part responsible for the British withdrawal from Palestine.[43] The Palestinian Diaspora, coupled with significant financial support by states and individuals, likewise backed the foundation of the PLO as an increasingly bureaucratic umbrella grouping of diverse Palestinian factions expelled from Palestine—which, in effect, has acted as a state without territory.

### Al-Qaida

It should be noted that Ossama bin Laden claimed to have pressed the Saudi Arabian leadership for peaceful change in accordance to Islamic law, as well as for the withdrawal of US forces from the Holy Lands.[44] Yet, once the effort to press for peaceful reform had ostensibly failed, bin Laden chose the path of extreme violence. In his 1996 Declaration of War, bin Laden provocatively stated, "Terrorizing you, while you are carrying arms on our land, is a legitimate and morally demanded duty." Then on 21 October 2001, he made the now infamous statement, "if killing the ones that kill our sons is terrorism, then let history witness that we are terrorists."[45] Concurrently, while claiming that it will not negotiate with terrorists, the US has tacitly agreed to one of bin Laden's key demands—the removal of American forces from Saudi Arabia and the Holy Lands located in Saudi Arabia (but not those located in Iraq or in Palestine).

What appears to be significantly different in the post-11 September 2001 era is that the previous terrorist, guerrilla, or partisan movements generally employed tactics that were dubbed as "hit and run." *Al-Qaida*'s innovation is a nomadic form of warfare that can use readily available quotidian technological capabilities as weaponry, and that involves "hit," but not "run." It thus goes beyond the concepts of 14th century Arab strategist Ibn Khaldun of "attack" and "withdrawal," but still in keeping with the conception of war as "trickery" and "deception." Moreover, as previously discussed, targets selected by post-modern terrorists now tend to be highly symbolic so as to attract the greatest media attention, regardless of the cost in human life: The World Trade Center and Pentagon represent the two of the most cherished symbols of American power, economy and society.

Bin Laden's pan-Islamic ideology stems, in part, from the 19th century political philosopher Jamal ad-Din Afghani of Persian Shi'ite background, who believed that the struggle in Afghanistan (following unmitigated British defeat in the 1839–42 Afghan war) should serve as an inspiration to overthrow British imperialism throughout the Islamic world. The late 19th century rise of both pan-Arab nationalism and the pan-Islamic movement provided one rationale for the long term British occupation of Egypt in 1882, in addition to control of the Suez "life line" itself. (Ironically, it was the opening of the Suez canal in 1869 that permitted Moslems to more easily visit Mecca and to inter-communicate.)[46]

Che Guevara's concept of *foco* argued that a band of elite forces could set off a revolution—even if the social conditions for revolution were not entirely "ripe." Similarly, the various cells of *al-Qaida* hope that that their appeals to martyrdom, plus unpredictable actions (even if major actions may take several years of planning) will be able to spark anti-Western movements throughout many Arab-Islamic countries. For the most part, however, *al-Qaida* appears to lack a truly popular base (except perhaps in northern Pakistan, some provinces in Saudi Arabia, and in much of Afghanistan). *Al-Qaida* partisans tend to be Saudis, Yemenis, Egyptians and Algerians.

Despite its limited popular base, *al-Qaida*'s leadership hopes that the nature of the counter-terrorist actions by the US, Israel, and Russia (among other powers) will help to fuel pan-Islamic movements within as many countries as possible. (In this sense, the US military intervention in Iraq was literally a "godsend.") Much as the tracking down of Che Guevara by US Green Berets made Che an "anti-hero" in much of Latin America, if not much of the world, the tracking down of bin Laden has made the latter into a mythological "anti-hero" in the eyes of many in the Arab/Islamic world.

Che Guevara could not spark world revolution (he failed miserably in Bolivia). Bin Laden, on the other hand, is playing in a highly politically charged region with tremendous, yet extremely mal-distributed, wealth and resources. Disaffected elites and wealthy warlords, mafias and individuals (perhaps with secret support of various states?) permit him or groups aligned to him to gain adherents willing to sacrifice themselves for the cause. At the same time, however, his ultimate ideological goals may be limited by political and military realities.

## State Terrorism, Chile, Argentina and "Democracy"

The Chile of Augusto Pinochet supported indiscriminate "state terrorism," against both peaceful and violent opponents of the regime as did Argentine Army General Leopoldo Galtieri, before his government collapsed after being defeated by the British in the Falkands/Malvinas war, once Buenos Aires had seized the island.

As an example of state over-reaction to terrorism, both Chile and Argentina, along with Uruguay, Paraguay, Bolivia and Brazil collaborated in the counter-terrorist Operation Condor. The latter had been established in 1975, in response to the formation of a joint revolutionary command in 1973, by the Argentine Revolutionary Army of the People, the Chilean Movement of the Revolutionary Left, the Uruguayan Tupomaros, and the Bolivian Army of National Liberation. Operation Condor was ostensibly intended to eliminate extreme leftwing movements, who were willing to use violence to achieve their ends, but went to a further extreme by imprisoning, torturing or assassinating those who advocated peaceful reform as well as those who were ostensibly associated with extreme movements. During the period 1976–1983, state-supported terrorism in Argentina killed an estimated 30,000 civilians, who were tortured to death in 341 death camps, or thrown into the ocean from airplanes, or otherwise "disappeared."

The case of Chile raised fundamental ideological questions in respect to US policy due to the fact that the Democratic Socialist government of Dr. Salvador Allende had been democratically elected by a simple majority in a state with long democratic tradition. In acts of state-supported terrorism in Chile, 3,100 people (labeled "the enemy within") were executed or forced to "disappear," while thousands of others were tortured or suffered arbitrary detention or forced into internal exile. Death squads with links to the secret police, such as the "September 11th Commandos," emerged to threaten, kidnap or assassinate opponents.[47] In late 2004, the National Commission on Political Imprisonment and Torture appointed by Chilean President Ricardo Lagos found that 94 percent of the people detained in the aftermath of the coup reported having been tortured.[48] The 1976 assassination of former Chilean ambassador, Orlando Letelier, exported state-supported terrorism onto the streets of Washington, DC.

The fact that the 11 September 1973 coincidentally represented the date of General Pinochet's violent military coup, backed by the United States, has tended to de-legitimize American claims to monopolize September 11 as a day to protest anti-state terrorism. In effect, US support for General Pinochet's 11 September 1973 coup in Chile has fortuitously tended to undermine American efforts to "expropriate" 11 September 2001 as the date that not only commemorates the most significant and destructive act of anti-state terrorism on US territory, but which would also justify an all out "war" against all forms "terrorism." The date thus signifies essentially contrasting views of the US as an innocent "victim of crime" (11 September 2001) or as a guilty "perpetrator of crime" (11 September 1973)— as regarded from very different social, political, historical and ethical contexts.

Yet the analogy of 11 September in relation to Chile has deeper implications than political numerology. The successful, yet illegal, CIA effort to destabilize and overthrow Allende's democratically elected Socialist regime appeared to de-legitimize the very democratic process, held sacred by the American creed itself. The Chile example also raised questions as to the validity of democratic peace theory that holds that democratic states do not fight one another—in the assumption that a *coup d'etat* represents a form of warfare.

After the coup in Chile, hardline socialists and communists could effectively propagandize that the democratic process was fraudulent; and that only more militant and violent actions could achieve "socialism." The US could thus be accused of "double standards" in its pretence to support democracy, on the one hand. But it would then display its abhorrence of the democratic process, on the other, should that process select leaders that oppose American liberal-democratic interests, by expropriating multinational corporations, for example. (From the Socialist perspective, however, expropriation meant placing Chilean industry under "democratic" state controls.[49])

The 1973 coup in Chile did not, however, discourage all Socialist parties from taking the path of elections and "non-violence." The question as to whether Socialist parties, once they came to power, would take the option to expropriate or nationalize multinational or domestic firms was always at the forefront. The Socialist president of France, François Mitterrand, initially nationalized the banks, as well as chemical, steel and electronics industries in 1981, and but then rapidly changed policy once the value of the French franc tumbled. Once coming to power in 1994, Nelson Mandela did not expropriate the South African mining industry—despite prior African National Congress propaganda to the contrary.

## "Democracy" and the 1992 Coup in Algeria

Perhaps not-so-dissimilarly to the case in Chile, the state-supported coup in Algeria in 1992 against the Islamic Salvation Front (FIS), poised as it was for victory after the first round of elections in December 1991, tended to discredit the democratic process in the eyes of many Islamic militants, who then argued that violent actions would prove necessary to achieve power. For a decade after 1992, when a "state of emergency" was implemented, the Algerian government used paramilitary forces and engaged in severe human rights violations in repressing the Islamic Salvation Front, and its military wing, the more radical Armed Islamic Group (GIA).[50] The latter's violent tactics against civilians, however, began to alienate the political leadership of the Islamic Salvation Front, many of whom were subsequently granted immunity after separating themselves from the GIA. Hence one tactic to end terrorism is to begin to split opposition groups and then co-opt the less militant factions.

A precursor to the 11 September 2001 attacks was consequently the attempt by the Armed Islamic Group, which had been formed after the crackdown on the Islamic Salvation Front, to fly a hijacked Air France passenger airliner into the Eiffel Tower in 1994. French commandos foiled the attempt, after the plane landed for refueling. The subsequent decade of terror and counter-terror from 1992–2002 between Islamic insurgents and government forces in Algeria killed tens of thousands. It is thus not entirely accidental that Algerians make up a significant contingent within the ranks of *al-Qaida*.[51]

The repression of Islamic parties has not, however, entirely discouraged all Islamic parties from choosing the route of democracy, however, as seen in the November 2002 parliamentary victory of the Justice and Development Party in Turkey, and of the participation of Islamic parties in elections in Jordan, Lebanon, and Iraq. It accordingly remains to be seen whether Islamic parties, once and if they come to power, will necessarily and fully implement Shar'ia law; how they treat multinational and foreign companies; and to what extent they might forge alliances against US and/or European interests. It remains to be seen what kind of government (given a 60% Shi'a majority in Iraq) might eventually be formed after the January 2005 elections and what policies the new government will pursue in respect to Islam, woman's rights, Iraq's massive debt, oil prices, and acts of terrorism.

In the case of Turkey, the democratically elected parliament opposed, by a slim majority, the deployment of 50,000 US forces in Turkey for purposes of military intervention against Iraq, checking the effectiveness of US operations. At the same time, the Justice and Development Party has not yet taken the country down the path of radical Islamization, as for example took place in Iran, Saudi Arabia, Pakistan, and then Afghanistan in the 1980s and 1990s. Turkey's entrance into the EU should, theoretically, moderate more radical Islamic factions; failure to enter, or failure to meet EU qualifications might, on the other hand, work to destabilize the country, or turn it toward an unexpected alliance with Russia. Issues involving "state terrorism" (demands that Turkey recognize the Armenian "genocide" and that Ankara try to integrate Kurds more fully into Turkish society thus weakening the popular base of the PKK) represent just two of the potential obstacles to Turkish membership in the EU. (See Chapter 9.)

**"Terrorists" become Respected Leaders**

The cliché is often the case, that "one man's terrorist is another's freedom fighter"; at the same time, it is also the case that a "partisan," once denounced by his political opponents as a "terrorist," may become a "respected" state leader in just a brief span of time. The issue raised here is the fact that the "terrorist" (who calls himself a "liberator" or "freedom fighter" or "soldier of god," etc, but rarely a "terrorist") can rationalize his violent actions, and even indiscriminate killing, on the basis of the perceived illegitimacy or injustice of the actions or policies of the state or states that he is combating. The "terrorist" thus believes that things will change once the government and society changes for the "better." Nobel Peace Prize laureates—Nelson Mandela, Yassir Arafat, Menachem Begin—were all considered "terrorists" at one point in their careers.

As a matter of political expediency, a number of leaders of groups identified as "terrorist" have suddenly been transformed into "freedom fighters" or vice versa. Raoul Salan fought patriotically for the French against the insurgencies in Indochina and Algeria, but then plotted to assassinate De Gaulle for retreating from

Algeria. Ex-Maoist, Jonas Savimbi and his UNITA "freedom fighters" were personally praised in 1986 by President Reagan as promising "a victory that electrifies the world and brings great sympathy and assistance from other nations to those struggling for freedom"—despite the horrid crimes of that particular group, among those of other US-supported "freedom fighters." On the other hand, Gulbuddin Hekmatyar, whose organization *Hizbi Islami* was the largest recipient of US military assistance during the war on Afghanistan, has transformed from "freedom fighter" to "terrorist"—in that his group has opposed the US-backed regime of Afghan leader Hamid Karzai in Kabul.

**Respected States Act like "Terrorists"**

During the Cold War, increasing evidence (which NATO leaders have thus far refused to openly discuss) has pointed to the establishment of a secret army code-named "Gladio" (the Latin word for "sword") within the Italian state that had a double purpose. Its first role was to operate as a "stay-behind" group in the case of a Soviet invasion and to carry out a guerrilla war in occupied territories. (A role evidently similar to that presently played by Saddam Hussein's remaining forces in Iraq after the US intervention in 2003.) The second goal of "Gladio" was to carry out domestic operations in case of "emergency situations," particularly against leftist groups. Terrorists, who were supplied by the secret army, carried out bomb attacks in public places, blamed those actions on the Italian left, and were thereafter protected from prosecution by the military secret service in order to create a "strategy of tension" that was intended to force the Italian public to turn to the state to ask for greater security.[52]

Secret networks were spread across Western Europe, yet in each country, the actions taken were different: "In Turkey, the 'Counter-Guerrilla' was involved in domestic terror and torture operations against the Kurds, while in Greece, the 'LOK' took part in the 1967 military *coup d'état* to prevent a Socialist government. In Spain, the secret army was used to prop up the fascist dictatorship of Franco, and in Germany, right-wing terrorists used the explosives of the secret army in the 1980 terror attack in Munich. In other countries, including Denmark, Norway, and Luxemburg, the secret soldiers prepared for the eventual occupation of their home country and never engaged in domestic terror or manipulation."[53]

In the case of Russia, it appears that Soviet style state supported terrorism has not completely ended. Explosions in Moscow apartment complexes in 1999 were blamed on Chechen "terrorists," but may have been either gas explosions, or else set by Russian security services, in order to justify Russian intervention in Chechnya. Even more dramatically, senior Russian officers and federal officials may have helped organize the hostage-taking raid in Beslan Northern Ossetia in which more than 330 people, half of them children, were killed.[54] Russian authorities have blocked demands for independent investigations. Moscow has consequently denounced American and European calls to work toward a political solution for the crisis in Chechnya and the Caucasus. The US and EU have argued that certain factions may accept a political settlement, although others will not. Russian President Putin responded rhetorically, "Why don't you meet Osama bin

Laden, invite him to Brussels or to the White House and engage in talks, ask him what he wants and give it to him so he leaves you in peace?"[55]

The contemporary "war on terrorism" and has accordingly been used as a pretext to avoid necessary political reforms, to strengthen the controls of state leaderships, to check immigration of specific groups, or to repress journalists, or attack political opponents, including those that do not advocate violence. These actions have been taken by a number of countries, such as Saudi Arabia, Egypt, Israel, Jordan, the Palestinian Authority, Columbia, India, Pakistan, Turkey, Liberia, Macedonia, Turkmenistan, Uzbekistan, not to overlook Malaysia and Indonesia, as well as Russia, Belarus, China, Eritrea, Iran, Syria, Zimbabwe, Nepal—as well as by the United States itself.[56]

## Dealing with Terrorism

Dealing diplomatically (with a mix of force and diplomacy) with "terrorists," or else with a regime that engages in "state terrorism," means choosing when to negotiate, and when to actually compromise (or appease) so as to reach a "deal" if possible—if it is believed the other side will reciprocate. While the eradication of some groups may be feasible, history has shown that "terrorists" have a habit of finding new supporters depending upon the geopolitical circumstances.

This implies that, in some circumstances, it may be possible to engage in a secret or open dialogue and negotiations with those individuals and movements who have been dubbed "terrorists" or "state terrorists" in previous campaigns of propaganda and counter-propaganda. At the same time, however, a prime target of partisan groups are not only those who attempt to eradicate, repress or prosecute them, but also those who wish to broker a compromise that appears to undermine the fundamental values and goals of hard line believers. Progress toward a possible resolution of a particular conflict can be long and hard.

An illustration of the dilemma caused by "double standards" is the question of state-supported terrorism. Serbian leaders, Slobodan Milosevic and Radovan Karadzic, who have been linked to both regular militias and para-militaries, engaged in acts of "ethnic cleansing" against Bosnian Moslems and ethnic Albanians. The latter, however, had formed their own militias and "terrorist" organizations to counter those of the Serbs, such as the UCK/KLA that was founded in 1992 by Kosovar Albanians after Milosevic took away Kosovo's autonomous status in 1989. The US had officially labeled the UCK a terrorist organization in 1998, but then provided it a degree of legitimacy in its battle against the "greater evil" of pan-Serb expansionism. Macedonians of Albanian background, who sought to secede from the Former Yugoslav Republic of Macedonia (now Macedonia), have been labeled "armed combatants" by NATO in the effort to prevent civil war, despite the protest of Macedonian officials.

Another example of dealing with states accused of supporting terrorism is that of Libya. In the years 2003–04, the US reached a political settlement with the former "terrorist" state, Libya—in steps taken since 1999 that pre-date the Iraq intervention.[57] Colonel Qaddafy, once considered the "mad dog" of Libya by American authorities, and accused of sending a terrorist hit squad to Washington,

DC in the 1980s, broke out of his status as a supporter of state terrorism by settling the case of the 21 December 1988 bombing of Pan Am 103 over Lockerbie, Scotland.[58] By 2004, Colonel Qaddafi had moved out of isolation; claimed to have given up his quest for WMD and support for international terrorism. That Qaddafi can reach an accord (even if oil may be at the bottom of the deal and despite tensions with Saudi Arabia) with the US and Europe indicates the possibility that other states in the Middle East and Persian Gulf can possibly as well.

Nelson Mandela represents the prime example of leader of a revolutionary party, the African National Congress (ANC), who formed the military wing of the ANC, *Umkhonto we Sizwe*, in 1961, and who then became president of South Africa—to the disbelief of Margaret Thatcher. Mandela was subsequently given life imprisonment for sabotage in 1963 until reprieved in 1990. As an explanation for Mandela's long-term imprisonment, it is very difficult for both governments and societies to distinguish between acts of "sabotage" and acts of "terrorism" which often get lumped together, as threats to order, stability and lives.

Mandela ultimately came to power through a more realistic strategy of "regime reform" brokered between the United States and the South African government of F.W. de Klerk. Knowing that South Africa could not forever repress the African National Congress, Secretary of State George Schultz, one of the few pragmatists of the Reagan administration, engaged in secret talks with the ANC. He also supported the truly conservative "appeasement" policies and reforms of South African President F.W. de Klerk, to bring Nelson Mandela to power without bloodshed—in a process of co-optation that helped draw the ANC away from Soviet support. (The Reagan administration had, at least inadvertently, also engaged in "regime reform" in the Philippines. After the assassination of Benigno Aquino, the leader of the opposition in 1983, his wife Corazon Aquino won the presidency with support of military leaders who turned against the cleptocracy of Ferdinand Marcos, after the latter had unexpectedly called for elections in 1986, and despite Marcos' efforts to claim victory through election fraud.)

An example of some of the threat options available to groups challenging state authority can be clearly seen in the policy options initially considered by the African National Congress (ANC). Nelson Mandela argued that the creation of the partisan organization *Umkhonto we Sizwe* was actually intended to prevent what he called "terrorism"—in the recognition that violence would largely become inevitable due to the refusal of the South African government to reform the system of Apartheid (seen as a form of *structural violence*)—in response to peaceful petition. In his 1964 address, he explained why the ANC chose the option of "sabotage" at that time rather than three other policy options that he identified as "terrorism," "guerilla warfare," or "revolution."[59] The purpose of *Umkhonto we Sizwe* was to "properly control violence" against the South African government and "to canalize and control the feelings of our people... (so as prevent) outbreaks of terrorism which would produce an intensity of bitterness and hostility between the various races of this country which is not produced even by war."[60]

Contrary to many revolutions, once the South African government under Nelson Mandela and his successors abolished Apartheid, it engaged in "truth and reconciliation"—instead of neck lacing enemies with burning tires as sought by some ANC militants.[61] Moreover, one can argue that this "managed revolution" led Pretoria to eliminate its nuclear weapons program in 1989 and destroy seven nuclear weapons. The change in political outlook toward the ANC and threat assessment thus came about from internal reforms. Nuclear weapons were no longer deemed necessary as a "deterrent" against third parties that had been supporting anti-Apartheid partisans—as if nuclear weaponry could deter an essentially internal struggle.

Another example involving dialogue with "terrorism" is the long-term peace process between Israel and Palestine. Despite many set backs, such as the assassination of Anwar Sadat by Islamic militants in 1981, dialogue took place between Yitzak Rabin and Yassir Arafat, yet only after their reluctant handshake was brought about by US President Bill Clinton. A militant Zionist student, however, subsequently assassinated Rabin in November 1995 for seeking compromise with Arafat. Radical Palestinian leaders, in turn, denounced Arafat for "selling out" the Palestinian cause. (The same reaction had occurred when Arafat proposed the creation of a national authority in the West Bank and Gaza Strip as a step toward Palestinian statehood.) The government of Ariel Sharon accused Arafat's *Al-Fatah* organization of supporting "terrorism" by the assassination of Israeli leaders; Palestinians counter-accused Sharon of "war crimes" during the 1981 invasion of Lebanon. Before Arafat's death in 2004, which, more than regime change in Iraq, appears to have catalyzed peace negotiations, Sharon simultaneously targeted *Hamas* leaders and threatened Yassir Arafat personally.

The capture of Sendero Luminoso (Shining Path) leader, Abimael Guzman, in 1992 led the latter to call for peace talks in 1993–94—although the drug financed movement has appeared to gain strength in the last few years. In the 1980s, Margaret Thatcher, as a target of the IRA, refused to deal with IRA "terrorists." In 1991–92, however, the UK began to engage in secret peace talks with Gerry Adams of the Sinn Fein, the political wing of the IRA, in part after being pressured by US President Bill Clinton, ultimately resulting in the Good Friday Agreement in 1998.[62] (The compromise then split the IRA, with the formation of the spin-off, Real IRA.) Accusations in January 2005 that the IRA engaged in a major bank robbery in Belfast may, however, have undermined 1998 peace accords; these allegations weakened the credibility of the Sinn Fein, the political wing of the IRA, and its ability to control the latter.

The Kurdish PKK leader Abdullah Ocalan called for a peace initiative and dialogue with Ankara in 1999 after being captured in Kenya. European Union pressure on Turkey (and the desire of Turkey to join the EU) appears to have prevented his execution—despite the fact that the EU has so far been reluctant to bring Turkey in as a full member. Yet in June 2004, the outlawed PKK or Kurdistan Workers' Party, now known as the Kurdistan People's Congress (KONGRA-GEL), ended its five truce with the Turkish government, with the claim that Turkish forces, backed by the US, has never kept to the truce.

In general, much as state leaderships might have problems in overseeing the actions of their military forces and secret services through civilian oversight, so too partisan groups have trouble controlling their military wings.

## Conclusions

In order to counter the destabilizing effects of accusations of "double standards" and help build international consensus, pro-regime propaganda may often need to be accompanied by concrete, visible and far-reaching social-economic and political reforms *tacitly* designed to compromise over the *legitimate* aspects of a revolutionary critique. One of the key questions may be how to establish confidence by ending the arbitrariness of state decisions, thus permitting greater transparency—in an effort to minimize acts of anti-state terrorism. In theory, this can be accomplished by co-opting various elements of the general population and by isolating the more militant, and least compromising, opponents of a particular regime. Failure of a particular government to engage in significant and worthwhile reforms, or failure to thoroughly pursue those reforms, however, could lead to the ultimate victory of anti-government partisans—or, to a stalemate or war of attrition involving continuing acts of terror and counter-terror in which no one wins.

Thomas Hobbes and Edmund Burke both recognized the role of "terror" in the affairs of men. For Hobbes, terror stems from the coercive power of the state, in order to assure that all citizens agree to the social contract.[63] For Burke, however, terror, and the threat to use force, may not necessarily succeed in obtaining agreement to the terms of the social contract and thus may not result in reconciliation between factions in dispute. The problem raised here is that the use of force may prove counter-productive; rather than eliminating a particular group it could strengthen its cause and support, or else provoke the wrath of other groups. Once one begins to use force, it is often difficult to back down. Edmund Burke recognized such a dilemma when he argued for conciliation with the American colonies, in stating that "the use of force… may subdue for a moment; but it does not remove the necessity of subduing again; and a nation is not governed, which is perpetually to be conquered."

Defining "terror" before the French revolution in the psychological sense of violent use of force by the state, Burke argued, "Terror is not always the effect of force, and an armament is not a victory. If you do not succeed, you are without resource; for, conciliation failing, force remains; but force failing, no further hope of reconciliation is left."[64] Burke additionally pointed out, "A further objection to the use of force is that you impair the object by your very endeavors to preserve it. The thing you fought for is not the thing which you recover, but depreciated, sunk, wasted and consumed in the contest."[65] Burke's comments must be taken into perspective. He was writing at a time when England considered George Washington and the signers of the Declaration of Independence, as traitors and when the Sons of Liberty, in addition to American militias and irregular forces, were engaging in violent actions against British loyalists.

Dealing with "terrorism" requires careful calculations as to when to threaten and actually use force if deemed necessary; it implies a sound analysis of the goals and ambitions of the terrorist organization (or state) and an assessment of whether such groups are open to any form of compromise despite often-vehement propaganda to the contrary. Dealing with "terrorism" requires calculations as to whether the leaderships of "terrorist" organizations (or of states) are truly willing to reach an agreement (and an accord in which the terrorist group does not see itself as being duped)—or whether containment (if possible) or forceful intervention should be the preferable options. Yet as "terrorists" and "state terrorists" are willing to take extreme positions and may risk death for their cause, bargaining may prove extremely difficult, if not impossible—as it is possible that no common interests or accords can be found.

Dealing with "terrorism" may require finding the appropriate path of secret negotiations though back channels; likewise dealing with legitimate governments that engage in terrorism may require either secret talks, or bilateral or multilateral mediation, or the engagement of international regimes, or other forms of mediation. At the same time, it also means recognizing that numerous groups or individuals, who may represent a multitude of conflicting factions, may seek to use all possible means, including acts of "terrorism," to stifle the negotiation process or block compromise that does not suit their interests. Some of the parties whose interests are affected by negotiations may be prepared for compromise, others not. The whole process can be derailed by events such as leaks to the press or terrorist reprisals and hostage taking, suicide bombings, etc.

In the battle between pro- and anti- government propaganda, it is easier for anti-government propaganda to obtain the upper hand. This is true as it is generally easier to simplify complex issues and then criticize the bad policies or repressive actions of regimes from a position outside of government, than it is to actually engage in the complicated process of governing a country—without, of course, excusing blatant disregard for human rights and overt "double standards." From this perspective, it is accordingly dubious that the sources of "terrorism" themselves can be eliminated unless the general conditions that help form the breeding ground for partisan or "terrorist" activities are either eliminated—or else somehow modified or ameliorated. More explicit multilateral military and intelligence cooperation can thus be effective against the immediate threat of "terrorism." But in order for there to be a lasting change that removes the very sources of the "threat," and that ends the political dichotomy between anti-state terrorism and state-sponsored terrorism, there must be deep structural change, both in the nature of political-social-economic conditions—and possibly in the nature of regional and international alliance and geopolitical relationships as well.

The key dilemma is how to be as flexible as possible in situations that may have very limited options or openings. The possible resolution of such extreme conflicts may involve steps toward independence (often with some form of security *assurances* or *guarantees*)—that is, if neither side can find the means and will to cooperate. It could also result in some form of power sharing in that power sharing may actually prevent simple majorities from ruling, in cases where majority rule is seen as oppressing a minority, or vice versa. Other options might include confederation, which grants greater self-rule or greater autonomy to one partisan group, but which still looks toward continual formal cooperation between differing and opposing groups. If, however, no options are available, the struggle often becomes one of mere attrition.

# Chapter 4

# The Risks of Nuclear Proliferation

In 1946, at the advent of the atomic age, J. Robert Oppenheimer forewarned of an international struggle for the control over nuclear power, similar to the struggle for raw materials, such as oil:

> The threat of atomic warfare and the rivalries for raw materials, industrial capacity, power plants, technical know-how, and scientific experience, which are inherent in any struggle to maintain superiority in the field of atomic weapons, must not be allowed to persist and be in themselves a sources of war. If you think of the dangerous situations that have arisen in the world because of the struggle for raw materials far less critical than uranium—oil, for instance—you will see what I have in mind.[1]

The rivalry for nuclear power capabilities has now been superimposed upon the rivalry for control over, and access, to oil, and thus adds an additional dimension to geo-political-economic rivalries. The struggle for access to oil had begun just before World War I following the shift from coal-fired to oil-fuelled fleets, but became even more acute in the years before World War II, as the military-industrial-consumer infrastructures became highly dependent upon supplies of, and access to, oil and natural gas. The struggle for nuclear power and technology began with Hitler's quest to obtain atomic weaponry. A new phase of rivalry is now beginning in the struggle to develop new forms of energy resources, particularly in the new era of hydrogen based fuels and "micro-power" (as indicated by Presidents Bush's January 2003 "Hydrogen Posture Plan")—at the same time that demand for oil and gas continues largely unabated. (See Chapter 8.)

The burgeoning demand for oil and gas reserves has instigated a number of post-Cold War geopolitical and economic crises. Since the 1970s and the rise of OPEC, the primary American focus has been on Persian Gulf reserves. The oil factor—and the effort to exclude the influence of Russia, China (and France) in the development of Iraq's oil industry—played a significant role in the US decision to intervene in Iraq, although it was not the only American concern. Oil pipeline rivalries have plagued the Caspian Sea region, and have represented a significant background factor in the wars in Chechnya, Georgia, as well as in Afghanistan, as well as in countries such as Columbia. China's claims to the oil rich Spratly islands also raised disputes with Malaysia, the Philippines, Taiwan, Vietnam, and Brunei, for example. Oil cartels, such as OPEC, have provided its members power and influence over non-oil producers; one of the rumored causes of US intervention in Iraq was to break the power of OPEC, yet the costs of the war, and of re-constructing Iraq, may require the new Iraqi government to maintain as high an oil price as possible (hitting between $40–$55 in 2004). Russian control over oil reserves gives it strategic leverage to influence states that cannot diversify their energy imports. (See Chapter 6.)

The struggle for access to oil and nuclear power is interrelated. States that seek a nuclear power capability, generally seek to reduce dependence upon imported oil. China, India, Pakistan and North Korea are all highly dependent upon oil imports and have sought to diversify energy resources through the use nuclear power—at the same time that each has sought to obtain a nuclear weapons capability. Oil rich states such as Iran likewise appear to possess other motivations than energy diversification in acquiring a "peaceful" nuclear power capability. All major and minor powers fear their potential vulnerability to being potentially cut off from energy supplies by means of accident, terrorist attack, or war—in a world characterized by *highly uneven* vulnerability and inter-dependence.

The nuclear industry poses a strategic-economic dilemma in that it represents a "dual use" technology that can be used for either peaceful or military purposes. The effort to develop a peaceful nuclear capacity, and acquire nuclear technology and expertise, can additionally serve as a conduit to obtain a nuclear weapons capacity, particularly if coupled with a weapons delivery and aerospace capabilities. In addition to purposes of energy diversification, and of obtaining technological expertise, one purpose of developing a nuclear power capability may be to amortize a nuclear weapons program. Not only does an atomic energy infrastructure help a country to develop nuclear weaponry, but it can also permit states to sell their nuclear technology to third parties. At the same time, such a program may be used, not necessarily for attack, but for deterrent purposes, and as a political tool of *strategic leveraging* intended to expand a state's influence and prestige, and to gain concessions from the US or other powers.

Clause three of Article IX of the 1967 Nuclear Non-Proliferation Treaty (NPT) formalized the fact that the five permanent members of the UNSC represented the only *legitimate* nuclear states. Yet the five permanent members ("P-5") have had only limited success in limiting the spread of nuclear weaponry. On the one hand, there have been some significant success stories, in that Ukraine, Kazakhstan, Belarus, South Africa, Brazil and Argentina, and Libya in 2003 (with negotiations beginning in 1999), for example, have claimed to abandon their nuclear programs. On the other hand, a number of states continue to pose various forms of missile and nuclear proliferation threats. The fact that the five permanent members of the UN Security Council can legally possess a nuclear capability following signing of the 1967 Nuclear Non-Proliferation (NPT) treaty has raised accusations of "double standards." Moreover, the NPT has done little to prevent nuclear modernization by the "P-5" itself, nor has it worked to prevent the spread of nuclear weapons to both NPT signers and non-signers.

India is believed to possess enough plutonium for 55 to 115 nuclear weapons; Pakistan may be capable of building a similar number with enriched uranium. Both countries have aircraft capable of delivering nuclear bombs. India's military has inducted short- and intermediate-range ballistic missiles, while Pakistan itself possesses short- and medium-range missiles (allegedly acquired from China and North Korea). Both Pakistan and India are assumed to be capable of delivering nuclear warheads over significant distances.[2] Both are trying to develop low yield tactical nuclear weapons, which, unlike Cold War megabombs, may be more useable in battlefield conditions.

Israel has pointed the finger to alleged nuclear programs in Iran, Syria, Egypt and Saudi Arabia, in addition to missile capacities of each of these countries, while Tel Aviv itself has opposed international inspection of its nuclear program. Egypt, in turn, has signed the NPT, but has strongly criticized the treaty, largely because the treaty has done nothing to influence Israel's undeclared nuclear arsenal. Cairo has urged the US to press Israel to sign the NPT, which would allow the IAEA to inspect suspected nuclear facilities, including the Dimona plutonium reactor.

One of the justifications for "pre-emptive" intervention in Iraq had been to eliminate the Iraqi WMD threat and send a clear message to other two "axis of evil" states, Iran and North Korea, that they should foreclose the nuclear option as well. Instead, US involvement in Iraq, and general loss of international prestige following that intervention in which "weapons of mass destruction" (WMD) were not found, may have led both North Korea and Iran to believe that the US is too bogged down in Iraq in battling "weapons of conventional destruction" to consider military action against their nuclear programs.

Both North Korea and Iran thus far appear to have dug in their heels in opposing US and multilateral efforts to prevent them from acquiring a full-scale enrichment capability that could possibly be used to develop a nuclear weapons capacity—if their nuclear programs are not accompanied by effective international inspections and control over fuel cycles. Although intelligence estimates are highly inadequate, North Korea may have developed enough fissionable material for two warheads—with some estimates range as high as ten, plus Nodong missiles for delivery.[3] Iran may be within two to five years from acquiring nuclear weapons. Both states could possibly be bluffing as well, and may be willing to negotiate—but only if given the right balance of incentives and threats.

The following appear to represent the strategies of a number of emerging "upstart" or "parvenu" states:

- Testing their nuclear arsenal in defiance of the five permanent members of the UN Security Council who each possess a nuclear capability since the 1967 NPT in order to obtain international recognition (Pakistan and India);
- Building or purchasing new nuclear systems and weapons delivery capabilities and renouncing the NPT (North Korea);
- Engaging in *non-weaponized deterrence*, that is, deterrence by coming technologically close to building nuclear weapons but not actually deploying (Germany and Japan);

- Basing deterrence upon uncertainty, i.e. not officially announcing their development, refusing to sign the NPT, but leading states to believe in their possession (Israel);
- Engaging in a number of diplomatic games in respect to nuclear weapons by trying to hide their nuclear or WMD capabilities despite signing the NPT (Iran???);
- Threatening to develop or purchase such weaponry, or else bluffing as to their actual capabilities (Iraq before 2003, Syria? Turkey? Egypt? Saudi Arabia? Taiwan? South Korea? North Korea? Iran?)

This chapter will accordingly examine the global problems of nuclear proliferation in general, with a specific focus on three "upstart" or "parvenu" states, Israel, Iran and North Korea. The following Chapter 5 will more thoroughly discuss the Indian-Pakistani question.

## Historical Background

Since the advent of President Eisenhower's *Atoms for Peace* program (which had been stimulated by Soviet efforts to break the US monopoly in nuclear capabilities in the 1950s), the US has attempted to engage in a two-fold balancing act. The first facet of US policy has been to permit the export of "peaceful" nuclear technology (to large extent intended to amortize initial investments in the "war" atom). The second facet has been to simultaneously attempt to control the nuclear fuel cycle in order to prevent the potential spread of a nuclear weapons capability.

Despite its intent to prevent nuclear proliferation to third parties, American nuclear export policy has largely been undercut by the ability and willingness of a number of states to seek out diverse high technology suppliers—in addition to the utilization of indigenous and/or acquired high tech knowledge. The failure to implement an International Atomic Development Authority in 1946 led to a largely uncontrolled nuclear arms race, once the Soviet Union largely surprised the United States by exploding an atomic device in 1949. (Soviet Foreign Minister Andrei Gromyko had argued in the UN that any agreement on the international control of atomic weapons must be preceded by a worldwide moratorium on their production and use—a position vehemently opposed by Washington.)

The US-Soviet duopoly in the nuclear field soon began to be challenged by French and Chinese, who, along with Germany, entered the global market of the "peaceful atom." By the late Cold War, other states entered the export field, including Pakistan, North and South Korea, Brazil and Argentina, Israel and South Africa, among others. The post–1991 break up of the Soviet Union also opened the door to potential access to nuclear technology and weaponry—and most crucially, scientific expertise. At present, the availability of nuclear technology on the global market makes it difficult to restrain states such as Iran and North Korea from acquiring such materiel. At the same time, prior to revisions, such as the Additional Protocol signed in 1997, the 1967 NPT treaty has been very lax: First, the IAEA possesses very limited intelligence gathering capabilities. Second, NPT countries could designate which sites could be inspected. Third, NPT signatories were not permitted to develop warheads, but they could still be part of nuclear alliances and delivery systems. Concurrently, states could develop missile delivery systems under the guise of space programs. Fourth, no sanctions prevented states from *not* signing the NPT accords. Fifth, although the Article VI of the NPT treaty urges declared Nuclear Weapon State parties to the NPT (the P-5) to engage in disarmament, nothing can really enforce this aspect of the Treaty.

American anti-proliferation policy has furthermore been undercut by the fact that the knowledge to make nuclear weapons is largely an open secret. Designs for the H-Bomb were conceived by Edward Teller as early as 1946; the *Progressive* magazine published an article "How to Make an H-Bomb" in 1979, which revealed that the process of making atomic weaponry could be based on publicly available technical information. A nation only needs the money, the technological infrastructure, the know-how, and the willingness to make the Bomb. The genie has been out of the bottle for quite awhile given the thousands of students who have studied nuclear physics in the US and Europe.

The US had initially opposed French efforts to acquire nuclear weapons. (The US refusal to support the French at Dienbienphu in 1954, followed by the 1956 Suez crisis, accelerated the French efforts to obtain nuclear weapons—which was an option first considered at the end of World War II.) The Nixon administration then decided to secretly support the French nuclear program, with the argument that an independent French nuclear deterrent provided greater uncertainty for Soviet planners. Henry Kissinger advanced the concept of "managed spread" as proposed by Charles De Gaulle, and supported steps toward a "multipolar" global system—a position now opposed by the neo-conservatives in the administration of George W. Bush.

Although the US (and USSR) initially opposed Chinese acquisition of nuclear weaponry, US efforts to play the "China card" against Moscow in the 1970s indirectly assisted the development of Chinese nuclear and weapons capabilities. Here, the US illegally bypassed Coordinating Committee (COCOM) restrictions against high technology sales to Communist countries. Sensitive technology included the sale of supercomputers to China that could help design and test nuclear weapons and ballistic missiles trajectories. Moreover, the 1985 US-China agreement for nuclear cooperation was seen as flawed in that it did not provide for strong safeguards or control over reprocessing.[4] The 1990–91 Persian Gulf war then led China to revamp its military and nuclear strategy—in that China saw Iraq's demands to absorb Kuwait as similar to China's demands to absorb Taiwan.

The People's Republic of China has also been involved in nuclear theft. Perhaps reminiscent of theft of US nuclear secrets by the Soviet Union in 1945, in 3 January 1999 the declassified version of the Cox Report stated:

> The People's Republic of China (PRC) has stolen classified design information on the United States' most advanced thermonuclear weapons. These thefts of nuclear secrets from our national weapons laboratories enabled the PRC to design, develop, and successfully test modern strategic nuclear weapons sooner than would otherwise have

been possible. The stolen U.S. nuclear secrets give the PRC design information on thermonuclear weapons on a par with our own. The PRC thefts from our National Laboratories began at least as early as the late 1970s, and significant secrets are known to have been stolen as recently as the mid-1990s. Such thefts almost certainly continue to the present.

Having initially acquired nuclear assistance in the late 1950s from the Soviet Union, Nikita Khrushchev then cut off relations and technological assistance in 1959—to slow up the Chinese nuclear program. A few decades after finally acquiring a nuclear capability in 1964, China assisted the nuclear program of Pakistan, Iran, South Africa, in addition to Brazil and Argentina. It sold Eastwind IRBMs to Saudi Arabia and has helped Iran acquire the ability to produce ballistic missiles. Moreover, the break up of the Soviet Union may have not only resulted in conventional weapons sales to Africa and Asia at bargain basement prices, but also major missiles sales: Allegations have surfaced that Ukraine, under the former leadership of Leonard Kuzma, sold six nuclear capable cruise missiles to China and twelve to Iran between 1999–2001.[5] It is also been alleged that Iran obtained tactical nuclear weapons after Soviet breakup.

Since the late 1980s, North Korea has been among the leading exporters of missile technology and components to Iraq, Egypt, Iran, Syria, Libya, UAE, Yemen and Pakistan. Political changes in Iraq, Yemen and Libya, however, mean that its main customers in the Middle East are no longer in the market. This fact could put additional pressure on the state to either find new markets, or else change industries—if it does not militarize further. North Korea has claimed that it would not sell nuclear weaponry to terrorist groups, particularly *al-Qaida*. However, Washington fears that economic circumstances and economic consequences of state collapse might result in a change of policy.[6]

In early 2005, International Atomic Energy Agency (IAEA) may have some found evidence of secret nuclear experiments in Egypt that could be used in weapons programs, including several pounds of uranium metal and uranium tetrafluoride—a precursor to uranium hexafluoride gas. Egypt had engaged in a nuclear technology program in the 1980s and 1990s, but claims to abide by the NPT treaty. Both the Soviet Union and China had opposed Egyptian requests for nuclear arms in the 1960s and 1970s. According to Israeli sources, it is believed that the network run by Abdul Qadeer Khan may have provided Syria, Egypt and Saudi Arabia with nuclear weapons technologies.[7] These accusations serve to deflect Syrian, Egyptian and Saudi efforts to bring Israel's nuclear facilities into the international inspection process, but likewise raise questions. Concurrently, charges in 2004 that South Korea and Taiwan may be engaging in nuclear development programs (both states had programs in the 1970s) seeks to deflect attention from North Korean and Chinese weapons programs, at the same time that it raises questions as to the veracity of these allegations.

Beijing has been using *strategic leverage* in an effort to gain geopolitical and economic concessions from Washington—in a game of "sweet and sour". On the "sweet" side, Beijing has claimed that it totally supports a nuclear free Korean peninsula, but has tacitly offered to trade its support for North Korean de-nuclearization in order to gain US support for China's unification with Taiwan. On the "sour" side, Beijing has threatened to forge a Sino-Russian military alliance, if not obtain high tech weaponry from EU countries. These aspects of "strategic leveraging" are intended as a means to pressure the US over the Taiwan issue (signing an anti-secession law in 2005)—even though such policies may risk a re-militarization of Japan and American sanctions. (See Chapter 6.)

Concurrently, Washington has regarded "peaceful" Russian nuclear assistance to Iran as inflaming regional tensions—in that it is not clear that Russia will be able to control the nuclear fuel cycle in such a way as to prevent Iran from upgrading enriched uranium for weapons purposes. The Russian purpose, however, is both strategic and economic. One the one hand, Russia seeks to back its own nuclear producers against both US and European competitors; on the other hand, it seeks to stabilize Shi'a Iran as a counterweight to Saudi Arabia and Sunni pan-Islamic movements that it sees as threatening the Caucasus and central Asia beneath the soft underbelly of the Russian federation.

**The Question of the Israeli Deterrent**

In March 1975, the US government had ranked countries as to their likelihood of seeking nuclear weaponry: India, Taiwan, South Korea, Pakistan, Indonesia and then Iran, were listed. Israel, however, was not mentioned—even though the US government knew of its nuclear weapons program. The US has been reluctant to engage in serious dialogue with Israel as to revelations of its significant, yet still publicly undisclosed, nuclear weapons capacity. Initially assisted by France as a form of security guarantee, Israel opted to develop a nuclear weapons capability in the midst of the 1956 Suez Crisis. During the latter crisis, Moscow had warned that Soviet missiles could strike Israel. The US refused to back the secret Anglo-French-Israeli thrust into Egypt (by threatening not to support the pound sterling if Britain did not pull back its forces). In this regard, Israel could not trust either the Russians or the Americans to back their interests.

The US had known about the French-assisted nuclear facility at Dimona, a plutonium reprocessing plant, as early as 1958 after U-2 spy flights. By May-November 1960, the French began to backtrack on support from the program, perhaps under US pressure. To the Israeli vexation, De Gaulle threatened an end to French assistance if Israel continued to oppose outside inspection. By November, a compromise was reached: the French government would end its direct involvement in Dimona plutonium reprocessing facility, but French companies would complete their contracts. Israel was requested to publicly declare its peaceful purpose (and sign a secret agreement with Paris not to develop nuclear weapons) and the French would drop its insistence upon outside inspection.[8]

At roughly the same time that the US Atoms for Peace Program had completed Israel's first research reactor at Nachel Soreq in 1960, a facility that was placed under international safeguards and IAEA inspections, the US began to discuss

Israel's nuclear program in top-secret meetings in 1960. The program was then leaked to the *New York Times* in December; at this point, the official Israeli response (after initial denial, including claims that the facility was a textile plant) asserted, "the new Israeli reactor, now in the early stages of construction, is for peaceful purposes only."[9]

Prime Minister David Ben Gurion told the Knesset that reports that Israel was building nuclear weapons were a "deliberate or unwitting untruth," and that Israel had proposed "general and total disarmament in Israel and the neighboring Arab states."[10] In conversations with the Eisenhower administration, Israel categorically ruled out any form of international inspections—although it might accept visits by scientists from friendly countries, but under strict Israeli supervision.

The US State Department appeared to accept Ben Gurion's "categoric assurances" that Israel had no plans to develop nuclear weaponry, although it was concerned over the ownership and possible sale of plutonium produced. In subsequent conservations with President Kennedy, who publicly claimed to be a strong advocate of non-proliferation, Ben Gurion did not entirely rule out the acquisition of nuclear weapons, but this future option would be based on events beyond Israel's control in the Middle East, or in relation to Soviet policy. One justification for the nuclear program was to develop sufficient energy capabilities to develop desalinization plants due to potable water shortage. At the same time, however, Ben Gurion did not hide the fact that Israel intended to develop a pilot plant for plutonium separation; an issue that Kennedy did not push.[11] Kennedy did not press for a firm commitment that Israel would not develop a nuclear weapons capability; he only urged Israel to "understand" US non-proliferation policy and for Israel to publicly stress its peaceful intentions. By 1963, just as the Dimona plant was to become operational, Ben Gurion sought US security assurances, while Kennedy expressed concern about Israel's weapons potential.[12] (Israeli efforts to obtain US military support against Egypt and for Jordan may have represented one reason for the US decision not to grant Israel strong security assurances.)

By 1987, Israel became a major non-NATO ally; it was purported that Israel assisted South Africa's nuclear weapons program, as well as the nuclear programs of other states. Israel is now reputed to possess as many 75 to 200 nuclear devices (purportedly including the hydrogen and neutron bombs). These systems have been combined with significant delivery capacities, including three submarines capable of launching cruise missiles and long-range F-16I fighters.[13] The Israeli question illustrates the political dilemmas involved in preventing nuclear proliferation, as well as the failure of uncoordinated American and French pressures. Most of all, US refusal or reluctance to provide Israel with strong security guarantees may have been at the roots of its decision to develop nuclear weapons. In today's situation, however, as the US expands its NATO-Mediterranean dialogue, it may be possible to draw Israel and other states into a new form of "regional security community" that will permit Israel to place its nuclear program under international safeguards. (See Chapter 8.)

## From Israel to Pakistan and India

The fact that the five permanent members of the UNSC declared the right to possess nuclear weapons raised the ire of India (in its rivalry with China for a seat on the UNSC and its desire to be recognized as an emerging power) in particular. In turn, this fact hastened Pakistan's efforts to acquire a nuclear capability as well, despite US efforts to sanction the regime. (See Chapter 5.) After India's underground test of nuclear weapon in 1974, Pakistan vowed that it would build an "Islamic bomb." Pakistani Prime Minister Zulfikar Ali Bhutto partly justified this quest by observing in "clash of civilization" terms that there was a Christian bomb, a Jewish bomb, and a Hindu bomb. He denounced what he saw as the US bias toward India and Israel; he also believed that a Pakistani bomb would help attract financial support and aid for Pakistan from other Arab/Islamic states.

Accordingly, Pakistan did not sign the NPT, and did not become a member of the Nuclear Suppliers' Group, which establishes guidelines for nuclear exports. By the 1980s and 1990s, Pakistani scientists (Abdul Qadeer Khan and his network) whose connections with the Pakistani government are still unclear; played a significant role in providing nuclear expertise to North Korea, Libya, as well as Iran, and possibly Malaysia, Saudi Arabia, and Egypt—actions that represented a major set back for US non-proliferation policy.[14] Due to the belated discovery of the Khan network, it may have been too late to stop the damage.

Following Chinese acquisition of a nuclear capability, India had argued that it should likewise possess the right to acquire a nuclear capability—assuming that other nuclear states would not begin the process of disarmament. India hence argued that the NPT is representative of "double standards": One for the UNSC members and one for every one else, and that Washington has tended to ignore both Israeli and Pakistani nuclear capabilities. India has argued that the NPT is ineffective in blocking the spread of nuclear weapons to non-nuclear states, as it does not provide adequate security *guarantees* to those states that are consequently pressured to give up their nuclear programs. Furthermore, the NPT does nothing to help limit or even eliminate the weapons systems of the major powers. Following the 1990–91 Persian Gulf war, Indian analysts had based the demand for nuclear weaponry upon the argument that if a state needed to assert its interests against the United States, or other major powers, it needed to possess a nuclear deterrent.

Both India and Pakistan then exploded nuclear bombs nearly simultaneously in 1998, while concurrently developing delivery capabilities. In an attempt to calm the situation, the Clinton Administration established five key "benchmarks" for India and Pakistan to follow based on the contents of U.N. Security Council Resolution 1172 (June 1998) which condemned the nuclear test by the two countries. These included: 1) signing and ratifying the Comprehensive Nuclear Test Ban Treaty (CTBT); 2) halting all further production of fissile material and participating in Fissile Material Cutoff Treaty negotiations; 3) limiting development and deployment of WMD delivery vehicles; 4) implementing strict export controls on sensitive WMD materials and technologies; and 5) establishing bilateral dialogue between India and Pakistan to resolve their mutual differences.[15]

**Question of Iran and the Region**

Following the Iranian revolution in 1979, and the taking of American embassy personnel as hostages, Washington broke off relations with the newly established Islamic Republic. The latter then began to re-consider the nuclear option at the start of the 1980–88 Iran-Iraq war. The Israeli *preclusive* strike upon the Iraqi Osirak nuclear site in 1981 effectively led both Baghdad and Teheran to accelerate the nuclear option. By 1982, two years into its bloody conflict with Iraq, Iran had turned to India, China and Pakistan for technological support. Some 15,000–17,000 Iranian students were sent abroad for training in nuclear physics.[16] Although attempting to play "divide and rule," by 1982–83, the US began to clearly tilt toward the Iraqi leadership of Saddam Hussein, who was seen as the "lesser evil" in comparison the Ayatollah Khoemeni—to prevent an Iranian victory. As Iran sought to develop a nuclear capability, the Bushehr nuclear site was "mysteriously" bombed, in former National Security advisor Richard Perle's words, six times from March 1984 to November 1987 during the Iran-Iraq "war of cities."[17] In September 1985, Iran, Syria and Libya stated they would obtain nuclear weapons to counter Israel's "nuclear threat" while Iraq reportedly obtained financing from Saudi Arabia for its nuclear program.

By 2002, it was revealed by an Iranian opposition group in exile (by members of the Mujahedin-e Khalq (MEK) which is ironically defined by the US as a terrorist organization) that Tehran had not declared two uranium enrichment facilities as required under the NPT. Subsequent IAEA investigation found that uranium had been enriched 20%—which is far higher than the two to three percent enrichment level required for nuclear fuel.[18] These facilities, located at Natanz, south of Tehran, have been built deep underground with heavily reinforced walls and roofs, indicating that the Iranians are either interested in hiding them or else concerned about the possibility of military strikes. Iran has also been constructing a breeder reactor at Arak (to be completed in 8–10 years) that is "ideally suited for producing weapons-grade plutonium."[19] After observing the effects of strikes against the Osirak and Bushehr reactors in the 1980s, Iran opted to spread its nuclear facilities throughout the country, and locate them in populous areas—making the possibility of successful air strikes and special force operations very uncertain.

By October 2003, Iran had finally admitted to conducting eighteen years of covert atomic experiments, including the unreported uranium enrichment in a breach of the NPT. Following IAEA revelations, Iran appears to fit somewhere between category 5 and 6 of the above categories. Teheran could either be developing such weaponry or else coming close to building nuclear weaponry, but not actually deploying—as, it argues, has already been the case with Germany and Japan. Iran could seek to back out of the NPT "Additional Protocol," as has been the case with North Korea. While the Bush administration seeks to revise the NPT, Teheran appears to want to push the NPT to its limits—by insisting upon its right under Article IV of the NPT to develop its own nuclear fuel cycle.

## Russia and Iran

Washington has been particularly concerned that Russian nuclear assistance to Iran at its Bushehr plant could help Teheran develop enriched uranium—if Russia, or other countries, did not thoroughly control the fuel cycle. Moscow, however, has argued that US efforts to block its nuclear deals, upon the pretext of Iranian nuclear weapons program, represented an instrument of unfair competition. Russia has also not wanted to renege on its Bushehr contact, due to the fact that Teheran may have promised to purchase an additional five reactors once the Bushehr plant is functioning (a promise reminiscent of Iranian promises to purchase Westinghouse reactors from the US in the 1970s under the Shah).

In order to block that deal, the Bush administration promised to compensate Moscow; yet Russia did not believe it could trust those promises due to the possibility that the US Congress, confronted with major budget deficits, might not allocate the funding as promised by the executive branch.[20] From a domestic perspective, the Putin administration additionally could not be regarded as kowtowing to Washington over an issue so "vital" to the national security and economy—despite the dangerous regional and global consequences.

Russian flips flops, as whether it would supply Iran nuclear fuel with or without conditions, angered Washington. The US preferred that Russia end all its support for Bushehr, yet insisted that if the project was to continue, that Russia demand that all nuclear fuel used by Iran must be returned to Moscow. (This issue subsequently raised a stink between Russia and Iran as to who would pay for shipping the spent fuel!) By mid–2003, Russia announced that the Bushehr facility would not be completed until 2005—providing more time for diplomacy. By 12 September 2003, the IAEA, of which Russia is a member, demanded that Iran provide full disclosure of its nuclear program, and freeze its uranium enrichment program, setting a deadline of 31 October. Teheran then walked out of the IAEA conference. (See below.)

By January 2005, there were unconfirmed reports that Russia had completed the installation of advanced radar systems around the Bushehr nuclear plant and at Iran's uranium enrichment plants for military purposes in Isfahan in central Iran. These reports, plus reports of Russian sales of "defensive" missile systems to Syria, appeared to indicate that Russia could be getting involved in the Middle East, with speculation as to whether Moscow might provide Syria or Iran with security *guarantees*—a dubious prospect at present.[21] By February 2005, Moscow claimed it would sign a nuclear deal with Iran in which the spent fuel would be reprocessed in Russia. Moscow appeared to indicate that some form of international inspections would be put in place.

## Iran and the European "Troika"

With the disclosures of the Iranian nuclear program, Iran and the EU-3 (the troika of the UK, Germany, and France) reached secret understandings about the nature of Iranian nuclear activities in 2001–03. As the US does not possess formal relations with Iran, only the Europeans (and Russians) can negotiate directly. As a result of the talks with European states, along with Russian pressures, Iran had unexpectedly announced, in October 2003, its willingness to sign the 'Additional Protocol' and then cease its actions in the field of uranium enrichment as a gesture of good will—in what was known as the 'Tehran declaration'. By 10 November, Teheran then declared that it would suspend all enrichment and reprocessing activities.[22] Then, in February 2004, Iran agreed to halt the production and assembly of centrifuge parts—in the "Brussels understandings."

Later in February, however, IAEA inspectors found advanced centrifuge systems for uranium enrichment, along with a program for polonium 210, which could be used as a neutron initiator for nuclear weaponry.[23] On 13 March 2004, Teheran announced that it had indefinitely suspended international inspections in response to IAEA censure. Iran argued that it postponed the inspections to the end of April due to the approach of the Iranian New Year on 20 March; the US representative to the IAEA stated that the freeze might be an attempt to buy time and hide covert activities before allowing inspectors access to new sites.[24] While the IAEA had warned of a possible break down of the NPT system, American neo-conservatives reiterated threats to intervene militarily, or somehow pre-empt its nuclear capability (perhaps through use of special forces or cruise missile strikes).

From the Iranian perspective, however, Europe has generally failed to meet its obligations to provide Iran with advanced nuclear technology and to close the investigation file against Iran's nuclear activities by the IAEA in return for a voluntary and temporary halt of enrichment activities, as it said was agreed in the Tehran and Brussels "understandings" in 2003. From Teheran's perspective, the Western countries were attempting to retain their monopoly on nuclear technology (likewise a complaint of Russia) and simply regard Iran as a mere nuclear fuel export market. Iran has thus argued that Europe is trying to coerce it to buy fuel despite the fact that it is cheaper for Iran to produce nuclear fuel than to import it from the West. In advocating national production, Iran argued that efforts by the international community and IAEA to deny its rights, or else the surrendering of this right by Iran, is to detriment to Iran's national interests.[25]

Then, on 31 October 2004, despite European efforts to achieve a diplomatic settlement, and despite (or because of) continued American threats to intervene in Iran following US intervention in Iraq, the Iranian Parliament unanimously approved a bill that supported the resumption of uranium enrichment process. In a session carried live on national radio, all 247 lawmakers of the 290-member body who were present voted for the measure. Some chanted "Death to America!" and "God is great!" As the vote came on the eve of the American elections, and as it appeared to reveal the fact the nuclear question had become one of national pride (much as is the case for both India and Pakistan), it seemed to serve as a warning to whichever candidate, George Bush or John Kerry, became president—not to intervene in the country.

Despite these theatrical events, by 15 November 2003, Iran and the European troika appeared to reach an agreement. They appeared to have obtained Iran's affirmation that it did not, and would not, seek to acquire nuclear weapons; that it would continue to implement Additional Protocol pending its ratification, which had been made more much difficult by its parliament's position (as pronounced on

October 31). Iran would voluntarily suspend "all enrichment-related and reprocessing activities." The Europeans, however, realized that there was a gap in commitment: The EU was calling for an indefinite suspension, Iran, however, was insisting that it the suspension should be limited in time.[26] In February 2005, French Defense Minister Michele Alliot-Marie stated that negotiations were hampered by lack of trust on both sides: "The Europeans don't want to concede anything in negotiations or give up something so long as the Iranians don't accept the controls that are being demanded.... And the Iranians don't want to give up a nuclear enrichment program because they are unsure that they will get anything tangible in return."[27]

The Troika has believed the best policy is to stall the program and has hoped that the Iranians would see for themselves that the acquisition of nuclear weapons would prove counter-productive. The Europeans have argued that they would join the US in applying sanctions in the UN Security Council if necessary, but do not support surgical strikes or sabotage of nuclear facilities, as the US and Israel have threatened. At the same time, however, as an aspect of the Iranian quest to obtain nuclear weapons is to obtain US recognition and economic assistance, EU policy will fail without US (and Russian) supports. If nothing can stall or stop the program, Iran could possibly acquire a nuclear weapons capability in 2–5 years.

By January 2005, in an ostensible turn around of policy, the US announced that it would back the multilateral European effort.

## Geo-strategic Concerns

Iran believes that it is confronted with a number of legitimate security issues. First, Iran argues that the possession of nuclear weaponry by Israel, Pakistan, as well as by India, have not been fully condemned by Washington. Second, the presence of US troops in Iraq, Bahrain, Qatar, Azerbaijan, and Afghanistan likewise remains a concern, in that Iran sees itself as "encircled." It fears that the US may be using Iraq as a base to send drones to spy upon Iran. Third, there is the fear of Israel's capacity to pre-empt Teheran's nuclear capability in which Israel, in a sense, redefined the traditional meaning of the word *pre-emption*. Israeli strategists argued that it may be necessary to strike reactors before they started producing fissionable material, rather than wait until later, when the threat would become unmanageable and when it would be more dangerous to strike.[28]

Here, Israel has attempted to pressure the US into action (as was the case for Iraq) by threatening unilateral strikes on Iran if the US does not act. US vice-president Dick Cheney reiterated this option publicly in January 2005, probably the first time a US government official has publicly threatened to play the "Israeli card"—as an aspect of strategic leveraging, with dangerous implications for perceptions in the Middle East. (In August 2004, Teheran had previously responded to US and Israeli threats to attack its Bushehr nuclear site by declaring that it would destroy Israel's Dimona nuclear facility, with its new 1300 km Shahab-3 missile.)

What is also driving Iranian concerns are communal clashes and acts of terrorism involving Shi'ia and Sunni Moslems in both Pakistan and Iraq. Political-ideological disputes with nuclear-capable Pakistan have raised tensions, as have Saudi-Iranian politico-religious rivalries—which have raised the threat of a Saudi-Pakistani "nuclear alliance." Iran will also await the final status of Iraq: The question as to whether the new Iraqi government will ultimately prove to be friendly or hostile to Iran may likewise play in Iranian strategic calculus in determining whether it does or does take the nuclear route. It is not yet clear how Iranian relations with the new Iraqi government after the 30 January 2005 elections will develop. Other issues concern the question of Shi'ite Holy Places in Iraq as well as more general relations between Iran and the majority of Iraqi Shi'ites (whose 'Quietist' views do not necessarily see eye to eye with their more militant Iranian counterparts). Events in Iraq in relation to the Kurdish question could likewise affect Iranian relations with Turkey, particularly as Ankara has threatened to intervene in northern Iraq, if the PKK is not put under control.

From the Bush administration perspective, Iran's nuclear program represents a significant question mark—contrary to Teheran's assertions that its nuclear program is designed for peaceful purposes only. A nuclear weapons deterrent could make it easier for Teheran to press its interests in the region, particularly in support of Shi'ite groups in Iraq, Afghanistan, Pakistan and central Asia, Lebanon, Bahrain—as well as in support of those Shi'ia groups located in the oil-rich eastern provinces of Saudi Arabia. The US will thus continue to pressure Iran to make certain that Iran makes a full disclosure of its nuclear capabilities. Tehran, however, has thus far insisted on its right under the NPT to develop its own nuclear fuel cycle. But Teheran also seeks US recognition and a firm promise not to press for "regime change."

Here, under neo-conservative influence, the danger is that Washington may put too much faith in the idea that the Islamic regime in Iran could be undermined by "regime change" in Iraq. Washington has appeared to believe that the Islamic leadership would be unable to co-opt the burgeoning numbers of Iranian youth who ostensibly seek "the American way" and who thus oppose the radical Islamic leadership. Much as Iraqi exiles obtained the ear of Washington, it appears that a much more influential lobby of Iranian exiles could likewise obtain Washington's support. It is dubious, however, that the US will want to repeat the Iraqi political situation in which the Iraqi National Council would be replaced by the Iranian National Council—in that neither group has had a real feeling for the changes in their respective countries after long years of exile.

**North Korea and the Far East**

While Japan has been concerned with China's burgeoning naval and nuclear capabilities, both North Korea and China have reciprocally been concerned with the rise of Japanese military, naval and Ballistic Missile Defense (BMD) capabilities, and may ironically fear that American withdrawal from the region could stimulate the rise of a more independent Japan. Concurrently, China has been concerned that North Korean nuclear and missile capabilities may provoke Japan, and has thus hoped to work with the Americans to contain North Korea, but not without a price. Beijing could pressure Pyongyang by cutting off food supplies, but has been reluctant to take strong measures—in fear that the regime could collapse or become more militant.

In this regard, Beijing has been using strategic leverage in an effort to gain geopolitical and economic concessions from Washington, in a game of "sweet and sour." On the "sweet" side, Beijing has offered to trade its support for North Korean de-nuclearization as a ploy to obtain US support for its reunification with Taiwan. On the "sour" side, it has tacitly threatened to forge a Sino-Russian military alliance, and obtain high tech arms from European countries. These aspects of "strategic leveraging" are largely intended, once again—as a means to pressure the US over the Taiwan issue. (See Chapter 6.)

On 4 October 2002, Washington accused North Korea of secretly developing a program designed to enrich uranium to weapons grade standards, in violation of the 1994 agreement that Pyongyang had signed with Washington to freeze its nuclear weapons capability. Arguing that North Korea had "cheated" on the "Agreed Framework," the Bush administration declared that the US was no longer bound by its side of the deal, and thus suspended the oil shipments which it had been providing North Korea under the 1994 agreement on 14 November 2002. Pyongyang then retaliated by expelling international inspectors; it was presumed to have restarted plutonium reprocessing.

Tensions over the nuclear question continued to mount since 1993 when the Clinton administration demanded that North Korea open its nuclear reactor facilities at Yongbyon, which were capable of producing weapons grade plutonium from spent fuel, to IAEA inspections. North Korea responded by threatening to drop out of the NPT treaty. It was purportedly at that time that Pakistan and North Korea may have made a deal: A. Q. Kahn's blueprints for making nuclear weapons in exchange for ballistic missile technology, based on North Korea's *Nodong* missile.[29] By 1998, Pakistan tested its *Ghauri* missile (based on the *Nodong*); both Pakistan and India tested nuclear weaponry in a series of underground explosions. In the summer of 2002, the CIA concluded that North Korea had begun to produce weapons grade materiel.

In November 2002 the United States, Japan and South Korea voted to suspend shipments of fuel oil to North Korea. President Bush declared that oil shipments would be cut if the North did not agree to put a halt to its weapons ambitions; he also issued a statement that the US had no intention of invading North Korea, so to indicate that Washington might provide North Korea with a security guarantee. Such a "promise," however, did not appear very sincere to Pyongyang, who wanted more concrete terms: North Korea demanded the signing of a "non-aggression" pact with the US, and argued that US had not kept its side of the 1994 Agreed Framework. The latter had stated that the construction of light water reactors would be completed in 2003, but the project was years behind schedule. By December 2002, the North threatened to reactivate nuclear facilities at Yongbyon for energy generation, arguing that it had no other option due to the American decision to halt oil shipments.

In January 2003, South Korea asked China to use its influence upon North Korea; Russia likewise offered to help convince Pyongyang to find a way to end its nuclear program. The IAEA threatened the possibility of sanctions. North Korea then announced it would withdraw from the NPT. South Korean President-elect Roh Moo-hyun proposed a face-to-face meeting with Kim Jong-Il, but this endeavor failed to break the impasse. In his January 2003 State of the Union address, President Bush declared that "America and the world will not be blackmailed." The IAEA found North Korea in breach of nuclear safeguards and referred the matter to the UN Security Council. At this time, North Korea fired a missile into the sea between South Korea and Japan, and then fired a second missile in March. The US and South Korea engaged in military maneuvers at the same time that the US intervened militarily in Iraq—as a deterrent against any possible North Korean aggression during the "preemptive" war against Iraq.

The UN Security Council expressed concern about North Korea's nuclear program, but did not condemn Pyongyang for pulling out of the NPT. North Korea then signaled that it was ready for direct talks with the US, which began in Beijing in April. American officials stated Pyongyang had admitted to possessing nuclear weapons, but that it was ready to destroy its nuclear program in exchange for normalized relations and economic assistance from the United States. Washington, however, refused to engage in direct bilateral talks, arguing that this would encourage bad behavior. By May, without any concrete response from Washington as to its demands for diplomatic recognition, Pyongyang threatened to tear up its 1992 agreement with Seoul to keep the peninsula free from nuclear weapons. In July, South Korea claimed that North Korea had started to reprocess a "small number" of the 8,000 spent nuclear fuel rods at its facilities in Yongbyon. In opposition to the neo-conservative Bush administration approach, former Defense Secretary William Perry stated: "You have to offer something, but you have to have an iron fist behind your offer."[30]

By August 2003, North Korea agreed to six-way multilateral talks on its nuclear program; these involved South Korea, the US, Japan, China and Russia. At these talks, the U.S. promised to resume heavy fuel oil and food aid and agreed in principle to a bilateral non-aggression pact; Washington would compensate North Korea for its loss of electric power and both the US and Japan would its normalize relations with Pyongyang. In turn, North Korea would agree in principle to scrap its nuclear program and institute a freeze on its "nuclear facility and nuclear substance"; it would permit inspections and then dismantle its nuclear facilities upon the completion of the light-water reactors promised under the 1994 Agreed Framework. North Korea would also conclude a treaty to halt its missile production and sales. Yet as the U.S. then refused to engage in direct substantive discussions, North Korea threatened to test a nuclear weapon.[31]

By December 2003, North Korea appeared to offer to "freeze" its nuclear program in return for a list of concessions from the US—in addition to a promised offer of a security guarantee and "non-aggression" pact. At that time, President George W. Bush declared Pyongyang must dismantle the program altogether. By February-June 2004, the second and third rounds of multilateral talks took place.

Here, the US made a brand new offer that would permit North Korea to obtain fuel aid—but only if Pyongyang froze, and then dismantled, its nuclear program. In other words, in a what seemed to be a new step-by-step approach designed to reduce tensions, the U.S. was no longer demanding that North Korea completely dismantle its nuclear weapons program before it would address North Korea's security and energy concerns.

The new US offer proposed a complete two stage dismantlement and elimination of North Korea's nuclear program in which a general three-month freeze was to be followed by the elimination and removal of all existing weapons as well as the plutonium program, the uranium enrichment program, and all civil nuclear facilities. These programs would be subject to verification by an undefined international body. The US and other states would promise not to invade or attack; each side would respect the territorial integrity of the other parties. The US, Japan and other states would assist North Korea with its energy needs; North Korea could then be shown a route through which it could be removed from the U.S. list of "State Sponsors of Terrorism" (North Korea was placed on the list in 1988). It would then achieve the gradual removal of sanctions.

While leaving open the possibility of further discussion, North Korea rejected the US proposals, arguing that it was being forced to take "unilateral" steps, that US policy in respect to uranium enrichment was "unreasonable" and that the US had not thoroughly renounced its hostile policy toward North Korea—in deeds as opposed to mere words. North Korea then reiterated its demand for compensation in the form of heavy oil and electricity.[32] At this point, it appeared that North Korea had taken offense to Japanese plans to purchase BMD systems from the US—to be deployed in 2007. North Korea saw the latter systems as undermining its own missile deterrent—and potentially offensive.

During these talks, Pyongyang argued that it was "entitled" to possess a powerful nuclear program in order to deter a pre-emptive US attack (as illustrated by the US intervention in Iraq). Pyongyang stated that it was entitled to pursue a "neither confirm nor deny" policy concerning the specifics of its nuclear capabilities (much like the US Navy neither confirms nor denies the presence of nuclear weapons aboard its ships). North Korea likewise raised allegations that South Korea had its own nuclear program, an accusation denied by Seoul (Seoul admitted to having such a program in the 1970s).

By 10 February 2005, North Korea declared itself a nuclear power and pulled out of the six-nation talks, stating that it was "prepared to mobilize all of our military force against any provocative moves by the enemy."[33] This opened the question as to whether the UN should apply sanctions (or whether the US might intervene militarily). Later in the month, in another of its many flip-flops, Pyongyang indicated that it *might* return to the discussions. The second term Bush administration stated that it has new tools to pressure Korea into compliance, once again raising the threatening rhetoric. Some South Korean analysts stated that North Korea may be bluffing: It was too early to consider North Korea as a nuclear power, as it has neither tested the nuclear devices nor provided any solid evidence of their possession.[34] In March 2005, US Secretary of State Condoleezza Rice proposed the resumption of multilateral talks—but at the same time that the US and South Korea engaged in military maneuvers.

## American and International Options

The fact that the nuclear genie is out of the bottle does not necessarily mean that states will develop nuclear weapons and delivery capabilities. A good number of states (Ukraine, Belarus, Kazakhstan, South Africa, Brazil and Argentina, and now Libya) have seen the positive aspects of the NPT and have realized that the development of nuclear weaponry is counter-productive, that it merely antagonizes regional and international diplomatic relationships, and that it can create more domestic and international political and economic dilemmas than it resolves. A nuclear program can additionally strain a country's financial capabilities.

Yet as it remains confronted with the proliferation of both nuclear capabilities delivery systems, US policy possesses a number of options, which are not necessarily exclusive. The first is strengthened IAEA inspections, as implemented by the 1998 "Additional Protocol" to the NPT. The second is economic sanctions and "containment." The third is the Proliferation Security Initiative (PSI). The fourth is to threaten, if not use, force. The fifth option is to try to "manage" the spread of nuclear weaponry. The sixth is a "nuclear free weapons zone." The seventh is the implementation of "Regional Security Communities" which would engage in *real dialogue* and multilateral diplomacy.

## Strengthened IAEA Inspections and Multinational Controls over Fuel Cycles

A number of steps have been proposed to strengthen international cooperation. These include: (1) the strengthening of national nuclear material export control systems by removing legal loopholes and by enacting legally binding controls in accord with the April 2004 UN Security Council Resolution 1540. (Washington has hoped that the latter would criminalize the proliferation of weapons of mass destruction, including nuclear weapons). (2) States should strengthen support of the aims of the Proliferation Security Initiative (PSI) by increasing international military, intelligence, and law enforcement cooperation. (3) The Convention for the Suppression of Unlawful Acts against the Safety of Maritime Navigation should be amended to make the transport of WMD on commercial vessels an internationally recognized offence.[35]

Though pointing in the right direction, a number of these issues remain problematic, however. In May 1997, the IAEA approved the "Additional Protocol," which was adopted primarily to strengthen the Agency's ability to detect undeclared activities in non-nuclear weapons states. All states party to the NPT have subsequently been asked to adopt this instrument as a complement to their full-scope safeguards agreement. The Additional Protocol imposes additional obligations on non-nuclear states and enlarges the IAEA's mandate by permitting inspections within 24 hour notice, and by reporting to the Nuclear Suppliers' Group (NSG) "Trigger List" items as well as uranium mining, enrichment and reactor activities.[36]

The latter demand, however, is problematic in the case of North Korea's program, for example, which is hidden deep underground along with its conventional weaponry. Along with the closed nature of North Korean society, it will be difficult to obtain full and unimpeded access with 24 hours notice. Another problem is that the Additional Protocol cannot stop states that drop out of the NPT altogether and opt to develop weapons, although it tries to create both positive incentives and negative sanctions for not doing so. If states do drop out of the NPT, then there should be an immediate review of that country's nuclear activities by the UNSC. The US, NATO and Russia should concurrently engage states that remain outside the NPT and that possess declared or undeclared nuclear weapons—such as India, Israel and Pakistan—and convince them to sign the IAEA Additional Protocol, the Comprehensive Nuclear-Test-Ban Treaty, so as gradually eliminate production of fissile material.[37]

Here, however, as part of the "double standards" written into the treaty, the Additional Protocol was signed by the US in Vienna in 1998—but as a declared Nuclear Weapon State party to the NPT, the US may exclude the application of IAEA safeguards on its activities. Under the Additional Protocol, the US also has the right to exclude activities and sites concerning national security in accordance with its National Security Exclusion. The latter is crucial to US acceptance of the Additional Protocol and provides the basis for the protection of US nuclear weapons-related activities, sites, and materials as a declared nuclear power. This fact, of course, raises concerns of those states that still feel threatened by US nuclear weaponry.

In negotiations with Iran and North Korea, and as was the case with Ukraine in 1994, the US and European position has been to permit non-nuclear weapons states to continue their civilian nuclear programs, but attempt to control their fuel cycles. This is to be done by importing the nuclear reactor fuel and returning any spent fuel—in order to make sure such fuel would not be upgraded to make fissile material. Yet instead of returning spent fuel to US or European facilities, another option is to place them in multinational facilities, which could then re-process nuclear fuels. The Bush administration has not yet endorsed the option of multinational facilities (which would ironically be close to the 1947 concept of the International Atomic Development Agency), but it has called upon members of the Nuclear Suppliers Group not to export enrichment and reprocessing equipment to states that do not already possess full-scale enrichment and reprocessing plants. As mentioned with the case of Iran, there is concern that such a process may prove to be more expensive, and that national industries could go out of business—if a multinational venture took over the sales and control of the fuel cycle.

**Sanctions and Containment**

If Iran or North Korea, for example, does not meet the IAEA's conditions, Washington will pressure the IAEA board of governors to send the issue to the U.N. Security Council. That step could result in the imposition of punitive measures, including tougher economic sanctions. The problem, of course, is the *degree of toughness that the UN should take involving a mix of positive incentives and threat of negative sanctions.*

Concerning North Korea, it will be difficult to obtain full multilateral agreement (that would be supported by Beijing) on any form of sanctions or coercive measures. China, Russia, Japan, as well as South Korea, have all been very reluctant to impose sanctions on North Korea. To obtain the backing of China in particular, the US needs to first propose, and then implement, a detailed plan of economic, high-tech and energy assistance, plus assurances of a nuclear fuel supply, as well as *conditional security assurances* leading to *stronger security guarantees.* These steps should be able to gain the confidence of China as a step toward finally obtaining an accord with Pyongyang.

Ideally, the US and the European troika could both offer incentives to draw Iran away from a nuclear weapons program—in an effort to split so-called "reformers" (centered around former president Hashemi Rafsanjani) and the anti-American hardliners. (Rafsanjani has warned that continual political disputes over the subject will lead to a cut off investment, as well as capital flight from the country.[38] Hardliners, however, argue that Iran can still play the oil card.) But these incentives would have to be accompanied by strong *threats* of sanctions by both parties, which would then carried out and coordinated by both sides. Under the pressure of American sanctions, Iran has already sought better relations with India, China, and Japan—which are desperate for oil.

If Iran, however, refuses to accept the carrots of incentives, sanctions could only be effective if the *entire* international community supports such actions. (See Chapter 6.) The US may find it very difficult, if not impossible, to get other powers to impose sanctions. It may be impossible to get "China to cancel its $100 billion gas deal with Iran; to force Turkey to cut off diplomatic ties with Iran or at least not buy natural gas from it; to tell India to avoid reaching an agreement with Iran for a $3.5-billion oil pipeline that will go through Pakistan; and maybe even to tell Russia not only to stop building the reactor at Bushehr, but also to cease its civilian investments as a punishment."[39] In addition, Japan has been negotiating with Teheran for $2 billion in oil contracts in 2003, despite US objections.

A more difficult problem to resolve is that the accords reached by the Europeans may not be sufficient to prevent Iran from obtaining a nuclear capability—particularly if the US does not become more *directly* involved in the negotiations due to the fact that it has not reached out to establish formal ties with Iran since the 1979 Islamic Revolution. On the one hand, there is no reason to assume (as do both Teheran and American neo-conservatives) that the Europeans, who live on Venus, will necessarily take the "soft" approach, while only the US, who lives on Mars, will take the "hard." The policies of the US and EU could well converge—*if* there is verifiable evidence of Iranian "deceit." On the other hand, the US could pressure the Europeans into accepting US directives—if Washington does not pursue all possible diplomatic options. If Washington does not soon take steps in Teheran's direction, as it has appeared to promise in January 2005, or if Teheran does not accept a compromise, the Europeans may be caught in the middle—and pressured to accept options—as largely defined by Washington.

**Proliferation Security Initiative (PSI)**

The September 2003 Proliferation Security Initiative (PSI) is intended to interdict lethal materials transported by land, sea or air, among other means, and to show American "willingness to use force when force is required." The Bush administration argues that the "Nuclear Suppliers Group should refuse to sell enrichment and reprocessing equipment and technologies to any state that does not already possess full scale, functioning enrichment and reprocessing plants."

Fourteen countries, including Russia, have signed the PSI agreement, yet the concept will need some fine-tuning in order to get Beijing and other countries fully on board. Beijing has questioned the legitimacy and legality of the interdiction plans, saying the best way to prevent the proliferation of weapons of mass destruction was "dialogue." Russia, which signed the agreement in the June 2004, had still questioned the legality of the plan, which involves seizing suspect shipments in the air and on the sea. Historically, interdiction on the high seas has been considered as a *casus belli*.

The problem remains: Which technologies need to be stopped, and which countries are to be targeted? Both major high technology producers such as China, as well as states with large shipping fleets (Panama and Liberia), need to cooperate as well.[40] The results have thus far been contradictory. PSI proponents claimed the seizure of a vessel carrying explosives and weapons by the Greek authorities in 2003 as a success. So was the stopping of a Malaysian ship off the Libyan coast n October 2003 that was carrying centrifuge components, and which indicated a possible A.Q. Khan connection with a private firm in Malaysia. (Malaysia is a signer of the Southeast Asia Nuclear Weapons Free Zone agreement.)[41] But the United States and Spain, after jointly seizing a North Korean vessel that was carrying missiles off the coast of Yemen, were forced to release the cargo—as the shipment had been destined for the Yemeni armed forces and thus did not violate international law.

**Military Intervention**

Covert actions in Iran and/or North Korea could sabotage facilities and stall nuclear programs, but at a risk of high tensions—and counter-action through acts of terrorism and war. Unilateral military intervention apparently remains an option and has not been ruled out as an option, even though US peacekeeping troops are dangerously overextended following deployment in Iraq in case another major military intervention proves "necessary."[42]

In April 2004, a massive explosion took place in Ryongchon near the Chinese border nine hours after Kim Jong-Il's train had passed through, raising questions as to what would have happened had Pyongyang interpreted the explosion to be an act of "terrorism" directed against its leader. North Korea possesses sufficient conventional force capabilities to set Seoul "in flames," with some 11,000 artillery tubes dug in the demilitarized zone. Its missile capabilities could strike Japan as well, assuming these systems are not pre-empted, or else checked by an effective BMD. North Korea's nuclear capabilities are presumed to be more concentrated and deeper underground than those of Iran—hence providing the Pentagon's rationale for the development of Robust Nuclear Earth Penetrator (RNEP), also known as "bunker busters."

In January 2005, it was rumored that the US was engaging in reconnaissance missions over Iranian territory with unmanned aerial vehicles (UAV) drones flown from Iraqi territory.[43] (If true, this would once again implicate Iraq in a potential conflict against Iran.) The Bush administration would not confirm such actions, but did not rule them out either. The day after the Presidential inauguration in January 2005, US Vice-President Dick Cheney charged that Iran was a major threat to world peace and accused Teheran of developing a nuclear weapons program and of sponsoring terrorism. He also played the Israeli card, "Given the fact that Iran has a stated policy that their objective is the destruction of Israel, the Israelis might well decide to act first, and let the rest of the world worry about cleaning up the diplomatic mess afterwards."[44] In February 2005, former UN weapons inspector in Iraq, Scott Ritter, a strong administration critic, claimed that President Bush had already signed executive orders to begin strikes on Iran in June 2005.[45] Even if not true, the "leak" appears intended to pressure Iran into compliance—in fear that the US or Israel would engage in preemptive strikes.

The "mess" (in Dick Cheney's words) created by such an attack, however, would not simply be "diplomatic" but "geo-economic" and "socio-political" as well: Pre-emptive strikes (whether or not aimed at regime change) could result in permanent socio-political instability, increased oil prices and involve acts of terrorism (with weapons of conventional destruction). Iran's mass media openly discuss Iran's military options, in case of US intervention. Iranian military leaders hope to deter a US military invasion by emphasizing the heavy costs that Washington is likely to incur once it has entered Iran. Teheran has also threatened to destabilize Iraq in order to keep US forces bogged down there for as long as possible.[46] Given US attempts to strike bin Laden and other targets, surgical strikes against nuclear sites will not necessarily succeed; and given the dispersed and advanced nature of the Iranian program, would enmesh the general population due to their close proximity to urban centers.

The real danger is that US or Israeli strikes against Iranian nuclear facilities may cause a backlash among the general population of 65 million, and help strengthen the regime, rather than weaken or undermine it. With large numbers of its population spread out in a world-wide diaspora, even limited pre-emptive strikes are likely to result in major terrorist attacks of all forms, much as Teheran struck out against members of the Shah's regime in the 1980s, and allegedly in support of *Hizb'allah* suicide attacks in Lebanon in 1983 against the US marines and French peacekeepers, following US actions in Lebanon and the tilt toward Saddam Hussein against the Ayatollah Khoemeni. The result might be long war of attrition in which Washington escalates its bombing, while Iran expands its terrorist actions to where ever it can send its revolutionary guards.

Should Iran adamantly refuse to fully disclose its nuclear capabilities and accept full transparency, it will also erode confidence and cause negative counter-reactions in countries throughout the Middle East/Persian Gulf/central Asia. A spiraling "security dilemma" of mutual fears could possibly result in a destabilizing nuclear, WMD and conventional arms race that Iran could hardly afford in either diplomatic, military or financial terms.[47] A nuclear Iran will most likely alienate Saudi Arabia, as well as Turkey, Egypt and Pakistan, in addition to risking an Israeli or US pre-emptive strike. The worst-case scenario is that an Iranian nuclear program is likely to provoke its neighbors to seek out nuclear weaponry and/or other forms of WMD, or else significantly increase their conventional armaments. The prospects of an Iranian nuclear force opened a debate in Israel (as early as 1998) as to whether the latter should make its nuclear force public, rather than maintain its present ambiguity of "don't ask don't tell."

In reaction to a potential Iranian nuclear program, Saudi Arabia has been rumored to look toward an alliance with a nuclear Pakistan, charges that have been vehemently denied by Riyadh.[48] (Saudi Arabia was also purported to have financed Saddam Hussein's nuclear program in the 1980s during its war with Iran.[49]) High placed military officials in Turkey have hinted of a possible nuclear option; another option would be to tighten Ankara's relations with nuclear Pakistan (perhaps to the detriment of Turkey's alliance with Israel). Turkey might consequently find itself caught between seeking NATO guarantees (but with an Alliance in dissolution), and seeking support from the European Union, which, however, is unlikely to possess a coordinated nuclear defense of its members, let alone for applicants such as Turkey. (See Chapter 6.) Another scenario is for both Saudi Arabia and Turkey to move toward "neutrality" and further distance themselves from American or Pakistani policies—rather than try to confront a nuclear Teheran with either nuclear weapons or with nuclear alliances.[50]

**Managed Spread**

A fourth possible option is the *neo-realist* view (as opposed to the *interventionist neo-conservative* stance) that atomic weapons capabilities are going to spread—whether the US likes it or not. The question then is how to *manage* that spread to only those states considered "stable" and "reliable." It is argued that nuclear weapons dampen hyper-nationalism and thus make war less likely on the domestic political side, while ostensibly creating an *equipoise* involving a "balance of power and threat" on the international military side.[51] In the neo-realist view, a more or less balanced nuclear spread should actually prevent war, as nuclear systems would, in effect, cancel themselves out in a "unit veto" system—through Mutual Assured Destruction. Nothing, however, prevents states with nuclear weapons to engage in either conventional or "limited" nuclear war, with nuclear weapons used to pre-empt or held as a last resort—or else to threaten nuclear blackmail.

After Soviet break-up, neo-realists, for example, advocated the spread of nuclear capabilities to Germany and Ukraine.[52] Germany, however, has remained stable; it has not attempted to develop an independent nuclear deterrent but one linked to France, and possibly Britain. A politically divided and financially strapped Ukraine has certainly not been stable. Kiev ostensibly abandoned the nuclear weapons remaining on its territory after Soviet break-up in 1994, under joint US-Russian pressures, combined with the promise of US, French, British, Russian and Chinese security *assurances*. This was to the dismay of Ukrainian "Gaullists," who believed Kiev should hold onto a nuclear capability so that it could sustain international prestige and be in a position to threaten Moscow—if not draw US attention to its cause. States, such as Iran or North Korea, appear even more instable than Ukraine—and thus may not capable of maintaining such weaponry in secure hands. They also cannot entirely be relied upon *not* to try to sell such weaponry to third parties.

While neo-realists may likewise consider both Iran and North Korea too unstable to possess a nuclear weapons capability, and not reliable enough to handle such a responsibility, they do tend to argue that the possession of nuclear weapons has thus far served the interests of both India and Pakistan. In this respect, the US had moved toward a rapprochement with nuclear India under the Clinton administration, while nuclear Pakistan represents one of the key allies in the "war on terrorism"—despite the fact that the US tried for years to prevent it from obtaining a nuclear capability.

Contrary to the neo-realist view, however, nuclear war could be initiated if either India or Pakistan tries to engage in a first strike against the other side. Perhaps more pertinently, the fact that both India and Pakistan have been developing tactical nuclear weapons indicates that both leaderships may be considering lowering the threshold for the use of such weaponry in "limited" battlefield situations. Unconfirmed reports also suggest that the US is secretly spending millions since the September 2001 attacks—in an attempt to safeguard and secure Pakistani nuclear installations (including the secret authorization codes for the weapons) against terrorist attack or else in the case of take over of the regime and its nuclear forces by pan-Islamic militants.[53]

## Middle East Nuclear Free Nuclear Zone

In July 2004, IAEA chief Mohamed El Baradei pressed Israeli officials to enter into talks on regional disarmament. Concurrently, the EU troika warned the Bush administration that the US would not win Iranian cooperation with the IAEA—unless Israel's nuclear program becomes part of the international effort. Egypt,

Syria and other Arab and Moslem states all pressed the IAEA to act. Egypt has likewise appealed to the US to press Israel to sign the Nuclear Non-Proliferation Treaty, which would allow the IAEA to inspect suspected nuclear facilities, including the Dimona plutonium reactor (which is protected by US made anti-aircraft defenses). At the same time, Sunni Moslem states generally do not want Shi'ite Iran to acquire nuclear weapons either—as it could use these weapons as strategic leverage to press its interests throughout the region. Moreover, should the US *not* sustain a military protectorate over Iraq, the new Baghdad (much like Hussein) might also want to acquire nuclear weapons—to counter those of Iran.

In this perspective, the US and EU need to bring back the Middle East regional arms control/ arms reduction discussions that have remained moribund since the 1990s—and as soon as possible. These discussions may now possess a much greater chance of success with the inclusion of both Iraq and Iran, the two countries that had been excluded from earlier talks—particularly now that the US has forcibly removed Saddam Hussein from power. Such an international conference could, at a minimum, aim at obtaining a no-first use pledge of WMD by all participants.

While the building of regional confidence measures should be a first priority, it is dubious that Israel will give up its presumed nuclear weapons capability altogether (thus making a nuclear free zone impossible). At the same time, however, much as China did not sign the NPT until 1992, Israel could put its nuclear program under international safeguards, if granted international security *guarantees*, as argued below.

## Regional Security Communities

During the Cold War, the US and Soviet Union often provided tacit or overt bilateral security accords to those states that might be considering the nuclear option, so as to dissuade their leaderships from acquiring nuclear weapons. In the post-Cold war period, the option of multilateral accords became a reality in respect to the former Soviet bloc state, Ukraine. Another example of a state giving up its nuclear program is Libya.

The US, Russia, China, France and the UK offered Ukraine multilateral security *assurances* to convince it to dismantle its nuclear weapons capability left over when the former Soviet empire collapsed. In 1994, after three years of bargaining and threats, and joint US-Russian pressures, Ukraine finally agreed to give up its nuclear capability and returned its nuclear warheads to Moscow. Belarus and Kazakhstan had previously returned their nuclear weapons to Russian and signed the NPT in 1993 (the date when North Korea first dropped out of the NPT.) Libya represents an example of a state that has unilaterally given up its claims to a nuclear capability. In 2004, after years of secret on-going discussions starting in 1999 (and that pre-dated US "preemptive" intervention in Iraq), Libya opted to give up its nuclear program, in exchange for an end to sanctions and US recognition of the oil-rich regime, whose leader the US once referred to as a "mad dog."[54] The US-Libyan deal related primarily to the explosion by Libyan terrorists of a passenger jet over Lockerbie, Scotland, as well as the US and EU desire to diversify petroleum supplies. In both these cases, diplomacy was able to achieve a positive result; it was not at all necessary for the US to engage in "regime change" by force. Moreover, neither regime could be considered "democratic."

The examples of both Ukraine and Libya offer the possibility that other states could agree to giving up their "rights" to possess nuclear weaponry in accord with an appropriate *irenic* strategy. Bilateral and/or multilateral security *assurances/guarantees* could be granted to those states willing to give up the nuclear option, or else willing to put their nuclear capabilities under international safeguards. Yet, in order to implement a policy of regional security communities, US policy would need to move toward a strategy of engaged *multilateral dissuasion*, leading toward normalization and reconciliation to those states that accepted the conditions.[55]

The United States may accordingly be confronted with the necessity to engage in a step-by-step process to *normalize* relations and then ultimately *recognize* both North Korea and Iran so as to end their isolation, as well as their nuclear programs. The question, of course, is on *what specific terms.* In order to achieve full Iranian and North Korean compliance, for example, the US may need to reciprocate by taking confidence-building measures and to deal objectively with their *legitimate* security concerns. At the same time, Washington would need to engage in *real dialogue*—as was the case with Libya—concerning Iranian and North Korean violation of human rights and support for terrorist activities.

The possibility of designing multilateral security *assurances*, possibly leading to security *guarantees*, creates a dilemma and dispute among US policymakers. The fundamental issue remains that multilateral security accords may *appear* to legitimize the regime. Concurrently, security guarantees do not necessarily preclude the possibility of evolutionary reforms—or even radical political change coming *from within*. At the same time, US or international promises not to attack or intervene in the country does not preclude such regimes from claiming that outside forces and exile groups (supported by foreign powers) are still attempting to undermine their leadership—and hence engaging in "regime change."

Multilateral regional security *assurances* (perhaps leading to security *guarantees*) have been promised North Korea, but the latter has also demanded a *bilateral* US-North Korean accord that guarantees that Washington will not attempt to engage in "regime change," the primary fear of Kim Jong-Il. The concept is for North Korea to not only obtain Chinese, Russian, and Japanese security guarantees, but also those of the United States—while concurrently reducing tensions between the two Koreas. The US has considered this option, but it has been reluctant to pursue it; it has also been reluctant to provide economic (and energy) assistance that keeps the regime (and its population) alive. This means Japan and South Korea would have to engage in the majority of financial aid, while Beijing provides food assistance.

The political approach is different with Iran. By contrast with Libya, Iran appears to need a face saving way out so that it is not regarded as merely bending to US pressures. Iran could likewise accept guarantees that the US would not try to engage in regime change by force *from without*. Here, however, the US cannot guarantee that internal domestic movements aligned with Iranian exiles would not seek to overturn or modify the Islamic regime. But the US can attempt to work toward a path of *regime recognition*, but without necessarily opposing far-reaching *regime reform* (as opposed to *regime change* by force). American *assurances* could be combined with multilateral supports and incentives from the troika of the UK, France and Germany. At the same time, the Iranian case will require a larger regional approach, which would likewise need to discuss WMD and delivery capabilities. A regional approach is, of course problematic: In the past it has been nearly impossible to bring Iran, Iraq and Israel to the conference table.

The implementation of confidence building measures would, in turn, seek to put Israel's un-proclaimed nuclear facilities under international safeguards and inspections. Next, the application of NATO-EU-Russian security guarantees to an Israeli-Palestinian "confederation" (under a general UN mandate and based upon agreements somewhat similar to the Geneva Accords) would seek to protect Israel (and Palestine) from potential nuclear and WMD threats emanating from the Middle East and Persian Gulf regions. The deployment of international peacekeepers made up of NATO, EU and Russian peacekeepers, along with Partnership for Peace countries acceptable to both Israelis and Palestinians under a UN mandate can play a triple role. It can help put an end to acts of terrorism and counter-terrorism; it can protect both Israel (and Palestine) against potential threats of WMD from neighboring states (including Iran). A multilateral NATO, EU, Russian security umbrella could be extended to cover the new Israeli-Palestinian bi-state "confederation"—and possibly to Iraq as well.

By thus integrating Israel more closely into a multilateral NATO-EU-Russian defense perimeter, such an approach would also seek to *restrain* the possibility of *unilateral* Israeli military intervention against Iran, or against other states in the region. Such a strategy of *multilateral dissuasion* would also seek to dissuade Iran from seeking a nuclear capability through the combined use of positive rewards and the threat of sanctions and pressures. It thus appears to be in the Iranian interest to accept full disclosure of its nuclear capabilities—in accord with IAEA specifications and the "Additional Protocol" of the NPT—to continue to build its credibility with countries in the region as well as the international community.

Here, through a tacit linkage to US-Iranian-IAEA discussions, the US, EU and Russia need to maintain pressure on Israel to engage in the Road Map for Peace and Geneva Accords, while simultaneously questioning Iran's refusal to recognize the state of Israel—assuming the latter will return to something approximating its 1967 borders. For its part, Iran should thus work to support the Saudi/Arab peace initiative to recognize Israel, retract its support for *Hizb'allah*, in accord with the goals of the Road Map for Peace, or in support of other international initiatives (involving an exchange of "land for peace"). As Teheran has been seeking to renew diplomatic relations with Egypt, relations that Iran cut off in the wake of the Camp David accords, bringing Iran to recognize the state of Israel (particularly if an Israeli-Palestinian peace agreement can be reached) appears plausible.

A regional peace settlement appears more plausible after the overthrow of Saddam Hussein, followed by the death of Yassir Arafat. Yet neither Israel nor Iran has thus far taken sufficient reciprocal steps to support regional peace efforts.

As part of the process of engaging states throughout the Middle East and Persian Gulf, positive incentives should be given to encourage gradual reforms, greater openness and "good governance" in the Arab/Islamic worlds (reforms instigated from *within* these societies and *not* forced upon them). Such a process would also mean taking steps to nudge India and Pakistan toward reconciliation over Kashmir and other disputes. The latter, in turn, should help ameliorate Iranian socio-political tensions with Pakistan. Accompanied by efforts to cool tensions in Asia over North Korea, such a radical strategy would ultimately involve the normalization, and then recognition, of both North Korea and Iran, and would be as significant as the Nixon-Kissinger opening to the People's Republic of China.

**Final Remarks**

Contrary to the tenets of neo-realist theory, it is not clear how nuclear weapons might dampen hyper-nationalism. It is extremely dubious that the possession of nuclear weaponry by Hitler would have dampened his quest to build the Third Reich, or would have stopped the Holocaust. It is unclear how the possession of WMD will necessarily dampen the policies of *any* leadership (including the American) that has determined that there are no other alternatives to the use of such weaponry! The possession of nuclear weapons, furthermore, permits states to pursue their regional interests behind a nuclear shield. Nuclear weapons also change the calculations for war, in that they can change the relative force capabilities of states in conflict, but do not necessarily prevent war altogether.

States regarded as attempting to develop nuclear weapons may be subject to pre-emption. US intervention in Iraq was based more on a hypothetical *future* Iraqi threat—and not the actual possession of nuclear weaponry. The US has threatened the possibility of "pre-empting" the North Korean and/or Iranian nuclear programs. The US, however, may not be willing to take the risk of a North Korean conventional force retaliation, or want to deal with geopolitical and economic instability caused by attacks against Iran.

Even if the possession of nuclear weaponry may possibly serve as an ultimate warning against a full-scale attack, and may possibly prevent a state from further escalating a conflict (unless one side thinks that it can launch pre-emptive strike), nuclear weapons may act *only as a partial deterrent* against conventional and unconventional forms of warfare. US nuclear weaponry did not prevent the Vietnam War, for example; nor did it not prevent the attacks of 11 September 2001. The possession of nuclear weapons by India and Pakistan has not prevented conventional clashes or wars of mutual subversion. Israel's undeclared "existential" deterrent has not stopped years of "asymmetrical" forms of warfare. In essence, rather than serving as an absolute guarantee against war, nuclear weaponry primarily represents a *symbol of prestige* and a *political power* factor intended to obtain recognition and support for a particular regime, and as a form of strategic leverage that would permit that regime to press its geopolitical and economic interests, even though such weaponry does not necessarily prevent revolutions and "regime change" from within.

In addition to problematic issues concerning radioactive waste management and transport, atomic infrastructure presents more general security concerns. One security drawback to the construction of atomic facilities is that they represent key targets for military operations or for terrorist attacks—to destroy a highly centralized source of energy that could put a country's economy out of business. Another goal would be to pre-empt a state's nuclear technological capacity, as was the case for the Israeli attack on the Iraqi nuclear reactor in 1981. Another problematic issue is that terrorists could seek to acquire radioactive materials for "dirty bombs" which spread nuclear waste products with conventional explosions—if they do not attempt attack a nuclear plant directly.

It is important to underscore the fact that the key difference between nuclear and conventional weaponry is not only the tremendous destructive potential, but that compared to most weaponry, nuclear weaponry is *genetically genocidal*. Moreover, trends toward the miniaturization of such weaponry lower the nuclear threshold—and make such weapons even more useable. Even the "peaceful" atom is problematic: Military or terrorist strikes upon nuclear power plants may produce irreversible genetic mutation in those who are exposed to high levels of radiation and as the radiation infiltrates the environment and enters the food chain—as revealed by the near total melt down of the Chernobyl plant in 1986.

Furthermore, the quest to modernize weapons systems is exacerbating arms rivalries. US efforts to acquire Ballistic Missile Defenses (BMD), for example, can be countered by cruise missiles flying in flattened trajectories. BMD systems put pressure on lesser nuclear powers to create as many delivery systems as possible and/or to seek clandestine methods for attacking behind BMD either within the opponent's territory or against its overseas interests by means of "asymmetrical" strikes. In February 2004, Russia claimed to have developed warheads and a new hypersonic vehicle (to be deployed by 2010) that can change trajectories to evade BMD systems. If so, this would mean the system of Mutual Assured Destruction (MAD) is still in effect for the US and Russia, while it is not clear that BMD systems will necessarily work to deter states that possess even more limited delivery capabilities—after the failure of US anti-missile tests in January 2005.[56] In effect, the Bush administration has placed US national security—as well as relations with Russia and other states on the line—by having unilaterally withdrawn from the ABM treaty (without negotiating a replacement)—and by gambling on an expensive and unproven technology.

Much as the NATO Parliamentary Assembly (which, unfortunately, does not have the same weight as the North Atlantic Council) has argued, North Korea should be urged to refrain from developing nuclear weapons, and to stop the marketing of ballistic missile technology. Iran needs to be persuaded to provide further information and explanations about its nuclear program and suspend all enrichment-related activities in order to promote confidence. States that remain outside the NPT and that possess declared or undeclared nuclear weapons, such as

India, Israel and Pakistan, should be convinced to sign the IAEA "Additional Protocol," the Comprehensive Nuclear-Test-Ban Treaty, and to gradually eliminate production of fissile material.

Beijing should refrain from developing new nuclear weapons, while Washington should be aware of the concern that US nuclear programs, such the Robust Nuclear Earth Penetrator (RNEP) or "bunker buster," which is specifically designed to eliminate underground hard targets, could affect international nuclear non-proliferation efforts—as it appears to contradict disarmament obligations under Article VI of the Nuclear Non-proliferation Treaty. And finally, NATO should seriously examine the issue of sub-strategic nuclear weapons in the context of the NATO-Russia Council and eventually submit a proposal on a phased and verifiable withdrawal of tactical nuclear weapons from Europe.[57]

All this points to the necessity to move as swiftly as possible toward a new "irenic" and "alternative realist" strategy that seeks the formation of "multilateral security communities"—as one means to put an end to the threat of nuclear proliferation. (See Chapter 8.)

# Chapter 5

# Manipulating US Global Power: Pakistan, "War on Terrorism" and Strategic Leveraging

Discussions of North South relations, particularly when examined in the "core-periphery" relationship, tend to focus on the "exploitation" of minor powers by the major powers or on the ability of the major powers to dictate the domestic or international policies of lesser states. Although there is truth to the argument that the major powers generally (but not always) get their way eventually, the characterization becomes stereotypical. It is possible for states, from positions of *relative* political military and economic "inferiority," to utilize their strategic position, as well as the nature of their entente and alliance relationships, to manipulate the policies of major powers.

As major powers seek to play games of "balance of power" *from above* by playing the interests of some states against others, lesser powers do their best to play similar games *from below* in order to extract as many concessions as possible. Such concessions can often be more substantial than generally anticipated. Although not succeeding in obtaining all of its demands, Islamabad has been able to manipulate Washington from a position of relative "weakness"—and in such a way as to "win" a significant number of its key goals.

In this regard, the Soviet invasion of Afghanistan initially provided Pakistan with an opportunity to press its own interests, which included the acquisition of nuclear weaponry—despite US opposition. By contrast, Soviet withdrawal from Afghanistan (combined with Pakistan's support for the Taliban) actually weakened Pakistan's ability to obtain US supports—and resulted in Pakistani isolation. The attacks on the World Trade Center and Pentagon on 11 September 2001 then, ironically, put Pakistan back in the limelight. This is true despite Islamabad's acquisition of nuclear weaponry, and despite US suspicions of Pakistan's secret support for Pakistani scientists (Abdul Qadeer Khan) in providing nuclear assistance to North Korea, Libya, as well as Iran—as well as US suspicion of continued Pakistani support for *al-Qaida*, among other "terrorist" organization.[1]

It must be stated that it was the US (and not Pakistani actions) which coaxed Moscow to intervene in Afghanistan, and which set the stage for US support for the Afghan resistance. In 1998, former Carter Administration National Security Advisor Zbigniew Brzezinski clearly stated that the United States "did not push the Soviets to intervene, but purposely augmented the chances that they would." When asked if he regretted the decision to assist Islamic fundamentalism with arms and

111

military supports, Brzezinski responded, "Which was more important in terms of the history of the world: The Taliban or the collapse of the Soviet empire?"[2] He furthermore stated that the Islamic world was too internally divided to pose any significant threat to the US.

Here, of course, the fact that bin Laden would launch his operations against the US on 11 September 2001 could not be foreseen. What, however, was known at the time was that there were a number of radical Islamic parties that were hostile to the US as well as the Soviet Union. Despite deep divisions within the Islamic world, these organizations could still engage in significant acts of terrorism against US and European (as well as Russian) interests. Perhaps more crucially, Brzezinski's statement indicates a failure to analyze the potential implications of Soviet collapse and disaggregation. A politically and economically instable Russia, could, on the one hand, pose a greater "threat" than the Soviet Union itself, and on the other, create a "shatterbelt" of potentially conflicting states in central Asia— what Brzezinski himself called the "arc of crisis." The Cold War quest to implode the Soviet Union from within fortunately succeeded without resulting in nuclear war, but the effort to impel the Soviet collapse left a tottering nuclear capable Russia in its wake, and led to the formation of an even greater "arc of crisis" than that which concerned Brzezinski in 1979.

This chapter will explore Pakistani efforts to manipulate US policy both before and after the 11 September 2001 attacks on the World Trade Center and Pentagon to better explain contemporary Pakistani foreign policy in its geo-historical context—in an area of the world in which nuclear weapons, oil, drugs and "terrorism" make a very explosive concoction.

## Soviet Invasion of Afghanistan

In many ways, US policy in support of the anti-Soviet resistance in Afghanistan represented revenge for Soviet support for Ho Chi Minh and the North Vietnamese; yet its implications have been even more far reaching. As an additional element of its Cold War strategy of containment, the US effort to undermine the soft Islamic underbelly of the Soviet Union was, in many ways, the key to not just rolling back Soviet global outreach, but also to impel the implosion of the Soviet empire itself. (On neo-conservative efforts to "implode" the Soviet Union, see Chapter 2.)

As Zbigniew Brzezinski stated in 1998, the US opted for clandestine activities in Afghanistan against the pro-Soviet regime in July 1979, six months before the Soviet invasion.[3] Then, after having taunted Moscow to intervene, Brzezinski then urged President Carter to grant stronger security guarantees to Islamabad; he also proposed overlooking the question of nuclear non-proliferation. In a memo dated 26 December 1979, Brzezinski told the President Carter that the US had no choice but to repair its relations with Pakistan: "It is essential that Afghanistan's resistance continues. This means more money as well as arms shipments to the rebels, and some technical advice. To make the above possible we must both pressure Pakistan and encourage it to help the rebels. This will require a review of our policy toward Pakistan, more guarantees to it, more arms aid, and, alas, a decision that our security policy cannot be dictated by our nonproliferation policy. We should encourage the Chinese to help the rebels also. We should concert with Islamic countries both in a propaganda campaign and in a covert action campaign to help the rebels."[4] A week after the above memo, Brzezinski wrote that "Our ultimate goal is the withdrawal of Soviet troops from Afghanistan... Even if this is not attainable, we should make Soviet involvement as costly as possible."[5]

Here, Moscow had most likely overthrown the Daoud regime in 1978 setting in power a more radical regime under Prime Minister Noor Mohammed Taraki, who nevertheless had support of the Pathan tribes. It was in September 1979 that Taraki was assassinated and replaced by President Hafizullah Amin, who was regarded as independent of Moscow—and *rumored* to be on the CIA payroll.[6] This provided a pretext for the Soviets to intervene—and as the failure to protect Taraki represented a loss of face and credibility for Soviet leader Leonid Brezhnev.

At the time, Prime Minister Aleksei Kosygin and Central Committee Secretary Andrei Kirilenko consistently opposed military intervention. Foreign Minister Andrei Gromyko belatedly recognized that Soviet intervention would lead to a self-fulfilled prophecy: The "encirclement" of the Soviet Union by the "capitalists" (NATO and Japan) which were then linked to the People's Republic of China (who were dubbed "capitalist roaders")—and also aligned with religious reactionaries (Saudi Arabia and Pakistan primarily). KGB Chief Yuri Andropov, however, pressed Brezhnev for intervention. From this standpoint, fears of stronger US, Chinese and Saudi and Pakistani influence, and the latter's support for pan-Islamic forces throughout Afghanistan and Soviet-controlled central Asia, led Moscow to reluctantly intervene.[7]

The Soviet intervention likewise coincided with increasing tensions between Saudi Arabia and Iraq versus Iran. The Iran-Iraq conflict led to Sunni-Shi'ite rivalries throughout the Islamic world, with Saudi Arabia seeking to encircle Iran through support of Iraq and Pakistan. Both Iran and the Saudi Arabia assisted the anti-Soviet "freedom fighters"—but more in rivalry than in mutual collaboration. In effect, the Iranian Islamic revolution led both Saudi Arabia and Pakistan to further "Islamicize" their respective regimes—to contain the symbolic and ideological threat posed by Iranian Shi'ite Islamic militancy.

As the Soviets fully engaged, President Reagan stepped up support for the Afghan resistance; the CIA significantly augmented military supplies to the Afghan *mujahedin* or "freedom fighters" by 1984. As the *jihad* against the Soviet invader intensified, Moscow looked for a diplomatic "face saving" way to withdraw. The US strategy transformed from merely increasing the costs of the defense burden to Moscow to that of "roll back" and "victory."

In essence, the United States itself was willing to back "radical" Sunni Moslem, as well as Saudi-backed *Wahhabist*, movements against pan-Shi'ite Iran, which was regarded as the "greater" of the two "evils." By 1982–83, the US, along with Saudi Arabia, fully supported Saddam Hussein's war with the Ayatollah Khomeini, which was instigated in reaction to Iranian support for Shi'a and Kurdish factions in Iraq. While Washington looked the other way, Saddam Hussein engaged in horrid war crimes in fighting Iran and against Kurdish and Shi'a factions, and other groups regarded as aligned with Iran, in the "war of cities" (a war resulting in the loss of over a million people).

The US also looked the other way as Saudi Arabia, one of its major arms clients, engaged in significant violations of human rights, refused to engage in democratic reforms, and the backed militant faction Hamas against Israel, and supported other radical Sunni pan-Islamic groups. The Saudis also backed the Pakistani Inter-Services Intelligence (ISI) who supported some of the most extreme Islamic factions, such as Gulbuddin Hekmatyar, whose *Hezbi Islami* was the largest recipient of US military assistance, which was channeled *through* Pakistan during the war on Afghanistan. During the Afghan war, the CIA became concerned that General Zia had been diverting a large share of the weapons to Hekmatyar whose organization's strategy appeared to be aimed at dividing the rest of the Afghan resistance so that it could take over in Kabul—with Zia's support.[8] The US and Pakistan also backed the efforts of Ossama bin Laden who was primarily a financier of the Afghan resistance, *mekhtab al khidemat* [MAT]).

## Soviet Roll Back and "Freedom Fighters"

Prior to the Soviet thrust into Afghanistan, the Carter Administration had flip-flopped on providing aid to Pakistan, largely due to justified fears that Islamabad was developing a nuclear capability. The Soviet invasion, however, led the Carter Administration to open the flood gates to massive US, Saudi and Chinese (as well as Japanese, French and UK) military and economic assistance to Pakistan as the centrally located state that would coordinate the Afghan resistance, while Pakistani efforts to acquire nuclear weapons were disregarded (if not encouraged). Allegations that Moscow intended to engage in a military thrust to warm water ports in the Indian Ocean were hyped in order to gain domestic and international support for the US strategy.

Once Moscow fell face first into the trap set by Brzezinski, Pakistan could then take advantage of its strategic position as a frontline state against Soviet intervention; the Carter Administration drew the line by firmly contending that a Soviet thrust into either Pakistan or Iran (which were both highly unlikely contingencies) would represent a *casus belli*. While Pakistan used Soviet pressures to gain US support for its policies, Moscow likewise used pressure on Pakistan as strategic leverage to support Cuba and Nicaragua against US pressures and intervention in those states (in support of the "Contras" versus the Sandinistas in Nicaragua). Yet in so doing, it was Moscow at that time, and not Washington, that risked overextending its resources, capabilities, and political will.

By March 1985, the US opened its arms to support almost any partisan group or regime that opposed Moscow in the belief that the "enemy of one's enemy was one's friend." Congressional debate over the sale of the shoulder-held Stinger ground to air launched missiles, for example, was symbolic of fears that US military support for radical pan-Islamic factions might ultimately turn against American interests. Between 900 and 1200 Stingers were sold to the Afghan resistance in 1986–87 despite CIA opposition, and in the fear that the Soviets would retaliate against the Afghan resistance based in Pakistan. Some of these weapons, or other systems, may have subsequently been used against civilian aircraft.[9] It has been estimated that a significant portion of the $6 billion in covert U.S. arms and training that went to Afghan rebel groups in the 1980s was funneled to pan-Islamic militant partisans that, in turn, utilized these resources to attack U.S. allies and U.S. citizens.[10]

As the *jihad* intensified, *mujahedin* and CIA targets included military installations, factories and storage depots *within* Soviet territory. This fact gives an indication of what kind of training these "freedom fighters" obtained. At the same time, there were some largely futile efforts to negotiate between the US and the Soviet Union over the war in Afghanistan. By November 1986, unable to convince Washington that a Soviet defeat by pan-Islamic forces would also represent a defeat for US interests in the region, Soviet leader Mikhail Gorbachev opted for withdrawal. Soviet steps to withdraw from Afghanistan were not taken without first extending new overtures to both Iran and to China. In respect to Beijing, Moscow addressed the "three obstacles" to peace (the withdrawal of Vietnamese troops from Cambodia, reduction of troops and weaponry along the Sino-Soviet border, plus removal of Soviet troops from Afghanistan). These Cold War Sino-Soviet accords set the stage for the Sino-Russian accords of the 1996 Shanghai Agreement, and to closer Sino-Russian defense accords in December 2004.

As previously mentioned, Pakistan was able to use military and financial supports from the US, Saudi Arabia and China to press its interests in the region, in the effort to gain a position of "strategic depth" between Pakistan, Afghanistan and Kashmir, as well as build a nuclear weapons capability. At the same time, factions of the *mujahedin* threatened to turn Afghanistan and Pakistan into "another Lebanon" if Washington or Islamabad did attempt to reach diplomatic settlement with Moscow and the Soviet-backed Kabul government of President Najibullah. These threats of terrorist action were consequently used as "strategic leveraging" in order to block irenic diplomacy intended to end the conflict. Yet once Moscow finally did withdraw (but only after reaching a rapprochement with China), the United States suddenly dumped the movement that it had helped to generate and sponsor—and became totally indifferent, losing interest in the region.[11]

Ossama bin Laden's *al-Qaida* (which emerged from the *mekhtab al khidemat* [MAT]) was founded around 1988–89 with headquarters in Afghanistan and Peshawar, Pakistan—in part to provide welfare for roughly 10,000 "Arab-Afghan freedom fighters." The latter (who were not always either Arab or Afghan) fought the Soviet Union in Afghanistan and then continued the struggle against the Russian-backed Afghan government. Following the Iraqi invasion of Kuwait, the US engaged in Operation Desert Shield (intended to protect Saudi Arabia from possible attack) and Operation Desert Storm, intended to force Saddam Hussein out of Kuwait. U.S.-UN military actions and economic sanctions against Iraq further alienated pan-Islamic factions (the Egyptian *al-Jihad* seen as responsible for the 1993 attempt to blow up the World Trade Center). The latter groups opposed U.S. military support for Egypt, Saudi Arabia as well as other "corrupt" pro-Western regimes that were not regarded as following "true" Islamic practices.

Ossama bin Laden's *al-Qaida* can thus be said to have arisen, in part, from the fact that the US was seen as suddenly abandoning the pan-Islamic cause—in addition to the fact that Washington sustained a troop presence in Saudi Arabia after the 1990–91 Persian Gulf war, contrary to Washington's promises. Continued US political and military support for Israel likewise represented a *casus belli*. It was thus in the 1990s that bin Laden began to transform his status of "freedom fighter" in the Afghan war against the Soviet Union (yet "terrorist" for the Russians)—to that of "terrorist" (for both the Americans and Russians).

## US Policy "Flip Flops" and Pakistan Post-Soviet Afghanistan

In 1992–93, the US came close (under Indian political pressures) to declaring Pakistan a state sponsor of terrorism, as Pakistan had hosted militants who had carried out a number of attacks on the Indian states of Punjab and Kashmir. Large numbers of kidnapping and bombings in Sindh necessitated the imposition of martial law there in 1992. Islamabad counter-claimed that these groups, most notably the *Jaye Sindh*, which the Pakistani government perceived as threatening to Pakistan's unity, were receiving help from India in their quest to establish a "Sindhudesh," an independent homeland for Sindhis. In July 1992, the US Congress imposed "Pressler amendment" sanctions on Pakistan, in order to prevent the latter from acquiring nuclear capable US F-16s.[12] (India was likewise banned from receiving F-16 fighter jets.) Then in January 1993, the US warned Pakistan that it was under "active continuing review" for possible inclusion on the Department of State list of terrorist countries; yet by July 1993, however, the US had withdrawn its threat, having determined that Pakistan had implemented "a policy for ending official support for terrorism in India." To reduce US political-economic pressures, Pakistan opted to move Kashmiri *jihadi* bases to eastern Afghanistan to continue in their struggle with India from there and to make Islamic parties responsible for the support of Kashmiri militants.

By 1994, pan-Islamic ideologues, the Taliban (the "students") seized power in Kabul. The Taliban had been created with the logistical assistance of Pakistan's Inter-Services Intelligence (ISI), working alongside the CIA, coupled with Saudi financing, as well as the profits from opium production. Between 1983 and 1997, it has been estimated that the ISI trained roughly 83,000 *mujahedin*, and used some of these to fight a proxy war against India in Kashmir province and to maintain control over Afghanistan. The ISI thus became a "state within a state," and increasingly Islamicist in world outlook.

In 1996 Osama bin Laden joined the Taliban after shifting his operations from the Sudan under US pressure and after having lost his Saudi citizenship in 1994. In Afghanistan, bin Laden sponsored bases for Kashmiri militants in Khost.[13] Afghan refugees in Pakistan studied pan-Islamic thinking in the Pakistani *madrassas*, and returned to join the Taliban. Pakistan accordingly supported the Taliban as a means to counter Indian, as well as Turkish and Iranian, influence in the region, and to ostensibly to provide itself with "strategic depth" in its nuclear and conventional military rivalry with India.

Here, however, the Taliban, combined with the Afghan Transit Trade (ATT), has indirectly worked to undermine Pakistani sovereignty. First, the rise of the Taliban worked to undermine the Pakistani economy through sale of un-taxed and/or illicit products. It has also afflicted Pakistani society with a male-centered social movement strongly opposed to woman's rights and education, and which has reinforced the "Kalishnikov culture" that had developed during the years of anti-Soviet warfare in Afghanistan. These influences have raised fears of the "Talibanization" of Pakistan, and has, at a minimum, made it difficult, if not impossible to control northern provinces: The Taliban had obtained significant support from Pakistan's Pathan population. The Pathans account for 50–60 percent of Afghanistan's estimated population of 20 million people.[14]

Prior to the October 2001 US intervention in Afghanistan, the US attempted to pressure Pakistan to bring the Taliban (and indirectly *al-Qaida*) in line, as only Pakistan, the United Arab Emirates, and Saudi Arabia had then recognized the regime. Washington had refused to officially recognize the Taliban when it came to power in 1994, but did not immediately put it on a list of states that supported terrorism. (It was not until in 1999 that the US and United Nations imposed economic sanctions on the Taliban regime for harboring bin Laden, despite previous evidence of Taliban support for international terrorism). US Secretary of State Madeline Albright thus reluctantly supported the Taliban as means of bringing stability to the region. At the same time, however, tensions between the US, Taliban and Pakistan erupted over rivalry between the Unocal consortium and that of the Argentine firm Bridas for the development of a pipeline from Turkmenistan through Afghanistan to Pakistan. Pakistani Prime Minister Benazir Bhutto initially supported the Argentine firm, Bridas, in developing a pipeline through Afghanistan but by November 1996, after Bhutto sacked her cabinet, accusing it of corruption, the new Prime Minister, Nawaz Sharif, backed the US-Unocal oil pipeline plans.[15]

The CIA was granted the go ahead to destroy bin Laden's network in March 1996. Despite US (and Saudi) efforts to persuade the Taliban to extradite bin Laden, the Taliban leadership refused. It was in August 1996 that bin Laden issued a Declaration of Jihad: "Message from Osama bin Laden to his Muslim Brothers in the Whole World and Especially in the Arabian Peninsula: Declaration of Jihad Against the Americans Occupying the Land of the Two Holy Mosques; Expel the Heretics from the Arabian Peninsula." In 1998, *al-Qaida* attacked US embassies in Kenya and Somalia.[16] These latter actions then led the Clinton administration to engage in cruise missile strikes in the Sudan and in Afghanistan, with missiles launched over Pakistani territory.[17] On the one hand, this action tended to bring the Taliban and *al-Qaida* even closer together as partners in crime; on the other, a reluctant Islamabad increasingly came under pressure to assist Washington in the "war on terrorism."

**September 11 and the US-Russian Diplomatic Revolution**

Before the tragic attacks of 11 September 2001, the US had begun a rapprochement with "Shanghai Cooperation Organization," which included the "Shanghai Five" (formed in 1996 by Russia, China, Kazakhstan, Kyrgyzstan, Tajikistan, then joined by Uzbekistan in 2001) and began to deploy US military advisors and NATO peacekeepers in central Asia. While reaching out to Russia, the US concurrently tried to tighten relations with India and forge a rapprochement with Iran, in effect "encircling" Pakistan, at the same time that US relations with China largely deteriorated.

In effect, the 11 September attacks can be regarded as kind of pre-emptive strike (even if a similar attacks had been planned since 1996). While the US and NATO had initiated a rapprochement with Russia in central Asia, Northern Alliance Afghan leader General Massoud had tried to gain financial and military support from the US and EU for his anti-Taliban cause—prior to being assassinated just two days before the 11 September 2001 attacks (dying a few days later). Earlier in the year, in late May 2001, four followers of Osama bin Laden had been found guilty of charges stemming from the 1998 US embassy bombings in Kenya and Tanzania and were convicted of charges including murder, conspiracy and perjury—thus giving Ben Laden additional rationale to attack.

From December 2001 to May 2002, Washington then accelerated its rapprochement with Moscow in a new "diplomatic revolution" through the formation of the NATO-Russia Council—in which NATO and Russia would meet in a "19+1" formula. (See Chapter 6.) Yet a number of obstacles remained to bringing the US and Russia closer together. In addition to problems in respect to NATO enlargement into former Soviet spheres of interest and security, Russia continued to complain about US backing for two key US allies, Saudi Arabia and Pakistan—due to their alleged support for pan-Islamic movements in Uzbekistan, Chechnya and elsewhere. Here, Moscow regarded Saudi Arabia and a nuclear Pakistan even more problematic than Iran and Iraq.

In addition to alienating China and most of the region by supporting the Taliban before US intervention in October 2001, Pakistan's policies had also alienated Iran, in that the Sunni Taliban persecuted Afghan Shi'ites. The latter was largely as a consequence of general socio-political tensions between Shi'ia and Sunni' Moslems, and have involved Sunni assassination squads targeting Shi'ia Moslems. (Interestingly, Pakistan has subsequently attempted to amends with Iran and other Islamic states by trying to link the Palestinian question and Kashmir, as two forms of the same struggle.)

In the 1990s, the US had become India's major trading partner. Spending roughly four times more in defense than Pakistan, India argues that Islamabad tends to rely upon nuclear weapons and unconventional or "asymmetrical" methods of warfare, in order to "bleed" its rival, out of relative inferiority.[18] While US-Indian relations improved at that time, there were still significant differences between Washington and New Delhi over Kashmir, nuclear and missile issues, policy toward Iran, the progress of India's economic reforms, not to over look distinct differences over the war on terrorism. India has tended to see US inability to pressure Pakistan to control terrorism as a sign of American "weakness."[19]

Pakistani support for Taliban in the 1990s also tended to alienate China, as the Taliban supported Sunni Moslem Uighurs in Xinjiang province. This fact, in part, initially led China to form the "Shanghai Five" and move toward a rapprochement with India, in an effort ameliorate tensions. There is additionally the implicit threat that if China continues to support Pakistan in Kashmir, then India will support Tibetan independence. (Concurrently China sought a rapprochement with the Taliban in an effort to deflect its support away from Uighur secession movements.) In late 2002, China sought a rapprochement with NATO despite NATO's bombing of the Chinese embassy in Belgrade during the war "over" Kosovo in 1999. As the US and NATO began to extend their presence in central Asia, in a rapprochement with the "Shanghai Five," in the late 1990s, China believed it was better to forge a closer relationship with NATO—in an effort to prevent the US from negatively affecting Chinese interests in the region.

From this perspective, Pakistani policies in the 1990s, prior to attacks of 11 September 2001 resulted in Islamabad's near total isolation. Islamabad's plans to create "strategic depth" through an Afghan-Pakistan federation created hostility with Russia, China, Iran, as well as with the US. The latter had only reluctantly accepted the Taliban's victory as "stabilizing" in the period 1994–98. At the same time, however, China did not entirely give up its support for Pakistan: Chinese efforts in 2002 to forge a rapprochement with India had been paralleled by Chinese efforts to bolster Pakistan's long range missile and conventional capabilities.[20] In effect, China continues to play its "sweet and sour" policy—or to mix metaphors, to place its bets on both sides.

## "War on Terrorism"

Following the 11 September 2001 attacks, Pakistan found itself caught between supporting Taliban versus hunting down *al-Qaida* operatives. Ironically, Pakistan was able to utilize its own capabilities of "strategic leverage" in order to re-gain American, as well as Chinese, supports, and remove itself from largely self-inflicted isolation. The US rapprochement with Pakistan served Chinese interests as well and permitted Pakistan to attempt to play its own version of the "China card"—as an additional lever against the US.

Immediately after 11 September, Pakistani President (General) Pervez Musharraf looked for a strategic trade off with the US. In return for supporting the US in the global "war on terrorism," Musharraf insisted upon the following conditions: (1) that Pakistani armed forces should not engage in actions outside Pakistan's borders (in Afghanistan and Iraq); (2) that the US-led coalition should seek to minimize collateral damage to Afghan civilians; (3) that any post-Taliban government should be friendly to Pakistan with the Pashtun majority fairly represented; (4) that the Kashmiri struggle for self-determination should not be defined as "terrorism" or considered part of a wider crackdown on terrorism; (5) that there should be no move by the United States to disarm Pakistan's nuclear and missile defenses.[21]

General Musharraf, under pressure from the United States, then gave the order to crack down on Islamic radicals. Within weeks, two thousand militants were rounded up and jailed, including several prominent militant clerics and leaders, but many were soon released: "Most of the militants have been released without charge, among them the heads of groups listed as terrorist organizations by Britain and the US. Pakistan has allowed militants backed by its own intelligence agency to continue their war in Kashmir even though it threatens to plunge India and Pakistan into a devastating conflict."[22]

Musharraf has accordingly been trying to walk a delicate tightrope, hoping that the conflict will not get too far out of hand, and trying to keep the US content. Although Pakistani leadership has genuinely attempted to hunt down *al-Qaida* and remnants of the Taliban, it does not want to be the one to turn Osama bin Laden over to the United States. That action would antagonize much of the Islamic world and possibly destabilize the country itself. The US has accordingly recognized that Pakistan has not turned over all *al-Qaida* suspects—although the capture of key *al-Qaida* operatives, such as Khalid Shaikh Mohammed in March 2003, helped to mitigate US-Pakistani relations in the public relations game. Musharraf has also banned a number of militant Pakistani groups, but their leaders have not always been prosecuted under Pakistan's Anti-Terrorism Act.

At the same time, acts of terrorism (such as the attack on India's parliament in December 2001 blamed on Pakistan-based *Lashkar-e-Taiba*) continue unabated. The horrific case of journalist Daniel Pearl, who was tortured and beheaded in 2002, involved overt demands by his captors for the US to supply the F-16s that had been denied Islamabad by the 1992 Pressler amendment. Exactly who was actually responsible for his murder remains uncertain, but suspicions that Pakistani security forces were involved continue to linger.[23]

### Geostrategic Leveraging

Pakistan has tried to show itself as front line US ally in fight against terrorism. It secured 70,000 troops to cover its border with Afghanistan despite the fact that it faces one million troops on Indian border. Yet Islamabad has also attempted to use this situation to its advantage by manipulating its now official possession of nuclear weapons as strategic leverage to draw US and international attention and support to the country.

In late 2001/early 2002, New Delhi and Islamabad hurled insults at one another. To counter Indian threats, Pakistan, in response, threatened to move troops who were guarding the border between Pakistan and Afghanistan to the border with India. This prospect meant that Pakistan would not patrol the Afghan-Pakistan border against the escape of *al-Qaida* operatives. In such a way, Pakistan was able to place pressure on Washington to mitigate the prospects for war, and more concretely, to make New Delhi withdraw demands for Pakistan to extradite suspected terrorists to India.[24] Concurrently, Islamabad believed that it could "facilitate infiltrations into Kashmir as long as it is of use to the US in the military campaign against the Taliban and the remnants of al-Qaida."[25]

### War with Iraq

The 26 March–11 April 2003 war with Iraq provoked major protests in Pakistan, raising questions as to whether pan-Islamic forces could use the Iraq war, as well as its chaotic and poorly planned aftermath, as a means to catapult themselves into power. In the 10 October 2002 elections, an alliance of Islamic parties (who supported the Taliban and bin Laden), and made up of the Pakistan Muslim League (PML-Q) and the *Muttahida Majlis-e-Amal* (MMA), had taken 20% of seats, plus two out of four provinces (the Northwest Frontier Province and Baluchistan).[26]

The war (combined with thinly veiled US neo-conservative threats to strike Pakistan which has been regarded as fostering nuclear proliferation) raised popular fears that Iran, and then Pakistan, might be next on the list, despite the fact that Islamabad was not officially mentioned as member of the "axis of evil" of Iran, Iraq, and North Korea. Another fear was that even if the US itself would not strike Pakistan, India might. It was thus feared that the US would support New Delhi, while the latter used the Bush administration doctrine of "pre-emption" against Pakistan. After just a week into the Iraq war, India and Pakistan engaged in a "tit-for-tat" testing of short-range nuclear capable missiles in March 2003. Both countries were reported to be developing tactical nuclear warheads and seeking to develop Ballistic Missiles Defenses.

## Afghanistan

Continued political-economic instability in neighboring Afghanistan also raised tensions with Pakistan. In October 2001, close to 1.5 million Afghan civilians had fled toward the Pakistani and Iranian borders, threatening, at a minimum, a humanitarian crisis, if not a greater not-so-long term political-economic disaster. (Iran has already absorbed 1.5 million Afghan refugees; Pakistan, 2 million). It was estimated that roughly 80% of the Pakistani population opposed U.S. actions in Afghanistan. Thousands of Pakistanis traveled to the border in October 2001 to join the Afghan resistance.

From Islamabad's perspective, it was not clear that the post-Taliban government truly represented Pashtuni interests, despite Harmid Karzoi's efforts to bridge relations with Pakistan. Much of the problem has to do with infrastructure development and the fact that the promised international assistance has either not been delivered, or else cannot be distributed properly—in part due the necessity to deal with rival regional warlords.[27] *Al-Qaida* began to build its alliances with warlords and former Taliban (at least fifteen districts in southern Kandahar have been openly controlled by the Taliban) in order to overthrow the Kabul government dominated by the US-backed Northern Alliance. Moreover, as opium production can be ten times more profitable than other crops such as cotton (raising questions as to whether the international assistance that does arrive is simply sinking into a black hole), it is dubious that a crackdown on the drug can be successful, without alienating the peasantry and warlords. As security conditions remain poor in the countryside, development prospects look bleak. NATO forces have had difficulty in securing Kabul itself.

The US has consequently been pushing a reluctant NATO to move peacekeepers beyond Kabul. In 25 June 2003, it was announced that NATO would take over the lead of the International Stabilization Force (ISAF) from the German-Netherlands Corps in Kabul. (Germany and the Netherlands had initially shared lead nation responsibilities and the command a multinational force of approximately 4,600 troops drawn from twenty-nine nations, including France.) Yet this fact has raised the question as to whether NATO forces could ultimately alienate Afghan countryside, as Soviet-backed forces once did—as they begin to extend their patrols away from Kabul. NATO itself had been reluctant to crack down on opium production, seeing that as police work, and detracting from its mission against *al-Qaida* and the Taliban.[28]

European members of NATO have worried that the US might push the war from Afghanistan into north Pakistan, inflaming the region and overthrowing the government of President Pervez Musharraf. The latter is desperately attempting to balance himself between pan-Islamic forces, the Pakistani ISA, and Washington— at the same time that his government has hoped to obtain some concessions from New Delhi over Kashmir. Yet by 2005, NATO made the decision to press ISAF into the west of Afghanistan. The US/NATO thus appears to be in a "Catch 22" situation in which it can neither move forward nor back.

## Arms Sales and the Return of "Balance of Power" Politics

Following the war with Iraq, in June 2003, after his meeting with General Musharraf at Camp David, President Bush asked Congress to approve a five year $3 billion security and development aid package to Pakistan, half of which would go to defense matters. But such a deal was ostensibly conditional upon Pakistani behavior in respect to Pakistan's cooperation in the "war on terrorism," improved relations with India and "democratization." Pakistan would not get new F-16s, but old ones could possibly be upgraded.[29]

General Musharraf continued to deny allegations of Pakistan-North Korean nuclear and technology ties. Pakistan did not bend to all US pressures and stated, for example, that it would only send peacekeepers to Iraq under a UN mandate, even though such a position was against general popular opinion, which has opposed *any* involvement that may appear to legitimize the US/UK military intervention in Iraq. Moreover, the issue of Abdul Qadeer Kahn's secret nuclear network continued to surface.

In June 2004, President Bush designated Pakistan as a Major Non-NATO Ally (MNNA). The designation makes Pakistan eligible for expedited access to excess defense articles and other privileges. The designation appears related to Pakistan's decision to purchase several major weapons systems.[30] At a 21 December 2004 press interview, Secretary of State Colin Powell indicated that Washington had accepted President Musharraf's statement that he had no knowledge of Khan's activities. Kahn, under house arrest, has not been permitted to discuss his nuclear activities with the IAEA, nor apparently, with Washington.[31] (The Khan nuclear network reportedly assisted Iran, Libya, and North Korea, as well as Syria, Egypt and Saudi Arabia with nuclear technical assistance. Libyan nuclear weapons designs may have passed by Khan from Chinese blueprints.) By March 2005, the Bush administration stated that it would permit the sale of F-16s to Pakistan, but would also permit India to buy F-16s as well, and would sell other defense technology, such as advanced radar warning systems. Here, rather than implementing a neo-conservative strategy of "pre-emption," against Pakistani

WMD, the Bush administration appears to be returning to the traditional "realist" strategy of "balance of power and threat" by playing India and Pakistan against one another.

## US Pressures for the "Democratization" of the "Illiberal Democracy"

In December 2004–January 2005, *Jamiat Ulema-e-Pakistan* criticized President Pervez Musharraf for reportedly objecting to Islamic symbols (the beard and veil). The *Muttahida Majlis-e-Amal* (MMA), the "United Action Front" in English, also protested throughout the Sind against President Pervez Musharraf's decision in 2004 to hold dual offices of both President and Chief of Army Staff. The MMA also protested against US intervention in Pakistan, and military operations against tribesmen in Waziristan. (Musharraf's government depends on an alliance of six Islamist parties, the MMA to maintain a majority in the national parliament.) The same alliance controls the assemblies in two provinces bordering Afghanistan — Baluchistan and the North-West Frontier Province (NWFP).

Musharraf's decision to break his commitment to step down as Army commander in 2004, has put the support of the Islamist parties into question in that it represented a promise he made in 2003 to secure the support of the MMA in parliament. The bargain struck with the Islamic parties served both to maintain a governing majority in the national assembly and to secure passage of the 17th amendment to the Pakistani constitution, which legitimatized Musharraf's 1999 military coup, popularly supported as an "illiberal democracy" (see Chapter 3). Musharraf has justified keeping his uniform as necessary to maintain "stability."[32]

The Bush administration has expected that the end of sanctions upon the "illiberal democracy" would facilitate its transition to truly "democratic" rule. In order to advance the "democratization" process, and to lessen the chances of electoral support for Islamic parties, Washington has urged Pakistan to reform the *madrasas* Islamic schools (which the US itself helped to support during the Afghan war against the Soviet Union as training grounds for Islamic militants). As of early 2004, only three model *madrasas* had been set up with an enrollment of a mere 300 students; yet as many as 1.5 million students attend unregulated *madrasas*.[33] To reform, Pakistan will need significant funding to update textbooks and help modernize and provide food and clothing for children who go to some 40,000–50,000 schools in areas in north. Once again, the terrorist threat ironically gives Pakistan more leverage to bargain for aid and development assistance. Such assistance, however, may not necessarily go to those who really need it due to extensive corruption, poor administration and Pakistan's dysfunctional system of taxation and revenue collection.

The issue is that Washington often selectively expects countries to "democratize" as a means to criticize and pressure the behavior of those states that do not follow US policies. At the same time, pressures to install "democracy" in such an unstable setting as in Pakistan raises the possibility that militant pan-Islamic partisans could ultimately come to power. The Musharraf government fears that too severe a crackdown on *jihadi* groups will cause significant political instability in Pakistan and further alienate Islamabad in the Islamic world—in a situation in which even Riyadh is afraid to crack down too severely.

### Toward Indian-Pakistani Reconciliation

The primary realistic option to the present non-satisfactory *status quo* would thus be for the US to makes good on its March 2003 pledge to work toward Indian-Pakistani reconciliation—and attempt to nudge both sides toward demilitarization and denuclearization, if possible.

Washington had initially projected that following the Iraq war, it would push for a diplomatic solution to the Middle East crisis. It then affirmed that the Road Map to Peace would be followed by steps toward an Indian-Pakistani rapprochement, as announced by US Secretary of State Colin Powell in March 2003. India initially denounced US meddling in the conflict, but appeared to play along. By April 2003, Indian Prime Minister Atal Bihari Vajpayee announced that he would attempt "one last" initiative for peace with Pakistan. In May 2003, India and Pakistan agreed to restore diplomatic ties. (Hopefully, these steps will not result in a repeat of the 1999 efforts undermined by the dangerous Kargil conflict.)

India has pushed the US to pressure Pakistan to end its support for terrorist groups altogether. India believes that Washington is obsessed with *al-Qaida* to the exclusion of other "terrorist" actors who the Pakistani's regard as "liberators." In August 2003, India, for example, blamed the Students' Islamic Movement of India and *Lashkar-e-Taiba* (which has been banned by both India and Pakistan) for terrorist attacks in Bombay. Yet as New Delhi was reluctant to blame Islamabad, it appeared that the peace initiative would still move forward.[34] Here, India has pressed for a Kashmir settlement based on the Line of Control (with minor modifications), while Pakistan had, at least up until 2003, argued that no India-Pakistani normalization would take place without resolution of the Kashmiri crisis in accord with "the wishes of the Kashmiri people." This position has implied a referendum, which has thus far opposed by New Delhi.

In Washington, in December 2003, President Musharraf stressed the importance of resolving the Israeli and Palestinian conflict and other "disputed points" (Kashmir) as the key to combating terrorism in the Middle East; he also hoped for better bilateral US-Pakistani trade (Pakistani textiles are a point of contention). Musharraf had narrowly escaped two assassination attempts in the military headquarters city of Rawalpindi that month, after announcing that Pakistan no longer insisted upon a UN Resolution on the Kashmiri question and after having initiated a unilateral cease-fire in November. In a statement that appeared to come closer to Indian demands, Musharraf argued that Pakistan would no longer insist upon a plebiscite, which, he argued, could heighten communal tensions in Kashmir rather than ameliorate the situation.[35]

In addition to the Islamicist MMA, other major Pakistani political groups opposed his Kashmir policy, however. The Pakistan People's Party (PPP), for example, rejected the Musharraf formula as premature in that it diluted the UN

Security Council resolutions without a *quid pro quo* from New Delhi. The PPP proposed safe and open borders without prejudice to the Kashmir dispute and has preferred modeling Islamabad's relationship with New Delhi on the model of Indo-China relations, which largely ignored the border issues.

Whether some form of greater Kashmiri autonomy can be worked out remains to be seen. Nelson Mandela, for example, has been proposed as a possible "facilitator." If reconciliation is at all possible, India will need to make greater visible strides in strengthening its commitment to human rights in Kashmir, while Pakistan will need to restrain acts of "terrorism." Greater international assistance to both Afghanistan and Pakistan that truly meets basic needs, that provides infrastructure development, and that engages in thorough changes in the educational system, will need to be forthcoming. Only the path toward a diplomatic and political settlement between India and Pakistan, backed by concerted US, Russian (and Chinese) efforts, can prevent tensions in South Asia from spiraling totally out of control. The past cycles of India-Pakistani-Chinese regional conflict must not repeat themselves.[36]

**Future Scenarios**

The US has been attempting to counter-balance a number of often conflicting policy and strategic objectives. The first is to prevent conventional, if not nuclear, war while simultaneously engaging in the "war on terrorism." The second goal is to maintain South Asian stability and build a long-term relationship with India as a counter-balance against China, while checking Russian efforts to strengthen ties with both India and China.[37] This geo-strategic situation has given Pakistan some room to maneuver in the pursuit of its own regional interests, and has helped to release it from its previous isolation of the 1990s.

Yet the situation is not at all stable. US neo-conservatives have not been convinced by Pakistani distinctions between *jihadi* freedom fighters in Kashmir and groups that are thought to possess links with *al-Qaida*. In this respect, they have urged the Bush administration to apply greater US (and Indian) pressure on the Pakistani regime of General Musharraf—in large part due to his efforts to tightrope between US interests and those of Pakistani *jihadists*.

US efforts to pressure Pakistan to hunt down the Taliban and *al-Qaida*, and crack down on Kashmiri "terrorists," could lead in a downward spiral toward destabilization. Ironically, however, the very threat of more chaos, instability and acts of terrorism has been used by Pakistan's leadership to bolster its ties with Washington: Here, General Musharraf has tried to convince Washington that he is the only alternative to radical Islamization or else chaos, *après moi, c'est le déluge.* In the assumption that a more capable leadership cannot ultimately come to power, and engage in serious political-economic reforms, Washington has been afraid of calling his bluff and is thus impelled to support his "illiberal democracy."

It has been argued that the US war with Afghanistan has actually strengthened the central Pakistani government at the expense of the ethnic separatists, and thus the break up of Pakistan is unlikely.[38] Although previously hesitant, NATO took the decision in 2005 to expand the International Security Assistance Force (ISAF) further west into Afghanistan. Yet there is still a risk that US/NATO actions may exacerbate Pathan irredentist demands for the creation of Pushtunistan. The formation of Pushtunistan would link the Pathan provinces (which backed the Taliban) in north Pakistan with those in southern Afghanistan by abolishing the hated Durand Line, the frontier drawn up by the British empire in 1893. This scenario could come into actuality if, over time, Afghanistan is partitioned with the essentially Tajik Northern Alliance controlling the north and a Pathan post-Taliban regime in control of the south.

Most tribal areas in Pakistan, except for South Waziristan, are not controlled by the Pakistani government, which permits *al-Qaida* and the Taliban to operate with relative ease in both Afghanistan and Pakistan. Furthermore, the Taliban has openly controlled at least fifteen districts in southern Kandahar. Concurrently, the ex- "freedom fighter"—now "terrorist"—forces, such as Gulbuddin Hekmatyar's *Hezbi Islami*, continue to oppose the US- and Russian- backed regime of Hamid Karzoi. Moreover, with its reconnaissance and security focus placed on Iraq, the Pentagon does not possess all the resources necessary to track these groups from outer space—or deal with them on land.[39]

Another, perhaps the more dangerous scenario, would be a pro-Islamic coup, or some form of demagogic radical movement, arising in Pakistan itself, permitting pan-Islamic forces or radical demagogues to control Pakistan's nuclear weapons. This possibility appears to be mitigated by the fact that militant Islamic parties appear to be at the limit of their popular support and need to widen their electoral base, which should, in turn, ostensibly dilute their ideological fervor. Yet these negative scenarios could be actualized if India and Pakistan fail in their reconciliation process which could possibly result in either Indo-Pakistani war or else Pakistani disaggregation.

# Chapter 6

# The Global Ramifications of American Military Expansionism

**Pentagon Re-posturing**

During the Cold War, the US strategy of containment was largely intended to impel a Soviet withdrawal from eastern Europe. Washington did not really expect (or welcome) the collapse of the Soviet Union into fifteen separate republics, of which four initially retained significant nuclear capabilities (Russia, Ukraine, Kazakhstan and Belarus). In addition to Soviet collapse, the collapse of neutral "buffer" states of Afghanistan and Yugoslavia opened up both internal and external power struggles for control over parts, if not the totality, of these formerly "neutral" territories. Moreover, the fact that a politically instable Russia has begun to splinter into numerous regional and ethno-political disputes has had significant implications for both Russian domestic political stability, as well as for the regions bordering Russia. This is particularly true as Russia has sought to re-assert its hegemony over former Soviet space, and has begun to seek out new overseas markets for sales of arms and oil.[1]

Without Soviet overseas outreach to serve a counterbalance to American efforts to achieve global hegemony, the US (with or without UN backing) has also opted to intervene militarily in regions throughout the world outside its former Cold War "spheres of influence and security." Seizing the "unipolar" moment, the United States has been moving into former Soviet spheres of influence and security as an integral aspect of a post-Cold War strategy of "strategic denial." Concurrently, the US has sought, largely single-handedly, to "mono-contain" the potential military and economic capabilities of Germany/Europe, Japan, China as well as Russia, not to overlook states such as Iran and North Korea.[2] Yet this strategy comes at the risk of political, military and economic overextension.

In a third wave of overseas "imperialism" (since expansion to Cuba and the Philippines and after World War II in which the US began to absorb overseas British and French spheres of security and influence), Washington has now engaged itself in regions in which it has little historical experience.[3] The US has begun to expand its military forces in eastern Europe, the Caucasus, central Asia, Northern Africa and Horn of Africa, as well as the Far East and Persian Gulf. In addition to numerous costly, but relatively minor, military interventions in the

127

1990s in global strategic terms, Washington opted for a major intervention in Iraq.

Following its March 2003 intervention in Iraq, the US began to downsize its forces in the "old" Europe (except Ramstein Airforce base in Germany, site of nuclear weapons storage). The Pentagon has thus begun to shift bases from the UK and Germany (downsizing 70,000 troops) to Italy; it has begun to implement more cost effective bases in the "new" Europe: Poland, Hungary, Romania and Bulgaria. With bases upgraded, some 5,000 to 10,000 troops are to be deployed, in Poland.[4] The "old" Europe is thus becoming more of a logistical center, with Italy at the center, rather than a Cold War encampment prepared for an "imminent" Soviet invasion. This new force re-posturing has raised questions as to whether the nature of US/NATO deterrence and reassurance is truly credible. It appears to assume that the "new" Europe could be rapidly defended from positions in eastern Europe.

The US reluctantly downsized forces in Saudi Arabia several years after Gulf war (except for small contingent in Dhahran) and shifted US forces to Qatar and Bahrain, as well as to Oman and the United Arab Emirates—in a tacit concession to bin Laden. Here, a long-term large-scale military and diplomatic presence in Iraq seems highly likely. The Pentagon appears to be planning 14 "enduring bases" with a drain on manpower resources for some time to come (over 100,000 troops through 2006)—at least until Iraqi oil fields can be developed and the country stabilized with a self-confident Iraqi police and military force.[5] It is highly probable (but not absolutely guaranteed) that the new post-January 2005 Iraqi government will agree to a continued American military presence.

US policy seeks both access to oil and strategic denial/interdiction capabilities in Persian Gulf. In order to guarantee access to oil and supply routes, to counterbalance both Russia and China, and to check pan-Islamic movements, Washington is also building bases in Kosovo, the Caucasus and central Asia, including Azerbaijan (some 15,000 troops), Georgia, Uzbekistan, Kyrgystan, Tajikistan, and Kazakhstan, as well as Afghanistan. Washington has reportedly built bases in Pakistan as well. The Pentagon also plans to reinforce its bases in Hawaii, Guam, and Diego Garcia (in the Indian Ocean), and French Djibouti at the Horn of Africa (5,000–6,500 troops), while seeking to regain basing rights in Philippines (after being forced out of Subic Bay in 1992). Semi-permanent bases are to be maintained in Algeria, Morocco, Tunisia plus Senegal, plus Ghana, Mali, Kenya. One of the primary goals in Africa is to protect an instable Nigeria, expected to provide some 25% of US oil needs in the future.[6] (It should be noted that many of these countries are former French colonies or protectorates.)

Interestingly, despite nuclear tensions with North Korea, the Pentagon is downsizing in forces by withdrawing 7,500 of its 32,500 troops in South Korea— thus appearing to reduce its trip wire in case of North Korean attack. Concurrently, Washington appears to be seeking out its former Vietnam War era naval base at Camh Ranh Bay (after the Russians left in 2003). Washington is also renegotiating its force position in Okinawa and elsewhere in Japan. Here, the US seems to be positioning itself for continuing conflict with pan-Islamic "terrorist" groups, if not seeking to counterbalance China and control sea lines of communication from the

Persian Gulf to Japan, but causing anxiety in Seoul.

In respect to the "war on terrorism," President Bush has signed a series of findings and executive orders that authorize Special Forces to conduct covert operations against suspected terrorist groups in as many as ten states in the Middle East and South Asia. Those moves enable the Defense Department, which accounts for 80% of the US$40 billion budget for foreign intelligence, and in which eight US intelligence agencies depend upon Defense Department funding or technical assistance, to run the operations free from legal restrictions that had previously been imposed on the CIA by Congress.[7] In the aftermath of 11 September, and in the long debate over "pre-emptive" intervention in Iraq, the Department of Defense has been able to outmaneuver the CIA, which has been regarded as being too tied down by bureaucratic and legal red tape for action.

Washington's overall purpose is to defend rimlands, shatterbelts and chokepoints by developing rapid reaction and expeditionary forces that are ready to move as fast as possible versus a "virtual" enemy, in which speed and stealth have replaced more visible troop commitments that generally serve as reassurance and deterrence. US intervention in Iraq was, in part, designed to put the Pentagon in a position to control the supply of oil from a potentially major producer of low cost high quality oil; to reduce Russian, Chinese and French influence over Iraqi oil production; and to shift bases in the region away from a potentially instable Saudi Arabia. These objectives were, to a large extent, based upon the Defense Department assessment that world energy demand, particularly for oil, will increase by 45 million barrels per day from roughly 75 million barrels per day in 2004 to 120 million barrels per day in 2025.[8] As Asia is expected to consume some 80 percent of the extra 45 million barrel per day increase, the possibility of conflict in that region looks very plausible—unless the US can take real leadership in shifting domestic and international energy habits and priorities soon enough and engage in irenic diplomacy to avert the real potential for conflict. (See Chapter 8.)

## Global Ramifications of the Iraq War

As the reasons for going to war with Iraq did not obtain international legitimacy from the UN Security Council (UNSC), or at a very minimum obtain some form of general international "consensus," the US-UK intervention has significantly damaged US relations with Germany and Turkey (the two most loyal US allies during the Cold War). US intervention has also tended to undermine the "legitimacy" of the UN and, indirectly, the "credibility" of NATO. It may have also undercut the US-UK "special relationship." Another consequence may have been to push the Russians, Chinese, Indians, and possibly the Turks, closer together. Alternatively, it could set the stage for an EU "Red Eiffel Tower" alliance with Beijing, which presently involves Franco-Chinese naval cooperation and the opening of the door to EU arms sales to China—albeit under a regulated "code of conduct" (which has not yet, however, been made legally binding, or in accord with international law).

There is furthermore a real risk that Bush administration neo-conservative policies could continue to divide an expanding Europe, force it out of its comfortable Kantian "out of history" nest on Venus (in Robert Kagan's stereotypes[9])—and then throw it once again into the "real" world of major power rivalries. US efforts to obtain the political-economic allegiance of eastern European states may consequently divide the EU, and isolate Moscow. The US had played the UK and Germany against France during the Cold War. Yet this new situation has opened a door in which the US can attempt to play the UK, Italy, Spain, Poland and other eastern European states against efforts to forge a common EU foreign policy, backed by what US Secretary of Defense Donald Rumsfeld dubbed the "old Europe" of France and Germany.[10]

Downsizing bases in the "old Europe" and rebuilding in the "new" Europe, however, coupled with US efforts to foster a Polish-Ukrainian alliance in respect to "coalition" peacekeeping in northern Iraq, among the other issues mentioned above, have tended to undermine the trust of the new-found post–11 September 2001 NATO-Russian entente, and have hurt American relations with Europe as well. These American actions have raised a number of risks that appear to violate US promises to Russia not to deploy forces in eastern Europe—although no formal treaty has been signed with Moscow.

A prime example is the $3.5 billion sale of forty-eight US F-16 fighters to Poland (for 2006–08), in direct rivalry with Swedish Gripin and French Mirage 2000-5 fighter jets, and which includes over $6 billion in a foreign military financing (FMF) loan package, forty-three offsetting projects and direct US foreign investment. This "contract of the century" has upset French and Swedish arms producers, Germany (the major investor in Poland), as well as EU Commission President Romano Prodi.[11] Ostensibly a reward for Polish support for the Iraq war, the sale of F-16s could also have the effect of alienating Belarus and Russia in that the sales are symbolic of a burgeoning military-industrial relationship with east-central Europe—which appears contrary to unwritten US promises not to expand NATO infrastructure into eastern Europe.

To counter American conventional and nuclear superiority, as well as the expansion of NATO into eastern Europe, not to overlook the Bush administration decision to unilaterally withdraw from the ABM treaty, Russia has attempted to modernize its missile capabilities, but has faced difficulties reforming its military. Ironically assisted by higher oil prices since the US intervention in Iraq, Russia has tested its "Satan" multiple warhead SS–18 missile—against the spirit of START agreements to abolish heavy land-based MIRVed missiles altogether. Moscow also claims to have developed new "hypersonic" weapons systems, with warheads that are ostensibly capable of evading BMD by rapidly changing trajectories.

Tensions over Russian opposition to US-UK intervention in Iraq had been accompanied by a number of Bush administration criticisms. These included: The Russian turn toward "authoritarianism"; hints that the US Congress might not forgive Russian debt; threats that the US might fail to repeal the Jackson-Vanik amendment—thus refusing to grant Russia Most-favored Nation (MFN) status, now called, "Permanent Normal Trade Relations" (PNTR); that Congress might not fully support Russian membership in the WTO; and that the US might cut Russian (as well as French and Chinese) oil companies out of pending contracts finalized with the regime of Saddam Hussein.

Russia's main concerns in Iraq were to sustain oil concessions granted by the regime of Saddam Hussein, retrieve roughly $8 billion in debt, and sustain trading relations. The significant increase in oil prices after the Iraq war, however, appears to have mitigated Russian demands for Iraqi debt repayment—as long as Russian companies could also augment their business in the new Iraq. At the same time, as France and Germany had led the opposition to US policy, Russia (and China, which also sought major oil concessions in Iraq) generally tried to stay in the background and not confront the US directly. (Which of the pre-war oil contracts will be honored remains to be seen, as will how US, European, Russian and Chinese firms might divide Iraqi concessions and market. Much largely depends upon the formation and nature of an new Iraqi government with perceived *legitimacy*, and how closely that new government depends upon the US for its security, and whether it opens its markets to truly competitive bidding or else relies on political favoritism.)

Despite the post–11 September NATO-Russian entente, and formation of the NATO-Russian Council, Russia only grudgingly accepted Baltic state membership in NATO. From the end of the Cold War, Russia has consistently warned that bringing the Baltic states into NATO would represent a *casus belli*. During the Yeltsin era, in December 2000–January 2001, there had been rumors that Moscow had begun to deploy tactical nuclear weapons in the region, allegations vehemently denied by Moscow. This media alarm appeared to represent an effort to speed NATO enlargement by magnifying the Russian threat, at the same time that it appeared to expose the EU's inability to deal with such a threat on its borders. The Putin government subsequently toned down its public opposition to NATO membership of three Baltic states somewhat, but such opposition is still at play in the background. In 2004, Putin warned that NATO flights over Baltic airspace could provoke an accident that might lead to confrontation. Baltic state membership in NATO puts Moscow and St Petersburg within easy striking range of NATO forces—should NATO decide to fully build up its defenses in the region.

Russia consequently demanded that all eastern European states sign the adapted Conventional Force in Europe (CFE) pact before entering NATO. New NATO members refused, however, arguing they would have greater bargaining leverage with Russia once they joined NATO. The Russian troop presence in Abkhazia and South Ossetia in Georgia and in Transdniester in Moldova, as well in Nagorno-Karabakh between Armenia and Azerbaijan, combined with Russian demands for a *droit de regard* over much of ex-Soviet eastern Europe (the Baltic states, Belarus, Moldova as well as Ukraine), have thus far represented major rationale for NATO members to refuse to sign the adapted CFE treaty. (Russia had previously promised to withdraw their forces from these regions in Istanbul in 1999.[12]) While Moscow has thus far tolerated, if not supported, limited US/NATO operations in former Soviet Central Asia, it has still questioned the purpose of some NATO activities, particularly those affecting the Caucasus.

Having given up its overextended empire in much of central and eastern Europe, the Russians have largely watched by the sidelines as the Americans and Europeans fill in the strategic "void." Whether NATO enlargement will, in fact, ultimately prove to be the "most fatal error of American policy in the entire post-Cold War era," as once prognosticated by George Kennan, will largely depend upon the reforms taking place in NATO itself, as well the nature of security accords reached by NATO with the EU, as the latter likewise expands into eastern Europe, and with Russia. Concurrently, however, as it reluctantly cedes control over former Soviet space in eastern Europe, and overseas in both Cuba and Vietnam, Moscow has been eyeing closer relations with China and India, and has begun to compete for control over former Soviet space in the Caucasus and central Asia, and open ties in the Middle East (Syria), Persian Gulf (Iran), and the Near East (Turkey)—as well as looking for new markets abroad.

### Russian PTNR Status

Following Soviet collapse, the US has thus far not granted Most-favored Nation (MFN) status, now called Permanent Normal Trade Relations (PNTR), to the new Russia. MFN status had initially been blocked by Senator Scoop Jackson along with his neo-conservative advisors, Richard Perle and Paul Wolfowitz. (See Chapter 2.) This fact, even though Russian emigration controls have been relaxed, coupled with the fact that China has been granted PNTR despite its horrendous human rights record, has raised cries of "double standards" among Russians.

The issue has thus remained a bone of contention between Moscow and Washington since the end of the Cold War. The Bush administration has supported providing PNTR status to Russia, but without a separate vote in Congress on the country's WTO accession. U.S. Trade Representative Robert Zoellick said that requiring a separate vote on Russia's WTO accession would "unfairly single it out among other countries seeking to join the WTO." There were additional fears that granting PNTR "prematurely" would hinder U.S. negotiators in securing Russia's entry to the WTO upon so-called "favorable" terms.[13]

### European Union Enlargement

While US policies during the 2003 intervention in Iraq appear intended to divide the "old" western and the "new" eastern Europeans, and place a wedge between the EU and Russia, they have been countered by European efforts to unify step-by-step, coupled with efforts to cooperate more closely with Moscow.

After the failure of European diplomacy to prevent the US from going to war "over" Kosovo at the 1998 Rambouillet Summit, the Europeans vowed to establish the *Euroforce*. Similarly, despite US efforts to play the UK, Spain and the eastern European states (particularly Poland) against France and Germany, the EU opted to expand its membership to twenty-five. Assuming the new European Constitution will ultimately be ratified (not an absolutely certain proposition), the EU appears to be moving closer together through the establishment of a single president and foreign minister.

So far after most major post-Cold War US-European confrontations over foreign policy, the Europeans have tended to grit their teeth and begun to unify, despite disputes over large and smaller state voting rights, the Common Agricultural Program, aid to underdeveloped regions, among other internal EU controversies. The term "convergent evolution"[14] depicts the process in which each crisis seems to represent a physical shock that forces new evolutionary changes upon each individual European state that, in turn, brings them toward convergence, despite real differences in policy and interests.

On the one hand, if the EU is to unify its security and defense posture, it will need to provide significant security supports to its new members. This is true in that eastern European states, which will soon be members of both NATO and the EU, will only begin to respect EU initiatives, once the latter can more truly guarantee their overall security. On the other hand, the EU will ultimately be compelled to reduce its dependence upon the US as the latter begins to re-deploy some of its bases (except Ramstein) and some of its 70,000 troops away from Germany as a means to cut costs and move closer to new theatres of conflict. The Pentagon is building up its bases in Naples—with a look to the south.

The latter downsizing had been a prospect foreseen in the Clinton era; yet German opposition to the war with Iraq had been cynically used by the Bush administration as a pretext for cutting back US forces in Europe. In addition to weakening the core NATO relationship with Berlin, downsizing may possess unexpected political economic consequences for US-German relations, including domestic demands to eliminate US nuclear weapons from German territory in the effort to strengthen the NPT.

A number of issues confront the transatlantic relationship. These include: The decline of the dollar relative to the Euro; trade disputes over agriculture (bananas) and the Common Agricultural Program; genetically modified organisms; subsidies for aerospace and for the steel industries. This is not to overlook trade sanctions on China (in respect to post-Tiananmen Square sanctions), as well as on Cuba, Iran— in addition to "horse trading" over Iraqi reconstruction and oil concessions. In respect to China, the EU seeks to open arms sales; the US has complained that EU Airbus sales to China (which cut into Boeing's market) have been highly subsidized by Brussels. The latter, in turn, has asked the WTO to investigate indirect US subsidies to Boeing from NASA and the Pentagon.[15]

Contrary to US expectations, the political fall-out from the decision of UK Prime Minister Tony Blair to side with the Bush administration in the war with Iraq (coupled with Blair's failed effort to influence US policy from behind the scenes) could ultimately press the UK closer to the EU. The US-UK justification for so-called *pre-emptive* war (in the argument that Iraq possessed WMD and posed an *imminent* threat) had been seriously criticized. The whole US-UK "special relationship" has been put into question. As the UK re-evaluates its relations with the US and Europe, London seriously looks like it could join "Euroland" in the not so long term, despite having ruled out such a possibility in 2003. Should the UK ultimately take steps to move closer to the European Union, as the 1998 St. Malo initiative initially indicated, then the possibility of a Common Foreign and Security Policy (CFSP) becomes much more plausible. From this perspective, Europe will soon be *impelled* by both extra- and intra- European considerations to develop more autonomous military capabilities. Both the regional and global aspects of European diplomacy will need to be backed by a credible force, if a CFSP is to be successful. In 2004, the EU announced the formation of a EU defense ministry and foreign ministry (EU-Consilium) in embryo, which would be strengthened following ratification of the European Constitution, which is expected, in 2006, but not without considerable debate. (The rejection by France, among other states cannot be ruled out; support is not universal and voter turn out has been low to the embarrassment of Brussels.)

## The EU, China and Russia

In the quest to establish a more multipolar world (an initiative initially supported by Henry Kissinger), France has been seeking a closer and "unique" relationship with Moscow, at the same time that both Paris and Berlin have been reaching out for a closer defense and economic relationship with China.

In April 2003, French Prime Minister Jean-Pierre Raffarin made a spectacular visit to China during the SARS (SRAS) crisis, to establish commercial and high technology cooperation with China. This trip, coupled with Franco-German overtures to open arms sales to Beijing, have raised questions as to the extent of the security relationship that might be established with China involving possible sales of advanced weapons systems and dual use technology. The prospect of Franco-German arms sales to China may put pressure on the US to break the arms embargo—imposed after the Tiananmen Square repression in June 1989.[16]

While Berlin and Moscow have engaged in closed-door talks, Paris and Moscow have formed "Le Conseil de coopération franco-russe sur les questions de sécurité (CCQS)" in the effort to forge a strategic partnership with an increasingly "authoritarian" Russia. Moscow has, in turn, hoped to forge a new relationship with the EU, similar to, if not more effective than, the NATO-Russia Council. Paris, however, rejected that approach and argued that NATO and the EU were not the same kind of organization. Not only has the EU has appeared to reject Russian overtures for a EU-Russian security cooperation, but it also appeared to dismiss Ukrainian membership in the EU as well, at least in the immediate future.

Paris does hope, however, to find common strategies with respect to North Korea, Iran and Chechnya. Here, the "troika" of France, Britain and Germany have hoped to obtain Russian cooperation in stemming Iran's quest for nuclear weaponry in seeking *real dialogue* with Teheran. Moreover, Paris no longer refers to the situation in Chechnya as a "*guerre ouverte,*" as depicted by Dominique de Villepin, but as a "*crise.*" (Paris likewise refuses the label of "appeasement" for its dealings with Moscow; it argues that one must take a "larger" perspective.)[17]

One of the most significant challenges for the EU is whether it can integrate Turkey, which has sought to enter the EU since 1987. The EU decided in late 2004 to formally invite Turkey to apply for membership in October 2005; yet the process will probably take more than a decade and could draw the EU into a number of regional hotspots in respect to Iraq, the Kurdish question, as well as the Caucasus (Georgia, Azerbaijan and Armenia). A divided Cyprus likewise threatens to postpone Turkish membership in the EU even further. The EU will also have to consider issues resulting from the Israeli-Turkish defense alliance.

The fact that Europe possesses roughly 14 million Moslems has raised the risks of xenophobic backlash. The immigration question in general; higher taxes; the costs of international assistance to poorer new members; the fears of the shift of jobs and industry to eastern Europe; the voting rights of larger countries—in additional to the fear that Europe will become a 'free trade zone' under the control of Brussels and not an effective strategic actor on the world scene—have all fueled a potential backlash to greater European integration. While Spain has voted "for," opinion polls in Denmark, the Czech Republic, Poland, as well as France, the Netherlands, and the UK, have expressed opposition to the new Constitution.

## The EU "Border Lands"

The fact that NATO and the EU have opted to expand in a largely uncoordinated "double enlargement" into eastern Europe puts both NATO and the EU alongside the Russian and Belarusian borders, but without the creation of a stable buffer region which could help reduce potential friction. This has helped to create an ambivalent situation in which the eastern Europeans in Belarus and Ukraine may find themselves increasingly caught between the "liberal-democratic" political-economic attractions of the European Union (and of the United States) versus the carrots and sticks of Moscow related to cheap energy, for example.

From the Russian perspective, the expanding NATO and EU presence is regarded as potentially drawing Kaliningrad toward secession, which, due to fissiparous tendencies throughout the ex-Soviet bloc, could have a "domino" effect in other regions, such as Murmansk, which, much like Kaliningrad, is in bad financial straits. Political stability in the north of Russia likewise depends upon the development of Karelia and St. Petersburg. The Yeltsin government had to deal with independence movements in Tatarstan, Bashkortostan, Udmurtia, Komi, Yakutia (Sakha), and Buryatia (along the Chinese border). Most problematic for both Yeltsin and Putin, however, have been secessionist movements in the Caucasus region, primarily Chechnya and Ingushetia.

Ukraine appears historically divided roughly along the Dneiper river between its "pro-Russian" and "pro-European" factions. The region of Lviv in Galacia tends to look toward the EU and Poland; pro-Russian factions of the more industrialized regions have sought closer cooperation with Russia and the Commonwealth of Independent States. Domestic tensions between eastern and western Ukraine were evident at the time of Soviet break-up (in which Moscow and Kiev haggled over dividing their gold reserves, financial assets, and military capabilities in a "civilized divorce" and when both the US and Russia pressured Ukraine not to sustain an independent nuclear weapons capability). These socio-political divisions then became increasingly evident in the November 2004 presidential elections. The latter, in effect, became "internationalized," as the US, EU, Russia, and Poland, attempted to influence the outcome. Moscow (and Minsk) strongly supported the candidate, Viktor F. Yanukovich, while Warsaw, Brussels and Washington, DC all supported the "reformist," Viktor A. Yushchenko, who had called for a general strike against the pro-Yanukovich Ukrainian leadership. (The situation appeared very similar to that which led to the resignation of Edvard Shevardnaze in Georgia in November 2003.)

The US (and OSCE) subsequently accused Ukraine of election fraud (denied by Russian and Ukrainian government spokesmen), ironically at the same time that accusations of significant election fraud also haunted both Democrats and Republicans in both the 2000 and 2004 US presidential elections. In the Ukrainian case, the accusations of fraud were then upheld by the Ukrainian Supreme Court, which in turn led to a new vote and the victory of Viktor A. Yushchenko, in the "orange" revolution. (In the American 2000 presidential election, the US Supreme Court opposed the appeal of the Democratic candidate, Al Gore, who had clearly won a majority of the popular vote throughout the USA, but who lost in the Electoral College, after allegations of voting fraud in Florida.)

While depicted as a "pro-Western" candidate, Yushchenko gave much emphasis in his campaign speeches to the fact that he desired to reaffirm Ukrainian ties with Russia, albeit on an equal footing with Ukraine's larger neighbor. Yushchenko's presidential campaign platform focused more specifically on domestic economic reform and on fighting corruption and mafias than on joining NATO or the EU. Membership in the latter was regarded as key, long-term goals. Yushchenko's major focus was accordingly on the general inability of Ukraine to reform its failing economy, which has jeopardized closer ties with both the European Union and the United States. Yushchenko will likewise need to patch the domestic cleavage between the pro-eastern and pro-western factions (some 80% of the pro-Russian eastern Ukraine voted against him). Here, he may have to grant greater autonomy to pro-Russian regions in the east, such as the Donbass coal producing region, as well as to western regions such as Lviv.

Moscow has expressed fears that Kiev may be seeking an anti-Russian alliance with NATO-member Poland through their "strategic partnership." Moscow has consequently opposed a "Baltic-Black sea alliance" and used oil as one weapon in the effort to pressure Ukraine, as well as other states, such as Georgia, into following a pro-Russian policy and to assure that these states do not enter NATO. US calls for National Ballistic Missile defense system, for example, led to calls for closer military cooperation between Russia and Ukraine, under the prior leadership of Leonid Kuchma. The latter's government has been officially accused of selling nuclear-capable cruise missiles to Iran and China between 1999–2001 in violation of non-proliferation treaties, along with efforts to supply Saddam Hussein's Iraq and other states with advanced defense systems.[18]

Acting Prime Minister, Yulia Tymoshenko, has likewise recognized the need to heal the rift in the country and argued that Russia, as well as Ukraine, should join NATO and the EU. Here, however, the fact that the billionaire Tymoshenko has been accused of bribery of Russian military officials could antagonize relations (not overlooking charges of corruption stemming from her alleged actions in Ukraine). In addition to the question as to whether the US would want Ukraine as a NATO member, is the question of whether Russia would accept assurances that Ukraine would lobby for Russian membership, without being accepted in NATO first, or at the same time.[19] From Moscow's perspective, the "internationalization" of the Ukrainian elections (with the US and EU taking opposing sides to Russia) and with former Solidarity Leader Lech Walesca speaking in Kiev, seemed to indicate a concerted Western effort to undermine what Moscow considers its "sphere of influence and security."

For its part, Moscow has sought to strengthen its bilateral alliance with Belarus, and has thus far unsuccessfully pressured Ukraine. In an effort to further integrate the region in trade terms, Russia had signed an agreement on 19 September 2003 to create a Common Economic Space (CES) with Belarus, Ukraine, and Kazakhstan. The economic zone represents approximately 90 percent of Russia's trade with the Commonwealth of Independent States (CIS), a loose affiliation of the former Soviet Republics, and roughly 219 million people. Moscow sees this as a step toward WTO status. At the same time, however, Russia and Ukraine remain competitors in steel, aerospace, and arms industries (as do the US and EU!) Moscow has also been looking toward enhancing its ties with Turkey, exchanging oil for Turkish consumer products, and may be able to take advantage of EU reluctance to bring Turkey in, as well as Turkish animosity with the US over the Kurdish question in Iraq.

While Moscow does seek WTO status (see analysis below), it has been projected that the development gap between those eastern European states that enter the EU and those that do not (Belarus, Moldova, Ukraine, as well as Russia) may continue to widen in the coming years. Most crucially, aid and assistance from the EU may not be a sufficient substitute for closer trade relations.[20] The EU, for example, would need to modify costs of enlargement, provide a means to make products from these regions more competitive, and minimize potential losses—if some of these countries were to enter. Without some form of special relationship, the gap between EU members and eastern European states could result in continuing political-economic instability within each of these countries, and tensions along NATO-EU borders due to smuggling of drugs, contraband and clandestine immigration—if not nationalist backlash and secessionist crises.

Citizens of both Ukraine and Belarus (as well as Russians in Kaliningrad) have begun to find themselves restricted by the "micro-electronic" curtain imposed by shifting Schengen arrangements, at the same time that they hope to sustain cross-border trade. While Schengen will not affect the formal economy and trade in raw materials, it will affect the informal cross border trade and make it more difficult to increase the volume of trade between Poland and Ukraine, for example. It may also reinforce and exacerbate nationalist or secessionist movements in Ukraine, as in Galacia—which could continue to splinter the country.[21] The crucial question as to whether economic relations between the EU and its non-EU neighbors, Belarus, Ukraine and Russia, will result in *trade creation* or *trade diversion* remains. Here, unlike the case for EU expansion from the 1970s to the 1980s, Europe has limited structural funds to assist central European states rise to the economic levels of the rest of the EU—and it has far less left over for non-EU border states in eastern Europe. Moreover, it is feared that Turkish membership in the EU (if at all possible) would squeeze Ukraine between Europe and Russia—particularly as Russia dominates the Black Sea.

## Belarus

In addition to Ukraine, US actions are interpreted as seeking to undercut other Russian spheres of influence. In January 2005, Belarus, whose failing economy inherited a large military-industrial complex from the Soviet empire is in desperate need of significant reform, was dubbed by US Secretary of State, Condoleezza Rice, as one of the "outposts of tyranny." President Aleksandr G. Lukashenko has increasingly led the country in an authoritarian direction, literally muffling the press, for example, whenever it has been critical the regime.

In October 2004, President Bush signed "The Belarus Democracy Act." The latter introduces US assistance for Belarus political parties, non-governmental organizations and independent media. It also prohibits U.S. government agencies from providing loans and investment to the Belarus government, except for humanitarian goods. While US support for the Polish Solidarity movement in the 1980s was more or less clandestine, US support for the Belarusian and Ukrainian opposition is very open and public. The key dilemma is consequently how to get Washington and Moscow to work together *against* Minsk (as Belarusian President Lukashenko hopes to win a third term in 2006, but can dubiously win without fixing the vote). This needs to take place before Russian hardliners begin to see themselves as encircled "as if it were a bear in a trap"—in opposition to public US efforts to draw Ukraine, Belarus and central Asia away from Russian influence.

## The Balkans

Russia did participate in the Contact Group in response to the Bosnian conflict; yet it was completely cut out of the decision-making process to engage in the war "over" Kosovo. (See Chapter 8.) The situation in Kosovo appears to be deteriorating with the failure to move forward on Kosovo's status. In what appears to be a reversal of roles and a strategy of "honest broker," NATO has appeared to back the new Serbian leadership of Vojislav Kostunica in cracking down against pro-Albanian secessionist movements in southern Serbia. Concurrently, NATO has also been backing Macedonia in its moves against pan-Albanian secessionists.

The war "over" Kosovo only froze its status, with Kosovar Albanians seeking national self-determination and many Serbian groups seeking ethnic partition. Whereas Serbs engaged in horrendous acts of ethnic cleansing and crimes against humanity in Bosnia and Kosovo, some 180,000–200,000 Serbs have moved out of Kosovo since 1999, leaving roughly 80,000–100,000 to live in ethnic enclaves.

The key to the issue is establishing confidence so that the displaced Serbs can return.[22] A related problem is that sanctions on Serbia tend to hurt the entire region, which is dependent upon trade along the Danube. EU commissioner Chris Patten has stated that economic stagnation, interethnic tension, and the potential for violence were linked and threatened the entire region: "There has been considerable progress in south-east Europe since 1999, but there is a danger of the whole process unraveling in Kosovo unless we grasp some nettles."[23]

## Turkey, Iran and Central Asia

Immediately following Soviet collapse, Russian hardliners initially tended to regard NATO links with Turkey, with its newfound interests in the Caucasus and central Asia, as a potential threat to its soft Turkic/Islamic underbelly. Moscow had claimed that a "Caucasus conspiracy" had been forming between NATO-member Turkey, Azerbaijan, and Georgia against Russia, Iran, and Armenia and that American policy sought to sponsor a GUUAM alliance against Moscow, linking Georgia, Ukraine, Uzbekistan, Azerbaijan and Moldova. This position had led Russia to pressure and cajole these latter states into towing the Russian line. (US support for Ukraine in the 2004 elections once again raised suspicions of US backing for a GUUAM alliance.)

Russia's concern has been to stem to rise of pan-Islamic and secessionist movements in the Caucasus, and throughout central Asia, in addition to stabilizing political conditions for the passage of oil pipelines from the oil rich Caspian Sea. Moscow likewise argued that the Taliban in Afghanistan, backed by Pakistan and Saudi Arabia, among other parties, have been lending support to the Chechen resistance. In this regard, Moscow has increasingly accepted the American military presence in the Caucasus and central Asia, although not without reservations. Moscow has also sought to make deals with Turkey, Iran and Saudi Arabia, at the same time that it plays "divide and rule" in the Caucasus and central Asia.

To better control the region, the "Shanghai Five" (China, Russia, Kazakhstan, Kyrgyzstan, and Tajikistan) was formed in 1996, in Shanghai. By August 1999, the "Shanghai Five" pledged to cooperate in fighting terrorism, drugs, arms smuggling, illegal migration, national secession and religious "extremism" in addition to demarcating borders and regulating trade relations. It was later joined by Uzbekistan in 2001—then calling itself the Shanghai Cooperation Organization (SCO) to counterpoint the Organization for Security and Cooperation in Europe.

In an effort to cooperate with Russia, Turkey argued that its policies were intended to check pan-Islamic movements supported by the Afghan Taliban, Iran, and the Islamic Movement of Uzbekistan/Turkestan and Uighur separatism that the "Shanghai Five" had been unable to contain. Ankara also expressed interest in joining the Shanghai Cooperation Organization in January 2005. NATO-member Turkey consequently signed military cooperation agreements with Kyrgyzstan and with the Uzbek leadership, which has thus far refused Russian supports against the Islamic Movement of Uzbekistan/Turkestan (the latter has launched incursions into Uzbekistan, Kazakhstan, and Kyrgyzstan). In addition, Turkey had previously signed an "anti-terrorist" agreement with Russia, in which it promised not to provide wounded Chechen rebels with medical treatment.

Turkey has looked closer to Russia for diplomatic supports and energy, particularly after refusing to participate in the US intervention in Iraq. Russia may be playing with Turkish discontent with US policy toward Iraq, which Ankara regards as fomenting a Kurdish independence movement. Turkey may also be looking for ways to normalize Turkey's relationship with Armenia, with Russian diplomatic assistance, and to end the Nagorno-Karabakh conflict. Ending the latter would, in turn, help Turkey enter the EU, as would Russian assistance on the Cyprus question, by urging the end of isolation of Turkish-controlled section.

In the mutual fear of secessionist movements and pan-Islamic terrorism, Russia has sought to bring China and India together, along with other states in central Asia, despite their geohistorical disputes. Xinjiang, Tibet, and Taiwan are of primary concern to China. India is primarily concerned with Kashmir and Sri Lanka (with militant Tamil movements seeking "self-determination" within the latter). Russia has sought to assert hegemony over the region as best it can after Soviet collapse. (Interestingly, different countries have used different forms of strategic leveraging to gain influence in the region. India has used its historical links; Saudi Arabia and Pakistan, their religious links; Turkey and Iran, their cultural links; South Korea and Japan, their economic links.[24] Washington has likewise used "democracy" as a tool of influence, at least in Afghanistan.)

China has signed agreements and/or territory swaps with Kyrgyzstan, Tajikistan, as well as Kazakhstan, which has significant energy reserves. Russia, in turn, has sought to strengthen ties with Uzbekistan and Kyrgyzstan, who are strong supporters of Russia's views on the war on terrorism. The Kyrgyz leadership has supported the concept of pre-emptive strikes; the Uzbek leadership has urged the creation of a common CIS list of terrorist organizations. (If so, it would be the Collective Security Treaty Organization (CSTO) of Armenia, Belarus, Kazakhstan, Kyrgyzstan, Tajikistan, and Russia that would engage rapid-reaction forces.[25])

Iran is the major Russian ally in the Persian Gulf region, despite disputes over ownership of oil reserves in the Caspian Sea. Russia represents Iran's major arms supplier and has assisted its nuclear program in addition to assisting Iran's ballistic missile capabilities—to the chagrin of the Americans. (See Chapter 4.) Moscow has regarded support for Teheran as the means to counterbalance Saudi influence in Chechnya and in central Asia. Moscow and Teheran supported the Northern Alliance against the Sunni Taliban, which, in turn, was supported by Saudi Arabia and Pakistan. Both have supported Orthodox Armenia against Islamic Azerbaijan (backed by the Americans)—as both powers seek to weaken oil rich Azerbaijan with claims to regions in Iran. Teheran's tacit support for Russia's intervention in Chechnya, which likewise appears contrary to the clash of civilizations thesis, may be one reason for Russian refusal to stop selling arms to Teheran.[26]

Russia has also sought to stabilize central Asia, working with the United States against *al-Qaida* and the Taliban in Afghanistan—as Moscow provided useful intelligence. Here, the US, EU and Russia did find some common ground in the war against *al-Qaida* and the Taliban in Afghanistan; both Russia and China acquiesced to US military bases in central Asia, with China engaging in a rapprochement with NATO in 2003. The American presence has *thus far* appeared, for the moment, to represent a stabilizing factor in the soft underbelly of the Russian federation—as long as Russia, China and the US possess common "threats" in the region. NATO and Russia appear to be cooperating against the return of the Taliban in Afghanistan, at the same time that Russia is tightening its links to key central Asian states. (See Chapter 5.)

## The Caucasus

Russia has sought to sustain military forces in Abkhazia and in the Ossetia region, in effect splintering Georgia, which appears in danger of losing the autonomous region of Ajara. Georgia has been excluded from participation in all major regional trade and East-West pipeline projects, such as the Baku-Ceyhan pipeline, largely because of its unresolved conflicts. Armenia sees itself as isolated by an alliance of Turkey, Azerbaijan and Georgia, which also includes Iran, in its conflict with Azerbaijan over Nagorno-Karabakh. While the region is badly in need of political-economic integration, and effective diplomatic mediation, Moscow has generally denounced American and European calls to work toward a political solution for the crisis in Chechnya and for the Caucasus in general. Moscow considers the Chechen issue an "internal affair" that is being manipulated by outside forces.

Following previous efforts to deal with Turkey and Iran, in the spring of 2003 Moscow implemented a four-fold approach in respect to the Chechen crisis. First, Moscow has attempted to institute a pro-Russian government in Chechnya (much as the US is doing in Iraq). Second, it has reached out to Saudi Arabia, in order to cut presumed Saudi assistance to Chechen militants, and attempt to keep oil prices stable, and as high as possible. Thirdly, it has reached out to other Islamic states, such as Malaysia. Putin referred to a major *al-Qaida* attack in Saudi Arabia in May 2003 to argue that Russia and the Saudi Kingdom were in the same boat in the "war on terrorism." Russia has also made a case for joining the Organization of Islamic States as an "observer"—in that 20 million Moslem live "peacefully and productively" in Russia, thus disproving the "clash of civilizations" thesis.[27] Fourthly, Moscow and Ankara have been attempting to find common accords in relation to the Caucasus, central Asia, as well as oil and trade.

It can furthermore be argued that Russia and the US appear to have accepted a tacit *quid pro quo* in respect to Russian intervention in Chechnya and US intervention in Iraq. Putin has conceded that Russian federal forces may have committed human rights violations in Chechnya, but he claims that these actions were not sanctioned by the top (as was not the case for US actions in Iraq in his view). Russia will also continue to transfer more authority to the pro-Moscow Chechen administration, and staff the police with Chechens in a staged withdrawal of some 80,000 Russian forces, much as the US is claiming to do the same in Iraq. Putin has also argued—in response to American criticism of his increasing "authoritarian" measures—that Russia will "democratize" at its own pace.

**Iraq**

The January 2005 electoral process in Iraq showed a significant turn out of Shiites and Kurdish voters, yet much more work must be done to achieve a stable "federal" government. The US intervention in Iraq has now largely alienated significant factions of both Sunnis and Shi'ites, and US policy has not entirely satisfied Kurdish factions who seek greater autonomy and who claim political control over the oil rich city of Kirkuk as part of their sector.

The continuing attacks by pan-Islamic partisans and former Ba'athists against those Iraqi police and military who dare work with the coalition forces and the Prime Minister Iyad Allawi's interim government, which has been racked with accusations of major corruption,[28] continue to destabilize the country. Sunni Arab Moslems, once placed in power by the British, now fear becoming a disenfranchised minority. Many did not vote in the 30 January 2005 elections, due to fears of violence within the so-called "Sunni triangle," but also in opposition to the "winner takes all" system that appeared to legitimize Shi'ite rule in an election process that is not regarded by all factions as entirely legitimate.

The Grand Ayatollah Ali al-Sistani, who had pressed Washington to support early elections, against the counsel of Iyad Allawi, created the new United Iraqi Alliance, which gained a majority of parliamentary seats. This group, which includes the pro-Iranian Supreme Council For the Islamic Revolution in Iraq (SCIRI) and the Shi'ite Al-Da'wah party, as well as representatives of radical Shi'ite cleric Moqtada al-Sadr and the ostensibly secular Iraqi National Congress (INC) of Ahmad Chalabi, who has been accused of exaggerating Iraq's WMD capability and manipulating US strategy through false intelligence. Lesser-known figures include independent Shi'ite leaders, as well as representatives of the Turkish-speaking Turkoman minority and the minority of Iraqi Kurds who are Shi'ite. The United Iraqi Alliance also includes representatives of one of Iraq's largest Sunni tribes, the Shammar, which extends from parts of the south of the country to Mosul in the north. The coalition thus consists of over two-thirds Shi'ites. In essence, al-Sistani has promised to secure sovereignty that is "full and unflawed in any of its political, economic, military or security aspects, as well as to strive to remove all the consequences of the occupation."[29]

The US-backed party of interim prime minister Iyad Allawi received only about 13 per cent in the elections for Iraq's 275–seat national assembly on 30 January 2005. The essentially Shi'ite coalition of the United Iraqi Alliance won some 48 per cent of the votes. The Kurdish Alliance gained around 26 per cent. Former UN weapons inspector Scott Ritter claimed that U.S. authorities in Iraq had manipulated the election results to reduce the percentage of the vote received by the United Iraqi Alliance from 56% to 48%, so that it would not obtain an absolute majority.[30] Yet even with such purported political manipulations, it will prove very difficult to prevent the new Iraqi government from pressing for policies that may go against US interests in respect to Iraq, oil, and the region. (See Chapter 1.) From a regional perspective, Riyadh fears that a victory of even moderate Shiites in Iraq will stimulate Shi'ite political movements in Saudi Arabia, Bahrain, and throughout the region, and indirectly strengthening the hands of Teheran.

**The Kurdish Question**

US intervention in Iraq has not-so-inadvertently opened the door to renewed Turkish conflict with the Kurdish PKK—in which Turkey has threatened to intervene against the latter if it continues to operate out of northern Iraq, along the Turkish border.[31] (Here, the PKK, now known as KONGRA-GEL, renewed fighting in June 2004 after a five-year unilateral truce.) Having fought with the PKK from 1984 until 1999, Ankara suspected the group as being supported by Syria, Iraq, Iran, and possibly Moscow. Now it suspects the Americans! (Turks complain that if the Americans do believe that the PKK is as bad as *al-Qaida*, then why don't they do anything about it!)

Kurdish nationalists have demanded that as many 200,000 Arabs (many Shi'ite Arabs, who had been relocated in the region by Saddam Hussein in accord with the latter's "Arabization" of the predominantly Kurdish region), be compelled to leave Kirkuk and those regions now controlled by the *peshmerga*, as tens of thousands of Kurdish refugees once forced out begin to return. The two main Kurdish parties, the Kurdistan Democratic Party (KDP) and the Patriotic Union of Turkey (PUK) want Kirkuk incorporated into an "enlarged autonomous" Kurdish region but have thus far opposed outright independence.

The proposal to include Kirkuk into an enlarged autonomous Kurdish region represents a demand similar to that made to Saddam Hussein when the latter had offered the Kurds a "comprehensive autonomy" plan in 1974. Failure to obtain major concessions from Saddam Hussein in respect to Kirkuk, among other demands, however, then led the KDP to split into two factions, the KDP and the PUK. This resulted in violent intra-Kurdish struggle in 1978–79, as well as intensified Iraqi efforts to repress the Kurds, which had been supported by the Shah of Iran, at least until the March 1975 Algiers agreement. The outbreak of the 1980–88 Iraq-Iran war resulted in another round of warfare and severe repression of the Kurds by Saddam Hussein, particularly after the KDP was seen as "spearheading" an Iranian thrust into northern Iraq.[32]

While relations between Kurds, Arabs and Iraqi Turkomen remain tense, some 40,000 Christians, among the wealthy elite of the country, have left for Syria and Lebanon. At the same time, roughly 100,000 Iraqis have returned to Iraq by 2004 after living in refugee camps in Iran. (Out of about 500,000 Iraqi refugees, roughly 200,000 were located in Iranian camps.) Turkey likewise fears that the Shi'ite victory in the January 2005 elections could lead Iraqi Kurds to solidify their semi-autonomous status in northern Iraq and encourage similar separatist developments in the Kurdish areas of Turkey. Iraqi Turkomen claim, for example, that Kurds were brought in from other areas to boost their votes in oil-rich Kirkuk against Turkomens and Arabs, in the January 2005 elections. Kurds counter that Saddam Hussein's "Arabization" program had forced Kurds to leave Kirkuk; the latter are presently returning to their original homes. How a relatively autonomous Kurdish region in Iraq, coupled with irredentist Kurdish claims, may affect Iraqi relations with Turkey, Iran and Syria remains to be seen.

**Pan-Islamic Strategy**

In the 1990s, the US had tolerated the Taliban (which harbored *al-Qaida* and other groups) in the hope that the latter would cooperate in bringing "stability" to the region, and, in turn, support US-backed multinational corporations to develop energy resources and oil pipelines in central Asia.[33] Ironically, while the US State Department did begin to express concern about the presence of *al-Qaida* on Afghan territory, following attacks in 1998 on the US embassies in Kenya and Tanzania, and then on the USS Cole in 2000, Afghanistan had not previously been put on the list of states sponsoring terrorism. This fact permitted US oil and construction companies to engage in business arrangements—despite the presence of bin Laden on Afghan territory since 1996 (moving from the Sudan).

After US military intervention in Afghanistan in October 2001 (only symbolically backed by both the UN and NATO), and following the rapid "defeat" of the Taliban by December 2001, the US attempted to work with each of the domestic Afghan factions, and with all the regional powers, including Russia, in the effort to reconstruct the country. Yet given the highly fractious nature of Afghan politics, bringing peace and development to the entire country will prove to be a long-term venture, primarily because aid and investment will not be forthcoming without strong commitment to political and military security. Much as was the case for ex-Yugoslavia, NATO has preferred to focus on peacekeeping and "security," and not in engaging in what it considers "police work" and in investigating drug production criminal activities. Moreover, NATO pressure on Pathan factions could destabilize northern Pakistan as well (see Chapter 5).

For the most part, *al-Qaida*, which was organized as a kind of veterans' organization for Afghan freedom fighters, appears to lack a truly popular base (except perhaps in northern Pakistan, some provinces in Saudi Arabia, and in much of Afghanistan). *Al-Qaida* partisans tend to be Saudis, Yemenis, Egyptians and Algerians (see Chapter 3), although a number of cells, or aligned groups, appear to be forming in Morocco, Egypt, Chechnya, as well as in Europe, largely in urban, immigrant districts. A Moroccan-based group, for example, attacked railway stations in Madrid on 11 March 2004, in an effort to impel Spain to withdraw its forces from Iraq. Spanish Prime Minister Jose Maria Aznar, who strongly supported the US intervention in Iraq, immediately tried to blame the Basque separatist group, *Euskadi Ta Askatasuna* ("Basque Fatherland and Liberty") or ETA, for the attacks, despite evidence that increasingly pointed to the Moroccan Islamic Combatant Group. The Spanish Socialist party then took office and withdrew Spanish peacekeepers from Iraq. (In addition to forcing coalition partners of the US to withdraw from Iraq, a more long-term strategy has been bin Laden's hope to return Andalusia to Muslim control, thus reversing the *Reconquista* of 1492!)

Despite their relatively small size, *al-Qaida* and aligned groups hope that forceful US, Israeli and/or Russian pressures and military actions will cause a backlash within states with predominantly Islamic populations, and thus create new enemies and antagonisms, in countries such as Pakistan (see Chapter 5), Saudi Arabia, Yemen, Jordan, Egypt, Morocco, as well as Afghanistan. It is hoped that US intervention in Iraq, military pressure on Syria, Iran and other Arab or Islamic states, the occupation of both Sunni and Shi'ite holy sites, Israeli repression of Palestinians, as well as Russian repression in Chechnya will all help fuel pan-Islamic movements within as many countries as possible. It is believed that these actions will help undermine or destabilize regimes that are seen as linked to the US—in order to ultimately form an Arab-Moslem *Ummah*, somewhat similar to that of the Ottoman empire. In this regard, inter-communal strife can serve the cause of anti-state organizations by opening the doors for "terrorist" recruitment, as was the case for Algeria from 1992 to 2002. (See Chapter 3.)

In Bosnia, Bosniac resistance to Serbian and Croatian "ethnic cleansing" in the 1990s obtained military support from both Shi'ite and Sunni countries. In Chechnya, a variety of groups, a few with links to *al-Qaida*, have resisted Russian intervention, and tried to widen the conflict to involve Dagestan and Georgia. Governments in Uzbekistan, Kazakhstan, Kyrgyzstan and Tajikistan likewise engaged in crackdowns on both peaceful dissent and militant pan-Islamic groups in 2004. China has continued to crack down in Xinjiang where the East Turkestan Islamic Movement (made up of Uighur Moslems) has been depicted a "terrorist" movement with links to bin Laden by Chinese authorities, as well as by the US.

Anti-state pan-Islamic movements have engaged in struggles in Indonesia which is the homeland of *Jemaah Islamiyah*, where significant anti-Western attacks have taken place in Bali and Jakarta. *Jemaah Islamiyah* seeks to create an "*Islam Nusantara*" that incorporates southern Thailand to Mindanao in the Philippines. Concurrently, at the beginning of 2005, the Indonesian government has attempted to engage in post-Tsunami peace negotiations with the Free Aceh Movement, which seeks secession. In Thailand *Jemaah Islamiyah* has also been seeking secession for the three southernmost provinces of Pattani, Yalla and Narathiwat. It is possible that Thailand agreed to deploy troops in Iraq in exchange for US assistance against pan-Islamic insurgents; yet the Thai House of Representatives then asked the troops return to Thailand to fight insurgents in the South. Along with the Philippines, Thailand obtained "major non-NATO ally status" in 2003 (as did Pakistan in 2004).[34] In February 2004, in an effort to co-opt less militant Moslems, Indonesia President Megawati denounced US policy as "unjust to Muslims." Pan-Islamic militants in Malaysia have tended to join the *Jemaah Islamiyah* movement based in Indonesia, while the Malaysian government itself has not supported what it sees as US policies directed "against" Moslems.

In the Philippines, government forces with US assistance have continued to engage in clashes in 2004–05 with the Moro Islamic Liberation Front (MILF) despite a seventeen-month truce; the government has also clashed with *Abu Sayyaf*, which split off from the MILF when the latter engaged in negotiations with the Philippine Government in 1991. While battling pan-Islamic militants, the Philippines has also been trying to engage in peace negotiations with the Communist Party's National People's Army (NPA). But here, however, as the US has labeled the political wing of the NPA, the National Democratic Front, as a terrorist organization, the NPA has threatened to continue its struggle.

In Africa, US forces have been reinforcing French controlled Djibouti in order to be in a better position to supervise the Horn of Africa. Kenya and Tanzania were the sites of US embassy bombings by *al-Qaida* in 1998. In January 2005, a brutal, decades long, conflict officially ended in the Sudan (which once housed *al-Qaida*, as well as Palestinian and Iranian militants). Genocide charges against the government have been "dropped"—but Darfur province remains in turmoil. This conflict between nomadic Arabic tribes of the north and essentially sedentary African tribes of the south was, to large extent, caused by mal-distribution of oil profits, scarce resources and water. China and India have both backed the Sudanese government, in order to maintain access to its southern oil fields.

The Moslem-Christian question is likewise in the background of continuing civil conflict in Ivory Coast, where some 27% of the Ivorian population is Moslem, but immigration has pushed the figure to over 50%. This fact led to the policy of "Ivorization" (which led to the political exclusion of those who were not born in Ivory Coast, which in turn led to inter-communal violence, and reluctant French intervention.) Ivory Coast, of course, was once depicted as the prime example in the 1980s of a "successful" developing country, along with Sri Lanka. Somewhat similarly, inter-communal tensions in Nigeria, which is 50% Moslem, and which has been plagued by corruption related to its petroleum industry, sparked rioting in the Islamic region of the north in 2003. Nigeria is expected to supply some 25% of US oil needs in the future.

Pan-Islamic proponents believe that a number of the above states may be impelled to shift sides against the US, or else their weak leaderships will simply lose control over their increasingly radicalized populations. New alliances of pan-Islamic forces (the Majlis-e-Amal MMA), for example, have hoped to overthrow the pro-US government of General Pervez Musharraf (though democratic opposition in elections or else by assassination) in order to forge a pan-Islamic theocratic state with nuclear weapons. (There were two assassination attempts on Musharraf in December 2003.) Another possibility is that pan-Islamic groups might lead a secession crisis in the north of Pakistan. (See Chapter 5.)

Bin Laden's goal in Iraq is to force the US out, but groups linked to *al-Qaida* may be divided between those who seek to re-establish Sunni leadership and foster civil war and those who seek to build a Sunni-Shi'a alliance. In Saudi Arabia, *al-Qaida* may be seeking to discredit the regime, rather than overthrow it. This is true in fear that if the regime becomes too instable, the US will occupy the oil fields.[35] There is also the fear that Shi'ite movements in the oil rich eastern provinces might demand secession.[36] In 2004, Saudi incentives to engage in greater reform measures and government accountability—which is really the key to offset further radicalization—appear minimal due to the rise of oil prices since the Iraq war. In seeking to crack down on militants aligned with *al-Qaida*, particularly since the beginning of the Iraq war in March 2003, the Saudi government succeeded in killing one of the major ringleaders in March 2004, yet it arrested a number of major reformists that same month.[37]

It is furthermore possible that *al-Qaida*, or another group, may attempt another major strike against the US, or other high profile targets, to demonstrate its resolve, and "prove" that it is not yet defeated.

**"Outposts of Tyranny"**

In some ways, Zimbabwe, designated one of the outposts of tyranny, represents South Africa's version of Russia's Belarus. A potentially wealthy state, Zimbabwe has the highest percentage in Africa of people fed by international aid—even though it once exported food. Once his eastern European style system of economics failed to spark growth, Mugabe turned to the World Bank for assistance in 1991, but market-oriented reforms were not implemented adequately. In 1997, he then adopted a limited land acquisition program that deteriorated into land seizures in 2000 and then the expropriation of predominantly white-owned commercial firms. The country has suffered from fuel shortages since 1999, as well as high inflation. Mugabe, once regarded as a "progressive" Socialist leader (despite his use of North Korean trained troops to crack down on the opposition party, Patriotic Front- Zimbabwe African People Union) has resurrected laws once used in Ian Smith's Rhodesia to pass repressive legislation and manipulate public opinion in order to sustain his ZANU party in power for as long as possible. He plans to stay in power into 2008. Manipulating youth militias, party activists, and war veterans, Mugabe has attempted to "terrorize" the press, civil society and the opposition political party, the Movement for Democratic Change (MDC). Continued political-economic instability in the potentially wealthy state of Zimbabwe adds just another dimension to sub-Saharan Africa's growing list of crises in terms of dire poverty, AIDS, and conflicts over oil and diamonds and other precious raw materials.

**Latin America and the Caribbean**

State Department reports indicate that for both the years 2000 and 2001 the majority of "terrorist" attacks did not occur in the Middle East, but in Columbia. There were 178 attacks against the Cano-Limon oil pipeline in Colombia by both Columbian Revolutionary Armed Forces (FARC) and its rival, the National Liberation Army (ELN). These actions "constituted 51 percent" of the total number of attacks in the year 2001; there were 152 pipeline bombings in Colombia, which accounted for 40 percent of the attacks in the year 2000. Here, however, the State Department made little distinction between acts of "terrorism" and acts of "sabotage." Columbian paramilitaries, such as the United Self Defense Forces of Columbia (AUC), allegedly backed by state authorities, have also been accused of equally severe human rights violations as have the "narco-terrorists" that they are fighting.[38]

Elected in May 2002, President Álvaro Uribe intensified the war on drugs and on "terrorism" with US assistance under "Plan Columbia", after the previous President Andrés Pastrana, was unable to achieve a negotiated solution to the conflict with the FARC. The latter, along with state-linked paramilitary forces of the United Self Defense Forces of Columbia (AUC), produce some 80 per cent of the world's cocaine while the ELN is responsible for a large proportion of about 3,000 kidnappings every year in Columbia. Four years of peace efforts under the Pastrana presidency, which included the granting of a large demilitarized zone to the FARC, ended in failure. There has furthermore been a risk of widening the conflict: As the irregular forces of the AUC and Colombia's military and police grow in power, armed groups from the ELN and FARC (which engaged in heavy clashes with government forces in February 2005) have passed into Venezuela and Ecuador and engaged in drug trafficking and hostage taking. The latter states, along with Columbia, are major oil suppliers to the US. Venezuela has been attempting to diversify its oil market, looking to oil and gas deals with China, and hopes to create an oil pipeline to Columbia for export to Asia. The US has accused Venezuela of supporting the FARC, while the populist Venezuelan President Hugo Chavez has accused the US of trying to destabilize his government and of plotting his assassination. Brazil, Cuba, and Peru have sought to defuse tensions.[39]

It has been harder for the US government to recognize government in Cuba than that of Vietnam, even though the US never fought a *direct* conflict with Fidel Castro, who was initially financed by US sources before turning against American interests by expropriating American-owned corporations without compensation. President Kennedy's blockade was largely responsible for turning Castro to the Soviet Union; and Cuba served as a generally pro-Soviet gendarme in support of Soviet backed movements in Central America and Africa throughout the Cold War. Following Soviet collapse, however, Yeltsin began to retract Russian assistance to the island; Vladimir Putin finally abandoned the Soviet installed electronic listening post at Lourdes in October 2003 (to the anger of Russian ultra-nationalists and the increasingly nationalist members of the Russian Communist Party). Tentative steps toward recognition of the Cuban government took place under Bill Clinton (but were checked, however, by the Elian Gonzales affair). The first term Bush administration clamped down on efforts to lift sanctions (and in opposition to European trade and diplomatic ties with Cuba in accord with the 1996 Helms Burton Act) just after former President Jimmy Carter gave a speech in May 2002 urging the end of sanctions if Castro restored human rights and civil liberties. Castro then imprisoned 75 peaceful political dissenters, giving them 6 to 28 year sentences. Following the latter crackdown, the EU likewise imposed sanctions in 2003. In January 2005, EU foreign ministers temporarily suspended those sanctions (to be reviewed in July), citing the need for constructive dialogue with the Cuban authorities in respect to civil liberties and human rights.

In response, the second term Bush administration, which labeled Cuba as one of the "outposts of tyranny,"[40] expressed concern that the end of EU sanctions would "embolden regime hard-liners and dishearten the peaceful opposition."

**The Middle East**

Part of the reason for the US-EU split over Iraq was a question of strategy. Prior to Iraq war, the question was that of "sequencing." Should one press for a Palestinian-Israeli peace agreement first, and then worry about Iraq—or intervene in Iraq first?

In general, Europeans sought a peace settlement in the Middle East first; the Bush administration promised a vaguely defined peace settlement through the Road Map for Peace, but opted for intervention in Iraq first. Yet given the initial outbreak of violence in Palestine and the wave of suicide bombings that followed the elimination of Saddam Hussein, it appears that US military intervention in Iraq in March 2003 did not ameliorate the situation. On the contrary, it initially emboldened Israel to engage in its own "preemptive strikes" against leaders accused of supporting "terrorism"—resulting in the assassinations of Sheikh Yassin and Hamas leader Abdel Aziz al-Rantissi, for example, in early 2004. At this point, Israel disagreed with at least fifteen points of the Road Map for Peace. From this perspective, it appears that Saddam Hussein, who had provided compensation for the families of "martyrs," and supported various Palestinian terrorist groups, appeared more as an external pretext to block Israeli-Palestinian reconciliation, than the actual cause of the conflict. Instead, it was the death of Yassir Arafat in November 2004 that has apparently provided the real impetus to break the dynamics of terrorism and counter-terrorism.

Newly elected Palestinian President Mahmoud Abbas obtained US and general international support upon the basis that he had opposed the "militarization of the intifada."[41] The death of Yassir Arafat, however, may have opened up a "power vacuum" within the Palestinian Authority, which, hopefully, will not spark a succession struggle that will pit Islamic Jihad and Hamas (who did not participate in the elections) against the more moderate factions of the PLO and *al-Fatah*. After an initial Israeli boycott of discussions with the new president Mahmoud Abbas, the two sides went back to negotiations once Abbas promised to control militant factions, and regain control of northern Gaza by deploying 2000 Palestinian security forces.

As the Palestinians began to show themselves ready to negotiate, Israeli Prime Minister Ariel Sharon found himself having to negotiate with the Labor Party in order to counter hard-line Likud opposition to his measures of unilateral withdrawal from Gaza. In order to remain on the Road Map to Peace, Israel will ultimately need to deal with the more complex issue of withdrawing the less prominent settlements from the West Bank, all the while containing the wrath of Israeli "colonists" who refuse to dismantle settlements in Gaza and the West Bank. Here, questions of the Palestinian "right to return" and joint controls over Jerusalem will remain open. In late January 2005, Sharon was quoted as believing a "historic breakthrough" was possible. At the same time, the Israeli approach has been *unilateral*, while the Palestinians seek a more comprehensive accord.[42]

From a regional perspective, Israel has instituted a new defense relationship with India (to check Pakistan), in addition to forging a close alliance with Turkey. Here, it appears Israel hopes to form a counter alliance against Iran, as well as against a Saudi-Pakistani connection, while Iran looks back to Russia and China for security supports. Concurrently, Israel may also supporting Kurdish partisans in Syria and in Iran in order to check the formation of a Syrian-Iranian alliance in support of Palestinians, as Israel begins to pull out of Gaza and potentially the West Bank (and as Syria pulls out of Lebanon). By operating out of Iraqi Kurdistan, Israel may also hope to keep a foothold in a highly instable Iraq (and to counter a pro-Shi'a, potentially pro-Iranian, government)—a factor seen as potentially upsetting Turkey, and undermining the Turkish-Israeli alliance.[43]

The possibility of fulfilling the Road Map to Peace (which may ultimately require long term peacekeeping of NATO, European and Russian forces under a general UN mandate) remains open. The question of a politically instable Syria (coupled with US accusations that Syria is assisting terrorist factions in Iraq and Lebanon), as well as the question of Iranian nuclear and missile program (see Chapter 4), means the route is not at all clear of landmines. It is possible that the assassination of the former prime minister of Lebanon, Rafic Hariri, in February 2005, was intended to set off a crisis between Syria, Lebanon, the US and Israel, particularly at the time that the Israelis and Palestinians had initiated negotiations.

As a sign of the "new multilateralism" promised by the Bush administration in January 2005, the US immediately began working with France, in particular, in the UNSC to pressure Syria to block its borders from terrorist infiltration into Iraq, and to withdraw from Lebanon, and to cease its support for *Hizb'allah*. The US has regarded the latter as a terrorist group, and has tried to press the EU to accept the same appellation. Yet the withdrawal of 14,000 troops Syrian troops and intelligence operatives could come at the cost of US recognition of the influential role of *Hizb'allah* in Lebanese politics. (*Hizb'allah* forces are stronger than those of the Lebanese army and increasingly backed by Iran as leverage against the US and Israel.)[44] Alternatively, withdrawal may risk destabilizing Syria, which is heavily dependent on the dynamic Lebanese economy—and Lebanon with it.

### China, India, Pakistan

US relations were largely frozen with India and Pakistan following the atomic testing by both countries in 1998. Yet after the events of 11 September, the US opened the doors to both countries. Since early 2002, the US and India have held numerous joint exercises involving all military branches; the US (and Israel as well) have also begun to sell advanced weaponry to India. While some analysts have called for India to serve as a counterweight to China, US-Indian strategy has diverged on a number of key issues, including India's role in the Persian Gulf and central Asia, approaches to countering terrorism, a potential U.S. role in resolving the India-Pakistan dispute, as well as the purpose of the Indian nuclear program.[45]

Following its intervention in Iraq, the US began to push for India-Pakistani reconciliation, as pressed for by Colin Powell in late March 2003. India, however, publicly denounced American meddling in its affairs and sent mixed signals to Pakistan. On the one hand, New Delhi threatened the possibility of a pre-emptive strike against Pakistani nuclear facilities; on the other, it opened up the possibility of talks over Kashmir. These included plans for a "peace" pipeline that could bring natural gas from Iran through Pakistan to India to fulfill burgeoning demand for energy. Another option includes Turkmenistan-Afghan-Pakistani pipeline, which would reach India, if it does not become a "pipe dream" due to security threats. If implemented, these oil pipelines could assist Indian-Pakistani reconciliation— although both states have proposed separate pipelines to Iran as well. Other options include north-south energy links to Russia, which would most likely disregard

Pakistan.[46] By contrast, the US has frowned upon closer Indian links to Iran and hopes to create a Silk Road pipeline through Baku, Tbilisi and Ceyhan.

At the same time that it develops a nuclear and missile capability, New Delhi, like Beijing, is expanding its naval outreach with the acquisition of a blue water navy. In January 2004, it signed a contract for Russia's Admiral Gorshkov carrier with of wing of MiG–29s.[47] India's army and air force is twice the size of Pakistan's, while its navy is second to that of the United States in the India Ocean. New Delhi has been seeking closer ties with Malaysia, Singapore, Thailand, Vietnam and South Korea (and possibly Japan) to counterbalance China's close ties to Pakistan and Burma/Myanmar. Beijing and New Delhi appear to be competing for control of the Andaman Sea on the west coast of Burma/Myanmar leading to the chokepoint at the Strait of Malacca. Indian strategy seeks to develop Myanmar oil reserves, gain access to the burgeoning markets of southeast Asia, to balance the influence of China and counter "terrorist" groups that have been operating in northeast India from Burma/Myanmar.

The Russian Federation under Boris Yeltsin had largely backed India's position on Kashmir; Vladimir Putin seems to be engaging Pakistan as well, but still tilting toward India. Moscow has been attempting to nudge China to resolve its border conflicts with India. Here, Russia, India and China all share common interests in respect for the principles of "state sovereignty" and "non-intervention" in separatist movements in Chechnya, Kashmir, Xinjiang, Tibet and Taiwan. China and India are to engage in talks over approximately 20 percent of Kashmir, presently held by China—after Pakistan's decision to cede a portion of the Kashmir and the Aksai Chin Ladakh regions to China in 1964. India continues to holds Jammu and Kashmir at the Line of Control. China also claims large parts of the northeastern Indian states of Sikkim and Arunachal Pradesh and deploys nuclear weapons in Tibet (once a "buffer" between India and China before the 1950 Chinese invasion). In effect, both Russia and China fear a radicalization of the situation in which both India and Pakistan might continue to engage in intermittent border clashes over Kashmir, possibly involving tactical nuclear weaponry. Further destabilization of the region could loosen China's grips over Xinjiang and Tibet—which historically have been claimed by India, and could possibly draw in China, as well as Russia on opposing sides.

**Japan and China**

In its December 2004 National Defense Program, Japan for the first time identified China as a potential security threat. Tensions have begun to mount over the possibility of conflict over oil and natural resources in their self proclaimed Exclusive Economic Zones in the disputed East China Sea, over the status of the Senkaku or Diaoyu islands, as well as over open Japanese support for the US if China should attempt to prevent Taiwanese secession by force. The fact that no peace treaty has been signed between Russia and Japan, and China and Japan, has meant that World War II never officially ended in Asia. North and South Korea have never signed an armistice either, thus adding to the uncertainty.

As a sign of increasing tensions, China and Japan confronted one another in November 2004 when Chinese nuclear-powered submarine moved into Japanese waters off the Okinawa islands. These kind of tensions have led Tokyo to change the laws governing the Japanese Self-Defense Force (JSDF) to give it an expanded role. The JSDF has recently engaged in non-combat and logistical support operations, such as providing medical support and provisions to U.S. forces. Despite popular opposition, the JSDF contributed peacekeepers to Iraq, probably to gain US support for Japanese defense and for Ballistic Missile Defenses (BMD).

Japan has consequently looked to Washington following Pyongyang's test firing of a long range Taepodong missile directly over northern Japan in 1998. North Korea did sign a moratorium on long-range missile testing in 1999—but has nonetheless threatened to engage in additional testing. Tokyo has accordingly enhanced defense spending and agreed to BMD cooperation with the US, after a review of the legal implications of its self-defense laws. Tokyo plans to develop a $6.5 BMD system, to be deployed between 2007 and 2011. Japanese politicians in the Diet had openly debated the constitutionality of unilateral pre-emptive strikes and the need for a counter-strike capability. At the same time, critics have feared that the development of BMD (which can be used either offensively or defensively) may further antagonize China and North Korea, as these systems could be combined with the development and deployment of American (and Japanese) offensive weapons systems. Yet, putting an end to the politics of "ambiguity" in December 2004, Tokyo and Washington openly announced their joint decision to coordinate their positions in the defense of Taiwan.

Here, Japan has accordingly been tightening its alliance with the US in opposition to potential ballistic missile threats from China and North Korea (despite China's efforts to mediate between the two Koreas)—at the same time that Tokyo hopes to deflect Moscow from supporting Beijing too strongly. On the one hand, Japan is concerned with greater Russian military assistance to Beijing and of a more assertive China. On the other hand, Japan needs Russian oil and gas to lessen its dependence upon the Middle East/Persian Gulf. Concurrently, Russia needs Japanese financing to help develop Sakhalin island and the Far East—also eyed by China which is rumored to support illegal immigration into the region.

Yet, despite some mutual Russo-Japanese interests, Japan continues to claim the Kurile islands (what the Japanese call the Northern territories) that were seized by the Soviet Union before the dropping of the atomic bombs on Hiroshima and Nagasaki by the US. Japanese demands have thus far been opposed by Moscow despite previous discussions with Khrushchev, Brezhnev, Gorbachev, Yeltsin, as well as Putin. On the one hand, Moscow hopes to obtain greater trade and aid from Tokyo; on the other, it fears giving up access to deep Pacific water for its submarine fleet for fear that Washington could use these islands to track its submarine movements. Despite a willingness to engage, Moscow also does not want to set any precedent for giving up remaining Russian territory following Soviet disaggregation. Talks in December 2004 between Russia and Japan ended in deadlock, as Russia would agree to give up only two, but not all four islands, in accord with the 1956 Japan-Soviet declaration. Russian commentators believe that US support for the return of all four Kuriles is selective—in that the US does not support Tokyo's claims against Beijing and Taipei for the Senkaku islands, nor does it support Tokyo's claims against Korea in respect to the Tokto Islands.[48]

In addition to seeking a new relationship with Russia, Japan could possibly link with India as a potential counterpoise to Beijing. Here, Japan has largely attempted to "balance" relations with both India and Pakistan in supporting the efforts of both parties to improve relations in late 2003. Tokyo, however, could tilt even closer to India, should its relations with China continue to deteriorate. The rise of China as a significant military and naval power; Russian military backing for a stronger China; the fears of possible US disengagement from the Asian-Pacific, China's claims to Taiwan and to the Spratly islands in the oil rich South China sea, all represent factors that bring Japan and India closer together. This is particularly true as India's navy can provide a counterweight to that of China and thus protect Japan's sea lines of communication (SLOC) to the South China sea.[49]

Both India and Japan appear to be taking countermeasures to China's burgeoning political-economic and naval influence. Concurrently, Moscow appears to be trying to bring China and India into closer cooperation—although it might prefer to deal with a wealthier Japan than with China. At the same time, Washington has been reticent to encourage closer Russo-Japanese relations.

**The Two Koreas**

Following US intervention in Iraq in 2003, the North Korean government stated that "The Iraqi war teaches a lesson that in order to prevent a war and defend the security of a country and the sovereignty of a nation, it is necessary to have a powerful physical deterrent."[50] On 10 February 2005, North Korea declared itself a nuclear power and pulled out of the six-nation talks that had been initiated by the US to persuade Pyongyang to give up its nuclear program. This opened the question as to whether the UN would apply sanctions—or whether the US might intervene militarily. (See Chapter 5.)

The South Korean unification minister, Chung Dong-young, stated that it was too soon to declare North Korea a "nuclear power," arguing that the country may be bluffing.[51] Despite the fact that some 6 million North Koreans depend upon international food assistance (particularly from China), North Korea's believes it can resist sanctions through its basic policies of "Juche" (self-reliance) and "Songun" ("army-first policy"). The presumed ability of North Korea to launch a devastating conventional force counter-strike on South Korea represents a major factor in deterring "pre-emptive" strikes by the US.

Despite fears of the North, South Korea had not been entirely convinced that Bush administration policy has worked in its best interests. In the 1980s and 1990s, South Korea's irenic "sunshine" policy opened the door to a rapprochement with North Korea. The model of German unification initially provided an inspiration, but a similar "buy out" seemed unworkable; another option considered was that of a new form of North-South "confederation." The 2005 budget presented to South Korea's National Assembly on 31 January 2005 increased allocations for cooperation with Pyongyang by more than fifty per cent.[52]

It is argued that six power talks are important, but not sufficient to bring North Korea back to the table. China and Japan, as well as the EU, can supply financial assistance and trade benefits; Russia can provide diplomatic and security assurances for North Korea. China has sought to prevent North Korea from antagonizing both Japan and the US, but fears pressuring its ally too strongly. It sees the North Korean economy progressing slowly, but likewise fears that the country might collapse, resulting in a humanitarian crisis, if pressured too strongly. At the same time, Beijing opposes a German-style unification. This, it fears, would raise the possibility that US troops might appear north of the Yalu—much as has been the case in respect to NATO enlargement to the Russian border, thus negating China's reasons for defending North Korea in the 1950 Korean war.

Critics furthermore believe that BMD (developed by Japan in cooperation with the US) has worked to upset the on-going inter-Korean détente. Critics have likewise feared that the deployment of BMD would lead American troops to withdraw from South Korea. This fear appeared to be actualized in 2004, when the Pentagon announced that it would downsize its forces (withdrawing 7,500 of its 32,500 troops)—raising questions as to whether the US military presence would still provide a tripwire to support South Korea in case of North Korean attack. The Pentagon appears to be redirecting its mission toward responding to terrorism and projecting force in the region in order to deter and counterbalance Beijing. This strategy, however, could result in a loss of American influence in the region and a strengthening of China's influence on South Korea.[53]

Bush administration rhetoric and support for "regime change," coupled with the fact that the South Korean military still label North Korea as the "main enemy," has thus far appeared undermine the possibility North-South cooperation. Caught between a rising China, with close trade links to South Korea, a potentially militarizing Japan, and an instable North Korea, Seoul may be impelled to either shift closer to Washington, or else develop its own high-tech military capabilities, including a nuclear option, to achieve a measure of strategic independence. Seoul appears to be engaged in difficult three-fold juggling act: (1) seek detente with Pyongyang; (2) move toward military self-sufficiency; (3) while maintaining, if not deepening, its alliance with Washington.[54]

## Asia and the Rise of China

Following years of secret and overt American assistance to China (following the Kissinger-Nixon opening to China), Bejing has begun to try to break out of its perceived U.S.-Russian "double containment." On the one hand, China has, in a geohistorical sense, felt "contained" by the "unequal treaties" signed with Russia since the late 18th century; on the other hand, it has also felt "contained" by continued post-1949 American support for Taiwan.

The Sino-Soviet rapprochement has strengthened since Gorbachev, and has led to an increasingly close strategic partnership with Russia in the post-Cold War period. In 2001, Russia and China signed a Treaty of Good Neighborliness, Friendship, and Cooperation; on 14 October 2004 they signed a Supplementary Agreement on the Eastern Section of the China-Russia Boundary Line, which has appeared to resolve issues regarding their 4,300 km frontier. China and Russia have augmented defense and aerospace cooperation, which, along with Ukrainian arms and military-technology sales, plus nuclear secrets acquired from the US, could greatly enhance China's military technological capabilities.

Closer Sino-Russian military ties appear designed to threaten the possibility of a Sino-Russian alliance in which Russia might possibly back Beijing's claims to Taiwan, which, according to the 2004 Chinese White Paper, represents a major "threat" in that it appears to be moving toward greater "independence." Second, a close Russian-Chinese defense relationship also seems to be directed at both the US/NATO and EU. It represents a form of strategic leverage intended to block a perceived NATO-EU effort to draw Ukraine away from its present neutrality and balancing act between east and west. Third, it seems aimed at Franco-German efforts to permit the sale of European arms to China, which could open a new EU-Chinese security relationship. In essence, the Russians seek to prevent a Sino-EU-American "encirclement" (and thus deflect Chinese claims away from central and northeast Asia and toward the Asian littoral) while China hopes to block the formation of a US-EU-Russian-Japanese alliance.

In February 2004, the EU announced that it would lift the arms embargo of China, after formulating a general "code of conduct" to regulate future arms sales to China. The US has thus far opposed lifting of arms sales to Taiwan citing human rights concerns remaining since the 1989 Tiananmen Square repression coupled by continuing threats to Taiwan. In that same month, however, the US renewed military to military talks that had been cut off in 2001 when Chinese F-8 fighter jet tipped into a slow flying U.S. EP-3E Aries surveillance aircraft, which was then forced into an emergency landing on the Chinese island of Hainan, where its equipment was stripped and reverse engineered.

China has become a net importer of oil. The fact that much of its oil supply comes from the Middle East means that it needs to diversify its supplies. Beijing is thus looking for oil reserves or investment and development projects in Canada, Venezuela, Brazil, Ecuador, Iran, Saudi Arabia, Angola, Sudan (and previously Iraq), as well as in Russia, with subsidized capital from government institutions. It is accordingly not surprising that increasing Russian-Chinese defense collaboration may include a Chinese share of 20% of Yukos (according to the Russian Energy Ministry). Yukos, the second largest Russian oil company, is facing bankruptcy, and wants to become a significant supplier to China through a major oil pipeline. Both Japan and China seek Russian oil deals.[55]

According to an internal report prepared for Defense Secretary Donald H. Rumsfeld. "China is building strategic relationships along the sea lanes from the Middle East to the South China Sea in ways that suggest defensive and offensive positioning to protect China's energy interests, but also to serve broad security objectives."[56] It is building a new naval base at the Pakistani port of Gwadar, which can monitor ship traffic through the Strait of Hormuz and the Arabian Sea, and is "seeking much more extensive naval and commercial access" in Bangladesh. China is upgrading its ability to "project air and sea power" from the mainland and Hainan Island. China is also looking at the possibility of pipelines that would traverse Pakistan, Bangladesh or Thailand, but mostly likely Myanmar/Burma—as part of its "string of pearls" strategy to bypass the narrow Straits of Malacca, and also seen as a strategy intended to encircle India.[57]

More importantly, Beijing has established a military alliance with Myanmar/Burma, one of the "outposts of tyranny." (Interestingly, Burma is to take the ASEAN chair in 2006). China maintains monitoring station on islets belonging to Myanmar/Burma in the Bay of Bengal, close to the Strait of Malacca, through which 80 percent of China's imported oil passes. The Straits handle between one-fifth and one quarter of the world's sea trade and half of all the world's oil shipments. Oil-tanker traffic through the Malacca Strait, increasingly a focus of piracy and terrorist activities since 2000 (an estimated 40 per cent of the world's piracy), is projected to grow from 10 million barrels a day in 2002 to 20 million barrels a day by 2020. China believes the US military would attempt to disrupt China's energy imports in case of conflict over Taiwan; particularly following the Iraq war, Beijing regards the US as unpredictable and seeking to "encircle" China.

On the positive side, cooperation against piracy, drug smuggling, and possibly "terrorism," for example, could help to bring China, Japan, India, Indonesia, Malaysia, Singapore and South Korea into mutually cooperative relations. On the negative side, China is embroiled in disputes with Malaysia, the Philippines, Taiwan, Vietnam, and Brunei over control of the Spratly (Nansha) and Paracel Islands, as well as with Indonesia over the Natuna archipelago, which has some of the largest gas reserves in the world. China, together with Taiwan, has asserted its claims to the Senkakus (Diaoyu Tai), controlled by Japan.[58]

Chinese-Taiwanese relations turned for the worse in April 2001 when George Bush, Jr. had approved the sale of the largest arms package to Taiwan since 1992; relations turned sour once again, when Taiwanese President Chen Shui-bian announced in September 2003 that he wanted a new constitution drafted by 2006, to be passed by referendum and then enacted by 2008. Chen then announced that he would hold a referendum in conjunction with the presidential election on 20 March 2004. The referendum asked Taiwanese whether Taipei should bolster its defense capabilities if China refused to remove the ballistic missiles aimed at Taiwan and renounce the use of force, and whether there was support for a negotiated "peace and stability" framework. While the US tried to downplay the referendum issue, it did attempt to pressure Beijing to reduce its missile deployments. Concurrently, President Chen appeared to flip-flop on the question as to whether he would seek "independence" if re-elected.[59]

In a sign of a potentially burgeoning EU "Red Eiffel Tower" alliance with China, French President Jacques Chirac bluntly stated at a banquet in honor of visiting Chinese President Hu Jintao on 26 January 2004 (when the Eiffel Tower glowed red in welcoming Chinese guests) that the referendum plan was "a grave error." France has claimed that it will somehow moderate Beijing's aims in respect to Taiwan, but it is unclear how the sales of selected arms and Airbus passenger planes will be able to alter Chinese determination to absorb Taipei.

Taiwanese analysts see the Chinese as engaging in a "sweet and sour" policy, by attempting to speak softly to Japan, the EU and the US to gain their trust, then putting pressure on Taiwan to unify. Taiwanese analysts argue that the mainland believes that time is on its side, although circumstances might impel it to intervene sooner than later. China has consequently reserved the "right" to use force, if need be. Chinese objectives appear to be: (1) prevent the Taiwanese "independence" movement from instigating new movements of secession within the People's Republic; (2) to eliminate Taiwan's export competition with China; (3) to assert control over the Spratly islands and other off-shore oil reserves; (4) to eliminate a potential strategic-military threat from the island and to be in a better position to defend China from potential rivals. Chinese threats to control Taiwan militarily furthermore represent a challenge to sea lines of communication and oil routes to Japan from the Persian Gulf. These factors have put pressure on Washington to engage in defense talks.[60]

By 2005, China stated that it would augment its publicly stated defense spending; with great media attention, its National People's Assembly then passed an "anti-secession" law designed to threaten Taiwan and check the US-Japanese defense measures in support of Taipei—in a façade of democracy designed to co-opt domestic support. While the US considered the law "unfortunate," Russia stated that the matter was a domestic Chinese concern. Pakistan (and Syria) supported the law as well. Japan and the EU appeared concerned that the law could legitimize the use of force; it was feared that the outbreak of conflict between China and Taiwan would force both Japan and Australia to chose between their alliance obligations with the US and their effort to make peace with China.[61]

With as many as five hundred IRBMs targeting Taiwan, Beijing has warned that it will increase its nuclear arsenal ten times from roughly 16–20 inter-continental ballistic missiles (ICBMs) to 200–250 ICBMs—if the US persists with the deployment of ballistic missile defenses to protect the island. Beijing's overinflated economy, undervalued currency, heavy oil consumption and importation, high internal debt, imbalanced population (a much higher proportion of males), and a fixation on Taiwan, does not augur well for the future...

**Emergence of New Regional Actors and Potential Political Economic Blocs**

The break down of the bipolar world has led to the emergence of potential regional powers with highly uneven political, economic and military capabilities and goals. In essence, rather than re-nationalizing industries, rival regional powers are attempting to integrate into new political and economic blocs. In the assumption that numerous geopolitical disputes do not get in the way, a number of new political-economic power blocs could emerge that will continue to challenge American interests well into the future.

The US has reached out to fill the security "void" created in the aftermath of Soviet collapse through NATO enlargement, it likewise sought to expand economically through NAFTA and support for "democratic globalism" through imperialist measures, culminating in its intervention in Iraq, which not only sought to preclude WMD, but also Russian, Chinese (and European) oil investments and linkages. The US appears to be countering Russian links to China through trade and alliance ties to Japan and increasingly with India, which is rising as a military and economic power in South Asia. Since the 1980s New Delhi has been engaging in market-oriented reforms and has a growing middle class and consumer society, despite its massive poverty. India has a highly developed information technology and computer center in Bangalore, which has been dubbed the world's second Silicon Valley, and is becoming a major region for the outsourcing of American jobs, but which is also outsourcing to the US!

Following Soviet collapse in August-December 1991, the Maastricht treaty formed the European Union in February 1992; the Single European market entered into force in 1993. The EU immediately began to incorporate Sweden, Austria and Finland, and then considered Poland, among other former Soviet bloc states, as full members. In turn, the United States formed its own economic bloc, the North American Free Trade Association in 1994 (bringing in Canada and Mexico), while concurrently seeking to expand NATO into eastern Europe, first drawing in Poland, the Czech Republic and Hungary by 1999, as means to counterbalance and check European enlargement. In a largely uncoordinated US-EU "double enlargement," more in rivalry than cooperation, the EU and NATO then began to expand deep into eastern Europe by 2004, reaching to the Russian, Belarusian and Ukrainian borders. The EU likewise expanded toward the Mediterranean to Malta and Cyprus, and began to seriously consider Turkey's membership in 2004.

By 2004, after years of discussion, Russia, Belarus, Kazakhstan, and Ukraine formed a trade bloc among the Commonwealth of Independent States (CIS), a loose affiliation of the former Soviet Republics that incorporates roughly 219 million people. In addition, Russia, Belarus, Kazakhstan, and Tajikistan all hope for simultaneous admission to the World Trade Organization (WTO). Russia has dropped its geo-strategic outreach in Cuba and Vietnam, but appears to be returning to the Middle East/Persian Gulf for trade and arms sales, as well as to countries such as Venezuela. It likewise appears to be looking toward India, Turkey and China. It is thus possible that Russia, Ukraine and Turkey, which already engage in bilateral Turkish-Russian economic co-operation and the BSEC (Black Sea Economic Co-operation), could form a free economic zone in the coming years. Russia is presently Turkey's second biggest trade partner, and could soon move to first place. Bilateral trade volume in 2004 was estimated at US$10 billion could expand to US$25 billion by 2007.[62] This trade could possibly rise even more once (and if) Russian and central Asian natural gas starts to flow to Turkey and Turkish consumer goods enter Russian markets. Turkey is likewise looking to enter the EU, but is more likely to obtain a special partnership, perhaps leaving it to seek closer ties with Ukraine and Russia, assuming geopolitical disputes over the Caucasus and elsewhere do not upset this new relationship.

While a Russian-Ukrainian-Turkish combo, perhaps linked to China's burgeoning economic potential (assuming the latter does not overheat) represents a not-so-long term chimera, the US-crafted NAFTA has been increasingly challenged by trade between the EU and Asia in general, at the same time that Russia and China appear to be moving closer together in terms of oil, aerospace and weapons deals. China and ASEAN (Association of Southeast Asian Nations) have reached a basic agreement that could create the world's largest trade zone beginning in 2010 and then form a European-style single market in 2020. This would put together 1.7 billion consumers with a combined gross domestic product of 2 trillion dollars. But ASEAN seeks to accommodate China (which signed ASEAN's Treaty of Amity of Friendship and Cooperation in 2003) without being inundated by it; to prevent China from gaining regional predominance it hopes to sustain its links with the US-Japanese alliance.

Russia and Japan have thus far been unable to reach agreements over the Kurile/Northern territories, which in turn could open greater Japanese investment in the Russian far east. Tokyo has simultaneously been concerned with growing Chinese political-economic influence in the region. This has been particularly true since the 1997-98 Asian economic crisis led to the overthrow of the anti-Chinese Indonesian President Suharto and the flight of Japanese capital from the region despite the fact that, in 2001, Japan's trade with ASEAN was still three times higher than that of China, and its investment far greater still. In December 2003, in the "Tokyo Declaration," Japan entertained the possibility of joining the China-ASEAN bloc in order to counterbalance China. A China-ASEAN-Japanese economic bloc would form a new, and largely unexpected, political-economic alliance, assuming tensions over North Korea and Taiwan and access to oil do not boil over into conflict. Japan has considered joining in a number of Free Trade Areas with Malaysia, Thailand and the Philippines; but much like the US and EU, Tokyo has had difficulty due to its policy of protecting agriculture at home.

In this regard, the evolution of the world into rival political-economic blocs and alliances appears to be in the making. The question as to whether regional blocs can remain in a relative *equipoise* and or whether these "blocs" will stumble into conflict over nautical chokepoints and shatterbelts resulting in a polarization of global alliances will, to a large extent, depend upon position of the three key *pivot* states, Turkey, Ukraine and the People's Republic of China. Beijing could either swing toward Russia or the EU. As long as it remains determined to reunify with Taiwan, it will not move too close to Japan, as Washington and Tokyo determined in December 2004 to coordinate strategy versus Taiwan. Likewise, the key *pivotal* state, Ukraine, seems increasingly likely to swing toward the US and EU and dubiously toward China—if it does not split apart of fall under Russian pressures. Should Ukraine lose its "neutral" position, it would definitely alienate Russia, which sees the US as increasingly interfering within its "spheres of influence and security" in Belarus, Ukraine, the Caucasus and central Asia. Concurrently, Turkey, one of the key NATO allies during the Cold war, could either shift toward the EU—or toward Russia.

**Conclusions**

The Bush administration and many of its neo-conservatives appear divided between those who want to contain both Russia and China and those who want to "co-opt" Russia. As revealed in the Bush Administration's first clash with China at the outset of its mandate, Paul Wolfowitz tended to see the predominant threat coming from China, Middle East and Persian Gulf. National Security Advisor Condoleezza Rice initially regarded Russia as a "threat," or a "potential threat," at least until 11 September.[63] Secretary of Defense Donald Rumsfeld, by supporting the position of the new eastern European members of NATO, opted to slow down the fast track designed to bring Russia closer to NATO. The post–11 September 2001 implementation of the NATO-Russia Council appeared to grant Russia a greater say in NATO policy, but appears to have disappointed Moscow, particularly once NATO expanded to the Baltic states.

After the Iraq war in 2003, steps toward a new US-Russian alliance appeared to flounder, leading Russia and China to tighten their defense and economic relationship, and permitting China to enhance its strategic leverage vis-à-vis Taiwan. These factors have led the Bush administration to engage in closer US-Japanese defense coordination in support of Taiwan. Whether the second Bush administration can begin to pry the two continental powers apart through a multilateral strategy remains to be seen. US pressures on Belarus as one of the members of the "outposts of tyranny," plus US-EU support for the "reformist," Viktor A. Yushchenko in the Ukrainian elections, as opposed to the candidate supported by Russia, Viktor F. Yanukovich, combined with American criticisms of growing "authoritarianism" in Russia itself, do not augur well for the future. Moreover, preventing the pivotal states of Ukraine, Turkey and/or China from completely shifting political-economic alliances should be one of the major focal points of an irenic US multilateral strategy designed to prevent such shifts from provoking conflict.

In its March 2005 National Defense Strategy, the Pentagon identified four methods of warfare that could by used both state and anti-state actors—in a world characterized by an increasing numbers of threats to American security and higher degrees of "uncertainty." These methods of warfare included the "traditional," the "irregular" (or asymmetrical), the "catastrophic" (the use of WMD, for example) and the "disruptive" (the innovative or unexpected use of new technologies). Yet if American global strategy cannot soon begin to restore the confidence and trust of both major and minor powers through concerted and multilateral action, its very counter-actions and responses to these methods of warfare will tend to *exacerbate* the very uncertainty posed by actual threats, as well as by the *fears* posed by *perceived* future threats. To prevent the situation from proving completely disastrous, will require that that Washington soon engage in a much more sophisticated and innovative global strategy. Such a strategy should emphasize truly concerted US, European and Russian "power" and "responsibility" sharing, and utilize a more complementary mix of diplomacy and *threat* to use force, combined with the restoration of confidence and trust through the establishment of new systems and norms of "global governance." (See Chapter 8.)

# Chapter 7

# "Clash of Democracies"
# or New Global Concert?

There is a real risk of a potential "clash of democracies" between an expanding EU and the global interests of the US. This is not to argue that the US and EU will necessarily "fight" with each other, but that the two may be unable to coordinate policies due to their divergent interests, the different ways in which they rank "common" values and norms, as well as the differing ways in which the two formulate foreign policy. It is furthermore argued that the American export of *liberal democracy*, seen as linked to *national self-determination*, has generally tended to emphasize nationalistic and majoritarian systems of governance—and has largely overlooked the possibility of implementing *consensual* forms of democracy as well as *confederal* models of political and social governance. The chapter then asks whether it is possible for the *consensual* model of "democracy," as being developed by the European Union, to be applied in such a way as to truly "strengthen" the UN, thus laying the foundations for an essentially *confederal* system of "global governance" or "world democracy"—with strong regional and civil society participation. In opposition to neo-conservative thinking, it is argued that the roots for such a strategy can be found in the 1948 Vandenberg Resolution, which not only sought US Senate ratification for the North Atlantic Treaty, but that also sought to "strengthen" the UN.

## "Clash of Democracies"

The term "clash" in the title of this chapter is obviously a take-off from Samuel Huntington's now famous (or infamous) "clash of civilizations." Yet, this conception of "clash" is not suggesting that the two democracies, US and Europe, will actually draw swords, or that they may, for some reason, enter into *direct* conflict. Rather it is to suggest that the disputes between the US and EU appear to becoming more and more acute, so that differences in strategy and action may actually exacerbate conflicts that already exist—or else help to spark new conflicts. In this regard, in the very expectation that the US and EU cannot formulate a common strategy, opposing states and/or "terrorist" organizations can attempt to play upon those "schisms" so as to expand their own power and influence, through inverse aspects of "strategic leveraging."

Huntington had initially characterized the "clash of civilizations" in terms of the "west" versus the "rest."[1] By this, he assumed that Americans and Europeans would remain aligned, based on the fact that both the United States and Europe belonged to the same "western" civilization. In his view, clashes between peoples were supposed to take place mainly *between* differing civilizations, and not *within* them. Yet it is evident that major conflicts can also be sparked by "intra-civilizational" schisms, such as that which plagued the Catholic Church, for example, in respect to the split between the Roman Catholic and Greek Orthodox churches, followed later by Lutheran rebellion, not to overlook schisms within Protestantism itself, between Calvin and Luther, among others. Included in the concept of schism, should be the profound differences in outlook between the two states of Great Britain and the United States of America, violently acted out in the American Revolution, despite the fact that both peoples belonged to the same English-speaking civilization. By downplaying "clashes" *within* the same civilization, and even those *within* Western civilization itself, Huntington's analysis reveals itself to be absurdly *ahistorical*. (See also Chapter 3.)

Francis Fukuyama has similarly depicted the US and Europe as aligned. In Fukuyama's neo-liberal (moving toward neo-conservative) conceptualization, the US and Europe were placed in the same alliance at the "end of history" in which the "idea" of liberal democracy had effectively gained ascendancy in the post-Cold War era despite its imperfections. In Fukuyama's perspective, there was no alternative ideology that could realistically challenge the predominant liberal democratic "idea"—and that could provide an effective alternative path of socio-political-economic development.[2] In this view, both the US and Europe were to remain aligned in a democratic federation of states. The "idea" of democracy thus promised a realm of peace for those "liberal democratic" states that had reached the pinnacle of their political possibilities, while all other states remained mired in history. But here again, much as Huntington tended to downplay conflicts *within* the same civilization, the "last man" at the "end of history" failed to recognize the fact that there is not just "one" idea of liberal democracy, but several competing post Cold War conceptions—which may or may not prove compatible. The latter include "consensual democracy," "national democracy," "democratic communitarianism," "participatory democracy," and "world democracy." There is also the apparently oxymoronic conception of "illiberal democracy" but which represents a kind of populist support for dictatorship. Consequently, emergent powers with alternative values, norms and interests, as well as domestic political-economic structures, as well as rival social movements, have increasingly challenged the predominance of the liberal democratic federal model.

American neo-conservative ideologues may like to flatter themselves that the American version of democracy is the best functioning version, but it is not the only viable form. *Liberal democracy*, as promulgated by Fukuyama, is not at all the same as *social democracy*, the form of democracy generally practiced by European states. Moreover, *consensual democracy* as represented by Switzerland, Belgium and the European Union represents an alternative form of democracy.[3] It cannot be overlooked that it was multilateral *consensual* diplomacy—that the US itself has historically helped to sponsor through the formation of the European Coal and Steel Community—that helped to solidify the glue that holds France and

Germany together. Franco-German cooperation represents the keystone that prevents the whole EU project from disintegrating.

The problem raised here is that neo-conservatives tend to place emphasis upon formal democratic structures; yet they do not highlight the need for even democratic states, let alone so-called "outposts of tyranny," to engage in democratic *practices* based upon established laws; hence the importance of "practicing what one preaches." This issue came to the forefront in the US itself during both the 2000 and 2004 presidential elections. After major anomalies involving election procedures in the 2000 presidential elections, OSCE observers (facilitated by the State Department) were placed in the midterm elections in 2002 and in 2003 (in the California gubernatorial elections) and in the Presidential elections in 2004. The presence of OSCE observers from 34 countries in Florida, Ohio and Minnesota, as well as in California, Nevada, Illinois, Maryland, Virginia, New Jersey, North Carolina and the District of Columbia in the 2004 presidential elections has appeared embarrassing for the US as the bastion of democratic belief and practice. The very fact, however, that the US opened itself to OSCE observers indicates a greater willingness to accept international, as opposed to national, standards for political behavior, even if US practices are not always up to par.

Here, a distinction must be made between the differing *formal* conceptions of democracy and *real democracy*. In contrast to differing formal conceptions, *real democracy* is defined as dialogue, negotiation and engaging in forms of power sharing despite significant differences in outlook—within *any* formal system of governance or even between governments. *Real democracy* thus represents a daily struggle that involves active engagement in *both* public *and* private spheres, even if those democratic processes may be *indirect* and *representative* at the local, regional, national and international levels. As not all individuals can or will participate *directly* in decision-making processes, or may not be qualified to participate in specialized areas of expertise, *real democracy* requires dialogue, oversight, transparency, and exchange of as many viewpoints as possible. This is to assure that elected officials, bureaucratic elites, as well as corporate leaders, remain open to alternative perspectives and options. The problem is to find a formal system of governance that best permits *real democracy* to express itself.

## The Export of the American Democratic Model

The complex nature of the American federal system, with its complicated systems of bicameralism, "checks and balances," as well as the *historically changing* meaning of "majority rule yet minority rights," coupled with the question of "states rights" vis-à-vis the power of the Federal government, is not well understood by either the American public or the world at large. Here, the concept of "majority rule yet minority rights," for example, did not, at the time of the American revolution, refer to the concept of "ethnic minority" groups, or other "minority" groups, who in some way differed from the general population. But rather, to a *secular* concept that emphasized differences in *class* in which the wealthy elites sought to protect themselves and their interests as a "minority."

It is furthermore not entirely clear that the American federal system effectively *represents* the growing differences among entire population. This appears true given its essentially two party system and strong executive branch, not to overlook its fifty states with their significant, and widely disproportionate differences in population size and ethnic backgrounds, in urban, suburban and rural concentration, as well as highly disproportionate distribution of wealth and economic capabilities.[4] These facts have raised questions concerning the system's very *legitimacy*—despite the fact that the American constitution has lasted so long without any significant revisions (only amendments).

The question of the *legitimacy* of the American democratic model has become even more pertinent in that US policy makers (and not just the neo-conservatives) have historically attempted to export US "democratic" processes in to various countries throughout the world.[5] While Woodrow Wilson is the first American president to export "democracy" overseas, the process initially began with the imposed export of the centralized Federal model of the North (the Union) to the highly decentralized confederal model of the South (the Confederacy). (See Chapter 2.) After World War I, Wilsonian concepts, linking "democracy" with "national self-determination," were first utilized as a tool to break down the Imperial German and Austro-Hungarian empires. Yet these concepts were then twisted by Hitler to assert German national "self-determination" through the irredentist quest to unify the German diaspora—forging a "national democracy" for Germans only. After World War II, and following the ratification of the "Made in USA" constitutions in Germany and Japan, the US attempted to sustain the single party predominance of the Christian Democrats and the Japanese Liberal Democrats for as long as possible during the Cold War.

The question of the *legitimacy* of the American system as a model for other countries consequently represents a crucial issue, particularly as the US faces greater political-economic competition with European social democratic models and their multiparty systems, and in face of the steps to ratify the new European constitution through a *consensual* approach to decision-making (assuming it eventually succeeds). The problem is that the export of the American democratic model overseas has generally taken place in post-Cold War conditions without deep consideration as to whether such a system of government is truly appropriate in that particular juncture of a society's socio-political history—particularly with respect to the fact that certain societies may consist of differing nationalities or ethnic groups of differing sizes, and with competing political-economic claims. While the export of American style democracy—generally linked to national "self determination" or "independence"—has represented a tool to break up the former empires, including that of the Soviet Union, it has also, and not so inadvertently, worked to undermine *consensual* or *confederal* models of "democracies" based upon cooperation between different nationalities or ethnic groups.

It is not at all clear that US efforts to export democracy by pressure or by force can or will result in the social and political transformations expected by neo-conservatives, especially in societies where democracy has been strongly linked to national or ethnic "independence." Certainly, the democratic process has *appeared* to have taken root in former Soviet bloc states, in eastern Europe, the Ukraine,

Georgia, as well as the Palestinian Authority, Afghanistan, Iraq and possibly Egypt. Voting at the municipal level (with women expected to vote later on) has taken place in Saudi Arabia in 2004 (yet few expect the Saudi royal family to become a constitutional monarchy any time soon). In Iraq, the second term Bush administration has hoped that the example of the US civil rights movement will prove exemplary in helping to bring greater social justice for all factions of Iraqi society. Bush administration officials have argued that the new Iraqi government, based upon a "majority" Shi'ite population, will not engage in the suppression of "minority" rights, through the implementation of Shari'a law, for example.[6]

The risk, however, is that neo-conservative neo-Wilsonian support for "liberal democratic" change through support for "civil society" movements and "national self-determination" may also instigate a backlash. This has been the case in countries such as China (repression of Tibet and students in Tiananmen Square in 1989), Russia (increasing steps toward authoritarianism or "national democracy" under Presidents Yeltsin and Putin), as well as a hardening of positions of states such as Iran, North Korea, Cuba, Burma and Belarus in opposing reforms. More and more states, such as Pakistan and up to now, Egypt, which have been unable to fairly balance competing interests and factions, have been opting for dictatorship or "illiberal democracy."[7] That the effort to spread democratic "values" and the American "way of life" abroad has been coupled with US actions in the "war on terrorism" that violate international law, not to overlook challenges to US constitutional rights, values, and norms, has resulted in a counter-reaction and a fundamental questioning of US democratic processes at both home and abroad.

**Roots of a "Clash"**

Differing conceptions of democracy suggest the emergence of a potential schism between the conceptions of liberal majoritarian democracy, as represented by the US, and the essentially social democratic models of separate European states, which are now forming an increasingly influential *consensual* model of the EU.

It is in the writings of the neo-conservative Robert Kagan that one sees the beginnings of a "clash" of values, norms, interests and strategic vision between the democracies of the United States and Europe as a whole. In Kagan's perspective, the world outlooks of the US and Europe are not at all aligned. The Europeans, in Kagan's view, have been able to escape the realities of power politics, and thus they downgrade the need for military force as a tool of geopolitics, largely due to the historical presence of American forces on European territory. Kagan's categorization accordingly implies that the American "Martians" and EU "Venusians" are not living at the "end of history," nor are they part of the same civilization—nor even on the same planet.

Yet to perceive the US-European relationship as a clash between "Mars" and "Venus" is not to present a fair characterization of their complex inter-relationship. What is most problematic now is a "clash of democracies" in which the US and Europeans possess differing forms and conceptions of the very concept of "democracy." While both Samuel Huntington and Francis Fukuyama argue that the two sides hold common values and norms derived from the same "civilization," the fact of the matter is that Americans and Europeans rank those values and norms very differently. Profound differences in the ranking of values, and norms joined by the problems raised by differing interests (which are, in turn, influenced by values and norms) make it difficult for the two sides to comprehend each other, even when they speak the same language.

## Other Conceptions of "Democracy"

American conceptions of "liberal democracy" and European conceptions (except perhaps for the UK) of "social democracy" differ greatly in respect to the role of the state in the society, and the nature of public welfare. The two "democracies" not only possess very different approaches to somewhat similar social problems, but also different ways of perceiving and enacting foreign policy.

Libertarian, "national-democratic" and communitarian models for political governance have begun to challenge the predominant majoritarian conceptions of both *liberal* and *social* democracy. The latter do not necessarily accept the freewheeling tenets of *libertarianism*. Liberal and social democrats also do not accept the views of *national democracy* (which asserts the rights of enfranchised groups over those not enfranchised or over those who have been disenfranchised), or of *illiberal democracy* (which rationalizes popular support for demagogic authoritarianism or dictatorship). Both liberal and social democrats generally do not agree with differing forms of "communitarianian democracy" which place community "rights" above individual "rights" (only with respect to what are considered *unjustified* individual claims) and which permits self-defined communities to seek greater autonomy *within* larger social-political units. Nor will all liberal democrats necessarily support conceptions of greater *participatory democracy* at all levels of society, nor will they agree to conceptions of *workplace democracy*, which involve employee decision-making in industrial management.

Moreover, even those who believe in "liberal democracy" may fundamentally disagree as to whether states should possess essentially two party systems, or multiple parties. Some "democratic" states, such as Mexico and Japan, have had single parties dominate their electoral systems—raising questions as to whether there is any competition for power involving alternative policies.[8] (In this regard, multiparty systems may be somewhat more tolerant of differing viewpoints than one or two party systems—although both systems can marginalize certain groups.)

Democrats may disagree, and possibly violently as was the case in the American Civil War, as to whether states should be highly centralized (or unitary), or else more decentralized and to what extent states, regions and localities should share power with the central, federal, or "confederal" government. In contemporary Iraq, for example, Kurdish groups are demanding a more decentralized "democratic federalism" versus Shi'ite (and Sunni) factions who urge a more "centralized democracy."[9] Serbs and Albanian Kosovars are in dispute over whether Kosovo should be independent, or part of a greater federation with Serbia or Albania. Even those who call themselves "democrats" may consequently disagree over to what extent the individual "state" should possess sovereignty in relation to larger confederal, federal or international structures of government.

Hence the concepts of global governance and "world democracy"—that transcend the traditional sovereignty of states—appear to be an anathema to traditional "liberal democrats"—and particularly to neo-conservative "democratic globalists."

Forces of "macro-nationalism," which include "national democratic" models, may seek to preserve "democracy" for specific ethnic groups or for national groups (based on "patriotism"). In general, "national democrats" often fear either losing their predominance to minority groups or immigrants, and thus demand the exclusion of other newly emergent social groups from the democratic process. "National democratic" ideology often comes to the forefront in opposition to a rise in immigration or in periods of recession. Samuel Huntington's latest writing in opposition to waves of Hispanic immigration in the US is representative of this "national democratic" perspective.[10] The National Front in France represents another form of "national democratic" movement. Israel, in the face of a growing Palestinian population, represents a "national democracy." Vladimir Putin's Russian "Unity" party (*Edinstvo*) is also "national" if not always "democratic."

The above ideologies have begun to provoke dissent within both liberal and social democratic models in the post-Cold War period. Contrary to Fukuyama's complacency, they can—rightly or wrongly—provide alternatives to emulate.

**Differing EU and US Foreign Policy Formation**

The US and EU accordingly possess differing systems of democratic governance that that will affect the strategic decision-making process, the nature of analysis, as well as political judgment and prognosis. Each system will handle both domestic and international ideological challenges to the legitimacy of their differing form of democratic governance very differently. At the same time, both are engaged in a rivalry in which both have been attempting to flaunt the benefits of their respective models so as to gain both domestic and international support for their actions.

The EU, as it attempts to frame a new constitution for a new *amalgamation* of states, somewhat stronger than a confederation, is developing a very different system of democratic governance than the more centralized federal system, which evolved in the US since the Articles of Confederation and the "Federalist versus Anti-Federalist" debates. These differing ways of making policy, plus clashing perspectives and interests, tend to lead to a clash of strategic culture and decision-making at the highest levels that makes it increasingly difficult to coordinate strategy—particularly in a situation in which the Europeans, as gradually evolving regional power, have been challenging America's global leadership role.

The American political system is essentially based upon two parties, which depends upon what is called "bipartisanship" or "bipartisan compromise" to function effectively. Thus a strong two-party system, in which republicans and democrats compete, often with very limited differences in viewpoint, has made it historically difficult for third party candidates to obtain credibility. The tradition of bipartisan compromise also makes it easier for the executive branch to play one party against another in order to achieve a set of political trade-offs. The nature of US election cycles furthermore leads American leaders to seek "quick fix" options or "satisficing" solutions in as rapid a time as possible—which generally do little to fully resolve a particular dispute or crisis in the long term. When Congress does not fully support presidential decisions, the executive often resorts to "executive agreements" to avoid possible congressional opposition or lack of support for Presidential policy. On the other hand, when Congress tries to initiate policy through the 1998 Iraq Liberation Act or 2004 Belarus Democracy Act, for example, Congressional politics tend to limit executive flexibility to deal with complex international diplomacy.

The EU political system, by contrast, represents a new multi-party multi-state hybrid, that may or may not be able to reach its decisions so rapidly. The EU is not a traditional territorial state, but an "amalgamation" of states, which possesses a *transforming* "regional sovereignty" as well as "multiple identities" at the EU, national, and sub-national levels. The EU is consequently characterized by complex inter-governmental, inter-regional, inter-bureaucratic and inter-party bargaining, compromises and trade offs, which govern its political culture. The EU is furthermore split between interests of larger, wealthier, more populous, states and smaller countries, a problem that is somewhat true for the American federal system as well. As unifying Europe is becoming increasingly aware of disproportionate extremes in its regional development, it hopes to make adjustments through both *inter-state* and *inter-regional* bargaining.

Because the upper levels of power are nominated, rather than elected, the EU model is generally more elitist, less populist, than the US model. To make up for its "democratic deficit," the new EU constitution has granted greater powers to the popularly elected Parliament. Assuming the new EU Constitution is eventually passed, the Parliament will have powers of "co-decision" with the Council of Ministers (which expresses the national interest of heads of state) for those policies requiring a decision by qualified majority.

In contrast with the US system, which has permitted the rise of a strong, directly elected, executive branch, with a potentially demagogic leader (whose two term mandate could possibly be limited to a single five year term), the EU President will be more of a figurehead, subject to the European Council, which "shall elect its President, by qualified majority, for a term of two and a half years, renewable once." The popularly elected European Parliament will then need to approve the Presidential candidate. The President will "chair (the Council) and drive its work forward and ensure, at his level, the external representation of the Union." The Minister of Foreign Affairs will be able to speak on the EU's behalf once a common policy is formulated. The new position will attempt to strengthen foreign policy decision-making by combining the present roles of the external affairs member of the Commission with the High Representative on foreign policy. The EU will also set up a diplomatic service to help strengthen the Minister's hand; at the same time, however, the new Foreign Minister may still become bogged down in intra-European debates in attempting to formulate a Common Foreign and Security Policy, and enter into disputes with the new Commissioner.

The EU also possesses "multiple sovereignties" in key policy areas: those countries that belong to the Schengen group and those that do not (Britain and Ireland); and those that belong to the Eurozone and those that do not (UK, Denmark, Sweden and eastern European states). Decisions on troop deployments and other military affairs will remain in the hands of individual states and not to the EU as a whole. Washington, for example, has recognized the "regional sovereignty" of the EU over economic affairs, beginning with the Uruguay round, but Washington has not yet recognized EU sovereignty over security and defense policy. Here, the US only recognizes particular "national sovereignties."

Moreover, only two states possess a nuclear deterrent (the UK and France). The fact that the UK remains within NATO's command, except in cases of supreme national emergency, and that France stands outside NATO's integrated nuclear command structure, makes it difficult for the two states to coordinate nuclear strategy. At the same time, a nuclear defense of the entire EU would be essential if the EU is to develop a true strategic identity. Moreover, nuclear cooperation between the US, EU and Russia may be of order in the coming years in the need to provide overlapping *security guarantees* to "regional security communities," and to help dissuade states from obtaining nuclear weaponry and delivery capabilities. (See Chapters 4 and 8.)

Most significantly for this discussion on European policy as it influences American global strategy, is that European armies will remain under the control of national leaderships—even if the new Constitution is ratified. State leaderships can still veto decisions despite the fact that the proposed Constitution calls for a Common Foreign and Security Policy (CFSP). Most foreign policy decisions will thus be subject to the principle of unanimity, while individual states will retain control over their national militaries. The new EU Minister of Foreign Affairs is to be appointed by the European Council, which will decide by qualified majority, with the agreement of the president of the European Commission, who will be elected for five years. The Commission, which represents the body that proposes and executes EU laws, is to be slimmed down from 25 to 18 members to better rationalize decision-making and policy execution. The fact that the EU cannot impose a CFSP, however, means that that US, or other states, can still play on differences between the individual states.

Problematically, the EU is still in the process of transformation, which could lead to its potential overextension. Will the EU bring in Turkey, Ukraine, or Russia into new forms of membership? If not, will it build high fences and border patrols along the Polish-Belarusian-Ukrainian-Russian borders? If so, how will it adjust its policies to incorporate these major states with all their political-economic problems, into a positive working relationship? The answer to the questions of may well determine the nature of strategic identity. With a single minister for foreign policy, the issue is not so much the question Henry Kissinger had raised as to what was Europe's telephone number—even though the US may still need to call all EU members plus the new foreign minister—but what is Europe's *next* location! So far, Europe has no fixed geographic boundaries, and this has prevented it from developing a consistent and stable strategic culture and identity.

**Clashing Strategic Visions**

In the post-Cold war era, the Europeans have begun to emphasize the necessity for a foreign policy based upon international political ethics and principles, with the emphasis on international law and *multilateral consensus* as a means to generate European unity—and to engage with states outside Europe.

In effect, the Europeans have, attempted to establish a new international legal order by strengthening UN-related activities in order to help provide the *legitimacy* for their very interaction as separate sovereign states. In this respect, the EU has adopted a largely secular (or Kantian universalistic) approach to domestic and foreign policy. EU members generally attempt to be neutral in conflicts, and play "honest broker" if possible. This new European international *political-ethical* approach can be seen by the clash between Germany and the US over the International Criminal Court (ICC).[11] Major political-ethical disputes can also be seen in such issues such as the death penalty—in which the US Supreme Court remains unwilling to ban the death penalty as "cruel and unusual" punishment. By contrast, the EU has officially banned the death penalty as a condition for joining. Europeans have also openly criticized US policy as violating the Geneva Convention in respect to individuals (including Europeans) taken prisoner in Afghanistan and Iraq. The EU has opposed the extradition of individuals accused by the US of acts of "terrorism" and who may face the death penalty.

**The Question of the Use of Force**

The EU emphasizes universal ideals, but also tries to be pragmatic as possible. French President Jacques Chirac, for example, argued that the option to go to war in Iraq should be considered only as a last resort. The Europeans in general have been reluctant to even *threaten* the possibility to use force, as urged by the Americans. By contrast, the US has tended to take a unilateral military approach to a number of crises, rather than let diplomacy take its course. While it is true that the Europeans may tend toward diplomacy, and the Americans toward military action, the key problem is not so much European "weakness" but the two-faced nature of US foreign policy. The latter—with its Janus gates unexpectedly and *selectively* swinging open or shut for war or peace—continues to insist on burden and responsibility sharing, but without accepting true European *power sharing*.

On the one hand, neo-conservative "Martians," complain that the US will only respect the EU once the latter truly begins to flex its muscles and take up its "responsibilities" by developing a war fighting capability. In this regard, the *Euroforce*, for example, must not remain an "empty shell." On the other hand, Martians have also opposed a Europe that can think and act for itself; they have tended to exaggerate the *future* EU capacity for *independent* military action. Yet as the EU represents a new form of geopolitical *amalgamation* (really going beyond a loose confederation), it will dubiously become a "hard pole" that can then wholeheartedly countermand the United States: Under the proposed new Constitution, foreign policy decisions will be subject to the principle of unanimity, while individual states will still retain control over their national militaries.

The American leadership complains that Europeans need to be prepared to both *threaten* and *use* force if necessary in order to achieve their objectives. In this regard, rather than attempt to restrict Europe's capacity to develop a truly unified

CFSP, the US should work with the Europeans to establish areas of greater *equity* and *complementarity* given their respective military and political-economic capabilities and differing interests—even if that implies a certain degree of asset duplication. On its side, the US tends to emphasize military capabilities, war fighting and intervention, but is reluctant to engage in peacekeeping. This leads Europeans to argue that they do not want to pick up the garbage after a US military intervention—in which they have had no input in the decision-making process. One of the reasons for not engaging in peacekeeping in Iraq is that opponents of the intervention do not want to provide the US with a *post-facto* justification for the "preemptive" intervention—that the EU had no power to prevent.

At present, while the Europeans tend to speak softly and offer incentives, the Americans carry the "big stick" and threaten sanctions and the use of force. Europeans argue that simply possessing force does not necessarily mean that the US has to use it; that both the threat and the use of force may prove counter-productive, if not dangerous. Although Europeans do not have the same military capacity as the US, it does not necessarily follow that their proposed strategies are necessarily impractical, and it does not mean that the threat, and then use of force, may necessarily be the best option in particular cases—although the use of force should never be entirely ruled out.

The key problem is that the two sides do not appear able to coordinate their "soft" and "hard" strategies. The future question is thus to what extent the US will heed the advise and interests of its allies, as well as Russia, and to what extent will it attempt to pressure its allies to go along with US goals and ambitions. There will always be a transatlantic link; the problem, however, is to devolve some aspects of defense, including both "power" and "responsibility" sharing to the Europeans themselves, as is now the case in Macedonia (Concordia) and then Bosnia in December 2004. The final status of Kosovo, which is presently under NATO's KFOR, likewise needs to be resolved. The US, EU and Russia also need to work toward a resolution of each of the crises in Chechnya, Georgia, Moldova, Armenia-Azerbaijan—perhaps through the ultimate formation of a joint NATO-EU-Russian Council. (See Chapter 8.)

**Clash of Policy Implementation**

The US-European dispute over the "new threats" largely came in the aftermath of the Cold War, when NATO was urged to "go out of area or out of business" in relationship to the crisis in Bosnia. During the Cold War, NATO had been regarded as a "collective defense" organization. NATO thus never ventured to oppose Soviet crackdowns outside NATO's sphere of influence, such as that of Prague Spring in 1968, to mention only one example. During the Cold War, it was, to a certain extent, easier to reach a common consensus as to how to deal with the perceived threats posed by the Soviet Union. (Even then, however, Allied consensus was not without its difficulties as indicated by the decisions to deploy nuclear weapons on European territory, for example, in the 1950s and 1980s.)

Following the collapse of the Soviet Union and Warsaw pact, however, a number of conflicts emerged just outside the territories of NATO member states.

This fact required that NATO and European states move beyond the conception of "collective defense" to that of "collective security" and "enforcement." Yet the move from collective defense to collective security and enforcement currently opened up the fundamental debate that threatened to forestall consensus and a common strategy. In the post-Cold War era, decisions based on collective security and enforcement have generally become more complex precisely because they involve intense debates over a wide range of political and military considerations.

Having initially failed to strongly warn Saddam Hussein that it would come to Kuwait's defense as a first step in *negotiating* the crisis, the US did engage in multilateral actions in relation to the 1990 Iraqi invasion. The US also engaged in a multilateral process through the formation of "Contact Groups" during the 1991– 95 Bosnian war (although the US and EU were disastrously unable to coordinate strategy, in part due to the US refusal to deploy peacekeepers in accord with the 1993 Vance-Owen plan).[12] The Clinton administration then attempted to work through multilateral processes in confronting conflicts throughout the developing world, at least until the disaster in Somalia in 1996.

At the advent of the Bosnian wars, the administration of George Bush, Sr. had given the EU the go-ahead to handle the crisis in ex-Yugoslavia, as demanded by Jacques Delors; the administration of George Bush, Sr. was generally pragmatic and multilateralist, not unilateralist. The US thus initially took a back seat in urging the EU and the UN to handle the crisis in ex-Yugoslavia. Yet, in this case, it was Germany (and the Vatican) who took the unilateral initiative in recognizing Croatian secession from Yugoslavia yet without seeking a way to guarantee rights of Serb minorities—against the counsel of the UN, EU and US. As the Bosnian crisis escalated, however, the US and Europeans could not agree on the appropriate strategy and tactics. There was a crisis in decision-making and tensions over UN-NATO "dual key" system of engagement. To simplify, France, the UK and EU tended to be pro-UN; the US tended to be pro-NATO.

Concerning Kosovo, the US opted out of multilateral efforts after the Rambouillet summit in 1998, engaging in aerial war "over" Kosovo in 1999, just a few weeks after Poland, the Czech Republic and Hungary joined an enlarged NATO alliance. Here, "humanitarian intervention" in Kosovo did appear to possess a greater international consensus than did military intervention in Iraq, despite the fact that neither war obtained UNSC authorization. Yet this did not mean aerial war "over" Kosovo was necessarily more legitimate. Other options, such as the deployment of a significant joint NATO-Russian inter-positionary force between Serbs and Albanian Kosovars, also appeared feasible. Yet the latter option was not carried out, ostensibly due to the fact that the Clinton administration was distracted by the *al-Qaida* bombings of the US embassies in Kenya and Tanzania in 1998.[13]

The repeated December 1992 "Christmas warning"—in which the US had threatened "to employ military force against the Serbs in Kosovo and in Serbia proper" if Serbia should extend the war into Kosovo—may have additionally limited US options by putting US and NATO credibility on the line.[14] The Clinton administration did not abide by its own promise of engaging in multilateral processes at the Rambouillet Summit; the latter's "Annex B" (which gave NATO sovereignty over Serbia proper) blocked the possibility of diplomatic compromise.[15] Here, US unwillingness or reluctance to deploy ground forces, even as peace keepers, played a major role in stalling the possibility of finding a political settlement in both Bosnia and Kosovo—despite the fact that it was clear that peace keeping would ultimately prove unavoidable in both cases. Multilateral US, Russian and EU/Finnish diplomacy then averted a possible ground war by convincing Milosevic to accept UN-backed NATO deployments in Kosovo alone.

After the 11 September attacks on the World Trade Center and Pentagon, the EU, NATO and the UN all backed US action against the Taliban in terms of a truly multilateral strategy. (NATO invoked Article V for first time in its history; yet it did not play a lead role in actual war fighting.) The US acted unilaterally, with some support from UK, France, and Germany, with supporting Special Forces. By contrast, the US military intervention in Iraq in 2003 was not backed by either the UN, EU or NATO. The US led the intervention with initial support from key allies, UK, Australia, as well as from Italy, Spain, Poland, Ukraine and other east European states. This intervention initially led to a division in Europe between essentially insular states of UK, Spain, Italy, plus much of eastern Europe, versus the essentially continental states of France, Germany and Belgium.

## Clash over "Terrorism"

In post 9/11 circumstances, the fact that the Americans have seen themselves in a "war on terrorism" and that the Europeans see themselves in a "fight against terrorism" indicates a significant difference in how to define the "enemy" and in which strategy and tactics to utilize. The US has regarded the conflict as a *qualitatively* different kind of conflict. The Europeans have tended to see the situation as a continuation of similar forms of terrorism, albeit with different political goals and more original tactics. The terrorist bombings on 11 March in Madrid, however, have not entirely brought the two sides closer—in that Spain then withdrew its forces from Iraq.

After the 11 March 2004 attacks in Madrid, the April High Level Policy Dialogue on Border and Transport Security, and the June 2004 US and EU summit, the US and EU have promised to coordinate strategy and tactics against specific terrorist groups. Yet they still have not closely coordinated strategy in relation to Iraq and may still differ in designing ways to eliminate the deeper social, economic and political factors that work to generate acts of terrorism. Most problematic will be deciding which groups might be fighting for "legitimate" causes against state "repression," and which groups represent "terrorists" but without a "just" cause.

Here, for example, the Americans and the Europeans have differed as to whether *Hamas* and *Hizb'allah* should be called "terrorist" organizations. The Russians have denounced American and European calls to work toward a political solution for the crisis in Chechnya and the Caucasus, at the same time that the Bush administration has been less willing to press the issue than the Clinton administration. The difference in US-EU perspectives is further magnified by the differences with the perspectives of Russia and China, thus illustrating the tremendous difficulty in achieving a truly multilateral and concerted approach to the crisis—whether from within the UNSC or from outside.

From this perspective, the US and EU appear to be drifting apart on a number of levels. The reality is that the US is capable of engaging in either unilateral actions or multilateralism—by choice. At the same time, the US and EU need to find a consensus on as many as of the new threats and crises as possible. The present crisis can be overcome, but only when Washington itself, still the pre-eminent global power, realizes that multilateral approaches, are, for the most part, in the national interest of the USA itself despite the fact that these often result in political and economic trade-offs. In any turn toward "multilateralism" involving the use of "contact groups," for example, the US will lead some projects, the EU others, Russia, China and Japan still others.

## Neo-conservatives and the UN

By contrast with the Europeans, the first term Bush administration has been less willing to accept the UN in framing global affairs. American neo-conservatives, in particular, are certainly skeptical of the concept of global governance and "world democracy" and of multilateralism in general and thus see the UN as *secondary* to sovereign states. They tend to argue that the UN has no real *legitimacy* because the UNSC does not consist of constitutional democracies, except for the US, France and UK; Russia is considered only half-democratic (if that), China, not at all.

The UN also disenchants neo-conservatives because the non-permanent UNSC members may not be "democratic" and the membership of states on various committees, such as the important Human Rights Commission, depends largely upon the role of dice—upon how states are selected for these committees. Another reason neo-conservatives oppose international regimes in general is that the financial accounting of these organizations is generally not well supervised and may be riddled with corruption. For these reasons, neo-conservatives largely oppose decisions made by international organizations in principle as not being truly "representative" or *legitimate* (even though the World Trade Organization [WTO], generally supported by neo-conservatives, is not truly representative either and needs to be opened up to differing viewpoints!) Yet rather than seeking to substantially reform UN practices, neo-conservatives appear content in attacking and sidelining the UN and most other multilateral organizations.[16]

Except perhaps for the WTO, neo-conservatives thus oppose "world democratic" attempts to legalize the conduct of foreign affairs and to subordinate the political will of nations to international enforcement regimes and norms as interpreted by international bodies and judges.[17] They essentially argue that the UN cannot act without US backing and support: "The whole system depends upon the national resolve of the US and this resolve cannot be maintained over the long run without a strong sense of national purpose."[18] (One could counter that the US may have difficulty sustaining its national goals in the long term—without strong support from other major powers, as well as the international community.)

Robert Kagan has argued that the French and German decision to act through the UN in an effort to check US actions in respect to Iraq was made because these states had no other recourse; the Europeans acted out of weakness, rather than strength. The relative weakness of the Europeans means that they need the UN as an international body (which the US helped to construct) to provide strategic leverage against the more powerful US. Other neo-conservatives similarly oppose "world democratic" attempts to "legalize" the conduct of foreign affairs and to subordinate the will of nations to international enforcement regimes and norms interpreted by international bodies and judges, such as the ICC, particularly as these actions are seen as "containing" the US. As James Caesar put it: "For many in Europe the rhetoric about the end of sovereignty, while it is clearly directed in the first instance at the outlaw or offending nations, also has a secondary target in the United States. It is designed to contain the US, to control Gulliver. Europeans are trying to defend their sovereignty by doctrines that deny sovereignty."[19]

In arguing essentially from the theoretical standpoint of Rousseau, Francis Fukuyama has posited a deeper analysis. He believes that Europeans are attracted to the UN because they regard the UN as the sole *legitimizing* body. Fukuyama argues that Europeans believe that "democratic legitimacy" flows from the will of the international community. The will of the international community is much larger than any individual nation-state, regardless of whether any particular state represents a democracy.[20]

## The Question of UN Security Council Legitimacy

The debate over the international legality and strategy of enforcement actions has consequently meant that the post-Cold War international decision–making process could only become more and more politicized and that heated political disputes would come more openly to the forefront than was the case during the Cold War when the Soviet threat generally held states together in mutual fear.

On a deeper level, from the European point of view, the key problem is to find the appropriate *balance* between the old conception of state sovereignty in which states accepted whatever other states did within their own territory (despite the fact that true sovereignty, has, at a minimum, implied mutual respect for international norms) and the new "rights" of first "humanitarian," and then "preclusive," intervention. For the French, intervention in Kosovo "was a legitimate enterprise and a political success"; but "it was also a source of divisions. Some saw it as the first instance of a customary right to intervene on humanitarian grounds without a UN mandate."[21] Intervention in Kosovo was thus considered tolerable, in this view, but as an *exceptional* case, as it was based upon "humanitarian" grounds. But as *preclusive* intervention in Iraq was not considered legally, morally, or strategically, justified, French Foreign Minister Villepin called for future international actions to be based upon the three principles of *Unity, Responsibility, Legitimacy*.[22] (It should be noted here that the concept of "humanitarian intervention" is now referred to as the "right to protect"—in the effort to downplay the military connotations of the term, "intervention.")

While all states should certainly follow the triad of legitimacy, responsibility and unity in engaging in any intervention or action involving the "right to protect," the call to adopt lofty principles does not entirely help to explain conceptual foundations of the *legitimacy* of the right of the UN Security Council (UNSC) to make decisions that affect individual state sovereignty. What is really an *internationalized* version of Rousseau's concept of the *general will* represents an essentially *ahistorical* argument as an explanation for the basis of the *legitimacy* of the UN as an international body, which can potentially frame laws and policies that *supercede* those of individual territorial states. (This, of course, assumes those states will find it in their interests to abide by those international laws.) The basis for the *legitimacy* for the decision-making power of the UN Security Council lies not so much in an abstract international *general will*, nor upon the formal basis of democratic structures and decision-making (see below), but in maintaining the larger *dynamic equilibrium* of an international *balance of power, interest and norm* in the aftermath of World War II.

From this perspective, the *legitimacy* of the UNSC stems from the fact that its members have represented the *predominant* centers of military, political, economic *and* normative power in the post-World War II period. The initial *legitimate* members of the UNSC were the victors in World War II: the US, Soviet Union, United Kingdom, China (soon to become Taiwan) and France. *Legitimacy* thus came with victory by military force, with France added on at the insistence of the UK—largely as an afterthought. Moreover, the initial legitimacy of the UNSC was based upon the US-UK-French-Soviet "double containment" of Germany and Japan (as well as of Italy and other former "enemy states").[23] All UN members had a *collective interest* in preventing the former "enemy states" from rising again as military threats. Likewise, all UN members ostensibly had an interest in establishing a new international order and normative structure.

The question of constitutional democracy as a *legitimizing* factor, however, was not raised at the time. The Soviet Union was at that time considered an ally; China was still in a situation of civil war, and Chang Kai Chek's nationalist KMT party could not be considered "democratic." The legitimacy of the UNSC was, accordingly, not based upon abstract harmonizing principles and the *general will* of the international community, but rather upon the *perceived necessity* to sustain a *dynamic equilibrium* among conflicting state interests, values and norms. UNSC *legitimacy* rested upon the UN's ability to sustain a dialogue over security issues, and between *conflicting* values and interests—in order to prevent conflict among its members. The membership of the UNSC did change to better reflect shifts in global *equilibrium* during the Cold War, but now needs a more radical re-appraisal after the Cold War, in order to *re-construct* its *legitimacy*.

## Role of NATO and the UN

Neo-conservative Richard Perle has made the argument that a community of democratic nations, such as NATO, possesses even greater legitimacy than the UN does—particularly in respect to taking military action.[24] He argues that this is true in that not all UNSC members can claim to be "democratic" and thus cannot claim *legitimacy* for actions based on democratic mandates. Richard Perle's point is formalistic, however—in that not all NATO members can claim to possess "democratic" histories. NATO members Portugal, Greece and Turkey have all had phases of dictatorship as members of NATO while NATO itself was not at all formed upon the basis of "democratic" criteria, as Perle seems to imply.

More crucially, Perle's argument overlooks the close relationship and interaction between NATO and the UN, and the fact that, in many ways, the two organizations represent two sides of the same coin. By 1947–49, the US began to consider options to counter the possibility that a Soviet veto in the UN Security Council might check vital European and US interests. It was feared that the UNSC might not function in case of potential disputes or conflict among its permanent members. A regional security organization was considered necessary in order to apply additional *strategic leverage* upon UNSC members, so that the international organization would, in fact, work. Consequently, NATO was given birth by Caesarian, plucked directly from Article 51 of the UN Charter, out of a mother UN paralyzed by Soviet veto. The subsequent relationship between the UN mother and NATO progeny has been troubled and uneasy—to say the least.

Contrary to the general myth, NATO, however, was not created solely to contain Moscow. Soviet membership in NATO was not ruled out *a priori*. In fact, the original framers of NATO never totally ruled out Soviet membership.[25] In addition to attempting to draw the US into a defense of Europe, NATO was created as a deterrent against any *potential* threat, which could have included a *revanchist* Germany, for example. Moreover, contrary to neo-conservative views, NATO was additionally created to "strengthen" the UN. One of the purposes of NATO, according to then Secretary of State George C. Marshal, was to "restore to international society the equilibrium necessary to permit the UN to function as contemplated at San Francisco.[26]

NATO's birth by caesarean did challenge the legitimacy of UN in the realm of security, but only on standpoint of collective *regional defense*. Yet in case of "out of area" actions, *enforcement* decisions that involved NATO were to go through UN Security Council—for better or worse.[27] In this regard, both US and NATO *enforcement* actions and non-Article V actions required—by the international laws that the US itself helped to establish—a UN Security Council mandate, if these actions were not clearly determined to be in "self defense" under Article 51 of the UN charter and thus under Article V of the NAT. These international legal factors, however, have tended to downgrade not just the UN, but also NATO, in the eyes of neo-conservatives.

## The Vandenberg Resolution

NATO itself developed out of a compromise between three conflicting visions of European security. The first option, initially supported by George Kennan, was to extend US security guarantees to the 1948 Western Union—in what was called the "dumbbell" approach designed to "equalize" the European and US security relationship and avoid American entanglement in European affairs. The second "America first" option was a more formal treaty arrangement, in view of the situation in Germany, and in light of French concerns. A third approach was to strengthen the UN. In this regard, UN Secretary General Trygve Lie initially opposed (prior to the Korean War) the concept of a regional defense pact as detracting from the UNSC's primary responsibility for international peace and security. Influential opponent of the NAT, Albert Einstein stated in May 1949 that he would have had no objections to the NAT—if the latter had been organized within the framework of the UN. Likewise, Senator Robert A. Taft, who voted against the North Atlantic Treaty (NAT), argued that NATO's presence would reinforce the division of Europe—and not strengthen the UN.[28]

In the tradition of Congressional compromise, Senator Arthur H. Vandenberg attempted to bring three conflicting visions of the future of Atlantic security together into one package. Senator Vandenberg hoped that any American association would be based upon reciprocity, mutual aid and self-help. In a concession to the pro-Western Union "dumbbell approach," Vandenberg sought to limit American engagement by watering down the automaticity of Article V security guarantees. In a concession to pro-UN advocates, he pressed for pro-UN language and attempted (but failed) to assert a clause in the NAT that promised support for "strengthening" the UN. As the Senator put it: "The Vandenberg Resolution was adapted to foster regional and other collective defense arrangements inside the UN but outside the veto."[29]

In addition to Senator Vandenberg's efforts to forge compromise between pro-UN, pro-European and pro-American options, UN principles were involved in the formulation of the North Atlantic Treaty—in the effort to *construct* NATO's very *legitimacy*. The UN helped sustain an open dialogue between the US, NATO and the Soviet Union (much as George C. Marshall repeated to critics of the UN throughout the years 1948–50)—and has continued to do so in relation to post-Soviet Russia. The complex UN-NATO interrelationship also helped to reassure France, and tacitly the Soviet Union, that German military power capabilities would remain "double contained."

Often overlooked is the fact that NATO has needed UN assistance in the effort to prevent or contain conflict not only in areas outside the NATO "area," but among NATO members themselves, both during and after the Cold War. Here, it was UN blue helmets who were deployed in Cyprus and not NATO forces, to create a buffer between NATO members, Greece and Turkey, in a major crisis involving "ethnic cleansing" in Europe in the midst of the Cold War. The Cyprus crisis (which still has not entirely been resolved)—more so that the US-UN role in the Korean war—represented the forerunner to post-Cold War conflicts in Bosnia, Kosovo, Afghanistan and Iraq that have likewise tended to exacerbate tensions between NATO, the UN, and Russia—not to overlook within NATO itself.

The Vandenberg Resolution likewise called for "Maximum efforts to obtain agreements to provide the United Nations with armed forces as provided by the Charter, and to obtain agreement among member nations upon universal regulation and reduction of armaments under adequate and dependable guaranty against violation." Significantly, the Resolution urged the US to "strengthen" the UN and work to revise the UN Security Council. (Vandenberg's efforts led to the April

1949 General Assembly debate, and then to the 1950 United for Peace Resolution that proposed a UN "peace patrol.")

After intense negotiation, however, references to "strengthening the UN" were not adopted in the final version of the North Atlantic Treaty. Although State Department discussions in 1948 pointed out that some hesitancy among the West Europeans to support the NAT might be resolved, "by stating explicitly on which articles of the UN Charter the security organization would be based,"[30] this advice was not followed. The founders of NATO sought near maximum freedom of political maneuver: In effect, NAT supported UN principles, but not necessarily, UN practices. At the same time, it was left purposely vague as to which of the contradictory UN principals and goals NATO would support.

In summary, the Vandenberg Resolution's proposal to "strengthen" the UN and its peacekeeping capabilities (along side the formation of NATO) represents one of the forgotten aspects of the Cold War, and reveals a significant *alternative* position to contemporary neo-conservative attacks on the UN. George Kennan's initial conception of a "dumbbell" approach of 1947–48 in which the Europeans and US would contribute equally to their defense likewise appears relevant and provides a possible model for an expanding EU defense capability, linked more equitably to US defense capabilities.

The possibility that Russia could enter into a new form of membership with NATO could likewise help "strengthen" the UN. In a surprise statement, at the US-Russian summit in Slovenia in October 2001, Russian President Putin revealed that the Soviet Union had requested the possibility of entering NATO in 1954 on the eve of NATO enlargement to West Germany—a fact that raises critical questions as to the nature of American estimations of the Soviet "threat." The publication of the Soviet demand was intended to reveal contemporary Russian interest in forging a closer relationship with NATO. Yet despite the formation of the NATO-Russian Council, the US has not yet taken further steps to draw Russia into deeper cooperation.

**Changes in the "P–5"**

By the 1970s, the *legitimacy* of Taiwan as a UNSC member was questioned by the US as well as by China and the Soviet Union. As was not to be the case in the 1950s, Beijing replaced Taipei without debate. As the UNSC reflected the global "balance" between the major centers of power, the Nixon administration accordingly brought Beijing into the UN Security Council. (Washington had previously opposed China's membership in 1950—a fact which represented one of the root causes of the Korean war.)

Chinese membership in the UNSC has consequently led to the erroneous belief that membership is based upon the possession of nuclear weapons, particularly after the 1967 Nuclear Non-Proliferation Treaty granted only permanent UNSC members the legitimate right to possess nuclear weaponry. China, however, had proposed its membership for the UNSC *before* acquiring nuclear weaponry. More importantly, the People's Republic was considered as the *legitimate* heir to the Dragon throne, as well as a victor in the struggle against Imperial Japan. (At the same time, however, one can still argue that China used nuclear weaponry as *strategic leverage* to gain entrance into the UNSC.)

In 1991, membership of the UN Security Council was questioned once again. Once the Soviet Union broke up, the Soviet position on the UNSC was taken by Russia (despite the fact that Ukraine wanted to debate the issue). Debate over UNSC membership was avoided despite the fact that German unification, followed by Soviet collapse, had challenged the very basis of the foundation of the UN Security Council—as the latter was founded to oversee the reconstruction of Germany and Japan and to prevent these "enemy states" from rising again as military threats. The unraveling of the "double containment" of Germany and Japan following German unification and Soviet collapse, has consequently undermined the initial purpose of the UN, and upset the *general equilibrium* of the entire global system as well—signifying the fact that the UNSC is in desperate need of re-evaluation, re-structuration and re-invigoration.

In sum, the basis for the *legitimacy* of the UNSC lies in helping to sustain the general political, economic and military *equipoise* among the major powers that had originally defeated Germany and Japan. Following German unification and Soviet collapse, coupled with the wars over Kosovo and Iraq, in which the role of the UN was largely relegated to the side, it is the time to *re-construct* the UN once again in accord with new transformations in the *global equilibrium*. The UNSC consequently needs to better reflect the major centers of political and economic power in order to be considered *legitimate* in post-Cold War circumstances. The purpose is to enhance the coordination of truly concerted global strategies to deal effectively with any number of challenges—from poverty to clean water to the prevention of war as well as the re-construction of war-torn states and societies.

**Reinvigorating the UN Security Council**

Rather than denigrating the UN, as the neo-conservatives tend to do, it is crucial that every effort be made to *re-legitimize* the UNSC, by re-structuring the latter to make it more representative of the post-Cold War world, and to take concerted efforts to minimize the use of the veto as much as possible. This proposal would seek to institute a more concerted approach to global policy, even if a number of policy decisions may still need to be taken in more informal "Contact Groups"— outside of even a revised UN framework.

The UNSC's non-permanent membership had been last expanded from 11 to 15 in a 1963 General Assembly vote that took effect in 1965. As previously mentioned, in 1971, the People's Republic of China took over the permanent seat on the UNSC that was initially occupied by Taiwan. Often un-recognized is the fact that Russia simply took the place of the Soviet Union after the latter's collapse—despite Ukrainian claims to be considered for UNSC membership.

In 2004, the UN "Open-Ended Working Group" officially recommended two options for reform of the UNSC. "Model A" provided for six new permanent seats, with no veto created for these new members, and three new two-year term non-permanent seats. "Model B" provided for no new permanent seats but created a new category of eight four-year renewable-term seats and one new two-year nonpermanent (and non-renewable) seat. Both involved a distribution of seats between four major regional areas, which are listed as "Africa," "Asia and Pacific," "Europe" and "Americas"—but excluding the "Middle East." In March 2005, Kofi Annan then called on the UN to choose between "Model A" or "Model B" by September 2005 at the 60th anniversary UN summit.[31]

The Working Group argued that members given preference for permanent or longer-term seats should be those States that are among the top three financial contributors in their relevant regional area to the regular budget, or among the top three voluntary contributors from their regional area, or the top three troop contributors from their regional area to UN peacekeeping missions. Neither option extended the veto power beyond the existing P-5, but did argue, much like the 1948 Vandenberg Resolution did, that the use of the "veto has an anachronistic character that is unsuitable for the institution in an increasingly democratic age and we would urge that its use be limited to matters where vital interests are genuinely at stake. We also ask the permanent members, in their individual capacities, to pledge themselves to refrain from the use of the veto."[32]

If Germany and Japan are to enter the UNSC, as appeared likely in Model A, it would mean the removal of the "enemy clause" from the UN Charter—a problem perhaps less difficult for Berlin, than for Tokyo due to the need to reconcile Japan with both UNSC members, Russia and China. Rome, however, has expressed some resentment that Berlin could be included, and not Italy. Poland has likewise expressed concerns over German membership. In 2004, the so-called "G-4" countries, Germany, Japan, India, and Brazil, all promised to support each other's membership on the UNSC. It appears that Pakistan would try to oppose Indian membership; both Mexico and Argentina have opposed Brazil's membership.

Despite Tokyo's argument that it has been heavily involved in dealing with key international issues, including Iraq, Afghanistan and Africa, and that it is a major financial contributor to the UN, China indicated hostility to Japan's candidacy. Beijing stated that the UN was "not a board of directors" whose composition could be decided by "the financial contribution of its members."[33] South Korea likewise opposed Japan's membership, while Japan itself thought new UNSC members should possess a veto. (The "G-4" proposal does not include states in Africa, such as South Africa, or Nigeria, or those of the Middle East/Persian Gulf either, in which Egypt, Saudi Arabia, Iran, if not Israel, might need consideration.) At the same time, Vladimir Putin asserted that any reform of the UNSC would be one-sided if new members did not have veto power. He stated that if there were no veto for the new members, all vetoes would have to go.[34]

The UN "Working Group" did propose the possibility that more far reaching reforms could take place in a review of the composition of the UNSC in the year 2020. It also proposed a review of the effectiveness of the Council in taking collective action to prevent, and remove, new and old threats to international peace and security, particularly in cases of genocide and large-scale human rights abuses.

The problem is that these new proposals for review have merely tended to postpone the crucial issues. Critics argued that some combination of the two plans should be considered; yet other, more radical options, still appear plausible. One is to place France and Germany, and perhaps ultimately the UK, into one rotating UNSC seat, assuming Europe can truly formulate a Common Foreign and Security Policy (CFSP), and truly begin to change concepts of national sovereignty. Japan could then come in as a permanent UNSC member. Here, it is theoretically possible for the EU to rotate UNSC membership among the UK, France, Germany, and Italy—if all EU states can agree on a CFSP, and permit their "core" powers to have a seat at the UNSC. As it is dubious that the US would ever give up its right to veto (without leading to a total collapse of the UN), permanent UNSC members should retain the veto, but if more than five permanent members did come in, then a two-veto system could be implemented, perhaps after a two-to-five year period.

While the UNSC would still be governed by the northern and more economically advanced states, this proposal would seek to permit a much wider representation for the second tier non-permanent UNSC members. The latter's membership could then be expanded, re-organized and rotated in such a manner so that key regional powers with *conflicting viewpoints* could *simultaneously* be represented—so as to permit *real dialogue*, as a step toward *world democracy*.

This more far-reaching option would thus diverge significantly from traditional conceptions of a state representation and state sovereignty in terms of power, wealth and population. Rather than think in terms of *individual* state representation, the proposal raised here is to look at states in terms of their strategic and political *interrelationships* in their specific regions and in terms of the vital issues and interests that most affect them. Why not find a way to include all three of the top contributors of finance and peacekeeping—plus some of the other major regional actors, and possibly rotate membership, if necessary?

States could also form groupings that reflect and affect their common interests, such as nuclear proliferation, development and re-construction issues, water questions, population, AIDS and other diseases, etc. Disputes would be arbitrated by UNSC members or else by Contact Groups that were more removed from the immediate issues or conflicts at hand. *Much as was the case in the League of Nations (Article 15), even permanent members directly accused in disputes would voluntarily give up the right to vote or veto wherever possible in areas deemed "non-vital." Such disputes would be handled in accord with the international legal principle of "complimentarity": Only if states fail to deal with the concerns raised would the matter be taken to the UNSC or other bodies.*

Moreover, as a companion to the UN General Assembly, a popularly elected "World Citizens Assembly," an idea conceived in the 1920s as a means to balance the state-led discussions of the League of Nations, could also be implemented.[35] This organization would provide a greater voice to the differing visions of global civil societies—particularly if such a body were granted the possibility to raise funding. A "World Citizen's Assembly" would perhaps be most effective if its members represented the populations of specific regions, such as major urban and agricultural areas, suburbs and industrial belts. Such a body would seek to make practical policy proposals and set guidelines, much as unofficial non-governmental organizations and businesses, representing differing interests and constituencies, do today. A "World's Citizen's Assembly" would also help to determine the basic values and norms for "global governance" and confederal "world democracy."

# Chapter 8

# Transcending the International Disequilibrium

How, given an apparently deepening global crisis following Soviet collapse, and after the attacks of 11 September 2001, can we establish new systems and norms of global governance? How do we transcend the new global disequilibrium? Reforming the UN alone will not change the dynamics of international geo-strategic, political economic and ideological rivalries. Washington, by itself, did not "cause" the global disequilibrium, yet the US will need to do more to address the roots of the present crisis, which, to a large extent, lies in the general failure of US diplomacy to establish new and more concerted norms for international state behavior in the post-Cold War era. As the US is still the predominant political and economic power, it will need to innovate a *truly* global strategy to point the way toward a more peaceful world, and help to guarantee a modicum of sustainable development, order and justice—to finally put an end to the "war on terrorism."

First, it is crucial for the US to move away from the rhetoric of "rogue states," "outposts of tyranny," and "war on terrorism" and toward a *multilateral strategy* of "engaged reconciliation" between conflicting parties. Here, the main problem will be deciding which groups might be fighting for "legitimate" causes against real state repression, and which groups represent "terrorists" without a "just" cause. Certain, but not all, militant organizations may need to be eradicated by force in situations where diplomacy appears impossible; one then cannot overlook the need to *threaten* the use of force, then to use force—if necessary. For the most part, however, without concerted efforts to bring conflicting sides together, there will be no end to the "war on terrorism" as long as anti-state organizations and established governments continue to counter-accuse each other of engaging in acts of "terrorism." Much as Edmund Burke argued in not entirely different historical circumstances, "Terror is not always the effect of force, and an armament is not a victory. If you do not succeed, you are without resource; for, conciliation failing, force remains; but force failing, no further hope of reconciliation is left."[1]

## European Security

The "war on terrorism" will not come to an end unless the US, EU and Russia can begin to fully cooperate in Europe and abroad, and begin to set the standards, values and norms for the rest of the world to emulate through the formation of "regional security communities."

The best option to achieve a new system of Euro-Atlantic Euro-Mediterranean security is through the formation of "regional security communities" that involve intensive interstate regional political-military and socio-economic cooperation. The deployment of multinational "war-prevention" forces throughout central and eastern Europe, where deemed necessary, could help reinforce stability and assist regional development. These measures can be combined with *overlapping* NATO, EU and Russian security guarantees to the states concerned, coupled with the signing of the adapted Conventional Force in Europe (CFE) treaty, which has remained a point of contention between an expanding NATO and Russia.

Obtaining an agreement over the adapted CFE treaty will, in turn, mean finding accords over Russian troop deployments in Moldova, Georgia, Chechnya, and Armenia and Azerbaijan, at the same time that the US and EU need to deal fairly with the *legitimate* security concerns raised by Russia and Belarus concerning the expansion of NATO. The US, EU, and Russia will need to work together in order to reform Belarusian behavior, and to prevent Ukraine from splintering. Labeling Belarus as one of the five "outposts of tyranny," and then criticizing the ostensible backtracking on "democratic" reforms in Russia, tends to push Russia and Belarus into a closer relationship—rather than working *with* Moscow to help *reform* Minsk.

As long as NATO continues to enlarge to the Russian border (without wholehearted Russian participation in the NATO decision-making process), Russian hardliners will propagandize against the NATO presence to oppose democratic reform and steps to develop greater transparency in Russian domestic and international relations. This is true as the deployment and modernization of NATO forces in the Baltic States and Poland have been regarded as threatening St. Petersburg and Moscow. The flight of NATO aircraft over the Baltic states may appear to represent a minor irritation to Russia from the US perspective, but it is an issue that is symbolic of the lack of NATO-Russian confidence. The option of joint NATO-Russian flights over the Baltic region might help build confidence among all parties—and thus help to break the ice.

If US-EU-Russian political-military tensions and mutual suspicions can soon be ameliorated, perhaps through greater cooperation in the "war on terrorism," a conjoint NATO-EU-Russian "War Prevention" Headquarters in Kaliningrad could be implemented, symbolically drawing East and West together. A new system of Euro-Atlantic Euro-Mediterranean security could then be initiated with the projection of overlapping NATO, EU and Russian security guarantees to the three Baltic states, and to other states as well, somewhat similar to the multilateral US, UK, French, Russian, Chinese accords promised Ukraine in 1994, after the latter gave up its nuclear weaponry. The US, EU and Russia will then need to deal with mafia activities, drugs and arms smuggling, as well as human trafficking—in the effort to reform states in the region.

Bringing both Russia and Ukraine into the World Trade Organization might help to integrate these economies into the global system. The US would like to prevent the emergence of a new Russian-dominated entity in Eurasia. Yet the best option is minimize Russian efforts to assert its hegemony is to work with Russia on key problems in a multi-pronged approach that seeks to *channel* Russian ambitions. First, the US should encourage both Russian and Ukrainian membership in the WTO as a step beyond the formation of a Common Economic Space within the CIS. To accomplish this, the US Congress would also need to grant Russia Permanent Normal Trade Relations (PNTR) status in order for Russia to enter the WTO as soon as possible.[2] (See Chapter 7.)

This latter step entails the difficult process of assisting Russia with economic reforms, and trying to put an end to forms of corruption that block trust. Granting Russia unconditional PNTR status will have little direct impact on U.S.-Russian trade, but would represent a step in the right direction for Russia to enter the WTO, and would help build Russian prestige, particularly as China had previously entered the WTO. By denying Moscow PNTR, long-term investment has been inhibited, as has potential for obtaining strategic leverage *over* Russian behavior. Moscow continues to see obtaining PNTR as an important political status, which could in turn provide Moscow with greater incentive to improve its commercial manufactures for export over the long term, and mitigate its efforts to forge a separate "Common Economic Space" with Ukraine, Belarus and Kazakhstan. PNTR status would also mean a more stable business climate for American multinational firms. (In January 2005, the Bush administration appeared to promise Russia PNTR status and to help it enter the WTO.)

These above steps will not, however, altogether check Russian claims to hegemony over the Eurasian heartland. In order to mitigate Russian claims, the US and EU will need to work with Russia in terms greater strategic cooperation in the "war on terrorism" and to find ways to cooperate in peacekeeping throughout eastern Europe, central Asia, and possibly, the Caucasus and the Middle East. Only once Russia feels secure in its relations with an enlarged NATO and with the new Europe, can it then focus on development and refurbish its economy, and work toward entry into the World Trade Organization, the OECD, and the EU (or build a form of associate membership). Although the modalities are far from being worked out, NATO, the EU and Russia could participate in the joint development of theatre ballistic missile defenses for the Euro-Atlantic region. Bringing Russia into a closer relationship with NATO and the EU, along with Ukraine and Turkey, in new forms of membership and power-sharing arrangements should work to forge a more concerted relationship in respect to other regions as well—with the brutal war in the Caucasus being the most problematic issue.

As a "neutral" Ukraine is essential to the stability of Europe, it is evident that present disputes over geo-strategic, political-economic and socio-cultural concerns still need to be thoroughly addressed and resolved—before complacency and indifference once again breed tensions and conflict. Unless both Russia and Ukraine can both be drawn into NATO and the EU in new forms of membership, maintaining Ukraine as a stable "buffer" between NATO and Russia appears key to maintaining the new post-Cold War European *equipoise*.[3] The dilemma is that both domestic and international factors seem to be working against the long-term establishment of an independent, neutral, and permanently non-nuclear, Ukraine— as the US, EU and Russia all appear to be competing for the political-economic allegiance of that key pivotal state—and, in the process, threatening its stability.

The adage attributed to the first NATO Secretary General, Lord Ismay, should be re-formulated. The implementation of a new system of European security would, in effect, necessitate building the European Union "up," drawing the United States "down" (but *not* "out")—at that same time that Russia is brought "in"—while, it should be added, keeping the Ukraine "happy" (i.e. "neutral" through overlapping NATO-EU-Russian security guarantees in a new form NATO-Euro-Atlantic "membership").

## Balkan Sectarianism

The US military strategy has emphasized war fighting capabilities and military intervention, but has been reluctant to engage in peacekeeping; the EU is prepared to engage in peacekeeping but does not want to simply clean up the mess after US intervention. The problem is thus to devolve some aspects of defense, including both "power" and "responsibility" sharing to the Europeans themselves, as has been the case in Macedonia (Concordia) and Bosnia in December 2004.

The 1995 Dayton agreement was never meant to be permanent: Socio-political tensions have not entirely ameliorated in Serbia, Montenegro, Bosnia-Herzegovina or Macedonia. The key problem is that the tension between "sectarian" demands for self-determination and "majority rule" (based in part on the Ottoman *millet* system fused with "nationalism," see Chapter 3) has been coupled with irredentist demands to change borders to better reflect the political and economic interests of rival groups—and so that no one group sees itself as "disenfranchised." Each state in the region deals with its majority/ minority questions in different ways. Croatia gives the Serb minority parliamentary representation, for example, but has not fully integrated Serbs into the society. Serbia has not recognized the political rights of minorities, particularly Albanians, but Hungarians and other groups as well. Slovenians have "separated" themselves from the Balkans, joining NATO and the EU—recognizing Italian and Hungarian minorities, but not former Yugoslavs. Montenegrins appear divided between maintaining a joint state with Serbia, or seeking independence. Moreover, a "technical" change in one border, between Serbia and Macedonia, for example, affects borders and the political-ethnic balance between Kosovo and Macedonia. Kosovars demand that Prishtina, and not Belgrade, determine the boundaries of Kosovo—while demands for Kosovar independence affect ethnic Albanians in Serbia, Macedonia and Albania.[4]

Despite the NATO intervention in 1998, the war "over" Kosovo/ Metohija in 1998 never resolved Kosovo's final status—and, in effect froze the situation. Albanian Kosovar demands for self-determination coupled with Serbian Radical Party gains in the December 2003 legislative elections (with a jailed Milosevic symbolically winning a seat) have indicated trouble. The year 2005 may represent a turning point, in that negotiations toward a final status for the region must begin soon—before both the Serbian and Kosovar Albanian sides turn to greater violence. Here the US and the EU need to bring Prishtina and a reluctant Belgrade together. On the one hand, Kosova self-determination would likely raise a spectrum of tensions throughout the Balkans region, as would partition as demanded by the Serbs. On the other hand, granting Serbian minorities in Kosovo some relative "autonomy within the autonomy"[5] in a loose confederal arrangement that guarantees power and profit sharing between the Kosovar Serb and Albanian communities, and which builds the confidence of both sides, may represent one option. The problem, however, lies in not only building trust between ethnic groups themselves (and obtaining strong guarantees for minority rights) but also in building trust between those groups and the European Union itself—which is not seen as moving rapidly enough to develop the region. It may be possible for looser confederal arrangements to work based on regional security communities, but this would require close cooperation with the EU.

## Peacekeeping beyond Europe

In respect to the disputes raging throughout much of the "developing world," the formation of multilateral contact groups much like that formed to deal with ex-Yugoslavia, or like the Quartet grouping of the US, the EU, Russia and the UN, should be given greater consideration—and made much more effective. Such Contact Groups need to engage in "behind the scenes" diplomacy, but they also must be prepared for multinational peacekeeping, backed by Rapid Deployment Forces under general UN or OSCE mandates, in a number of *post-conflict*, or even *pre-conflict*, situations. Having forces for peacekeeping ready for possible deployment under UN mandates would go a step further in implementing the initial intent of the 1948 Vandenberg Resolution that worked to establish NATO—and that was originally intended to "strengthen" the UN.

If Israel continues the process of withdrawal from the Gaza, and ultimately from lesser settlements in the West Bank, and then return to its approximate 1967 borders, the deployment of NATO, EU, and Russian multinational peacekeeping forces may prove necessary to prevent acts of both "state-supported" and "anti-state" terrorism. Such peacekeeping forces would seek to guarantee the long term security of an Israeli and Palestinian "two-state solution"—or what would really be a loose "confederation" that would require close cooperation between the two sides over water, energy, trade, and security, for example. The concerted effort upon the part of the US-EU-Russian-UN Quartet may be necessary to help achieve the Road Map to Peace and a compromise similar to the "Geneva Accords" (October 2003)—assuming these or similar accords (involving an exchange of "land for peace") can be accepted as viable and implemented by both sides.[6]

The deployment of NATO-EU-Russian peacekeepers would not only seek to stabilize the Israeli-Palestinian relationship, but would also work to provide US and multilateral security guarantees for a new "confederation." Whether such security guarantees could have been implemented before the Iraq war is now a moot question. But in light of the fact that new "threats" appear on the horizon (despite or because of) US intervention in Iraq, the extension of NATO-EU-Russian security guarantees to Israel and Palestine—and possibly to other interested states in the Euro-Mediterranean—appears crucial.

Following the 30 January 2005 elections in Iraq, and assuming a new relatively independent and "sovereign" government can soon be established (a big assumption), it may be possible for the UN to finally undertake a greater development role, that would include a greater role for US, NATO, European, Russian, or other peacekeeping forces under a general UN mandate. Working with Iraqis under a general UN mandate might help build greater domestic Iraqi support, as well as greater international *legitimacy*, for a new Iraqi government that can truly work to stabilize and reconstruct the country (and its oil industry) after the chaos of the US-UK "occupation."

A peacekeeping force under the UN would, of course, need to fight against acts of terrorism that have been destabilizing the country; it would need to help to re-integrate the Sunni populations or other groups, such as the Christian and Turkomen communities, that have become alienated. The UN presence would also help to establish confidence that US or Iraqi military forces would not engage in interventions throughout the region—as a number of neo-conservatives have threatened. Failure to internationalize peacekeeping forces, however, may well mean a very long term and very costly US presence (over a decade)—or else the eventual withdrawal of US and coalition forces overshadowed by the possible threat of a wider civil war and intervention by regional powers.

In 2003, India and Pakistan opened negotiations after a number of years of nuclear "brinksmanship" and acts of terror and counter-terror. One of the possible options would be the temporary deployment of international peacekeepers along the Line of Control (LoC) between India and Pakistan, for example—or in accord with whatever political settlement can be reached. Here, India, as the predominant regional power, appears that it might accept territorial modifications along the LoC, but, thus far, has not gone further to accept possible Kashmiri autonomy. At the same time, Pakistan appears to be dropping its previous demands for a plebiscite in Kashmir, for example—to the dismay of pan-Islamic *jihadis*.

As recent experience has shown, however, peacekeeping *by itself* does not necessarily keep the peace. Peacekeeping needs to be preceded by viable political accords. The latter may necessitate the tough work of changing boundaries and engaging in territorial compensations. Finding new modes of power-sharing through the process of *consensual* democracy and through the establishment of autonomous regions or *confederal* arrangements may also play role. Here, it may prove necessary to *mediate* the "sectarian" interests of various ethnic or religious factions so that these groups may be able to *share* control over the vital political and economic issues that affect them—assuming such arrangements can ultimately be reached through *persuasive* multilateral diplomacy.

### "Real Dialogue"

On the question of so-called "rogue states" or "outposts of tyranny," it is important to emphasize that the issues of massive human rights abuses, support for "terrorism," as well as proliferation of WMD, can only be effectively dealt with by engaging in a *real dialogue*. The latter seeks to determine the precise nature of the concerns and interests of these so-called "rogue states," and those of their regional rivals. Appropriate deliberation can subsequently determine exactly which of these concerns may be truly "legitimate" or "vital"—before making policy decisions.

The dilemma posed here is that US government rhetoric tends to impel states and political movements to choose sides, thus polarizing situations and preventing the possibility of compromise and concession. Concurrently, if Washington continues to pressure "tyrannies" to "democratize," it can only do so if it likewise puts pressure on some of its own allies to reform—so as to set appropriate standards. Concurrently, rather than pressing to obtain perfect democracies which could take years to achieve, the US may need to set more limited goals of "good governance" while, at the same time, realizing its own domestic and international limitations in its ability to impose reforms on unwilling states.

The point here is that one cannot impose "democracy" by force; real reforms can rarely be achieved in highly politically charged conditions in which parties have become polarized. At the same time, one cannot stop the realization and implementation of *legitimate* reforms as demanded by generally competing political movements within a given society. The question as to whether "problematic" states are best *reformed* by containment and sanctions; by the threat and possible use of force; by support of civil society and exile movements against the regime; or by some form of combination of these options, can really only be resolved in a multilateral context. Such a context should involve the engagement of the key concerned actors, much as was the case with the Contact Groups that dealt as effectively as possible, albeit not perfectly, with the war in Bosnia. The primary question is consequently to what extent the US, as the global hegemonic power, will heed the advice and interests of its own Allies and friends and to what extent will it seek to pressure its Allies and friends to go along with American goals and ambitions. Will the US seek to trap the Europeans into obeying its designs, after engaging only half-heartedly in a multilateral strategy?

Now that the Bush administration has, for example, labeled Zimbabwe as an "outpost of tyranny," the US, EU and UN need to work closely together, along with the Southern African Development Community (SADC), the African Union (AU), and the Commonwealth to press for reform in the forthcoming March 2005 elections, and beyond. The US likewise needs to work with South Africa, which is in the best position to influence Zimbabwe, but which has thus far preferred quiet diplomacy, contrary to the American position.[7] (See Chapter 6.)

While the US may need multilateral supports to help provide incentives (and truly coordinate sanctions), Washington may be soon need to engage in a step-by-step process to *normalize* relations and then *recognize* states, such as Iran and North Korea. This would represent one of the conditions to end their isolation—and to prevent them from acquiring nuclear weapons. Instead of pressing for *regime change*, the US may find that it has to accept *regime recognition*, but without necessarily ignoring the need for far-reaching *regime reform*.

The question, of course, is *on what terms.* The option of designing *conditional security assurances*, possibly leading to stronger security *guarantees*, creates a dilemma and dispute among US policymakers as to the *degree* of toughness that the US approach should take involving a mix of positive rewards and negative sanctions. The fundamental dilemma here is that multilateral security accords *appear* to *legitimize* the regime, but they do not preclude the possibility of evolutionary reforms—or even the possibility of radical political change coming *from within*. Of course, efforts to change societies *from within* does not prevent such regimes from claiming that foreign forces and exile groups are purposely attempting to undermine their leadership, and hence engaging in "regime change."

The concept of overlapping US, Chinese, Russian, Japanese and South Korean security assurances leading to stronger security guarantees, plus economic incentives (see Chapter 4) for Pyongyang, in exchange for a pledge not to develop nuclear weapons, appears to be moving in the right direction, despite Kim Jong-Il's decision to back out of multilateral talks in 2004. (This approach appears far more productive than confrontation with North Korea as a "rogue state" and member of the "axis of evil.")[8] In March 2005, the US urged North Korea to return to multiparty talks, and likewise urged the Chinese to put greater pressure on Pyongyang, but concurrently engaged with South Korea in military maneuvers. Here, it appears that Washington will need to take additional bilateral steps to resolve the crisis—particularly as Pyongyang has demanded an apology for calling it one of the "outposts of tyranny."

In order to achieve full North Korean compliance on the nuclear question, and convince it to put its nuclear program under international safeguards, the US may need to engage in confidence-building measures and incentives, as well as *conditional security assurances* that could ultimately lead to *stronger security guarantees* for Pyongyang through some form of a "non-aggression pact." North and South Korea can then work toward a *confederal* solution that would avoid an expensive and provocative "buy-out" of the North by the South, and that would likewise allay Chinese fears of possible US military expansion north of the Yalu. At the same time, Washington will need to engage in *real dialogue* concerning North Korean violation of human rights, and support for "terrorist" activities— much as it has done in the case of Libya. If the US cannot soon find a path toward diplomatic normalization, however, the situation on the peninsula will remain tense—and increasingly explosive.

A concerted American global strategy would simultaneously seek to dissuade Iran from seeking a nuclear capability through the combined use of *positive* rewards and the *negative* threat of international sanctions and pressures, while, once again, engaging in *real diplomacy* to deal with human rights violations and support for terrorism. As long as the US appears intent on supporting "regime change" in Iran *by force* (with dubious prospects for success despite the fact that the general Iranian population and youth appear attracted to American culture), the two sides will remain at loggerheads. This is true despite the fact that the overthrow of Saddam Hussein (and of the Taliban) could be used diplomatically to open the door to better US-Iranian relations—that is, if the US is ready to deal in more *realistic* terms with the Islamic Republic. The continued occupation of Iraq, including Shi'ite holy places, coupled with US refusal to recognize the Islamic Republic due its repression of dissent, its support for *Hizb'allah*, not to overlook the seizure of the US embassy in Teheran in 1979, have all checked progress.

Reviving Middle East regional arms control discussions that have been frozen since the 1990s should also be considered. A regional approach, which would need to discuss WMD and delivery capabilities, is problematic, but feasible. Israel, Iraq and Iran would need to develop confidence-building measures. The implementation of confidence building measures would seek to put Israel's un-proclaimed nuclear facilities under international safeguards and inspections. Moreover, Iran appears to need a "face saving" way out so that it is not regarded as merely bending to US pressures. Iran could possibly accept *conditional security assurances* leading to *stronger security guarantees* that the US would not try to engage in regime change by force. Here, however, Washington cannot absolutely guarantee that internal domestic movements (in part backed by Iranian exiles) will cease their efforts to overturn the Islamic leadership—or else, try to "neutralize" the power and role of the Mullahs through abolishment of the Guardian Council.

These *conditional security assurances*, possibly leading to *stronger security guarantees* could still be combined with multilateral supports from the *troika* of the UK, France and Germany, plus Russia. The end result could be full American recognition of the regime—but under the condition that it would put an end to its support of terrorism, and accept the "two state" (or *confederal*) solution to the Israeli-Palestinian conflict. Since Teheran, for example, has been seeking to renew diplomatic relations with Egypt—relations that Iran cut off in the wake of the Camp David accords—bringing Iran (and with it the *Hizb'allah*) to recognize the state of Israel (particularly if an Israeli-Palestinian peace agreement can be reached) appears plausible.

Moreover, as previously proposed, the deployment of NATO-EU-Russian peacekeepers (under a general UN mandate) *and* application of *multilateral security guarantees* to an Israeli-Palestinian "confederation" would, on the one hand, protect both Israel and Palestine from potential missile/nuclear and WMD threats emanating from the Middle East and Persian Gulf regions. On the other, by integrating Israel more closely into a multilateral NATO-EU-Russian defense perimeter, such an approach would also seek to *restrain* the possibility of *unilateral* Israeli military intervention against other states in the region.

The deployment of international peacekeepers made up of NATO, EU and Russian peacekeepers, along with Partnership for Peace countries acceptable to both Israelis and Palestinians under a UN mandate can consequently play a triple role: 1) It can help end to acts of terrorism and counter-terrorism. 2) It can protect both Israel (and Palestine) against potential threats of WMD from neighboring states (including Iran, if still necessary). 3) It can restrain the threat of unilateral Israeli actions so as to build help confidence throughout the region.

As part of the process of engaging states throughout the Middle East and Persian Gulf, positive incentives should be given to encourage gradual reforms, greater openness and "good governance"—reforms that would be instigated from *within* these societies and not *forced* upon them. Such a process would also mean the not so easy task of taking further steps to nudge India and Pakistan toward reconciliation over Kashmir and other disputes (which should, in turn, lessen Iranian tensions with nuclear Pakistan), while simultaneously seeking to cool tensions in Asia over North Korea through the formation of a North and South

Korean "confederation" backed by UN and multilateral security accords. Such an alternative strategy would ultimately involve the US recognition of both North Korea and Iran, as argued above, and would represent as significant a step as the Nixon-Kissinger diplomatic opening to the People's Republic of China.

## Averting Major Power War in Asia

A truly multilateral strategy would seek a Russian and Japanese entente over the Kuril islands/Northern territories backed by confidence building-measures, but at the same time, seeking to retract Russian military support for China and other regional powers. Russia, China and Japan have thus far played a positive role in trying to dissuade North Korea from developing nuclear weapons; but it seems more steps are needed to reduce tensions and build confidence. A multilateral US-Russian-Japanese entente would bring concerted diplomatic pressure on China, and to prevent it from playing Russian, Japanese, and European interests against those of the US—in its destabilizing efforts to regain Taiwan by force.

Such a policy would not, however, be designed to "contain" a rising China, but rather to *channel* its rise by seeking to foster the development of a loose *confederal* arrangement to the PRC-Taiwan dispute based upon the principle "one nation with cooperative states and several systems." This proposal would not permit the People's Liberation Army onto Taiwan, but would try to find other international security accords, and ways to engage in Taiwan-PRC military cooperation and confidence building measures through ASEAN, for example. Moreover, by working with China to develop new alternative energy sources and technologies such as non-polluting options to coal, nuclear power and oil, the US, EU and Japan can attempt to reduce China's burgeoning demand for oil and wean it away from its claims to the oil rich reserves of the South China sea.

The US and EU have yet to show Russia the positive benefits of joining the Euro-Atlantic community versus the downside of supporting China militarily in its quest to reunify with Taiwan. Failure to begin a concerted process of US-EU engagement with Russia threatens to provoke it away from "neutrality" and into becoming a "spoiler" in Eurasia—in a self-fulfilling prophecy. Russian actions may increasingly become entirely "unpredictable" and "irrational." Moscow may ultimately resort to the use of threats, if not the actual use of force, to obtain its goals.[9] If not soon brought closer to the US and EU, a *revanchist* Russia (literally fueled by high oil prices) could strengthen its ties with states such as China, India, Iran, as well as an increasingly independent Turkey—if not provide overt support to various pan-Islamic movements.

## The Question of Energy and Geopolitics

One of the major long-term concerns of American global strategy should be to sponsor ecologically sound technologies and manage excessive habits of consumption more effectively so as to significantly reduce the exploitation of non-renewable resources—with an eye toward a more fair distribution of the world's productive capabilities through "sustainable development." At the same time, there is no need, nor does it seem possible, for much of the developing world to follow in the same wasteful, consumer-oriented, path of the major developed countries. The dilemma is not only assist world development, but also indirectly help to wind down the "war on terrorism"—assuming *homo geopoliticus* can pass through a geo-economic and ecological *danger zone* in the next several decades.

By the year 2020, US and European energy demand could increase by 35%, with US dependence upon oil imports rising from 50% to 67%, even assuming increased efficiencies. European demand for imported oil alone could rise to a whopping 90%, with gas imports rising to 60%. The developing countries' energy and oil demand is similarly expected to double, rising close to the combined consumption of the US and EU, which presently represent 20% of the world's population and declining.[10] Asia alone is expected to consume some 80% of the developing world's increase in energy consumption.[11] Beijing is already the world's number one coal consumer and the third largest oil user, soon to be number two after the US. This puts the US and China in particular at loggerheads with each other and the rest of the world, unless the two can work together, along with other countries and multinational firms, as has been proposed, to develop new energy and technology alternatives.

A heavy dependence upon imported oil affects geo-strategy: US natural gas imports come from Canada, yet its oil comes from four key countries, Canada, Mexico, Venezuela and Saudi Arabia. The Middle East still holds some 67% of the world's proven oil reserves, while the Persian Gulf holds 90% of the spare oil production capacity. This is true despite recent efforts to diversify to the Caspian Sea, to Russia (the second largest oil producer after Saudi Arabia), as well as to Iraq, Libya, Nigeria, Angola, and other African countries. In May 2003, Presidents George W. Bush and Vladimir Putin launched the US-Russian Energy Dialogue, to create an "East-West" energy corridor that will permit oil from Azerbaijan, Kazakhstan, and Turkmenistan to reach world markets at competitive prices. Here, however, finding new sources of oil does not help resolve the longer-term dilemma of rising consumption (and a number of multinational oil companies have overestimated their reserves while political instability in oil rich countries has been cutting back on production).

The first term Bush administration appeared, at first, to be retrogressing in its outmoded support for coal, oil and nuclear power. The Bush administration's opposition to the Kyoto protocol on global warming was symbolic of its general reluctance to move beyond the fossil fuel economy and to develop alternative energy resources and energy-saving capabilities for the future. Alternative forms of energy contribute only about 5.5 percent of total US energy supply at present—almost the same situation as in 1970, in the previous energy crisis.

This negative position toward alternative energy technologies appeared to alter somewhat, however, in January 2003—following the announcement of the President's "Hydrogen Posture Plan" that is intended to reduce fossil fuel energy dependence by developing new hydrogen-based energy resources. Yet to what extent this program will be supported and funded remains to be seen. Now that oil prices have reached over $40–$55 a barrel and rising in 2004 to early 2005 (despite unofficial propaganda that the war in Iraq was fought to reduce oil prices and to break OPEC!), the US, Japan, the EU, as well as China and India, may take alternative energy sources more seriously. Oil utilization will remain high for the coming years, of course, but can be replaced by alternatives, step by step. The US, EU, Japan, as well as China, as the major importers of oil, will need to work together to develop, and then diffuse, those alternatives throughout the world.

## Toward Alternative Energy Sources

In effect, the first term Bush administration had initially proposed cuts in the research budget for hydrogen-based fuels, adopting a "go slow" approach that has further exacerbated dependence upon fossil fuels. The Bush administration then belatedly promised $1.2 billion in January 2003 to implement a four phase "Hydrogen Posture Plan" to accelerate the development of advanced fuel efficient technologies, such as hybrid gas-electric and fuel cells, coupled with producer and consumer tax incentives—so as to fully realize a hydrogen economy and infrastructure by 2030–40.[12] In this regard, President Bush announced his "Hydrogen Posture" Plan in his State of the Union address; yet nevertheless opted for intervention in oil-rich Iraq in March 2003—seemingly indicating a "lack of faith" in the alternative energy initiative.[13] By April 2005, although advocating more tax incentives for renewable energy and energy saving measures, President Bush pushed primarily for augmenting oil refinery space and nuclear power.

The effort to reduce the use of fossil fuel consumption, at first glance, has appeared to strengthen the argument for nuclear development. Yet a number of factors indicate that, with a truly concerted effort, the world's energy infrastructure could be weaned away from dependence upon fossil fuels—and without an excessive dependence upon the global spread of the "peaceful" atom. The Three Mile Island and Chernobyl nuclear accidents virtually doomed the nuclear industry; nuclear plants additionally make perfect targets for terrorist activities. The fact that the "war" atom and the "peaceful" atom are closely inter-related provides additional incentives to move away from the worldwide nuclear infrastructure—not to overlook genetic risks and the problems involving the transport and long-term storage of radioactive waste products. In this respect, it will soon be time for nuclear energy to wither away.[14]

First, the microchip revolution has led to the development of "micro-power" and the generation of energy by more decentralized, compact, and efficient units. Microchips allow for greater energy efficiency in industry, home construction, consumer products; they permit energy usage to be tailored to homes and communities. National and international attention needs to be given to full-scale development of alternative energy resources, bio fuels, solar, wind geothermal, greater emphasis on public transport and recycling industries, which all need to be better integrated into community energy infrastructure and industrial production. Wind Power and solar photovoltaic cells represent the fasting growing energy sources, while hydrogen power, linked to fuel cell technology, may represent the primary energy source of tomorrow.[15] The problem is not to think in terms of one option, but to utilize many technologies in combination.

**The Danger Zone**

In effect, even assuming the technological aspects of this "alternative energy infrastructure" plan can be implemented and provided sufficient financing and corporate interest in the coming years, this means *homo geopoliticus* will remain in a *danger zone* both during and after the implementation of the plan. Such a technological revolution could be, without too much exaggeration, as significant for the Middle East/Persian Gulf as the voyage of Columbus—in relation to the European effort to bypass the levies of the Ottoman Empire and the bandit-ridden routes to the Silk Road by crossing the Atlantic and Pacific.

The first facet of this *danger zone* will be characterized by increasing global rivalry for imported energy by the US, EU, China and India, among the rest of the non-oil producing countries. This is true as many of these countries will scramble to guarantee access to energy by seeking to protect sea lines of communication (SLOC), as well overland routes and pipelines, and links to key allies, by military means. The problem is to diversify energy supplies as much as possible—as high energy dependence upon politically instable countries in the Middle East/Persian Gulf in particular is not necessarily in the interests of any oil consuming country.

The second facet could be characterized by a potentially dangerous negative backlash by the oil producing countries themselves. The political-economic pressures to engage in technological and economic change will also result in revolutionary political and social changes, if not upheavals, throughout the world. As the alternative energy infrastructure is being put into place, oil producing states, such as Russia, could fear significant cut backs in demand—assuming they cannot first diversify their economies sufficiently to adjust to new geo-economic and technological circumstances. Even oil producing states may thus turn to the so-called "peaceful" atom, for example, as Iran appears to be doing—in planning to diversify future energy needs. Rather than to "liberalizing," such leaderships may attempt to dig in their heels and become even more dogmatic and dictatorial. They may accordingly seek to suppress (or eliminate) minority groups and political dissidents that criticize their policies, while possibly opting for military intervention in order to monopolize their control over resources and/or to sustain geo-strategic controls over pipelines and supply routes. (See Chapter 6.)

Artificial scarcity induced by multinational energy firms (which have been generally reluctant to diversify to alternative forms of energy production), as well as by cartels, corruption, and political instability, have all combined to diminish energy production on the international scale. Due to increasing demand for energy among both the developed and developing countries, the general rise in world prices has already begun to hit the non-oil producing states the hardest—making it even more difficult for these societies to get off the ground.

**Issues of Sustainable Growth and Development**

The question of scarce resources adds an additional burden upon the question of sustainable growth and world development.

The coming geo-economic *danger zone* may be accompanied by greater ecological disasters caused by global warming (involving a melting of the polar ice caps and more frequent hurricanes), more dangerous concentrations of carbon dioxide in the atmosphere, and a deepening of pollution throughout the eco-system. In just a few years, flooding may swamp some regions; other regions, however, may become more arid. Lack of water and other resources has partly been the cause of decades of inter-communal conflict in the Sudan, for example. Israel justified its "peaceful" nuclear program (and indirectly its nuclear weapons program) on the need for energy to desalinize water in a region without potable water (see Chapter 4). India, Bangladesh, Turkey, Iraq, Syria, Israel and Palestine, for example, all sustain disputes over the sharing of potable water.[16] It is possible, much as former UN Secretary General Boutros Boutros Ghali has frequently warned, that the next wars in the "Greater Middle East" could be fought, not over oil, but over water—as the latter is becoming more valuable than black gold.

Perhaps more so than in previous famines and catastrophes, the horrors of the 2004–05 Tsusami crisis (not related to global warming) in the Indian Ocean have awakened many in the US, Europe and Japan to the necessity to provide greater aid and assistance to the poorer regions of the planet. In this case, the major donors vowed to make certain that aid gets to the people who most need it. It is also clear that the major states (the US, China, Japan and the EU) all sought to use assistance to the Tsusami victims to strengthen their political influence in the region, yet there still appeared to be a general recognition that it is possible for aid to go directly to those who most need it. Poverty, by itself, does not cause "terrorism" but it can help provide plenty of potential recruits—particularly in an increasingly globalized world where the world media starkly reveals the differences between rich and poor, thus exacerbating resentment, envy and frustration.

In January 2005, the UN report, "Investing in Development: A Practical Plan to Achieve the Millennium Development Goals" recommended that rich countries double their official development assistance for poor countries in order to reach the Millennium Development Goal of halving extreme poverty by 2015. This kind of project should be considered in the national "self interest" of the US, and of the other major industrial powers—in that eliminating poverty can help open up new markets and can attempt to reduce the numbers of potential recruits for terrorist and mafia activities. Other initiatives include the use of the IMF as a lender of *first*, rather than *last*, resort.[17] Another is the much-debated Tobin tax.[18] Another option would be a more systematic utilization of "conditional cash transfers" and "micro-credits." A fourth option to enhance development would be to implement "controlled temporary immigration."[19] Given their "moralist" and "compassionate conservative" streak, one wonders why elements of the neo-conservative movement cannot lend more support to some of these development proposals—except perhaps that these proposals require a more effective multilateral approach and steps toward "global governance" and confederal "world democracy."[20]

In addition to the fact that significant American and international financial resources will continue to go to Iraq rather than to many other needy countries, the "war on terrorism" may even more negatively influence the process of world development. The issues raised here is that "war on terrorism" strengthens protectionist impulses by both major and minor states that are already afflicted by the political, economic and social instabilities caused by the "globalization" of trade, finance, immigration, as well as by the hype of the international media. On the one hand, it is not certain that such measures will necessarily put an end to terrorism; on the other, the high costs and political-economic effects of such security restrictions (hurting US airlines, for example) may cause considerable harm to the prospects for global economic recovery. In this respect, state security measures have generally tended to strengthen state controls and supervision over immigration, travel, capital flows, trade and technology transfer. The "war on terrorism," in effect, assists state efforts to restrict the processes of globalization, and both directly and indirectly undermines the prospects for true world development, with tendencies to polarize groups within differing societies.

Here, it is clear that in the capital rich petroleum producing states, the problem is not lack of capital, but corruption and the mal-distribution of income and benefits. Corruption that appears rampant in many oil rich states, along side extreme wide gaps between rich and poor, helps to explain popular support for *al-Qaida* attacks upon these governments—but does not justify either "terrorist" methods or goals. "Development" of many of these countries is largely a issue of finding ways to more proportionately distribute the wealth and resources that are already available—in part by both diversifying the economy and demanding greater government openness and transparency—even if the implementation of truly "democratic" processes appears a long way off, if not utopian.

It is possible that the search for energy alternatives by the major energy consumer countries could help press the oil exporting economies to open and diversify their economies in a positive fashion. It is possible that the pressure for political-economic-technological change could assist "civil society" movements to press for sound and dependable governance that protect human rights and work toward reducing poverty, while simultaneously engaging in sustainable development. This may not mean total "democratization" for all oil producing states, but political movements within some of these societies could press for an end to the general corruption that has become associated with petroleum production. Yet this kind of demand for change, assuming it is not crushed, cannot be imposed *from outside*—without setting up new systems of corruption in turn.

In the case of poorer countries without capital, development assistance and the more systematic use of financial incentives, as mentioned previously, can help to cultivate entrepreneurial skills that enhance product differentiation (that make products more distinct, interesting and competitive on a regional and world market). At the same time, however, development assistance rarely works to abolish elements of domestic monopoly and corruption that plague these countries and that prevent real competition among both domestic and international producers. It remains problematic that even crucial development assistance and debt relief, granted by the major industrial countries, largely patches over the deeper problems stemming from *structural* and *institutional* barriers to world development—barriers that are raised by differing national jurisdictions.

If the US and other industrial powers were really serious about world development, they should consequently take the lead in the formulation of policies that deal with how the immigration practices of states should be shaped in the general global interest.[21] They should take the lead in making policies that examine which states or regions need greater or lesser capital and financing; and how the trade and fiscal policies of differing states should be adjusted in accord with a common set of priorities. Concerted policies would also determine how best to deal with the aftermath of international conflicts (or natural and man-made disasters)— in terms of state and society building.[22] The fact of the matter (from the traditional realist perspective), however, is that states do generally not want to give up their national jurisdictions—over these kind of issues.

True *human* development and *real democracy* may only be possible with greater popular or indirect participation in enterprises, municipal and regional councils, as well as in national parliaments and international organizations (through the creation of a UN "World Citizen's Assembly" based upon regional representation—and not states—as proposed in Chapter 7). True development may furthermore involve *power sharing* or *shared* ownership and/or control of resources and enterprises. Finding constructive ways that truly engage popular political participation, without permitting destabilizing demagoguery will remain a major challenge. The *majoritarian* principle of "majority rule with minority rights" may not always work in situations where minority groups with a strong communal identity possess a long history of discrimination, repression or exploitation by majorities in power, or where minorities have a long history of repressing majorities. The majoritarian "liberal-democratic" model, which was trumpeted by post–1989 "end of history" theosophy, may not necessarily prove to be the best option—in that it largely ignores *consensual, communitarian* and *confederal* models, as well as other alternative models based on "good governance."

It goes without saying that development assistance that encourages greater regional integration that permits the poorer countries and regions a real say in world affairs, must further be accompanied by the fostering of an *ecological aesthetic consciousness*. The latter would seek out new alternative technologies and work to implement political-economic systems capable of sustainable development, thus intending to make "virtue out of necessity"—although not necessarily in the "neo-conservative" sense of term, "virtue."

Steps toward greater regional integration should be coupled with concerted multilateral strategies in the "war on terrorism," or other crucial social, political and ecological concerns. These steps, in turn, need to be reinforced by institutions and norms of local, regional, and global governance—or confederal "world democracy." Such an approach must work toward the reconciliation and reconstruction of war-torn societies upon the basis of greater fairness and justice, and to assist basic development goals in the ultimate aim to abolish the political-economic conditions that help give rise to all four forms of "terrorism." (See Chapter 3.) Perhaps most fundamentally, these processes should be backed by an *open* and *pragmatic* approach intended to look for diplomatic alternatives and diverse options to *prevent* disputes and crises before they break out. Such an open and pragmatic approach must be based upon a "morality of decent instincts tempered by the knowledge of human imperfection"—as opposed to the "morality of absolute self-assurance fired by the crusading spirit."[23]

# Notes

## Notes: Introduction

1   See Hall Gardner *Surviving the Millennium* (Westport, CT: Praeger, 1994), Introduction; Chapters 1–2.
2   Although other powers attempted to develop nuclear weapons during the Cold War (South Africa, Brazil, Argentina) or else maintain weapons already in their possession after the Soviet collapse (Belarus, Kazakhstan and Ukraine), these states ultimately gave up their nuclear programs under international or joint US-Russian pressures.
3   Hall Gardner, *Dangerous Crossroads* (Westport, CT, 1997), Chapter 1. See also Hall Gardner "Toward New Euro-Atlantic Euro-Mediterranean Security Communities," in *NATO and the European Union: New World, New Europe, New Threats*, ed., Hall Gardner (Aldershot and Burlington: Ashgate, 2004), Chapter 8.

## Notes: Chapter 1

1   See interview with Zbigniew Brzezinski, *Le Nouvel Observateur* (Paris, 15–21 January 1998).
2   Steve Coll, *Ghost Wars* (Penguin, 2004), 51.
3   See, for example, the initial nostalgic "neo-realist" reaction to the end of the Cold War, John J. Mearsheimer, "Why We Will Soon Miss the Cold War," *The Atlantic Monthly*, Vol. 266, No. 1 (July 1990).
4   See, for example, "Treading Water in Iraq: The Opportunity Cost of $82 billion," Center for American Progress (14 February 2005). See http://www.american progress. org / site/ pp.asp?c=biJRJ8OVF&b=34593.
5   *New York Times*, 26 January 2005, 9.
6   Richard A. Clarke, *Against All Enemies* (New York: Free Press, 2004). US intelligence officials informed President Bush on 6 August 2001 that bin Laden was capable of a major strike against the US, including the hijacking of American aircraft.
7   Paul Wolfowitz, quoted in Bill Keller, "The Sunshine Warrior," *New York Times Magazine*, 22 September 2002, 97, cited in, *Carl Kaysen Steven E. Miller Martin B. Malin, William D. Nordhaus John D. Steinbruner*, American Academy of Arts and Sciences (2003) http://www.amacad.org/publications/monographs/War_with_Iraq.pdf.
8   The first coup was "planned" in 1994–95 by the Iraqi National Congress (generally favored by the Defense Department), but the Clinton Administration refused to back it. The second coup was better organized in 1996 by the Iraqi National Accord (generally favored by the CIA), but failed as Hussein's intelligence executed the plotters. See Liam Anderson and Gareth Stansfield, *The Future of Iraq* (Palgrave, 2004), 95–96. See also Robert Baer, *See No Evil* (New York: Crown Publishers, 2002).
9   The Iraq Liberation Act (Public Law 105-338) raised two questions: the first was how to achieve regime change. The second was how to promote the emergence of a "democratic" government.
10  Paul Alexander, "The Generals Speak" *Rolling Stone* (3 November 2004).
11  George F. Kennan, *American Diplomacy: 1900–1950* (University of Chicago, 1953).

12　"Afghan alumni have been involved in most major terrorist plots or attacks against the US in the past 15 years and now engage in international militant and terrorist acts throughout the world.... The leaders of some of the most dangerous terrorist groups to emerge in the past decade have headquarters or major offices in Afghanistan... This is why the Taliban's continued support for these groups is now recognized by the international community as a growing threat to all countries." Office of the Coordinator for Counter-terrorism, *Patterns of Global Terrorism - 2000,* 30 April 2001.

13　Ahmed Raschid, *Taliban* (New Haven: Yale University Press, 2001).

14　On US intervention and problems of "nation-building," see Minxin Pei, "Lessons of the Past" *Foreign Policy*, July/August 2003. On international assistance to war-torn societies, see François Jean and Jean-Christophe Rufin (eds), *Economie des guerres civiles* (Paris: Fondation pour les Etudes de Defense, 1996).

15　See Anthony Lake, "Confronting Backlash States," *Foreign Affairs* (March/April 1994). The Clinton administration subsequently moved away from the expression, "rogue states," using instead the term, "states of concern."

16　Madeline Albright's assertion that the deaths of 500,000 children "was a price worth paying" for the containment of Iraq was manipulated by bin Laden's propaganda in his 1998 declaration of *jihad* on the US, even if the US argued that the humanitarian crisis was the responsibility of Saddam Hussein and not caused by UN sanctions. Liam Anderson and Garth Stansfield *The Future of Iraq*, op. cit., 99. Populations in Iraqi Kurdistan (in the no fly zone) generally fared better under UN and NGO assistance than populations under Hussein's control. One can also question whether 500,000 children was an accurate figure: 100,000 may be closer to the mark. See Matt Welch, "The Politics of Dead Children: Have sanctions against Iraq murdered millions?" *Reason Online* (March 2002). http://www.reason.com/0203/fe.mw.the.shtml.

17　Chalmers Johnson, *Blowback* (Little Brown, 2000), 216. Focusing primarily on Japan, China and the two Koreas, Johnson argues that American "double standards" and "stealth imperialism" have caused great resentment and potential *revanchist* movements—or "blowback"—in many countries throughout the world. One could add the danger of a potential, but not inevitable, *revanchist* movement in Russia as well.

18　Hans Morgenthau, *Politics Among Nations,* (Boston, MA: McGraw Hill, 1985), 381.

19　On Saddam's policy of *tarhib wa-targhib* ("terror and enticement"), see Anderson and Stansfield *The Future of Iraq*, op. cit., 53.

20　Hussein brutally repressed the Kurdish Democratic Party and the clan of its leader Massoud Barzani, in 1983, in that the latter aligned itself with Iran at the time in which the US began to give Iraq more open support. In 1989, Iraq used chemical weapons against the Kurds, as it did again in 1999 in the *al-Sadr* uprising against Shi'ite protestors in southern Iraq. On the latter, see *Human Rights Watch*, 17 February 2005.

21　See, for example, Peyman Pejman "Iraq: Officials Say U.S. Was Wrong To Dissolve Army, Intelligence Apparatus" *Radio Free Europe/ Radio Liberty (RFE/RL)*, 13 November 2003. Much like the trial of Serbian leader Slobodan Milosevic, the December 2003 capture (and eventual public and national or international trial?) of Saddam Hussein may close some wounds, but open new ones.

22　On proposed "vigilant containment," see John Mearsheimer and Stephen Walt, "An Unnecessary War," *Foreign Policy* (January–February 2003).

23　Bob Woodward, *Plan of Attack* (Simon and Schuster, 2004), 71. The CIA's assessment that "covert action is not going to remove Saddam Hussein," due to the fact that he had perfected his security apparatus, assumed that his intelligence agencies, the army, as well as his own family, would continue to support him in the long term. Moreover, more muscular weapons inspections involving armed troops, as proposed by Paris and Berlin may have created a new internal dynamic and power struggle and provided greater protection for NGOs and international assistance workers (in political conditions more stable than in the post-Saddam post-military intervention crisis).

24    Hall Gardner and Simon O'Li, "Unpublished Interview" with Dominique de Villepin, (Paris, May 2003).

25    James Risen, "Iraq offered a Deal as the War Loomed," *International Herald Tribune*, 7 November 2003, 1.

26    Paul Alexander, *The Generals Speak*, op. cit. General Zinni additionally argued that "when (he) was commander of CENTCOM, we had a plan for an invasion of Iraq, and it had specific numbers in it. We wanted to go in there with 350,000 to 380,000 troops. You didn't need that many people to defeat the Republican Guard, but you needed them for the aftermath. We knew that we would find ourselves in a situation where we had completely uprooted an authoritarian government and would need to freeze the situation: retain control, retain order, provide security, seal the borders to keep terrorists from coming in." To muster this number of troops, the US needed to consider other options, or else obtain a UN mandate for intervention.

27    The first US Director of Reconstruction and Humanitarian Assistance for Iraq, General Jay Garner inadvertently admitted in mid–May 2003 that planning for reconstruction represented "an *ad hoc* operation, glued together over about four or five weeks time."

28    "Iraq: U.S.-Led Forces Failed to Secure Key Evidence" *Human Rights Watch* (4 November 2004).

29    A dozen retired US military officers sent a signed letter to the Senate Judiciary Committee criticizing the nomination of White House counsel Alberto Gonzales for the post of Attorney General—as the latter had approved a series of memorandums arguing that the US could lawfully disregard portions of the Geneva Convention and that some forms of torture could be justified in the war against terror. *International Relations and Security Network (ISN) ISN Security Watch* (5 January 2005).

30    See "The New Iraq?" *Human Rights Watch* (25 January 2005).

31    Bloomberg School of Public Health at Johns Hopkins University in Baltimore, cited in *ISN Security Watch* 29 October 2004. See also, "The Lancet Iraq Mortality Survey: The UK government's response is inaccurate and misleading." *Cambridge Solidarity with Iraq* (1 November 2004). Had the Fallujah sample been included, the survey's estimate would have been of an excess of about 298,000 deaths, with 200,000 concentrated in the 3% of Iraq around Fallujah; http://www.casi.org.uk/briefing/041101lancetpmos.html.

32    See estimates of insurgents, civilian and military deaths compiled by the Council on Foreign Relations, "Iraq: The Insurgency by the Numbers" (6 January 2005). http://www.cfr.org/background/ iraq_insurgnum.php.

33    National Intelligence Council (NIC), "Mapping the Global Future" (Washington, DC: CIA, 2004). http://www.cia.gov/ nic/NIC_2020_project.html.

34    See Walter Pincus "U.S. Says More Iraqi Police Are Needed as Attacks Continue" *Washington Post*, 28 September 2004, A23. According to Condoleezza Rice, the Bush administration's exit strategy is "directly proportional" to the country's ability to defend itself against "terrorists" after the 30 January 2005 elections.

35    General Wesley Clark, cited in, Paul Alexander, "The Generals Speak," op. cit. The US Army has been operating on the assumption that the number of American troops in Iraq would remain above 100,000 through 2006.

36  See Hall Gardner, "From Egypt of 1882 to Iraq of 2003" *Sens Public,* No. 3 (March 2005). http://www.sens-public.org/article_paru3.php3?id_article=114.

37  See, Stephen Hemsley Longrigg, *Iraq 1900-1950* (Oxford: 1953); Yitzhak Nakash, "The Shi'ites and the Future of Iraq," *Foreign Affairs* July/ August 2003; Henry A. Foster, *The Making of Modern Iraq* (Norman, University of Oklahoma Press, 1935).

38  It has been alleged that the British used chemical weapons (backed by Winston Churchill in 1920) against Iraqi Kurds in the 1920s. Phosphorus bombs and a rudimentary form of napalm were used to subdue Iraqi Kurdistan. See Geoff Simmons *Iraq from Summer to Saddam* (St. Martin's 1994), cited in Liam Anderson and Garth Stansfield *The Future of Iraq* (Palgrave, 2004), 23.

39  Karl Marx, "The Future Results of British Rule in India," 22 July 1853.

40  As General Wesley Clark put it: "It wasn't until the last minute that they came up and said, 'Hey, by the way, we are going to create a wave of democracy across the Middle East.' That was February of 2003, and by that timethey hadn't planned anything. Paul Alexander, "The Generals Speak" op. cit.

41  See Robert D. Kaplan, "A Post-Saddam Scenario," *The Atlantic Online* (November 2002). http://www.the Atlantic.com/issues/2002/11/Kaplan.htm.

42  Former UN weapons inspector Scott Ritter claimed that US authorities in Iraq had manipulated the election results to reduce the percentage of the vote received by the United Iraqi Alliance from 56% to 48%, so that it would not obtain an absolute majority. "Scott Ritter Says U.S. Plans June Attack On Iran," (21 February 2005). http://electroniciraq.net/news/. Even without such purported manipulations, it will prove very difficult to prevent the new Iraqi government from pressing for policies that may go against US interests in both its domestic and foreign policies.

43  The Paris Club agreed to write off a portion of Iraq's debt in three stages. See Zaid Al-Ali, "The IMF and the Future of Iraq" (08 December 2004). http://usa.mediamonitors. net/content/ view/full/11850/. See also debates demanding a write-off of all "odious debts." *Jubilee Iraq News* http://www.jubileeiraq.org/cgi-bin/mtsearch.cgi?Template= jubileeiraq &search = %22Paris% 20club%22.

44  This updates my definition of the "global equipoise." See Hall Gardner *Surviving the Millennium,* op. cit. Introduction; Chapters 1–2.

45  See Hall Gardner, "Aligning for the Future" *Harvard International Review,* Vol. 2. No. 4 (Winter 2003). See also http://www.nthposition.com/reflectionsontheseptember.php.

## Notes: Chapter 2

1   J. William Fulbright, *The Arrogance of Power* (1967).

2   Charles Krauthammer, "Democratic Realism" (Washington, DC: American Enterprise Institute, 12 February 2004). Krauthammer reveals his "realist" side. http://www.aei.org/news/newsID.19912/ news_detail.asp.

3   Socialist Michael Harrington and *Dissent* magazine coined the term "to describe their old friends who'd moved to the right." See Jonah Goldberg, "The Neoconservative Invention: No New Kid on the Block," *The National Review* (20 May 2003). http://www.nationalreview.com/goldberg/goldberg052003.asp.

4   The US assured all companies that they could ultimately bid for contracts; but, at the same time, AID claims it has enacted (1) a "fast track" and special exemption to reduce bidding so as to speed up the process; (2) that firms are chosen according to US security clearance; (3) that foreign firms can be chosen for subcontracts.

5    See David Calleo, "Hegemony and Decline: Reflections on Recent American Experience" in *Sens Public* No. 3 (May 2005). http://www.sens-public.org/rubrique_paru3.php3?id_ rubrique=47.

6    See Steve Coll, *Ghost Wars*, op. cit.

7    The following Bush, Jr. officials were in the Reagan Administration: Pentagon: Paul Wolfowitz, Douglas Feith; Defense Department Policy Board: Richard Perle; State Department: Richard Armitage, John Bolton; UN Ambassador: John Negroponte (now US ambassador to Iraq); NSC: Elliott Abrams. On the other hand, Dick Cheney served in the administrations of both Bush Sr. and Bush Jr. Neo-conservatives, Elliott Abrams (Middle East) and Robert Joseph (arms proliferation), obtained key positions in the Bush Jr. administration; I. Lewis Libby has been Cheney's advisor. Richard Perle, former CIA chief, James Woolsey, former arms-control negotiator Kenneth Adelman and military historian, Eliot Cohen served on Rumsfeld's Defense Policy Board (DPB). Two of the individuals most responsible for the Iraq war, Douglas Feith and Paul Wolfowitz, however left the Pentagon in 2005 in the second Bush administration.

8    For text of NSC-68, see Steven L. Rearden, *The Evolution of American Strategic Doctrine* (Boulder, Colo/ SAIS Foreign Policy Institue, 1984).

9    Paul H. Nitze and Robert W. Chandler, "At What Price an Enlarged NATO" draft editorial, unpublished (16 May 1995).

10   Max Boot, "Think Again: Neocons," *Foreign Policy*, January/February 2004.

11   See Hall Gardner "From Balance to Imbalance of Terror" in Hall Gardner, ed. *NATO and the European Union,* op. cit.

12   Nathan Thayer, in Committee on Foreign Affairs, *United States-Japanese Relations* (Washington, DC: GPO, 1982), 218–20.

13   "Z," To the Stalin Mausoleum" Daedalus 19, 1 (Winter, 1990).

14   Jim Lobe "Baker's Return Equals Cheney's Heartburn" 13 December 3003 www.antiwar.com/ips /lobe121303.html.

15   *International Herald Tribune* 18 February 1992; 12 March 1992; 25 May 1992.

16   "The 1992 draft of the Pentagon's Defense Planning Guidance advocated 'discouraging the advanced industrialized nations from even aspiring to a larger global or regional role.' The United States may at times seek help from others, but not too much help, lest it lose its leading position in one part of the world or another. The document, when it was leaked, provoked criticism. In response, emphasis was placed on its being only a draft, but its tenets continue to guide American policy." Kenneth N. Waltz, "Globalization and American Power" *The National Interest*, No. 59 (Spring 2000).

17   See neo-conservative *Project for a New America* website http://www.newamerican century.org/statementofprinciples.htm.

18   *Committee on the Present Danger*. http://www.fightingterror.org/whoweare/index.cfm.

19   See "An Open Letter to the Heads of State and Government Of the European Union and NATO" 28 September 2004. http://www.newamericancentury.org/russia-20040928.htm. The letter, signed by many neo-conservatives, strongly criticizes Putin's steps toward an "authoritarian regime." A counter-letter argues for concern, but against exaggeration: See "A response to the open letter to heads of state and government of the European Union and NATO of Sept. 28, 2004." http://washingtontimes.com/upi-breaking/20041013-055300-4000r.htm. Or else, www.npetro.net/openletter.html.

20   John Mearsheimer and Steven E. Miller in *Foreign Affairs*, 72, 3 Summer, 1993. John J. Mearsheimer, "Why We Will Soon Miss the Cold War," *The Atlantic Monthly*, Vol. 266, No. 1 (July 1990). See debate between John J. Mearsheimer, "Back to the Future"

International Security 15 (Summer 1990): 5-56. Reprinted in Lynn-Jones and Miller, eds., *The Cold War and After* (Cambridge, Mass: MIT Press, 1993), 141–92.

21   Richard Perle, "...The question is how imminent must the attack be to justify the preemptive response. Here, we need to think more carefully about the concept of imminence.... ...the Israelis decided to strike (the Osirak reactor in 1981) some years in advance of the production of the nuclear weapon that they were concerned about... because the Iraqis were about to load fuel into the reactor and once they did so, (the Israelis) would not have had an opportunity to use an air strike... because radioactive material would have been released into the atmosphere. So from an Israeli point of view, what was imminent and what had to be acted against in a pre-emptive manner was not the ultimate emergence of the threat but an event that would lead inexorably to the ultimate emergence of the threat... What is imminent about Iraq and what may be imminent in some other situations requires you to look back and decide when a threat becomes unmanageable." http://www.newamericancentury.org/iraq-20030224.htm.

22   "National Strategy to Combat Weapons of Mass Destruction" (12 December 2001).

23   The anti-Iranian pro-Iraq shift was perhaps not so accidentally accompanied by the October 1983 Hizb'allah suicide bombings of the US marine barracks and French peacekeepers in Beirut, and followed by terrorist attacks from both pro-Iranian and Palestinian groups, and culminating in the Lockerbie bombing. Although the 1983 suicide attack was more closely linked to the US military presence in Lebanon, after the 1981 Israeli intervention, it may have had a double message. The 1983 bombing resulted in US withdrawal from Lebanon.

24   George Bush, Sr.; Brent Scowcroft, *A World Transformed* (Knopf, 1998), 489.

25   Richard A. Clarke, *Against All Enemies* (New York: Free Press, 2004), 32.

26   Bob Woodward, "Decision Iraq: Would Kerry Have Done Things Differently?" *Washington Post* (24 October 2004, B04).

27   James W. Caesar, "The Great Divide" in *Present Dangers* ed by Robert Kagan and William Kristol (San Francisco: Encounter Books: 2000), 37.

28   Robert Kagan, "Multilateralism, American Style" *The Washington Post* 13 September 2002. See also Robert Kagan, *Of Paradise and Power* (New York: Knopf, 2003).

29   Robert Kagan, "Multilateralism, American Style," ibid.

30   See Eqbal Ahmad, "Terrorism: Theirs and Ours" (1998) in *Terrorism and Counter-Terrorism* ed. Russell D. Howard and Reid L. Sawyer (Gilford: McGraw Hill, 2003).

31   Paul Wolfowitz, "Statesmanship in the New Century" in *Present Dangers*, eds. Robert Kagan and William Kristol (San Francisco: Encounter Books: 2000), 314.

32   Ustina Markus, "CIA in Decline; Pentagon on the Rise" *ISN Security Watch* (24 January 2005).

33   See 1854 "Ostend Manifesto" by James Buchanan, J.Y. Mason, Pierre Soulét, *American History Leafets, Colonial and Constitutional* No. 2. http://xroads.virginia.edu /~HYPER/ HNS/Ostend/ostend.html.

34   For a comparison of Iraq in 2003 with the Philippines in 1900, see Frank Gibney, "Is President Bush Repeating McKinley's Mistake in the Philippines?" *History News Network*. http://hnn.us/articles/1595.html.

35   "My paramount object in this struggle is to save the Union, and is not either to save or to destroy slavery. If I could save the Union without freeing any slave, I would do it; and if I could save it by freeing some and leaving others alone I would also do that. What I do about slavery, and the colored race, I do because I believe it helps to save the Union." *Abraham Lincoln in a letter to Horace Greely* (22 August 1862).

36    William Appleton Williams, *Empire as a Way of Life* (Oxford: Oxford University Press, 1980), 53.

37    Dana Milbank, "Another Ol' Hickory in the White House?" *Washington Post* (17 September 2002), A19.

38    William Appleton Williams, *Empire as a Way of Life*, op. cit., 53.

39    See Donald Kagan, *On the Origins of War and the Preservation of Peace* (Doubleday: New York, 1995). Opposition to appeasement in any form runs through most of Kagan's work. Paul Kennedy, on the other hand, points to late 19th century British policy toward the US as one of successful "appeasement," for example. See Paul Kennedy, *Strategy and Diplomacy* (Unwin-Hyman, 1984).

40    Douglas Porch, "Europe, America, and the 'War on Terror'" *Strategic Insights*, Vol III, No. 4 (April 2004).

41    Steven Lenzner and William Kristol, "What Was Leo Strauss Up To?" *The Public Interest* (Fall 2003). "To understand political life in terms of regimes is to recognize that political life always partakes of both the universal (principles of justice or rule) and the particular ("our" borders, language, customs, etc.). The concept of regime... is one that avoids the unhealthy extremes of utopian universalism and insular nationalism. President Bush's advocacy of "regime change"—which avoids the pitfalls of a wishful global universalism on the one hand, and a fatalistic cultural determinism on the other—is a not altogether unworthy product of Strauss's rehabilitation of the notion of regime."

42    Strauss, Leo, *History of Political Philosophy*, ed. Leo Strauss and Joseph Cropsey, (Chicago: University of Chicago Press, 1987); Leo Strauss, *The Early Writings*, 1921-1932, ed. Michael Zank (Albany: NY: State University of New York, 2002).

43    Steven Lenzner and William Kristol, "What Was Leo Strauss Up To?" op. cit. See also critical commentary, John G. Mason, "Leo Strauss and the Noble Lie" *Logos* (Spring 2004). http://www.logosjournal.com/mason.htm.

44    See argument of Marcel van Herpen, "Six Dimensions of the Growing Transatlantic Divide" in Hall Gardner, ed. *NATO and the European Union*, op. cit., Chapter 11.

45    See commentary by Leo Strauss, in Carl Schmitt, *The Concept of the Political* (Chicago: University of Chicago, 1995).

46    See Hall Gardner, "NATO Enlargement and Geohistory" in *NATO for a New Century,* ed., Carl Hodge (Westport: Praeger, 2002).

47    Ronald Wintrobe, *Dictatorship*, University of Western Ontario (25 April 2002). www.ssc.uwo.ca/economics/faculty/ Wintrobe/DICTATORSHIP_SURVEY.pdf.

48    Immanuel Kant, "Appendix 1: On the Opposition between Morality and Politics with Respect to Perpetual Peace" *Perpetual Peace.* http://www.mtholyoke.edu/acad/intrel/kant/append1.htm.

49    Immanuel Kant, "Appendix 1," ibid.

50    As Abraham Lincoln put it, "If the end brings me out all right, what is said against me won't amount to anything. If the end brings me out wrong, then ten angels swearing I was right would make no difference."

## Notes: Chapter 3

1    On strategic leveraging, see Hall Gardner, *Surviving the Millennium*, op. cit.

2    The term "propaganda by deed" derived from the Italian, Carlo Pisacane. George Woodcock, *Anarchism* (London, 1962), 308.

3    See Bruce Hoffman, *Inside Terrorism* (Columbia University Press, 1998).

4     For description, see Daniel Gross, "Terror on Wall Street—A Look at a 1920 Bombing" *TheStreet.com* (20 September 2001).
5     In *Mein Kampf*, in the battle against Marxist ideology, Hitler argued in support of total regime change: "It has invariably happened in the history of the world that formal State authority has failed to break a reign of terror, which was inspired by a *Weltanschauung*. It can only be conquered by a new and different *Weltanschauung* whose representatives are quite as audacious and determined..."
6     France, Russia and China experienced stages of "totalitarian terrorism" yet unlike France (after Napoleon's defeat in 1815), the Soviet Union and China continued to sustain a repressive domestic state apparatus.
7     Hannah Arendt, *Origins of Totalitarianism* (Harcourt: 1976).
8     Hannah Arendt, ibid., 6. See also Chapter 13.
9     A complete political sociology of terrorism is necessary. but while suicide bombers come from poor classes, leaders such as Abu Nidal and Saudi-Yemeni Ossama bin Laden, come from extremely wealthy backgrounds. Abu Nidal who, in his quest for revenge against Israel's confiscation of his father's lands, split with the PLO in 1974 and set up a rival Fatah Revolutionary Council. The Abu Nidal Organization was given support by Iraq; in addition to attacking Israelis, it also assassinated Palestinians that sought compromise with Israel.
10    In an ever-widening definition, the "war on terrorism" has opened a wide legal gap in which it is not at all clear which groups and specific actions can be defined as "terrorist." On the one hand, an Italian judge defined actions of a group in Afghanistan as "guerrilla" rather than "terrorist." On the other hand, a Bronx district attorney accused members of the St. James Boys street gang of shootings "committed with the intent to intimidate or coerce a civilian population" under New York's state terrorism laws. *ISN Security Watch* 2 February 2005.
11    Initially backed by Saudi Arabia in the 1980s, Islamic charities have financed *al-Qaida*. Funds for the Irish Republican Army were also collected by "charities," but often from Irish pubs located in the USA and elsewhere (without any official backing).
12    See, OECD, "FATF Special Recommendations on Terrorist Financing," 31 October 2001. http://www1.oecd.org/fatf/pdf/SRecTF_en.pdf.
13    National Intelligence Council (NIC), "Mapping the Global Future," op. cit.
14    Immanuel Wallerstein, *Geopolitics and Geoculture: Essays on the Changing World-System* (Cambridge: Cambridge University Press, 1997).
15    Samuel Huntington, *The Clash of Civilizations and the Remaking of World Order* (New York: Touchstone, 1997).
16    Cited in James S. Robbins "Bin Laden's War" in *Terrorism and Counter-terrorism* ed. Russell D. Howard and Reid L. Sawyer (Gilford: McGraw Hill, 2003), 365, fn 11.
17    Bruce Hoffman "Combating Terrorism," Subcommittee on National Security, Veterans Affairs, and International Relations, House Committee on Government Reform 27 March 2001. http://www.mipt.org/ srchnatl strat 03272001d.asp.
18    See Howard and Sawyer, *Terrorism and Counter-terrorism*, op. cit. 557. *Aum Shinrikyo* had purportedly been cooperating with North Korea, Russian mafia groups, and indirectly with Iran, in smuggling nuclear materials out of the ex-USSR.
19    Tariq Ali, "Who really killed Daniel Pearl?" *The Guardian* (5 April 2002).
20    Stefan Wolff, "Conflict Management in Northern Ireland," *International Jounral on Multicultural Studies*, Vol. 4, No. 1 (2002).

21 On detention camps in ex-Yugoslavia, see Final Report of the United Nations Commission of Experts established pursuant to security council resolution 780 (1992) Annex VIII - part 1/10 Prison camps S/1994/674/Add.2 (Vol. IV) 27 May 1994.

22 As Bernard Lory put it: "An interpretation of the recent war in Bosnia as a war of religion is an erroneous one. It has been a war between millets shaped by nationalism. See Bernard Lory, "Rusty Ottoman Keys to the Balkans Today" in Hall Gardner, ed., *Central and Southeastern Europe in Transition* (Westport, CT: Praeger, 2000), 38. It may also be possible to apply this theory to Lebanon in 1975 and Iraq in 2003.

23 Anneli Botha, "Terrorism in Africa" *Defense Journal* Vol. 1, No. 1. January 2005.

24 Huntington's ideological interpretation of history appears to overlook that fact that Hitler sought a real war of "civilization," to exterminate specifically identified groups (Gypsies, Jews, Slavs, socialists, communists, homosexuals, as well as Christians). In *Mein Kampf*, Hitler had considered Christianity as a religion imposed by "spiritual terror," and proposed counter-terror to create the Third Reich.

25 See also Gilles Kepel, *Fitna: la guerre au Coeur de l'Islam* (Gallimard, Paris: 2004).

26 See Karl Marx, cited in "Revolutionary Spain," http://www.marxists.org/archive/marx/ works/ 1854/revolutionary-spain/ch05.htm.

27 Napoleon's response to irregular partisan warfare was the following: "*Il faut opérer en partisan partout où il y a des partisans*. Cited in Carl Schmitt, *La Notion de Politique*; *Theorie du Partisan* (Paris: Flammarrion, 1992), 216.

28 Walter Laqueur, *The Age of Terrorism* (Boston: Little, Brown and Co: 1987), 11.

29 Mikhail Bakunin, *The Immorality of the State Ethics: Morality of the State*. http://www.etext.org/text/Bakunin%20Mikhail%20%20The%20Immorality%20of%20 the%20State.txt. "For there is no terror, cruelty, sacrilege... or foul treason which has not been committed... by representatives of the State, with no other excuse than this elastic, at times so convenient and terrible phrase: *Raison d'état*."

30 See Noel O' Sullivan "Terrorism, Ideology and Democracy" in *Terrorism, Ideology and Revolution*, ed. Noel Sullivan (Sussex: Wheatsheaf Books, 1986), 14–16.

31 As Roosevelt argued, "Anarchy is a crime against the whole human race, and all mankind should band together against the Anarchist. His crimes should be made a crime against the law of nations . . . declared by treaties among all civilized powers. See Richard B. Jensen, "The United States, International Policing the War against Anarchist Terrorism," *Terrorism and Political Violence* 13, 1 (Spring 2001), 19.

32 David C. Rapoport, "The Four Waves of Rebel Terror and September 11" *Anthropoetics* Vol. 8, No. 1 (Spring / Summer 2002).

33 Hedley Bull, *The Anarchical Society* (New York: Columbia University, 1995), 259.

34 On the re-invention of *jihad* as the rationalization of terror, see Khalid Duran, "Middle Eastern Terrorism: Its Characteristics and Driving Forces" in *Terrorism: Roots, Impact, Responses*, ed. Lawrence Howard (Westport, CT: Praeger, 1992).

35 *ISN Security Watch* (5 January 2005).

36 See also Gilbert Achcar, *The Clash of Barbarisms* (New York: Monthly Review Press, 2002).

37 In 1797, Robert Fulton stated: "Should some vessels of war be destroyed by means so novel, so hidden and so incalculable the confidence of the seamen will vanish and the fleet rendered useless from the moment of the first terror." Captain Brayton Harris, USN (Retired), *World Submarine History*, 1580–2000. http://www.submarine - history.com/NOVAone.htm.

38 Thomas A. Edison predicted that "There will one day spring from the brain of science a machine or force so fearful in its potentialities, so absolutely terrifying, that even

man, the fighter, who will dare torture and death in order to inflict torture and death, will be appalled, and so abandon war forever." New laser weaponry designed to blind and terrorize the enemy is also intended to end warfare.

39  For a Cuban view, see http://www.un.int/cuba/Pages/fidelbarbados061001 _ing.htm.

40  Paul Virilio argues that Palestinian suicide tactics have nothing to do with either Christianity or Islam, but was "inseminated" by the "Red Queen," Fusako Shigenobu, leader of the Red Army Faction, into the region. She was arrested in 2000 in Japan. See Paul Virilio, *Crepuscular Dawn* (New York: *Semiotext(e)*, 2002).

41  Khalid Duran, "Middle East Terrorism" in *Terrorism: Roots, Impact, Responses*, ed. Lawrence Howard (Westport, CT: Praeger, 1992), 52.

42  Despite the fact that bin Laden himself is Sunni, his organization may have obtained some support from Iranian Republican Guards—contrary to the view that Sunni and Shi'ite Moslems would not cooperate.

43  Menachin Begin, cited in Walter Laqueur, *The Terrorism Reader* (New York: New American Library, 1978), 142. Nelson Mandela identifies the *Irgun* as the model for the formation of the military wing of the ANC. See Mandela, "I am Prepared to Die," Nelson Mandela's statement from the docket in the Rivonia Trial Pretoria Supreme Court (20 April 1964) http://www.anc.org.za/ancdocs/history/ rivonia.html.

44  See "1996 Declaration of War Against the Americans Occupying the Land of the Two Holy Places" in Yonah Alexander and Michel S. Swetnam, *Usama bin Laden's al Qaida: Profile of a Terrorist Network* (Ardsley, NY: Transnational Publishers, 2001). In shifting US forces from Saudi Arabia to Qatar, the US tacitly gave in to one of bin Laden's key demands.

45  "1996 Declaration of War," ibid.

46  Louis Snyder, *Macro-Nationalisms* (Westport, CT: Greenwood, 1984).

47  Edward C. Snyder "The Dirty Legal War: Human Rights and the Rule of Law in Chile 1973-1995" *Tulsa Journal of Comparative and International Law 1995* http://cyber.law.harvard.edu/evidence99/pinochet/HistoryGeneralArticle.htm.

48  For details, see *Human Rights Watch*, "Chile: Government Discloses Torture Was State Policy" (29 November 2004).

49  On this issue, it is generally overlooked that individual US states had expropriated the property of British loyalists after the American Revolutionary war; that lands of various Indian tribes were likewise expropriated for America's Manifest Destiny, as was the property of Japanese Americans during World War II.

50  In its 2002 Annual report, Amnesty International reported: "The authorities stated in October 2001 that Algerian security forces had "neutralized" 20,000 "terrorists" since 1992, without specifying how many had been killed and how many apprehended. http://web.amnesty.org/web/ar2002.nsf/mde/algeria!Open.

51  Therese Delpech, *International Terrorism and Europe* Chaillot Papers, No. 56 (Paris: EU Institute for Security Studies, December 2002).

52  Daniele Ganser, "NATO's secret armies linked to terrorism?" *ISN Security Watch* (15 December 2004). See also Daniele Ganser, "NATO's Secret Armies: Operation Gladio and Terrorism in Western Europe" (London: Frank Cass, 2005).

53  Ibid.

54  *ISN Security Watch* (28 January 2005).

55  *Moscow Times*. The Moscow Times.com (8 September 2004).

56  See Taras Kuzio, "AL-Qaeda Regroups. State Misuse of the Anti-Terrorism Campaign," *RFE/RL* Vol. 3, No. 5 (13 February 2003). For details, see Human Rights Watch, "Opportunism in the Face of Tragedy, Repression in the name of anti-terrorism" http://www.hrw.org/campaigns/september11/opportunismwatch.htm.

57    Anjali Bhattacharjee and Sammy Salama, "Libya and Nonproliferation" *Monterey Center for Non-Proliferation Studies* (24 December 2003).

58    This was possibly an act of revenge for the shooting down an Iranian commercial Airbus in the Gulf by the U.S.S. Vincennes. (American apologies for the "accidental" shooting were never accepted by Iranian and pan-Islamic revolutionaries). Another reason for the bombing of the *Pan Am* flight was for revenge against US attacks in 1986 that had killed Qaddaffi's adopted daughter that were, in turn, revenge for a Libyan bombing of a Berlin disco, which had been staged to avenge the sinking of two patrol boats by the US over Libyan claimed waters in March 1986.

59    "Four forms of violence were possible. There is sabotage, there is guerrilla warfare, there is terrorism, and there is open revolution. We chose to adopt the first method and to exhaust it before taking any other decision. In the light of our political background the choice was a logical one. Sabotage did not involve loss of life, and it offered the best hope for future race relations. Bitterness would be kept to a minimum and, if the policy bore fruit, democratic government could become a reality. "I am Prepared to Die," Nelson Mandela's statement, Rivonia Trial Pretoria Supreme Court, 20 April 1964, op. cit.

60    Mandela, op. cit.

61    See John Paul Lederach, "Civil Society and Reconciliation" in *Turbulent Peace*, edited by Chester A. Crocker, Fen Osler Hampson, Pamela Aall (Washington, DC: US Institute for Peace, 2001).

62    For details on the peace talks in Northern Ireland, see Stefan Wolff, "Conflict Management" in *Northern Ireland International Journal on Multicultural Studies*, Vol 4, No. 1 (2002).

63    Thomas Hobbes, *Leviathan*, The Second Part of Commonwealth, Chapter XVII "Of the Causes, Generation and a Definition of a Commonwealth." "Therefore before the names of just and unjust can have place, there must be some coercive power to compel men equally to the performance of their covenants, by the terror of some punishment greater than the benefit they expect by the breach of their covenant.... "

64    Edmund Burke, "Speech on the Conciliation with the Colonies" in *The Portable Edmund Burke* ed. Isaac Kramnick (Penguin 1999), 259–73.

65    Edmund Burke, "Speech on the Conciliation with the Colonies," 259–73. Burke likewise remarked that, "we have no sort of experience in favor of force as an instrument in the rule of our colonies" and that "the *temper and character* of the American colonies in particular would make them impossible to govern, in that the colonies stem from the English heritage." In this quote, Burke's argument reveals the clash *within* the same civilization. From the Burkean perspective, the use of force to achieve "democracy" *from outside* that society is a contradiction in terms—unless one is prepared, much as Burke advocated in respect to the American colonies, to make Iraq the 51st state or part of a new American "commonwealth"—a highly unlikely prospect!

## Notes: Chapter 4

1    J. Robert Oppenheimer, "International Control of Atomic Energy" in *The Atomic Age*, eds. Morton Grodzins and Eugene Rabinowitch (New York: Simon and Schuster, 1963), 54. Oppenheimer is perhaps most responsible nuclear weapons miniaturization.

2   CRS Issue Brief, *India-US Relations* (Washington DC: Congressional Research Service 4 November 2004.) http://fpc.state.gov/documents/ organization/ 37996.pdf.

3   Unification Minister Chung Dong-young, "It's definite that North Korea possesses 10 to 14 kilograms of plutonium that can make one or two nuclear weapons," but it is too early to call is a nuclear power. *ISN Security Watch* (14 February 2005).

4   Eldon Greenberg, "Memorandum: Legal Deficiencies in the US-China Agreement" Galloway and Greenberg, Attorneys at Law September 9, 1985; the US Arms Control and Disarmament Agency, however, backed the accord.

5   *ISN Security Watch*, 2 February 2005.

6   *International Crisis Group* "North Korea: Where Next for the Nuclear Talks?" *Asia Report* No. 87 (15 November 2004).

7   *ISN Security Watch* (5 January 2005).

8   Avner Cohen, "Most Favored Nation" *The Bulletin of Atomic Scientists* (January/ February 1995).

9   Ibid.

10  Ibid.

11  Ibid, 52.

12  In a letter to President Kennedy, Ben Gurion linked the Holocaust and Israel's need for deterrent strength to counter the numerical superiority of the Arabs. See Avner Cohen, op. cit., 45.

13  See Seymour M. Hersh, "The Coming Wars: What the Pentagon can now do in secret" *The New Yorker* (24–31 January 2005). See also Amy Goodman, "Interview with Mordechai Vanunu" Counterpunch (18 August 2004). http://counterpunch.org/ goodma. See also MSNBC "Strategic Israel" http://www.msnbc.com/news/ wld/graphics/ strategic_ israel_dw.htmn08182004.html.

14  Here, according to the CIA, the Khan network may have sold North Korea a very similar package that it sold to Libya, including nuclear fuel (raw uranium hexafluoride), centrifuges and one or more warhead designs. "US Sees More Arms Ties Between Pakistan and Korea" *New York Times*, 14 March 2004. Although not publicly stated, the implications are that Iran may have made a similar deal in the late 1980s and continued at least until the mid–1990s. One report says that cooperation between Pakistan and North Korea expanded into the nuclear and missile areas in Benazir Bhutto's second term (1993 to 1996) to include exchanges of scientists and engineers. B. Raman, "The Pakistan-North Korea Nexus," 10 March 2004. http://www.rediff.com. Assistance to Libya began in the early1990s and continued into 2002. Assistance to North Korea may have continued until 2003. However, a German intelligence investigation concluded as long ago as 1991 that Iraq, and possibly Iran and North Korea, obtained uranium melting information from Pakistan in the late 1980s. Khan may have provided Iran with centrifuges; but Pakistan denies that it was aware of the illegal transfer.

15  *CRS Issue Brief for Congress*, India-US Relations, op.cit.

16  It should be noted that in February 1975 the Shah stated that Iran "has no intention of acquiring nuclear weaponry but if small states began building them, then Iran might have to reconsider its policy."

17  Richard Perle, http://www.newamericancentury.org/iraq-20030224.htm, op.cit.

18  Shannon Kile, Stockholm International Peace Research Institute (SIPRI), cited in, Charles Recknagel, "Iran: Tehran Seen As Progressing Along Two Tracks To Develop Nuclear Weapons (Part 2)" RFE/RL Wednesday, 22 December 2004.

19  Shannon Kile, cited in Charles Recknagel. Ibid.

20  Parenthetically, this issue of "potential compensation" promised by the executive branch but then blocked by Congress has plagued not only US-Soviet/Russian relations, since Congressional refusal to extend Lend Lease in 1945, but US relations with states, such as Turkey, after the 1990-91 Persian Gulf war, which had been promised compensation for a cut off of Iraqi oil through Turkey was not forthcoming.

21  See Tom Regan, "Is Russia Rebuilding its Mideast role?" *Christian Science Monitor* (26 January 2005).

22  Director General, "Implementation of the NPT Safeguards Agreement with the Islamic Republic of Iran," International Atomic Energy Agency (10 November 2003).

23  Scott Peterson, "Evidence of possible work on Nuke tests Iran's credibility," *Christian Science Monitor* (26 February, 2004).

24  "Iran Freezes Nuclear Inspections After It Is Censured by the UN," *New York Times* (14 March 2004).

25  "Iran Rejects the European offer to Supply it With Nuclear Fuel" *Middle East Media and Research Institute, Inquiry and Analysis Series* No. 191 (21 October 2004).

26  International Crisis Group, "Iran: Where Next on the Nuclear Standoff" (24 November 2004).

27  Lisa Bryant, "France Defends talk with Iran on Nuclear Fuel" (4 February 2005).

28  Richard Perle, http://www.newamericancentury.org/iraq-20030224.htm. op. cit.

29  David E. Sanger, "In North Korea and Pakistan: Deep Roots of Nuclear Barter" *New York Times* (24 November 2002).

30  *Washington Post* (15 July 2003).

31  *International Crisis Group*, "Iran: Where Next on the Nuclear Standoff", op. cit.

32  Ibid.

33  "U.S. Struggles to Place Pressure on North Korea" PINR (23 march 2005).

34  *ISN Security Watch* (14 February 2005).

35  NATO Parliamentary Assembly Venice Italy – Resolution on Confronting Nuclear Proliferation, November 2004. http://www.nato-pa.int/default.asp?TAB=595.

36  On additional protocol, see http://www.armscontrol.org/factsheets/IAEAProtocol.asp1.

37  NATO Parliamentary Assembly Venice Italy, op. cit.

38  Kenneth Pollack; Ray Takeyh, "Taking on Tehran," *Foreign Affairs*, March/April 2005.

39  *See* Zvi Bar'el, *"The Charm of the Iranian threat" Haaretz* 1 December, 2004.

40  See Jeremy Bransten "World: Russia Joins U.S.-Led Initiative On WMD" *RFE/RL Reports* (2 June 2004).

41  Sheldon W. Simon, "A WMD Discovery in Malaysia" Pacific Forum, Center for Strategic and International Studies (CSIS) (January-March 2004).

42  In case of conflict with North Korea, the US would need 2000 fighter jets and 690,000 military personnel—more than four times the current US troop presence in Iraq. Erich Marquardt, "US Struggles to Place Pressure on N. Korea" *PINR* (23 March 2005).

43  Seymour M. Hersh, "The Coming Wars," op. cit. *ISN Security Watch* 14 Feb. 2005.

44  Dick Cheney, cited in *New York Times* (21 January 2005).

45  "Scott Ritter Says U.S. Plans June Attack On Iran" (21 February 2005). http://electroniciraq.net/news.

46  "Iranian military rhetoric reflects outside pressures" *RFE/RL Reports* (11 November 2004).

47  In this regard, it can be argued that the Shah's efforts to develop a large-scale nuclear program in the 1970s, for example, strained resources and in part, worked to create international and domestic opposition that discredited and destabilized the regime.

48  See James M. Goldgeier and Michael McFaul, *Power and Purpose: US Policy Toward Russia After the Cold War* (Washington, DC: Brookings, 2003), 302. Cited in Robert O. Freedman, "Russia—A Partner for the US in the Post-Saddam era?" *Strategic Insights* Vol. 3, No. 4 (5April 2004).

49  Between 1985–90, Saudi Arabia purportedly paid up to five billion dollars for Saddam Hussein to build nuclear weapons on condition that some of the bombs be transferred to the Saudi arsenal. One can also mention Saudi financing for Hamas, as well as the Taliban. See Leslie and Andrew Cockburn, "Royal Mess" *The New Yorker* (28 November 1994). http://www.newyorker.com/printable/?archive/ 011015fr_archive 01.

50  On Turkey and Saudi Arabia moving toward neutrality, see Jonathan Feiser, "Nuclear Iran: Repercussions for Turkey and Saudi Arabia" *PINR* (28 January 2005).

51  "… (H)ypernationalism is least likely when states can rely on small professional armies, or on complex high-technology military organizations that do not require vast manpower. For this reason nuclear weapons work to dampen nationalism, since they shift the basis of military power away from pure reliance on mass armies, and toward greater reliance on smaller high-technology organizations." John J. Mearsheimer, "Back to the Future" *International Security*, Vol. 15, No. 1 (Summer, 1990), 21.

52  John Mearsheimer and Steven E. Miller in *Foreign Affairs*, 72, 3 (Summer 1993). (A better option for Germany is to integrate its defenses into an all-European nuclear force backed by the UK and France, and, if possible, in coordination with Russia, should NATO and the American deterrent begin to wither away or no longer appear reliable. See Hall Gardner, in *NATO and the European Union*, Chapter 8, op. cit.).

53  Seymour M. Hersh, "The Coming Wars: What the Pentagon can now do in secret" *The New Yorker* 24 and 31 January 2005; posted January 17 2005.

54  Martin Indyk, "The Iraq War Did Not Force Gadaffi's Hand," *London Financial Times* (9 March 2004). Libya approached the US in 1999 to discuss eliminating its WMD.

55  On the concept of *multilateral dissuasion*, see Hall Gardner, ed., *NATO and the EU*, Chapter 2, op. cit.

56  The failure of US BMD tests in February 2005 could mean a substantial cut in President Bush's 2006 BMD budget, by as much as $1 billion, in that BMD has been the single largest US defense research and development project.

57  NATO Parliamentary Assembly, "Resolution on Confronting Nuclear Proliferation," op. cit. Congressional funding for RNEP was demanded by the Bush administration in January 2005 after Congress had sliced funding from the previous year's budget.

## Notes: Chapter 5

1  "Ironically, not only did Pakistan develop its nuclear weapons capability while receiving some $600 million annually in U.S. military and economic aid, but the leadership ranks of *al-Qaida* and the Taliban include some of the very same radical Islamists nurtured by Pakistan's Inter-Services Intelligence (ISI) organization and supported and armed by the CIA in the successful effort to drive the Russian Army out of Afghanistan." Congressional Research Service, *Pakistan's Nuclear Proliferation Activities and the Recommendations of the 9/11 Commission (Washington, DC: CRS Report for Congress, 25 January 2005*.

2  Brzezinski in *Le Nouvel Observateur* (Paris, 15–21 January 1998), op. cit.

3  Brzezinski, op.cit.

4  Steve Coll, *Ghost Wars: The Secret History of the CIA, Afghanistan and bin Laden, from the Soviet Invasion to September 10, 2001* (New York: Penguin Press, 2004), 51.

5    Coll, ibid., 51.
6    Coll, 47. Coll does not cite Brzezinski's remarks from the *Le Nouvel Observateur*. Yet US efforts to discredit Amin may have been the trick to draw Moscow into invasion.
7    See Odd Arne Westad, "Concerning the Situation in 'A'" *Cold War International History Project,* Nos. 8–9 (Winter 1996/97), 130–31 and passim.
8    Edward Jay Epstein "Who Killed Zia?" *Vanity Fair* (September 1989) http://edwardjayepstein.com/archived/zia.htm.
9    See Ken Silverstein, "Stingers, Stingers, Who's Got the Stingers?" *Slate* (3 October 2001). http://slate.msn.com/id/116582.
10   William D. Hartung, *U.S. Weapons at War* (New York: World Policy Institute, June 1995), 1–3. In the "boomerang effect," U.S. arms or U.S. military technology also found its way into the hands of U.S. adversaries in Panama, Iraq, Somalia, and Haiti.
11   See Tariq Ali, "The Color of Khaki," *New Left Review* January/February 2003. Ali states that the CIA dumped its unofficial agents and worked with the Pakistan ISI.
12   "Pressler Amendment" Nuclear Non-Proliferation Conditions on Assistance for Pakistan Amendment to the Foreign Assistance Act of 1961, amended. *Federation of American Scientists.* http://www.fas.org/news/pakistan/1992/920731.htm.
13   Ahmed Rashid, *Taliban* (New Haven: Yale, 2000).
14   Ahmed Rashid, *Taliban*, op. cit.
15   Kleveman, 243.
16   Ibid 186. Benzar Bhutto saw the unity of Afghanistan as more important than its gender policy, which she asked it to moderate. For Islamabad, a Taliban victory was to provide the country with "strategic depth." Madeline Albright also criticized the Taliban's policy toward women, but initially supported its effort to unify the country.
17   It was rumored that some of the unexploded cruise missiles and parts recovered from the strikes were sold to China and Pakistan by *al-Qaida.*
18   Support of Kashmiri militancy to "bleed India" was seen by Islamabad as a low cost strategy that buys leverage versus India. Deepa Ollapally, "South Asia's Politics of Paranoia" *The World and I*, Vol. 18, No. 5 (May 2003).
19   Mohan Malik, "High Hopes: India's response to US Security Policies" *Asian Affairs* Vol. 30, No. 2 (Summer 2003).
20   Mohan Malik, "The China Factor in the India-Pakistan Conflict" *Parameters*, Carlisle Barracks. Vol. 33, No. 1 (Spring 2003).
21   Robert G. Wirsing, "Precarious Partnership: Pakistan's response to US security policies" *Asian Affairs* Vol. 30, No. 2 (Summer 2003).
22   *The Guardian* (25 May 2002).
23   Tariq Ali, *The Guardian* "Who really killed Daniel Pearl?" (5 April 2002). It is rumored that the Pakistani ISI, may have been involved. Other rumors tried to put the blame on India. The question of F-16s, demanded by Pakistani military for 20 years, seems a bit too blatant: Such is the shadowy world of terrorism.
24   See Sten Widhalm, "Kashmir and a New Cold War" in Hall Gardner, ed., *NATO and the European Union*, op. cit.
25   Sunit Ganguly, "Kashmir, caught in the Middle" *Bulletin of the Atomic Scientists*, Vol. 59, No. 4 (Jul/Aug 2003).
26   See Centre for South Asian Studies, *Pakistan: General Elections 2002* (Geneva: 29 Rue de Neuchatel, 2002).
27   US Institute of Peace, "Unfinished Business in Afghanistan: Warlordism, Reconstruction, and Ethnic Harmony," No. 105 (April 2003). www.usip.org/pubs/ special reports/ sr105.html.

28   *International Security Network* (3 January 2005).
29   Rose Gordan, "Bush Ok's $3 billion aid Package to Pakistan, but no F-16s" *Arms Control Today* Vol. 33, No. 6 (July/August 2003).
30   Congressional Research Service, *Pakistan's Nuclear Proliferation Activities,* op. cit.
31   "As Nuclear Secrets Emerge, More Are Suspected." *New York Times* (26 December 2004), 1: 12.
32   Congressional Research Service, *Pakistan's Nuclear Proliferation,* op. cit.
33   International Crisis Group, "Unfulfilled Promises: Pakistan's Failure to Tackle Extremism" *Asia Report* No. 73 (16 January 2004).
34   *Wall Street Journal* (27 August 2003), A10.
35   "PPP Punjab President Qasim Zia clarifies remarks about conciliation, Kashmir, Kalabagh," *The Pakistan Newswire* (27 December 2004).
36   In the late 1950s, and early 1960s, India, China and Russia appeared to be moving toward rapprochement in the *pancheel* concept; India and Pakistan also sought to negotiate their differences. Yet the Sino-Indian border conflict (in which both the US and USSR supported India against China) ended that possibility. The strategic importance of Kashmir to India lay in the defense of Ladakh against China. In October 1962, India and China then went to war, at roughly the same time as the Cuban missile crisis. See S.M. Burke and Lawrence Ziring, *Pakistan's Foreign Policy* (Oxford: Oxford University Press, 1990), 224–25; 271–284.
37   Jean Luc Racine, *Cachemire: Au Peril de la Guerre* (Paris: Autrement/CERI: 2002).
38   Stephen Philip Cohen, "The Nation and the State of Pakistan" *Washington Quarterly* (Summer 2002), 119.
39   Michael Scheuer, "Interview," Jamestown Foundation, *Terrorism Monitor* (10 December 2004).

## Notes: Chapter 6

1    See for example, Bogdan Szajkowski, "Will Russia disintegrate into Bantustans?" *The World Today*, Vol. 49, Nos. 8–9 (August–September 1993). The fact that as many as 204 ethno-territorial disputes have plagued the ex-USSR helps to explain Russian vehemence in suppressing the Chechen movement in order to ostensibly prevent that struggle from blazing the trial for the independence of other regions.
2    Kenneth N. Waltz, "Globalization and American Power," op. cit.
3    On the role of US military bases in the expansion of the overseas American empire, see Chalmers Johnson, *The Sorrows of Empire* (New York: Henry Holt, 2004), 214–15.
4    NATO decided to base aircraft in Lithuania to defend Baltic airspace. NATO reportedly plans to modernize "installations" (rather than build full scale bases) in Poland. This means updating or expanding four command centers, fuel-storage facilities, seven air bases, and installing six long range radars. *RFE/RL Reports* Vol. 8, No. 52, Part II (18 March 2004).
5    *New York Times* (26 January 2005).
6    Greg Jaffe, "In Massive Shift, U.S. is Planning to Cut Size of Military in Germany," *Wall Street Journal* (10 June 2003).
7    See Ustina Markus, "CIA in Decline; Pentagon on the Rise" *ISN Security Watch* (24 January 2005).
8    Bill Gertz, *The Washington Times* (18 January 2005).
9    Robert Kagan, *Of Paradise and Power* (New York: Knopf, 2003).

10  See Nile Gardiner and John C. Hulsman, "The Bush-Blair Summit: Iraq, the U.N., and the Future of Europe," *Heritage Foundation WebMemo* No. 239 (26 March 2003).

11  *RFE/RL Reports* "Poland, Belarus, Ukraine" Vol. 5, No. 15 (22 April 2003).

12  See Final Act of CFE Treaty: http://www.osce.org/docs/english/1990-1999/cfe/cfefin act99e.htm.

13  "U.S.-Russia poultry trade progresses" *The Voice of Agriculture* Vol. 82, No. 8 (14 April 2003). http://www.fb.com/news/fbn/03/04_14/html/u_s_-russia.html. Russian Jews, such as Natan (Anatoly) Sharansky, have demanded that the Jackson Vanik amendment be lifted. American Jews, however, "would like guarantees from Russia, in view of a rising wave of anti-Semitism, that Jews in its territory will go unharmed. They also demand the right of unhindered and unsupervised self-organization for Jewish communities and a return of Jewish communal property confiscated by the Soviet regime." See Sam Vaknin, "Let My People Go: The Jackson-Vanik Controversy." http://samvak.tripod.com/pp149.html.

14  Costanza Musu, "European Foreign Policy: A Collective Policy or a Policy of 'Converging Parallels?" *European Foreign Affairs Review* Vol. 8, Nos. 35–49 (2003).

15  *ISN Security Watch* (16 March 2005).

16  Frank Umbach, "EU's Links with China Pose New Threat to Transatlantic Relations" *European Affairs,* Spring 2004.

17  "La France et la Russie vont renforcer leurs relations militaries," *Le Monde* (22 January 2005).

18  Ian Hayes, "Lifting the China Embargo," *ISN Security Watch* (2 February 2005).

19  In the past, NATO has simultaneously brought rivals in pairs into the alliance: Greece and Turkey, Poland and Czech Republic, for example.

20  See for example, "Europe's Eastern Enlargement: Who benefits" *Current History* (November 2001). Darius K. Rosati, "Economic Disparities in Central and Eastern Europe and the Impact of EU Enlargement" (Warsaw: Central European Initiative and the UN Economic Commission for Europe, 1999).

21  Kasia Wolczuk, "Ukraine and EU Enlargement: The Potential Consequences at the Regional Level" University of Birmingham (25 April 2001). www.bham.ac.uk/crees/statehood/ukraineandeuenlargement.htm.

22  See comments of Kosovar Minister for Returns Slavisa Petkovic, the only Serb in Prime Minister Ramush Haradinaj's cabinet, and his criticism of the International Crisis Group's report, urging independence for Albanian Kosovars. *ISN Security Watch* (2 February 2005).

23  *ISN Security Watch* (28 January 2005).

24  Chietigj Bajpaee, PINR (2 February 2005)

25  At the CIS summit in September 2004, Kyrgyz President Askar Akaev stated, "I am a decisive supporter of a strategy of preemptive strikes," Uzbek President Karimov suggested the creation of a CIS-wide list of terrorist organizations and individuals.

26  Robert O. Freedman, "Russia—A Partner for the US in the Post-Saddam era?" *Strategic Insights* Vol. 3, No. 4 (5 April 2004).

27  Robert O. Freedman, ibid.

28  "Mystery in Iraq as $300 Million is Taken Abroad," *NY Times* (22 January 2005). By Aug. 2004, $8.8bn in Iraqi Development Funds was distributed without accountability.

29  The Shi'ite community remains divided between four predominant factions: the "Quietists," (supports separation of church and state but also seeks majority Shi'ite rule); the al-Sadr faction (nationalist tendencies), the Supreme Council for the Islamic Revolution in Iraq (pro-Iranian tendencies), and the *D'awa* Party (nationalist tendencies). See Sammy Salama, Kathleen Thompson, and Jennifer Chalmers, "In

Post-War Iraq, Placating the *Shi'a* is Paramount" *Monterey Center for Non-Proliferation Studies* Research Story (30 January 2004). For details, see Charles Recknagel, *RFE/RL Reports* (December 2004).

30  "Scott Ritter Says U.S. Plans June Attack on Iran" (21 February 2005). http://electroniciraq.net/ news/.

31  Commander of U.S. Central Command, John Abizaid, stated that, largely due to lack of available forces, he could not to assist Turkey in its conflict with PKK operating out of Iraqi territory. See *International Herald Tribune* (13 January 2005), 3.

32  The March 1975 Algiers agreement recognized the principle of *thalweg* as the boundary in the Shatt al-Arab river; it dropped all Iraqi claims to Iranian Khuzestan and to the islands at the foot of the Gulf, and ended the Iranian support for the Kurds (at that time). http://reference.allrefer.com/country-guide-study/ iraq/ iraq 19. html.

33  Ahmed Raschid, *Taliban* (New Haven: Yale University Press, 2001). See Chapter 5.

34  In June 2004, President Bush designated Pakistan as a Major Non-NATO Ally (MNNA) as provided for by Section 517 of the Foreign Assistance Act of 1961, as amended. Thailand, another important antiterrorism ally, received the same status in 2003. The designation makes Pakistan and Thailand, along with Japan, South Korea, Australia and other allies eligible for expedited access to excess defense articles and other privileges. The designation also appears related to Pakistan's decision to purchase several major weapons systems. Congressional Research Service, *Pakistan's Nuclear Proliferation Activities*, op. cit.

35  Michael Scheuer, in *ISN Security Watch* (4 January 2005), op. cit.

36  The Saudi Islamic movement is divided into roughly four groups, *jihadists* (like bin Laden); reformists of "Islamic Awakening" who seek a broad coalition of factions to reform the society; Islamic rejectionists (who reject the corrupt Saudi State as well as *jihadists'* position on religion) and Saudi Shi'ites, who make up roughly 10% of the overall Saudi population but who inhabit the eastern oil rich Saudi provinces.

37  International Crisis Group, "Saudi Arabia Backgrounder: Who are the Islamists?" Middle East Report No. 31 (21 September 2004). http://www.icg.org//library/docu ments/middle_east___ north_africa/iraq_iran_gulf/31_saudi_arabia_backgrounderpdf.

38  On state and anti-state terrorism in Colombia, see *ICG Reports*, http://www.intl-crisis-group.org/projects/showreport.cfm?reportid=634.

39  *ISN Security Watch* (25 February 2005).

40  The case of anti-Castro militant, Luis Posada Carriles, who has applied for political asylum in the US, although wanted for committing acts of terrorism by Venezuela, may be a test case for Bush policy in the war against all forms of "terrorism."

41  Abbas argued that the militarization of the *intifada* resulted in world condemnation, and not condemnation of Israel. "Interview with former PA Prime Minister Mahmoud Abbas (Abu Mazen) in Jordanian *Al-Rai* published in *The Middle East Media Research Institute Special Dispatch Series* - No. 793, (5 October 2004). http://www.memri.org/ bin/articles.cgi? Page= countries&Area= palestinian&ID= SP79304#_edn1.

42  By March 2005, it looked like *Hamas* might accept a one-year suspension of violence. Yet Israel announced it that would build 3500 new homes in the largest West Bank settlement in an area Israel regards as part of greater Jerusalem.

43  Seymour M. Hersh, "Plan B: As June 30th approaches, Israel looks to the Kurds." *The New Yorker* (28 June 2004). Israel denied Hersh's story.

44    *ISN Security Watch* (10 March 2005). Washington will only recognize Hizb'allah if gives up its arms; yet the latter (backed by the Lebanese anti-Syrian opposition) claims that it will only do so once Israel withdraws from areas in Lebanon that it holds.

45    CRS Issue Brief, *India-US Relations* (Washington, DC: Congressional Research Service, 4 November 2004). http://fpc.state.gov/documents/organization/ 37996.pdf.

46    Pipelines and pipeline dreams," *RFE/RL Reports* (2 March 2005).

47    John C.K. Daly, "China brief: Can the Dragon Swim? The Naval Balance in the Taiwan Strait" *China Brief The Jamestown Foundation* Vol. 4, No. 2, 20 January 2004.

48    Pravda, 12/15/2004 http://english.pravda.ru/world/20/91/368/14721_kuril.html.

49    Dr. Subhash Kapila, "Japan-India Strategic Co-operation," *South Asia Analysis Group*. http://www.saag.org/papers2/paper126.html.

50    Cited in Colin Robinson, "Stand-off with North Korea: War Scenarios and Consequences" *Center for Defense Information* www.cdi.org. David Shambaugh "China and the Korean Peninsula: Playing for the Long Term," *The Washington Quarterly* Vol. 26, No. 2 (Spring 2003). See comments by William Perry, "US, North Korea Drifting Toward War," *Washington Post* (15 July 2003).

51    As Chung Dong-young put it: "To encourage North Korea to become a member of the international community, economic cooperation and engagement are more effective than military pressure or containment." http://www.koreaemb.org/archive/ 2005/2_1/foreign/ foreign3.asp.

52    Dr. Michael A. Weinstein *PIRN*, 14 February 2005.

53    Ibid.

54    Ibid.

55    Beijing seeks a 2,400 kilometer route from Angarsk in Siberia to Daqing in China's northeast Heilongjiang province. Tokyo is pushing for a 4,000–km pipeline from Taishet to the Pacific port of Nakhodka. Chietigj Bajpaee, "China's quest for energy security" PINR (2 February 2005).

56    Bill Gertz, *The Washington Times* (18 January 2005).

57    Chietigj Bajpaee, "India recovers lost ground in energy game" *PINR* (16 March 2005).

58    John C. K. Daly, *Jamestown Foundation* (20 December 2004).

59    International Crisis Group, "Taiwan Strait IV: How an Ultimate Political Settlement Might Look," Appendix A (26 February 2004).

60    *ISN Security Watch* (2 February 2005). US and Chinese talks touched on the issues of counter-terrorism, regional security, tensions in the Taiwan Strait and North Korea.

61    "World reacts to Chinese Anti-Secession Law," *Christian Science Monitor* (15 March 2005).

62    *ISN Security Watch* (13 January 2005).

63    Causing a scandal in Russia and upsetting the French, Condoleezza Rice, asserted in an interview, "I believe that Russia is a threat to the West in general and to our European allies in particular." *Le Figaro Magazine*, No. 1059 (10 February 2001). In April 2001, a Chinese fighter jet tipped into a US spy plane, causing a major diplomatic incident.

## Notes: Chapter 7

1    Huntington, *The Clash of Civilizations and the Remaking of World Order*, op. cit.

2    Francis Fukuyama, *The End History and the Last Man* (New York: Macmillan, 1992).

3    See Arend Lijphart, *Patterns of Democracy* (New Haven: Yale University, 1999). Lijphart's analysis lumps US and European systems together as "majoritarian" even

though liberal conceptions of majoritarian democracy may differ substantially from *social democratic* conceptions. He analyses three *consensual* democracies, Switzerland, Belgian and the European Union, which are all multi-ethnic. Although he does not closely analyze the foreign policy formulation in respect to wars, he does argue that *consensual* democracies may be "even more peace loving." (298)

4      As one measure to re-adjust growing regional imbalances, and make for more efficient government, it might be possible to amalgamate the 50 states into larger regional units—with more balanced populations and economies. This "revolution" would require a constitutional amendment that would bypass state legislatures.

5      G. John Ikenberry, "Why Export Democracy?: The 'Hidden Grand Strategy of American Foreign Policy" *The Wilson Quarterly*, Vol. 24; No. 2 (Spring 1999).

6      Condoleeza Rice, *Remarks at Institut d'Etudes Politiques de Paris—Science Po* (8 February 2005). http://www.state.gov/secretary/rm/2005/41973.htm.

7      Farreed Zakaria, *The Future of Freedom* (April 2003).

8      See Marco Rimanelli, *Comparative Democratization and Peaceful Change in Single-Party Dominant Countries* (New York: St. Martin's, 1999).

9      Kurds seek to maintain a potential veto over the new Iraqi constitution. The Transitional Administrative Law permitted the three provinces with a majority of Kurds to veto the draft constitution by a two-thirds majority in each province, a position opposed by rival Shi'ite factions, but so far accepted by the new Constitution.

10     Samuel Huntington, "The Hispanic Challenge" *Foreign Policy* (March/April 2004).

11     For a critique of US ICC policy, Remigius Chibueze "United States Objection to the International Criminal Court," *Annual Survey of International and Comparative Law*" (Vol. 9:1, 2003). The American Service Members Protection Act of 2002 (dubbed "the Hague Invasion act" permits to use all necessary and appropriate means to bring about the release of US citizens or allies held by the ICC, and threatens a withdrawal of US military assistance to countries that sign the ICC and allows for US participation in UN peacekeeping missions to be contingent upon immunity. This position has put the US at odds with EU members.

12     David Owen, *Balkan Odyssey* (New York: Harcourt, Brace, 1995), Chapters 3–4.

13     See William D. Hartung, "The Costs of NATO Expansion Revisited" *World Policy Institute Issue Brief* www.worldpolicy.org/projects/arms/ reports/april99.html. See also

14     Hall Gardner, "The Genesis of NATO Enlargement" in *Central and Southeastern Europe in Transition*, ed. Hall Gardner (Praeger, 2000), 162, ft. 20, p. 182.

15     "… Rambouillet was not a negotiation—as is often claimed—but an ultimatum. This marked an astounding departure for an administration that had entered office proclaiming its devotion to the U.N. Charter and multilateral procedures. The transformation of the Alliance from a defensive military grouping into an institution prepared to impose its values by force occurred in the same months that three former Soviet satellites joined NATO. It undercut repeated American and allied assurances that Russia had nothing to fear from NATO expansion, since the Alliance's own treaty proclaimed it to be a purely defensive institution." Henry Kissinger, "New World Disorder," *Newsweek*, US Edition (31 May 1999).

16     Neo-conservative focus on corruption in the UN "Oil for Food" program appears to distract attention from "kickbacks" and "pork barrel" spending by US contractors in Iraq, as well as corruption in the provisional Iraqi government. Which is worse?

17     James W. Caesar, "The Great Divide," in *Present Dangers*, ed. by Robert Kagan and William Kristol (San Francisco: Encounter Books: 2000), 35.

18     James W. Caesar, 36.

19     James W. Caesar, op. cit. 37.

20  Francis Fukuyama, "Has History restarted Since September 11?" *Center for Independent Studies*, Australia (8 August 2002). http://www.cis.org.au.

21  Dominique de Villepin, "Law, Force, Justice," *International Institute of Strategic Studies* (27 March 2003). http://www.iiss.org/ showdocument.php?docID=114.

22  Ibid.

23  See Hall Gardner, *Surviving the Millennium*, op. cit.

24  Chris Patten and Richard Perle, "Patten vs. Perle: Is the U.S. a Unilateralist Hegemon?" *European Affairs* (Winter 2003). Perle questioned, "Why should not NATO be as legitimate as the UN, which happens to contain a lot of dictatorships?"

25  Ira Straus, *Center for Eastern Europe and Russia in NATO*, "Russia in NATO" December 1994 http://www.fas.org/man/nato/ceern/rus_in.htm.

26  Hall Gardner, "NATO and the UN: The Contemporary Relevance of the 1949 North Atlantic Treaty" in *A History of NATO*, ed, Gustav Schmidt (New York: Palgrave, 2001).

27  See Hall Gardner, "NATO and the UN," op.cit.

28  Hall Gardner, "NATO and the UN," ibid.

29  Arthur H. Vandenberg, *The Private Papers of Senator Vandenberg* (Houghton Mifflin, 1952), 474.

30  Sir Oliver Franks, quoted in *Foreign Relations US*, Vol. 3 (1948), 169.

31  UN Secretary General Kofi Annan called for the abolishment of the Human Rights Commission, accused by neo-conservatives and other critics of defending tyrants, and its replacement by a new Human Rights Council, elected by a two-thirds vote of the General Assembly. (A "World Citizen's Assembly" might represent a better legitimizing force for such a Council.) Annan also proposed the creation of a peace-building commission and a fund to promote democracy. He called for a "responsibility to protect" that would authorize international action, including the use of force, when nations are unwilling or unable to protect their own citizens. See http://www.globalpolicy.org/reform/initiatives/annan/2005/followupreport.pdf.

32  *Report of the High Level Panel on Threats, Challenges and Change* (2 December 2004). http://www.globalpolicy.org/reform/initiatives/panels/high/1202report.pdf.

33  G4 Nations Bid for Permanent Security Council Seat *Deutsche Welle* (22 September 2004). http://www.globalpolicy.org/security/reform/cluster1/2004/0922permbids.htm.

34  *RFE/RL Newsline* (4 December 2004).

35  See David Held, "Democracy and Globalization" *MPIfG Working Paper* (May 1997). http://www.mpi-fg-koeln.mpg.de/pu/workpap/wp97-5/wp97-5.html. See discussion, Allison Van Rooy, *The Global Legitimacy Game* (Houndmill: Palgrave, 2004), 133–3.

## Notes: Chapter 8

1  Edmund Burke, *Speech on the Conciliation with the Colonies*, 1775.

2  In March 2003, Senator Richard Lugar introduced "The U.S.-Russia Trade Act of 2003," to abolish the Jackson-Vanik amendment. The legislation would also allow Congress to vote on Russia's WTO accession (opposed by the Bush administration), in addition to providing Russia with PNTR. US-Russian trade tensions over poultry, beef and pork have thus far worked to block its implementation.

3  To bring both Russia and Ukraine into NATO, see Ira Straus, "Now it is Russia and Yanukovych who are dividing Ukraine," *Untimely Thoughts* (18 November 2004).

4  See *RFE/RL Balkan Report* Vol. 9, No. 9 (26 March 2005).

5  USIP Briefing "Kosovo: Final Status in 2005" US Institute for Peace (February 2005).

6   "The Geneva Accord" Haaretz.com http://www.haaretz.com/hasen/pages/ShArt.jhtml? Item No=351461. Annex X, unpublished, was to propose multinational peacekeeping.

7   See *International Crisis Group*, Zimbabwe Africa Report, No. 78 (19 April 2004).

8   See, for example, Colin Robinson, "Stand-off with North Korea: War Scenarios and Consequences" *Center for Defense Information* www.cdi.org; David Shambaugh "China and the Korean Peninsula," *The Washington Quarterly* Spring Vol. 26, No. 2 (2003). See also Chalmers Johnson, *Blowback*, op. cit.

9   On domestic sources of potential Russian *revanchism*, see Gordan Hahn, "Is Russia's next revolutionary wave beginning?" *Untimely Thoughts* (2 February 2005).

10  Marcel Rommerts, "Shaping an EU Energy Strategy has become More Urgent" and Laura Sikes "Energy Facts and Forecasts" *European Affairs* (Winter 2003).

11  Bill Gertz, *Washington Times* (18 January 2005).

12  Department of Energy, "The Hydrogen Posture Plan" (February 2004). http://www.eere.energy.gov/hydrogenandfuelcells/pdfs/hydrogen_posture_plan.pdf.

13  Could the billions spent on the Iraq war been better spent in developing alternative energy sources, not to overlook fostering sustainable development programs throughout the developing world? The dictator could have fallen later.

14  For German efforts to phase out nuclear power, see Rolf Linkohr, "German Energy Policy" *Uranium Policy Institute* http://www.world-nuclear.org/sym/1999/ linkohr.htm

15  See *World Watch Institute*, "The Choice: An Energy Strategy for the 21st Century." http://www.worldwatch.org/features/security/briefs/1.

16  In 88 developing countries, with nearly 40 per cent of world's population, water shortages are already a serious constraint on development. See general discussion, Global Water Fund, http://www.globalwaterfund.com/page/page/579700.htm.

17  Richard Portes, "Towards a Lender of First Resort," *Working Paper Series*, American University of Paris (9 December 2004).

18  For the "Tobin Tax Initiative," see http://www.ceedweb.org/iirp/; http://www.cheb ucto. ns.ca/Current/P7/bwi/ccctobin.html.

19  Rodrik proposes "controlled temporary immigration." See Dani Rodrik, *Feasible Globalizations,* Harvard University (May 2002). http://ksghome.harvard.edu/~drodrik/ Feasible.pdf. See below, ft. 21.

20  The nomination of the neo-conservative Paul Wolfowitz, one of primary advocates of war with Iraq, as head of the World Bank, in 2005, represented an effort to *channel* development assistance in such a way as to serve American interests in the "war on terrorism." One of his first actions was to telephone the rock star Bono, an activist for world development, for advice!

21  "... Liberalizing cross-border labor movements can be expected to yield benefits that are roughly 25 times larger than those that would accrue from the traditional agenda focusing on goods and capital flows!" Yet for any national leader to dare suggest the need to increase immigration would be to commit political suicide. Hence, Rodrik proposes "controlled temporary immigration." He additionally argues that the forces of globalization create "trilemna" in that the nation state, democracy, and deep economic integration appear mutually incompatible. Only two out of the three can co-exist at the same time. As a feasible alternative, I am proposing steps toward greater regional integration coupled with additional steps toward "world democracy," Rodrik, op.cit. See also, Dani Rodrik, "How Far Will International Economic Integration Go?" http://ksghome.harvard.edu/~drodrik/JEPrev1.PDF.

22  Hedley Bull, *The Anarchical Society* (New York: Columbia University, 1977), 87.

23  J. William Fulbright, *The Arrogance of Power* (Random House, 1967).

# Selected Bibliography

Alexander, Yonah and Swetnam, Michel S., *Usama bin Laden's al Qaida: Profile of a Terrorist Network* (Ardsley, NY: Transnational Publishers, 2001).

Anderson, Liam and Stansfield, Gareth, *The Future of Iraq* (Palgrave, 2004).

Arendt, Hannah, *Origins of Totalitarianism* (Harcourt: 1976).

Baer, Robert, *See No Evil* (New York: Crown Publishers, 2002).

Bull, Hedley, *The Anarchical Society* Second Edition. (New York: Columbia University Press, 1977).

Bush, George, Sr. and Scowcroft, Brent, *A World Transformed* (Alfred A. Knopf, 1998).

Clarke, Richard A., *Against All Enemies* (New York: Free Press, 2004).

Coll, Steve, *Ghost Wars: The Secret History of the CIA, Afghanistan and bin Laden, from the Soviet Invasion to September 10, 2001* (New York: Penguin Press, 2004).

Etzioni, Amitai, ed. *The Essential Communitarian Reader* (Lanham: Rowman and Littlefield, 1998).

Foster, Henry A., *The Making of Modern Iraq* (Norman: University of Oklahoma Press, 1935).

Fukuyama, Francis, *The End of History and the Last Man* (Penguin, 1992).

Fulbright, J. William, *The Arrogance of Power* (1967).

Gardner, Hall, *Dangerous Crossroads* (Westport, CT: Praeger, 1997).

—*NATO and the EU: New World, New Europe, New Threats* (Aldershot, UK: Ashgate, 2004.

Hoffman, Bruce, *Inside Terrorism* (Columbia University Press, 1998).

Howard, Lawrence, ed., *Terrorism: Roots, Impact, Responses*, (Westport, CT: Praeger, 1992).

Howard, Russell D. and Sawyer, Reid L. ed. *Terrorism and Counter-terrorism* (Gilford: McGraw Hill, 2003).

Huntington, Samuel, *The Clash of Civilizations and the Remaking of World Order* (New York: Touchstone, 1997).

Johnson, Chalmers, *Blowback* (Little Brown, 2000).

—*The Sorrows of Empire* (New York: Henry Holt, 2004).

Kagan, Donald, *On the Origins of War and the Preservation of Peace* (Doubleday: New York, 1995).

Kagan, Robert, *Of Paradise and Power* (New York: Knopf, 2003).

Kagan, Robert and Kristol William, eds., *Present Dangers* (San Francisco: Encounter Books: 2000).

Kennan, George F., *American Diplomacy: 1900–1950* (University of Chicago, 1953).

Kennedy, Paul, *Strategy and Diplomacy* (Unwin-Hyman, 1984).

Kepel, Gilles, *Fitna: la guerre au Coeur de l'Islam* (Gallimard, Paris: 2004).

Laqueur, Walter, *The Age of Terrorism* (Boston: Little, Brown and Co: 1987).

—*The Terrorism Reader* (New York: New American Library, 1978).

Lijphart, Arend, *Patterns of Democracy* (New Haven: Yale University, 1999).

Longrigg, Stephen Hemsley, *Iraq 1900-1950* (Oxford: 1953).

Miller, Steven E. and Trenin, Dmitri, eds. *The Russian Military* (Cambridge, MIT, 2004)

Morgenthau, Hans, *Politics Among Nations: The Struggle for Power and Peace* Brief Edition (Boston, MA: McGraw Hill, 1985).

O'Sullivan, Noel, *Terrorism, Ideology and Revolution*, (Sussex: Wheatsheaf Books, 1986).
Raschid, Ahmed, *Taliban* (New Haven: Yale University Press, 2001).
Rearden, Steven L., *The Evolution of American Strategic Doctrine* (Boulder, Colo/SAIS Foreign Policy Institue, 1984).
Rimanelli, Marco, *Comparative Democratization and Peaceful Change in Single-Party Dominant Countries* (New York: St. Martin's, 1999).
Ruggie John Gerard, *Multilateralism Matters* (New York: Columbia University, 1993).
Schmitt, Carl, *The Concept of the Political* (Chicago: University of Chicago, 1995).
—*La Notion de Politique*; *Theorie du Partisan* (Paris: Flammarion, 1992).
Schmidt, Gustav, ed., *A History of NATO* (New York: Palgrave, 2001).
Strauss, Leo; Cropsey, Joseph ed., *History of Political Philosophy* (Chicago: University of Chicago Press, 1987).
—*The Early Writings, 1921–1932*, ed. Michael Zank (Albany: NY: State University of New York, 2002).
Van Rooy, Allison, *The Global Legitimacy Game* (Houndsmill: Palgrave, 2004).
Virilio, Paul, *Crepuscular Dawn* (New York: Semiotext(e), 2002).
Wallerstein, Immanuel, *Geopolitics and Geoculture: Essays on the Changing World-System* (Cambridge: Cambridge University Press, 1997).
Williams, William Appleton, *Empire as a Way of Life* (Oxford University Press, 1980).
Woodward, Bob, *Plan of Attack* (Simon and Schuster, 2004).
Zakaria, Farreed, *The Future of Freedom* (April 2003).

## Web Sites: Electronic Journals

*CIAO: Columbia International Affairs Online:* http://www.ciao.org
*Congressional Research Service Reports and Issue Briefs*:
    http://fpc.state.gov/c4763.htm
*Connections PfP consortium*: http://www.pfpconsortium.org/info-pages/pubs_en.htm
*European Union Institute for Security Studies*: http://www.iss-eu.org/
*Federation of American Scientists* http://www.fas.org/
*Foreign Affairs:* http://www.foreignaffairs.org/
*Foreign Policy:* http://www.foreignpolicy.com/
*Heritage Foundation:* http://www.heritage.org/
*Human Rights Watch:* http://www.hrw.org/
*International Herald Tribune:* http://www.iht.com/
*International Security Network*: http://www.isn.ethz.ch/
*Jamestown Foundation*: http://www.jamestown.org/
*Jubilee Iraq News* http://www.jubileeiraq.org/
*Moscow Times:* http://www.moscowtimes.ru
*National Intelligence Council:* http://www.cia.gov/nic/NIC_2020_project.html
*National Interest*: http://www.nationalinterest.org/
*Nthposition Online:* http://www.nthposition.com
*NATO Parliamentary Assembly:* http://www.nato-pa.int/default.asp?TAB=595
*Power and Interest News Report:* http://www.pinr.com/
*Radio Free Europe/Radio Liberty (RFE/RL):* http://www.rferl.org/
*Sens Public:* http://www.sens-public.org/
*Stratfor*: http://www.stratfor.com./
*The National Security Archive:* http://www.gwu.edu/~nsarchiv/NSAEBB/NSAEBB82/
*Untimely Thoughts:* http://www.untimely-thoughts.com/
*World Watch Institute:* http://www.worldwatch.org/features/security/briefs

# Index